Statistics 3 & 4

Statistics 3 & 4

Jane Miller

Series editor Hugh Neill

CAMBRIDGE
UNIVERSITY PRESS

PUBLISHED BY THE PRESS SYNDICATE OF THE UNIVERSITY OF CAMBRIDGE
The Pitt Building, Trumpington Street, Cambridge, United Kingdom

CAMBRIDGE UNIVERSITY PRESS
The Edinburgh Building, Cambridge CB2 2RU, UK
40 West 20th Street, New York, NY 10011-4211, USA
10 Stamford Road, Oakleigh, VIC 3166, Australia
Ruiz de Alarcón 13, 28014 Madrid, Spain
Dock House, The Waterfront, Cape Town 8001, South Africa

http://www.cambridge.org

First published 2001

Printed in the United Kingdom at the University Press, Cambridge

Typefaces Times, Helvetica   *Systems* Microsoft® Word, MathType™

A catalogue record for this book is available from the British Library

ISBN 0 521 78605 3 paperback

Cover image: Getty One Stone

Contents

Introduction

Cambridge Advanced Level Mathematics has been written especially for the OCR modular examination. It consists of one book or half-book corresponding to each module. This book contains the third and fourth Statistics modules, S3 and S4.

The books are divided into chapters roughly corresponding to syllabus headings. Occasionally a section includes an important result that is difficult to prove or outside the syllabus. These sections are marked with an asterisk (*) in the section heading, and there is usually a sentence early on explaining precisely what it is that the student needs to know. In S4 probability and moment generating functions have been treated consecutively in Chapters 3 and 4 because they are closely related, but they need not be taken this way. Chapter 3 may be taken before Chapter 2 if a break between the abstract chapters is desired.

Occasionally within the text paragraphs appear in *this type style*. These paragraphs are usually outside the main stream of the mathematical argument, but may help to give insight, or suggest extra work or different approaches.

The author has assumed that the students have access to calculators with built-in statistical functions.

Numerical work is presented in a form intended to discourage premature approximation. In ongoing calculations inexact numbers appear in decimal form like $3.456\ldots$, signifying that the number is held in a calculator to more places than are given. Numbers are not rounded at this stage; the full display could be either $3.456\,123$ or $3.456\,789$. Final answers are then stated with some indication that they are approximate, for example '1.23 correct to 3 significant figures'.

Several chapters contain Practical activities or Computer activities. These can be used either as an introduction to a topic, or, later on, to reinforce the theory. These activities also present opportunities for working on Key Skills.

There are plenty of exercises, and each chapter contains a Miscellaneous exercise which includes some questions of examination standard. Questions which go beyond examination requirements are marked by an asterisk; other questions which the author believes may be harder than A level questions though within the specification are marked by a dagger (†). At the end of each module book there is a Revision exercise and two practice examination papers. The author thanks Chris Hockley and Norman Morris, the OCR examiners who contributed to these exercises, and also Peter Thomas, who read the books very carefully and made many extremely useful comments.

The author thanks OCR and Cambridge University Press, and in particular Diana Gillooly, for their help in producing this book. However, the responsibility for the text, and for any errors, remains with the author.

Module S3

Statistics 3

1 Continuous random variables

This chapter develops ideas about continuous random variables which you first met in S2. When you have completed it you should be able to

- use probability density functions for continuous random variables which are defined 'piecewise'
- understand the relationship between the probability density function and the cumulative distribution function
- use either the probability density function or the cumulative distribution function to evaluate the median, quartiles and other percentiles
- find the cumulative distribution function and probability density function of Y from the cumulative distribution function of X when Y is a function of X
- use the general result $E(g(X)) = \int g(x)f(x)\,dx$ where $f(x)$ is the probability density function of the continuous random variable X and $g(X)$ is a function of X.

1.1 Defining a probability density function 'piecewise'

The data in Table 1.1 give the frequency distribution for the ages of a random sample of people diagnosed with diabetes.

Age (years)	0–	5–	15–	25–	35–	45–	55–	65–	75–	85–99
Frequency	1	5	2	18	18	35	51	65	48	21
Frequency density	0.2	0.5	0.2	1.8	1.8	3.5	5.1	6.5	4.8	1.4

Table 1.1. Frequency distribution of ages of a random sample of people diagnosed with diabetes.

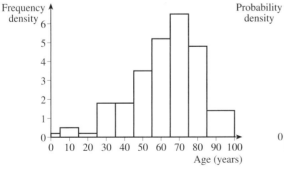

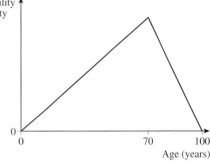

Fig. 1.2. Histogram of ages of a random sample of people diagnosed with diabetes.

Fig. 1.3. Possible probability density function for the age of a person suffering from diabetes.

The data are illustrated by a histogram in Fig. 1.2. How can the age of a person with diabetes be modelled? The histogram is not symmetrical and therefore, since the sample size is large, it is unlikely that the underlying population is symmetrical either. This means that the normal distribution is not appropriate as a model. Rather than trying to find a single curve to fit the data you can use more than one function and combine them 'piecewise'. Fig. 1.3 shows an attempt to model these data using two different straight line functions, one between 0 and 70 years and another between 70 and 100 years. In order to make the numbers involved smaller it is better to measure X, the age of a person with diabetes, in tens of years. Fig. 1.4 shows the suggested probability density function for X. The unknown constant, k, on this diagram can be found by using the property of a probability density function that you first met in S2 Section 1.2, namely

$$\int_{-\infty}^{\infty} f(x)\,dx = 1. \qquad (1.1)$$

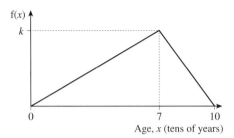

Fig. 1.4. Probability density function for X, the age of a person diagnosed with diabetes, in tens of years.

In this particular case it is not necessary to integrate because the region under $f(x)$ is a triangle. The area of this triangle is $\frac{1}{2} \times 10 \times k$, so $k = \frac{1}{5}$.

The equations of the two parts of the probability density function can be found using coordinate geometry. It is left for you to confirm that the equation of the left-hand line is $y = \frac{1}{35} x$ and the equation of the right-hand line is $y = -\frac{1}{15} x + \frac{2}{3}$. Thus the probability density function is defined by

$$f(x) = \begin{cases} \frac{1}{35} x & 0 \le x < 7, \\ -\frac{1}{15} x + \frac{2}{3} & 7 \le x \le 10, \\ 0 & \text{otherwise.} \end{cases}$$

Whether you rescale or not is a matter of preference. If you do rescale, then you need to remember to convert back to the original scale when you are finding the mean and variance (see Example 1.2.1).

The probability that X lies in a particular interval can be found by integrating $f(x)$ over that interval. The method is illustrated in part (c) of the following example.

Example 1.1.1
The time, X, in minutes, spent waiting for a prescription to be supplied at a chemist's is modelled by the probability density function

$$f(x) = \begin{cases} \frac{1}{64} c & 0 \le x < 16, \\ cx^{-\frac{3}{2}} & x \ge 16, \\ 0 & \text{otherwise.} \end{cases}$$

(a) Sketch the probability density function.
(b) Find the value of c.
(c) Find the probability that a person chosen at random will wait between 5 and 25 minutes.

(a) Fig. 1.5 shows a sketch of the probability density function.

(b) Since $\displaystyle\int_{-\infty}^{\infty} f(x)\,dx = 1$,

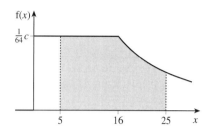

$$\int_0^{16} \frac{1}{64}c\,dx + \int_{16}^{\infty} cx^{-\frac{3}{2}}\,dx = 1,$$

$$\left[\frac{1}{64}cx\right]_0^{16} + \left[-2cx^{-\frac{1}{2}}\right]_{16}^{\infty} = 1,$$

Fig. 1.5. Probability density function for Example 1.1.1.

$$\frac{16}{64}c - \left(-\frac{2}{4}c\right) = 1,$$

giving $c = \frac{4}{3}$.

Thus the probability density function is

$$f(x) = \begin{cases} \dfrac{1}{48} & 0 \leq x < 16, \\[2mm] \dfrac{4}{3}x^{-\frac{3}{2}} & x \geq 16, \\[2mm] 0 & \text{otherwise.} \end{cases}$$

(c) The area which gives $P(5 \leq X \leq 25)$ is shaded in Fig. 1.5.

$$P(5 \leq X \leq 25) = \int_5^{16} \frac{1}{48}\,dx + \int_{16}^{25} \frac{4}{3}x^{-\frac{3}{2}}\,dx$$

$$= \left[\frac{1}{48}x\right]_5^{16} + \left[\frac{4}{3}\times(-2)x^{-\frac{1}{2}}\right]_{16}^{25}$$

$$= \frac{11}{48} - \frac{8}{3}\left(\frac{1}{5} - \frac{1}{4}\right) = \frac{11}{48} + \frac{8}{60} = \frac{29}{80}.$$

1.2 Finding the expectation and variance of a continuous random variable

In S2 Sections 1.4 and 1.5 you learnt how to find the expectation (or mean) and variance of a continuous random variable using the equations

$$E(X) = \mu = \int_{-\infty}^{\infty} x\,f(x)\,dx, \qquad (1.2)$$

$$\mathrm{Var}(X) = \sigma^2 = \int_{-\infty}^{\infty} x^2 f(x)\,dx - \mu^2. \qquad (1.3)$$

The same equations give the expectation and variance of variables whose functions are defined piecewise, the only difference being that there are several parts to the integration.

Example 1.2.1

Find the mean and variance for the continuous random variable X whose probability density function is defined by

$$f(x) = \begin{cases} \frac{1}{35}x & 0 \leqslant x < 7, \\ -\frac{1}{15}x + \frac{2}{3} & 7 \leqslant x \leqslant 10, \\ 0 & \text{otherwise.} \end{cases}$$

This is the model which was used in Section 1.1 for the age, measured in tens of years, of people diagnosed with diabetes.

From Equation 1.2,

$$E(X) = \mu = \int_{-\infty}^{\infty} x\, f(x)\, dx = \int_0^7 x \times \frac{1}{35} x\, dx + \int_7^{10} x\left(-\frac{1}{15}x + \frac{2}{3}\right) dx$$

$$= \int_0^7 \frac{1}{35} x^2\, dx + \int_7^{10} \left(-\frac{1}{15}x^2 + \frac{2}{3}x\right) dx$$

$$= \left[\frac{1}{35} \times \frac{1}{3} x^3\right]_0^7 + \left[-\frac{1}{15} \times \frac{1}{3} x^3 + \frac{2}{3} \times \frac{1}{2} x^2\right]_7^{10}$$

$$= \left(3\frac{4}{15} - 0\right) + \left(11\frac{1}{9} - 8\frac{32}{45}\right) = 5\frac{2}{3}.$$

From Equation 1.3,

$$\text{Var}(X) = \sigma^2 = \int_{-\infty}^{\infty} x^2 f(x)\, dx - \mu^2$$

$$= \int_0^7 x^2 \times \frac{1}{35} x\, dx + \int_7^{10} x^2 \times \left(-\frac{1}{15}x + \frac{2}{3}\right) dx \; - \left(5\frac{2}{3}\right)^2.$$

It is left as an exercise for you to show that this integration gives $\text{Var}(X) = 4\frac{7}{18}$.

If you wish to give the answers in terms of years, rather than tens of years, then the expected value for age given by the model is $10 \times 5\frac{2}{3} = 56\frac{2}{3}$ years. Since the standard deviation is $\sqrt{4\frac{7}{18}}$, where X is measured in tens of years, it is $10\sqrt{4\frac{7}{18}} = 20.9$ years (to 3 significant figures). Therefore the variance in years^2 is $\left(10\sqrt{4\frac{7}{18}}\right)^2 = 100 \times 4\frac{7}{18} = 438\frac{8}{9}$.

Exercise 1A

In Questions 1 to 5, the continuous random variable X has probability density function $f(x)$ and c is a constant.

1 $f(x) = \begin{cases} c & 0 \leqslant x < 1, \\ c(2 - x) & 1 \leqslant x \leqslant 2, \\ 0 & \text{otherwise.} \end{cases}$

(a) Sketch the probability density function.   (b) Find c.

(c) Find $P(0.5 \leqslant X \leqslant 1.5)$.   (d) Find $E(X)$.   (e) Find $\text{Var}(X)$.

2 $f(x) = \begin{cases} cx & 0 \leqslant x < 3, \\ c(6-x) & 3 \leqslant x \leqslant 6, \\ 0 & \text{otherwise.} \end{cases}$

    (a) Sketch $f(x)$.   (b) Find c.   (c) Find $P(X \leqslant 2)$.

    (d) Find $P(2.5 \leqslant X \leqslant 5)$.   (e) Find μ.   (f) Find σ^2.

3 $f(x) = \begin{cases} cx & 0 \leqslant x < 2, \\ \frac{1}{2}cx(4-x) & 2 \leqslant x \leqslant 4, \\ 0 & \text{otherwise.} \end{cases}$

    (a) Sketch the probability density function.   (b) Find c.

    (c) Find $P(1.5 \leqslant X \leqslant 3)$.   (d) Find μ.   (e) Find $\text{Var}(X)$.

4 $f(x) = \begin{cases} cx & 0 \leqslant x < 1, \\ c & 1 \leqslant x < 3, \\ c(4-x) & 3 \leqslant x \leqslant 4, \\ 0 & \text{otherwise.} \end{cases}$

    (a) Sketch the probability density function.   (b) Find c.

    (c) Find $P(0.5 \leqslant X \leqslant 2.5)$.   (d) Find μ.   (e) Find $\text{Var}(X)$.

5 $f(x) = \begin{cases} \frac{1}{4}c(2-x) & -1 \leqslant x < 0, \\ \frac{1}{2}c & 0 \leqslant x < 1, \\ \frac{1}{2}cx & 1 \leqslant x \leqslant 2, \\ 0 & \text{otherwise.} \end{cases}$

    (a) Sketch the probability density function.   (b) Find c.

    (c) Find $P(-0.5 \leqslant X \leqslant 1.5)$.   (d) Find μ.   (e) Find $\text{Var}(X)$.

6 (a) The lifetime, in thousands of hours, of a light bulb is modelled by a continuous random variable, X, having probability density function

$$f(x) = \begin{cases} \frac{2}{5}x & 0 \leqslant x \leqslant 1, \\ \frac{1}{10}(5-x) & 1 < x \leqslant 5, \\ 0 & \text{otherwise.} \end{cases}$$

      Using this model,

      (i)   sketch the graph of $f(x)$,

      (ii)   find the probability that the lifetime of a randomly chosen light bulb is less than 2000 hours,

      (iii) find the expected lifetime of a light bulb in hours.

    (b) A different model is proposed in which the probability density function is

$$g(x) = \begin{cases} xe^{-x} & x \geqslant 0, \\ 0 & \text{otherwise.} \end{cases}$$

      (i)   Using this revised model, find the expected lifetime.

      (ii) Describe what you consider to be the principal difference between the models.

(OCR)

7 The continuous random variable X has probability density function

$$f(x) = \begin{cases} \lambda(a - x) & 0 \leqslant x < a, \\ \lambda(x - a) & a \leqslant x \leqslant 2a, \\ 0 & \text{otherwise.} \end{cases}$$

(a) Sketch the probability density function.

(b) Find λ in terms of a.

(c) Show that $P\left(X \leqslant \frac{1}{2}a\right) = \frac{3}{8}$.

(d) Find the mean of the distribution.

(OCR, adapted)

1.3 Cumulative distribution functions

Probability density functions are used to calculate probabilities, and each time such a calculation is performed the probability density function is integrated. Consider, for example, the probability density function

$$f(x) = \begin{cases} 2e^{-2x} & x \geqslant 0, \\ 0 & \text{otherwise,} \end{cases}$$

which is shown in Fig. 1.6.

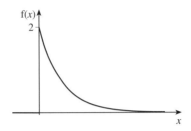

Fig. 1.6. Probability density function $f(x) = 2e^{-2x}$, $x \geqslant 0$.

This form of probability density function involving an exponential term is a suitable model for the interval between random events. Question 7 in Exercise 1B shows how it is related to the Poisson distribution.

Suppose that you wish to calculate $P(X \leqslant 3)$, $P(X \leqslant 4)$ and $P(X \leqslant 5)$. Then

$$P(X \leqslant 3) = \int_{-\infty}^{3} f(x)\,dx = \int_{-\infty}^{0} 0\,dx + \int_{0}^{3} 2e^{-2x}\,dx = \left[-e^{-2x}\right]_{0}^{3} = 1 - e^{-6},$$

$$P(X \leqslant 4) = \int_{-\infty}^{4} f(x)\,dx = \int_{-\infty}^{0} 0\,dx + \int_{0}^{4} 2e^{-2x}\,dx = \left[-e^{-2x}\right]_{0}^{4} = 1 - e^{-8},$$

and $P(X \leqslant 5) = \int_{-\infty}^{5} f(x)\,dx = \int_{-\infty}^{0} 0\,dx + \int_{0}^{5} 2e^{-2x}\,dx = \left[-e^{-2x}\right]_{0}^{5} = 1 - e^{-10}.$

Rather than perform the integral every time you take a different value for the upper limit, it would be more convenient to have an expression of the integrated function with this upper limit as a variable. In place of the integrals above you can write

$$P(X \leqslant x_1) = \int_{-\infty}^{x_1} f(x)\,dx = \int_{0}^{x_1} 2e^{-2x}\,dx = \left[-e^{-2x}\right]_{0}^{x_1} = 1 - e^{-2x_1}$$

where x_1 stands for different values of the upper limit. This equation gives $P(X \leqslant x_1)$ as a function of x_1.

The function obtained by integrating the probability density function in this way is usually denoted by $F(x_1)$. It is called the **cumulative distribution function** (or sometimes just the **distribution function**) and is abbreviated as c.d.f. Note how a capital F denotes the cumulative distribution function whereas a lower-case f denotes the probability density function.

In order to define $F(x_1)$ completely you need to specify the appropriate function for both of the intervals $x_1 < 0$ and $x_1 \geqslant 0$ in Fig. 1.6. For $x_1 \geqslant 0$, $F(x_1) = 1 - e^{-2x_1}$ as found above. For $x_1 < 0$, $F(x_1) = 0$. Thus the cumulative distribution function is

$$F(x_1) = \begin{cases} 1 - e^{-2x_1} & x_1 \geqslant 0, \\ 0 & \text{otherwise.} \end{cases}$$

You met the concept of a cumulative distribution function of a continuous random variable in S2 in connection with the normal distribution. There you used tables or a calculator to find values of the cumulative distribution function since for a normal distribution the function cannot be expressed exactly.

Once the cumulative distribution function has been found by integration the suffix '1' on the x term is usually omitted. Thus for the example above, the cumulative distribution function can be written as

$$F(x) = \begin{cases} 1 - e^{-2x} & x \geqslant 0, \\ 0 & \text{otherwise.} \end{cases}$$

Dropping the suffix '1' is possible because the function F is the same whether it is defined by writing

$$F(x) = \begin{cases} 1 - e^{-2x} & x \geqslant 0, \\ 0 & \text{otherwise,} \end{cases}$$

or by writing

$$F(t) = \begin{cases} 1 - e^{-2t} & t \geqslant 0, \\ 0 & \text{otherwise.} \end{cases}$$

The letters x in the first case and t in the second are called dummy variables because they do not affect the function F. See P4 Section 2.1.

Similarly in the expression $\int_{-\infty}^{x} f(t)\, dt$ the variable t is a dummy variable because, when you integrate and evaluate, all trace of t disappears. Thus $\int_{-\infty}^{x} f(t)\, dt = \int_{-\infty}^{x} f(u)\, du$. They can both be interpreted as the area up to the value x under the graph of the function f.

As well as giving the probability that X lies below a certain value x the cumulative distribution function can be used to find the probability that X lies within a certain interval. For example, using the cumulative distribution function above

$$P(1 \leqslant X \leqslant 2) = P(X \leqslant 2) - P(X \leqslant 1)$$

$$= F(2) - F(1) = \left(1 - e^{-2 \times 2}\right) - \left(1 - e^{-2 \times 1}\right)$$

$$= e^{-2} - e^{-4} = 0.117, \text{ correct to 3 significant figures.}$$

For a continuous random variable, X, the **cumulative distribution function** (c.d.f.), $F(x)$, is defined by

$$F(x) = P(X \leqslant x) = \int_{-\infty}^{x} f(t)\, dt,$$

where f is the probability density function of X.

The probability that $a \leqslant X \leqslant b$ is given by

$$P(a \leqslant X \leqslant b) = F(b) - F(a).$$

Example 1.3.1
A continuous random variable, X, has probability density function

$$f(x) = \begin{cases} \frac{3}{7}x^2 & 1 \leqslant x \leqslant 2, \\ 0 & \text{otherwise.} \end{cases}$$

(a) Sketch the probability density function.
(b) Define the cumulative distribution function completely.
(c) Calculate $P(1.2 \leqslant X \leqslant 1.5)$.
(d) Calculate $P(X > 1.5)$.

(a) Fig. 1.7 shows the probability density function.

(b) The cumulative distribution function will have three separate parts corresponding to the intervals $x < 1$, $1 \leqslant x \leqslant 2$ and $x > 2$.

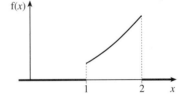

Fig. 1.7. Probability density function for Example 1.3.1.

For $x < 1$, $F(x) = \displaystyle\int_{-\infty}^{x} f(t)\, dt = \int_{-\infty}^{x} 0\, dt = 0.$

For $1 \leqslant x \leqslant 2$, $F(x) = \displaystyle\int_{-\infty}^{x} f(t)\, dt = \int_{-\infty}^{1} 0\, dt + \int_{1}^{x} \frac{3}{7}t^2\, dt$

$$= F(1) + \left[\frac{3}{7} \times \frac{1}{3} x^3 \right]_1^x$$

$$= 0 + \left(\frac{1}{7} x^3 - \frac{1}{7} \right) = \frac{1}{7} x^3 - \frac{1}{7}.$$

For $x > 2$, $F(x) = \displaystyle\int_{-\infty}^{x} f(t)\, dt = \int_{-\infty}^{2} f(t)\, dt + \int_{2}^{x} 0\, dt$

$$= F(2) + 0 = 1 + 0 = 1.$$

So $F(x) = \begin{cases} 0 & x < 1, \\ \frac{1}{7} x^3 - \frac{1}{7} & 1 \leqslant x \leqslant 2, \\ 1 & x > 2. \end{cases}$

(c) $P(1.2 \leqslant X \leqslant 1.5) = F(1.5) - F(1.2)$

$$= \left(\tfrac{1}{7} \times 1.5^3 - \tfrac{1}{7}\right) - \left(\tfrac{1}{7} \times 1.2^3 - \tfrac{1}{7}\right)$$

$= 0.235$, correct to 3 significant figures.

(d) $P(X > 1.5) = 1 - P(X \leqslant 1.5) = 1 - F(1.5)$

$$= 1 - \left(\tfrac{1}{7} \times 1.5^3 - \tfrac{1}{7}\right)$$

$= 0.661$, correct to 3 significant figures.

For functions defined piecewise a similar approach is used, as illustrated in the following example.

Example 1.3.2

A continuous random variable has probability density function given by

$$f(x) = \begin{cases} \tfrac{1}{6}x & 1 \leqslant x < 2, \\ \tfrac{1}{3} & 2 \leqslant x \leqslant k, \\ 0 & \text{otherwise.} \end{cases}$$

(a) Find the value of k.
(b) Define the cumulative distribution function completely.

(a) Fig. 1.8 shows a sketch of the probability density function. The area under the probability density function is made up of a trapezium and a rectangle.

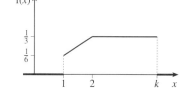

Fig. 1.8. Probability density function for Example 1.3.2.

Area of the trapezium $= \tfrac{1}{2}\left(\tfrac{1}{6} + \tfrac{1}{3}\right) \times 1 = \tfrac{1}{4}$.

Area of the rectangle $= (k-2) \times \tfrac{1}{3}$.

Since the area under the probability density function is 1 it follows that

$$\tfrac{1}{4} + \tfrac{1}{3}(k-2) = 1, \quad \text{giving} \quad k = 4\tfrac{1}{4}.$$

(b) The cumulative distribution function will have four separate parts corresponding to the intervals $x < 1$, $1 \leqslant x < 2$, $2 \leqslant x \leqslant 4\tfrac{1}{4}$ and $x > 4\tfrac{1}{4}$.

For $x < 1$, $F(x) = 0$.

For $1 \leqslant x < 2$, $F(x) = F(1) + \int_1^x \tfrac{1}{6}t\,dt = 0 + \left[\tfrac{1}{12}t^2\right]_1^x = \tfrac{1}{12}\left(x^2 - 1\right)$.

At $x = 2$, $F(x) = \tfrac{1}{12}\left(2^2 - 1^2\right) = \tfrac{1}{4}$.

For $2 \leqslant x \leqslant 4\tfrac{1}{4}$, $F(x) = F(2) + \int_2^x \tfrac{1}{3}dt = \tfrac{1}{4} + \left[\tfrac{1}{3}t\right]_2^x = \tfrac{1}{3}x - \tfrac{5}{12}$.

At $x = 4\tfrac{1}{4}$, $F(x) = 1$.

For $x > 4\tfrac{1}{4}$, $F(x) = 1$.

Thus the cumulative distribution function is

$$F(x) = \begin{cases} 0 & x < 1, \\ \frac{1}{12}(x^2 - 1) & 1 \le x < 2, \\ \frac{1}{3}x - \frac{5}{12} & 2 \le x \le 4\frac{1}{4}, \\ 1 & x > 4\frac{1}{4}. \end{cases}$$

The cumulative distribution function can be used to find the median, quartiles and other percentiles. For example, since the median, M, is defined by $P(X \le M) = \frac{1}{2}$, the median will be determined by the condition $F(M) = \frac{1}{2}$. Similarly the lower quartile, Q_1, will be determined by $F(Q_1) = \frac{1}{4}$ and so on. When a cumulative distribution function is defined piecewise some common sense is needed when deciding which part of the function should be used in these equations and it is helpful to write down the values of $F(x)$ where the pieces join as was done in the example above.

Example 1.3.3
(a) For the probability density function defined in Example 1.3.2 find the median and lower and upper quartiles.
(b) If $P(X < h) = 0.2$, find the value of h.

(a) Since $F(2) = \frac{1}{4}$, the lower quartile is 2.

This means that the median is greater than 2, so it is found from

$$F(M) = \frac{1}{3}M - \frac{5}{12} = \frac{1}{2}, \quad \text{giving} \quad M = 2\frac{3}{4}.$$

The upper quartile, Q_3, will be greater than this and is given by

$$F(Q_3) = \frac{1}{3}Q_3 - \frac{5}{12} = \frac{3}{4}, \quad \text{giving} \quad Q_3 = 3\frac{1}{2}.$$

(b) Since $P(X < h) = 0.2 < 0.25$, h is less than the lower quartile. So it is given by

$$F(h) = \frac{1}{12}(h^2 - 1) = 0.2.$$

The roots of this quadratic equation are $\pm 1.843\ldots$. The value of h is clearly given by the positive root, so $h = 1.84$ correct to 3 significant figures.

Note that finding the median, for example, in effect involves finding the inverse of F since solving $F(M) = \frac{1}{2}$ means putting $M = F^{-1}\left(\frac{1}{2}\right)$. In order to do this F^{-1} must be well-defined. You know that F is an increasing function because of the way in which it is defined. However, in order for it to be one–one it must be strictly increasing for the interval under consideration.

If a continuous random variable is defined in terms of its cumulative distribution function, $F(x)$, then the probability density function, $f(x)$, can be found by differentiating $F(x)$ with respect to x. This follows from the fact that the cumulative distribution function is found by integrating the probability density function. You should verify this statement by differentiating the cumulative distribution function, found in Example 1.3.2. Note that $F(x)$ will not be differentiable at the 'joints' of its parts but this does not matter since the value of $f(x)$ at a point has no practical interpretation. It is conventional to assign the end-points to the same piece for f as for F.

The probability density function, $f(x)$, can be found by differentiating the cumulative distribution function, $F(x)$, with respect to x:

$$f(x) = F'(x).$$

Example 1.3.4

The cumulative distribution function of a random variable, X, is

$$F(x) = \begin{cases} 0 & x < 0, \\ 4x^3 - 3x^4 & 0 \leqslant x \leqslant 1, \\ 1 & x > 1. \end{cases}$$

Find the probability density function.

For $x < 0$, $F(x) = 0$ so $F'(x) = 0$.

For $0 \leqslant x \leqslant 1$, $F(x) = 4x^3 - 3x^4$ so $F'(x) = 12x^2 - 12x^3$.

For $x > 1$, $F(x) = 1$ so $F'(x) = 0$.

So the probability density function is

$$f(x) = \begin{cases} 12x^2 - 12x^3 & 0 \leqslant x \leqslant 1, \\ 0 & \text{otherwise.} \end{cases}$$

Exercise 1B

1 The probability density function of a random variable, X, is

$$f(x) = \begin{cases} \frac{1}{8}x & 0 \leqslant x \leqslant 4, \\ 0 & \text{otherwise.} \end{cases}$$

(a) Find the cumulative distribution function of X.   (b) Find the median.

2 The probability density function of a continuous random variable, X, is

$$f(x) = \begin{cases} \dfrac{2}{3} & 0 \leqslant x < 1, \\ \dfrac{4}{3} - \dfrac{2}{3}x & 1 \leqslant x \leqslant 2, \\ 0 & \text{otherwise.} \end{cases}$$

(a) Find $F(x)$.   (b) Find the lower quartile.   (c) Find the 85th percentile.

3 The probability density function of a continuous random variable, X, is

$$f(x) = \begin{cases} \dfrac{3}{14}x & 0 \leqslant x < 2, \\ \dfrac{3}{28}x(4 - x) & 2 \leqslant x \leqslant 4, \\ 0 & \text{otherwise.} \end{cases}$$

(a) Find $F(x)$.   (b) Find the median.   (c) Find $P(2.5 \leqslant X \leqslant 3)$.

4 Daily sales of petrol, X, at a service station (in tens of thousands of litres) are distributed with probability density function

$$f(x) = \begin{cases} \frac{3}{4}x(2-x)^2 & 0 \le x \le 2, \\ 0 & \text{otherwise.} \end{cases}$$

(a) Find $F(x)$.   (b) Find the median in litres.

5 The cumulative distribution of a random variable, X, is

$$F(x) = \begin{cases} 0 & x < 0, \\ \frac{1}{108}\left(9x^2 - x^3\right) & 0 \le x \le 6, \\ 1 & x > 6. \end{cases}$$

Find the probability density function of X.

6 The cumulative distribution function of a random variable, X, is

$$F(x) = \begin{cases} 0 & x < 0, \\ \frac{1}{18}x^2 & 0 \le x < 3, \\ \frac{2}{3}x - \frac{1}{18}x^2 - 1 & 3 \le x \le 6, \\ 1 & x > 6. \end{cases}$$

Find the probability density function of X.

7 Consider a Poisson process with mean μt for a time interval t. Let T be the random variable, the time interval between successive events.

Show that $f(t)$, the probability density function of T, is given by

$$f(t) = \begin{cases} 0 & t < 0, \\ \mu e^{-\mu t} & t \ge 0. \end{cases}$$

Hint: $P(T > t) = P(\text{no events in time interval } t)$.

1.4 Cumulative distribution functions of related variables

Consider the following problem. Cubical boxes are made so that the length, X (in cm), of an edge has a uniform distribution over the interval $9 \le X \le 11$. What sort of distribution will the volume, Y, of the boxes have, where Y is measured in cm^3?

This question can be answered by relating the cumulative distribution functions of X and Y. The first step in this process is to define the probability density function and hence the cumulative distribution function of X. A sketch of the probability density function of X for the cubical box example is shown in Fig. 1.9. In order for the area under the probability density function to be 1, the value of the constant c must be $\frac{1}{2}$. So the probability density function of X is

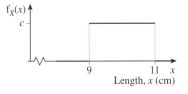

Fig. 1.9. Probability density function of the length, X, of the edge of a cubical box.

$$f_X(x) = \begin{cases} \frac{1}{2} & 9 \le x \le 11, \\ 0 & \text{otherwise.} \end{cases}$$

It is left as an exercise for you to show that the cumulative distribution function of X is

$$F_X(x) = \begin{cases} 0 & x < 9, \\ \frac{1}{2}(x-9) & 9 \leqslant x \leqslant 11, \\ 1 & x > 11. \end{cases}$$

Now, over the interval $9 \leqslant x \leqslant 11$ for X, which corresponds to the interval $729 \leqslant y \leqslant 1331$ for Y,

$$F_Y(y) = P(Y \leqslant y) = P(X^3 \leqslant y) \qquad \text{(since } Y = X^3)$$
$$= P(X \leqslant y^{\frac{1}{3}}) = F_X(y^{\frac{1}{3}}) = \frac{1}{2}(y^{\frac{1}{3}} - 9).$$

The cumulative distribution function of Y is thus

$$F_Y(y) = \begin{cases} 0 & y < 729, \\ \frac{1}{2}(y^{\frac{1}{3}} - 9) & 729 \leqslant y \leqslant 1331, \\ 1 & y > 1331. \end{cases}$$

The probability density function, $f_Y(y)$, of Y can be found by differentiating $F_Y(y)$ with respect to y.

For $729 \leqslant y \leqslant 1331$,

$$f_Y(y) = F_Y'(y) = \frac{1}{6}y^{-\frac{2}{3}}.$$

Elsewhere $f_Y(y) = 0$.

So the probability density function of Y is

$$f_Y(y) = \begin{cases} \frac{1}{6}y^{-\frac{2}{3}} & 729 \leqslant y \leqslant 1331, \\ 0 & \text{otherwise.} \end{cases}$$

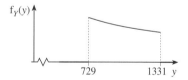

Fig. 1.10. Probability density function of the volume, Y, of a cubical box.

This function is shown in Fig. 1.10.

Example 1.4.1

The radius, X, of a circle is a random variable with probability density function

$$f_X(x) = \begin{cases} x^2 & 0 \leqslant x \leqslant 1, \\ 0 & \text{otherwise.} \end{cases}$$

Find the probability density function of Y, the area of the circle.

The cumulative distribution function of X is

$$F_X(x) = \begin{cases} 0 & x < 0, \\ \frac{1}{3}x^3 & 0 \leqslant x \leqslant 1, \\ 1 & x > 1. \end{cases}$$

When $X = 0$, $Y = 0$; and when $X = 1$, $Y = \pi$.

The relation between X and Y is $Y = \pi X^2$ over the interval $0 \leqslant X \leqslant 1$. This relation is one–one on this interval. Thus

$$F_Y(y) = P(Y \leqslant y) = P(\pi X^2 \leqslant y)$$

$$= P\left(X \leqslant \sqrt{\frac{y}{\pi}}\right) = F_X\left(\sqrt{\frac{y}{\pi}}\right) = \frac{1}{3}\left(\frac{y}{\pi}\right)^{\frac{3}{2}} \qquad \text{for } 0 \leqslant y \leqslant \pi.$$

The probability density function of Y is found by differentiating the cumulative distribution function. This gives

$$f_Y(y) = \begin{cases} \dfrac{1}{2}\sqrt{\dfrac{y}{\pi^3}} & 0 \leqslant y \leqslant \pi, \\ 0 & \text{otherwise.} \end{cases}$$

In the following example the relation between Y and X is not one–one on the interval of interest, so care is needed in relating the values taken by Y to those taken by X.

Example 1.4.2

Find the probability density function of the continuous random variable Y where $Y = X^2$ and X has probability density function $f_X(x) = \frac{3}{2}x^2$ for $-1 \leqslant x \leqslant 1$, and $f_X(x) = 0$ otherwise.

The cumulative distribution function of X is

$$F_X(x) = \begin{cases} 0 & x < -1, \\ \frac{1}{2}x^3 + \frac{1}{2} & -1 \leqslant x \leqslant 1, \\ 1 & x > 1. \end{cases}$$

The domain of X is $-1 \leqslant x \leqslant 1$, so the variable Y takes values between 0 and 1.

$$F_Y(y) = P(Y \leqslant y) = P(X^2 \leqslant y) = P\left(-y^{\frac{1}{2}} \leqslant X \leqslant y^{\frac{1}{2}}\right).$$

The fact that the relation between X and Y is not one–one leads to a double inequality in the last probability above.

So $\quad F_Y(y) = P\left(-y^{\frac{1}{2}} \leqslant X \leqslant y^{\frac{1}{2}}\right) = F_X\left(y^{\frac{1}{2}}\right) - F_X\left(-y^{\frac{1}{2}}\right)$

$$= \left(\frac{1}{2}y^{\frac{3}{2}} + \frac{1}{2}\right) - \frac{1}{2}\left(-y^{\frac{3}{2}} + \frac{1}{2}\right) = y^{\frac{3}{2}}.$$

Differentiating with respect to y gives $f_Y(y) = \frac{3}{2}y^{\frac{1}{2}}$ for $0 \leqslant y \leqslant 1$, and $f_Y(y) = 0$ otherwise.

The theory of this section has an application in simulation studies, for example, in a study of traffic queues at a road junction controlled by traffic lights. One aspect of such a simulation would require generating random values for the time interval between one car and the next arriving at the junction. The behaviour of traffic at the junction can then be investigated for different traffic densities and for different settings of the traffic lights, something which would be impractical to do with real traffic.

The following example introduces a method for simulating random samples from a given distribution.

Example 1.4.3
X is a continuous random variable with a cumulative distribution function F such that F^{-1} is a well-defined function (see the discussion after Example 1.3.3).
(a) Show that if $Z = F(X)$, then Z has a uniform distribution on the interval from 0 to 1.
(b) Show that, conversely, if Z has a uniform distribution on the interval from 0 to 1 and $X = F^{-1}(Z)$, then the cumulative distribution function of X is F.

(a) Consider first the form of the cumulative distribution function for the random variable U where U has a uniform distribution on the interval from 0 to 1:

$$P(U \leqslant u) = \int_0^u \mathrm{d}t = u.$$

Now consider the cumulative distribution function of Z:

$$P(Z \leqslant z) = P(F(X) \leqslant z) = P\left(X \leqslant F^{-1}(z)\right) = F\left(F^{-1}(z)\right) = z.$$

So Z has a uniform distribution on the interval from 0 to 1.

(b) Finally consider the cumulative distribution function of X:

$$P(X \leqslant x) = P\left(F^{-1}(Z) \leqslant x\right) = P(Z \leqslant F(x))$$

$$= F(x). \quad \text{(since } Z \text{ has a uniform distribution)}$$

So the cumulative distribution function of X is F.

Computer activity
The second result proved in Example 1.4.3 provides the basis for simulating measurements from a distribution with a given cumulative distribution function. Pseudo-random numbers in the interval from 0 to 1 can be generated by computer. Then the function F^{-1} is applied to these numbers to simulate a random sample from the distribution with cumulative distribution function F. Use this method on a spreadsheet to simulate a random sample from the distribution which was defined in Section 1.1:

$$f(x) = \begin{cases} \frac{1}{35}x & 0 \leqslant x < 7, \\ -\frac{1}{15}x + \frac{2}{3} & 7 \leqslant x \leqslant 10, \\ 0 & \text{otherwise,} \end{cases}$$

where X is the age, in tens of years, of people diagnosed with diabetes.

1.5 The expectation of a function of a random variable

In the previous section you learnt how to find the probability density function of a variable, Y, from the probability density function of a related variable, X. That knowledge puts you in a position to calculate the expected values of both X and Y.

Consider again the cubical boxes of Section 1.4. By symmetry $E(X) = 10$. The expected value of the volume Y can be found as follows.

$$E(Y) = \int_{729}^{1331} y \times \frac{1}{6} y^{-\frac{2}{3}} \, dy = \int_{729}^{1331} \frac{1}{6} y^{\frac{1}{3}} \, dy = \left[\frac{1}{8} y^{\frac{4}{3}}\right]_{729}^{1331} = \frac{1}{8} \times 1331^{\frac{4}{3}} - \frac{1}{8} \times 729^{\frac{4}{3}} = 1010.$$

Note that $E(X^3)$ is not equal to $(E(X))^3$.

If you do not need to know the distribution of Y, then there is a quicker way to find its expected value. The expected value of Y, $E(Y)$, can be found directly from the probability density function of X using the following relation.

> If the continuous random variable X has probability density function $f(x)$ and $g(X)$ is a function of X, then
>
> $$E(g(X)) = \int_a^b g(x)f(x) \, dx, \qquad (1.4)$$
>
> where a and b are the limits appropriate to the situation.

Applying Equation 1.4 to the cubic box example, where $Y = g(X) = X^3$, gives

$$E(Y) = E(g(X)) = \int_a^b g(x)f(x) \, dx = \int_9^{11} x^3 \times \frac{1}{2} \, dx = \left[\frac{1}{8} x^4\right]_9^{11} = \frac{1}{8} \times 11^4 - \frac{1}{8} \times 9^4 = 1010.$$

The appropriate limits here, 9 and 11, are the lowest and highest values of x.

This is the same result as was obtained before.

Example 1.5.1
Find the mean of the random variable Y in Example 1.4.1 directly from the probability density function of X.

Since $Y = g(X) = \pi X^2$,

$$E(Y) = E(g(X)) = \int_a^b g(x)f(x) \, dx = \int_0^1 \pi x^2 \times x^2 \, dx = \left[\frac{1}{5} \pi x^5\right]_0^1 = \frac{1}{5}\pi.$$

You can verify for yourself that you obtain the same result by using the probability density function of Y directly.

Exercise 1C

1   The continuous random variable X has probability density function $f(x)$. Use Equation 1.4 to show that $E(cX + d) = cE(X) + d$, where c and d are constants.

2 The length, X, of a side of a square has a uniform distribution over the interval from 1 to 6.

    (a) Find the probability density function of Y, the area of the square.

    (b) Find $E(Y)$.

    (c) Find $E(X^2)$, using Equation 1.4.

    (d) Why are your answers to parts (b) and (c) the same?

3 The radius, X, of a circle follows a uniform distribution over the interval from 1 to 4. Find the probability density function of Y, the area of the circle.

4 The continuous random variable X has probability density function

$$f(x) = \begin{cases} \frac{3}{4}(1 - x^2) & -1 \leqslant x \leqslant 1, \\ 0 & \text{otherwise.} \end{cases}$$

Find $E(X)$, $E(X^2)$, $E(X^3)$, $E(X^4)$.

5 The continuous random variable X has probability density function

$$f(x) = \begin{cases} \frac{1}{2} & 0 \leqslant x \leqslant 2, \\ 0 & \text{otherwise.} \end{cases}$$

Find $E\big((X-1)^3\big)$.

6 The continuous random variable X has probability density function

$$f(x) = \begin{cases} \frac{3}{8}x^2 & 0 \leqslant x \leqslant 2, \\ 0 & \text{otherwise.} \end{cases}$$

Find $E(3X^3)$, $E(2X)$, $E(3X^3 + 2X + 1)$.

7 The continuous random variable X has probability density function

$$f(x) = \begin{cases} \frac{1}{9}x & 0 \leqslant x < 3, \\ \frac{1}{9}(6 - x) & 3 \leqslant x \leqslant 6, \\ 0 & \text{otherwise.} \end{cases}$$

Find $E(X^3)$ and $E\left(\dfrac{1}{X}\right)$.

Miscellaneous exercise 1

1 The random variable X has probability density function given by

$$f(x) = \begin{cases} kx & 0 \leqslant x \leqslant 1, \\ k & 1 < x \leqslant 2, \\ 0 & \text{otherwise,} \end{cases}$$

where k is a constant.

    (a) Show that $k = \frac{2}{3}$.

    (b) Find $E(X)$ and $E(X^2)$.

    (c) Show that the median M of X is 1.25, and find $P\big(|X - M| > \frac{1}{2}\big)$.   (OCR)

2 The random variable T has probability density function given by

$$f(t) = \begin{cases} k(t-2) & 2 \leqslant t \leqslant 4, \\ 0 & \text{otherwise,} \end{cases}$$

where k is a constant. Find, in terms of k, the cumulative distribution function.

Hence, or otherwise, find the value of k.

Show that $P(T > 3) = \frac{3}{4}$. (OCR)

3 The continuous random variable X has cumulative distribution function F given by

$$F(x) = \begin{cases} 0 & x < 0, \\ a\left(6x^2 - x^3\right) & 0 \leqslant x \leqslant 4, \\ 1 & x > 4, \end{cases}$$

where a is a constant. Find a.

Find the probability density function of X, and use the fact that the graph of this function is symmetrical about $x = 2$ to write down the expectation of X. (OCR)

4 The continuous random variable X is such that

$$P(X > x) = \begin{cases} 1 & x < 0, \\ k(3-x)^3 & 0 \leqslant x \leqslant 3, \\ 0 & x > 3. \end{cases}$$

Show that $P(X > 1) = \frac{8}{27}$.

Find the probability density function of X, and hence find $E(X)$. (OCR)

5 The continuous random variable X is the distance, measured in hundreds of kilometres, that a particular car will travel on a full tank of petrol. It is given that

$$P(X \leqslant x) = \begin{cases} 0 & x < 3, \\ ax^2 - 8ax + b & 3 \leqslant x \leqslant 4, \\ 1 & 4 < x, \end{cases}$$

where a and b are constants. Show that $a = -1$, find the value of b, and verify that $P(X \leqslant 3.5) = \frac{3}{4}$.

Find the probability density function of X. (OCR)

6 The continuous random variable X has probability density function given by

$$f(x) = \begin{cases} \dfrac{k}{x} & 1 \leqslant x \leqslant \mathrm{e}, \\ 0 & \text{otherwise,} \end{cases}$$

where k is a constant.

(a) Show that $k = 1$.

(b) Find the cumulative distribution function F of X, and sketch the graph of $y = F(X)$.

(c) Find $E\left(\dfrac{1}{X}\right)$ in terms of e. (OCR)

7 The continuous random variable X has (cumulative) distribution function given by

$$F(x) = \begin{cases} \frac{1}{8}(1+x) & -1 \leqslant x < 0, \\ \frac{1}{8}(1+3x) & 0 \leqslant x < 2, \\ \frac{1}{8}(5+x) & 2 \leqslant x \leqslant 3, \end{cases}$$

with $F(x) = 0$ for $x < -1$, and $F(x) = 1$ for $x > 3$.

(a) Sketch the graph of the probability density function $f(x)$.

(b) Determine the expectation of X and the variance of X.

(c) Determine $P(3 \leqslant 2X \leqslant 5)$. (OCR)

8 The continuous random variable X has cumulative distribution function given by

$$F(x) = \begin{cases} 0 & x < 0, \\ 2x - x^2 & 0 \leqslant x \leqslant 1, \\ 1 & x > 1. \end{cases}$$

(a) Find $P\left(X > \frac{1}{2}\right)$.

(b) Find the value of q such that $P(X < q) = \frac{1}{4}$.

(c) Find the probability density function of X, and sketch its graph. (OCR)

9 If X is continuously uniformly-distributed between 0 and 1, and $Y = \ln X$, find $P(Y \leqslant y)$, and hence deduce the probability density of Y. Obtain the expectation of $\ln X$. (OCR)

10 The object distance, U, and the image distance, V, for a concave mirror are related to the focal distance, f, by the formula

$$\frac{1}{u} + \frac{1}{v} = \frac{1}{f}.$$

U is a random variable uniformly distributed over the interval from $2f$ to $3f$. Show that V is distributed with probability density function

$$\frac{f}{(v-f)^2},$$

and state the range of corresponding values for V. Obtain the mean and median of V. (OCR)

2 Linear combinations of random variables

This chapter studies the distribution of linear functions and linear combinations of random variables. When you have completed it you should be able to apply the following results.

- $E(aX + b) = aE(X) + b$ and $Var(aX + b) = a^2 Var(X)$
- $E(aX + bY) = aE(X) + bE(Y)$
- $Var(aX + bY) = a^2 Var(X) + b^2 Var(Y)$ for independent X and Y
- if X has a normal distribution, then so does $aX + b$
- if X and Y have independent normal distributions, then $aX + bY$ has a normal distribution
- if X and Y have independent Poisson distributions, then $X + Y$ has a Poisson distribution.

2.1 The expectation and variance of a linear function of a random variable

In the last chapter you studied functions of a random variable. This chapter starts by looking at one particular type of function of a random variable, X, namely a linear function $aX + b$, where a and b are constants. If you have done Question 1 of Exercise 1C, then you already know that for a random variable

$$E(aX + b) = aE(X) + b. \qquad (2.1)$$

If you have not done this question, try it now.

There is also a relation between $Var(aX + b)$ and $Var(X)$, which is

$$Var(aX + b) = a^2 Var(X). \qquad (2.2)$$

You may be surprised that this second relation does not include the constant b. However, the result is reasonable when you remember that variance is a measure of spread and that adding a constant to X (or subtracting a constant from it) does not affect the spread of the values.

Example 2.1.1
The temperature in degrees Fahrenheit at a seaside resort is a random variable with mean 59 and variance 27. Find the mean and variance of the temperature in degrees Centigrade.

Let X be the temperature in °F. Then $E(X) = 59$ and $Var(X) = 27$.

If Y is the temperature in °C, then $Y = \frac{5}{9}(X - 32) = \frac{5}{9}X - \frac{160}{9}$.

So $E(Y) = E\left(\frac{5}{9}X - \frac{160}{9}\right) = \frac{5}{9}E(X) - \frac{160}{9} = \frac{5}{9} \times 59 - \frac{160}{9} = 15$,

and $Var(Y) = \left(\frac{5}{9}\right)^2 Var(X) = \frac{25}{81} \times 27 = \frac{25}{3}$.

Here are proofs of Equations 2.1 and 2.2 in the case when X is a discrete random variable.

Theorem   For a discrete random variable, $E(aX + b) = aE(X) + b$.

Proof   Let the discrete random variable X take values x_i with probabilities p_i. Then from S1 Section 8.1,

$$E(X) = \mu_X = \sum x_i p_i \ .$$

Now define a new variable Y such that $Y = aX + b$. This variable Y takes values y_i, where $y_i = ax_i + b$, with probabilities p_i.

The expected value of Y is given by

$$E(Y) = \mu_Y = \sum y_i p_i = \sum (ax_i + b) p_i$$
$$= a\sum x_i p_i + b \sum p_i$$
$$= aE(X) + b, \qquad \text{(since } \sum p_i = 1.)$$

Since $Y = aX + b$, $E(Y) = E(aX + b)$; it follows that $E(aX + b) = aE(X) + b$.

Theorem   For a discrete random variable, $\text{Var}(aX + b) = a^2 \text{Var}(X)$.

Proof   From S1 Section 8.2,

$$\text{Var}(X) = \sum (x_i - \mu_X)^2 p_i = \sum x_i^2 p_i - \mu_X^2 \ .$$

The first form of the formula for variance is more convenient for this proof.

Now define a new variable Y such that $Y = aX + b$. This variable Y takes values y_i, where $y_i = ax_i + b$, with probabilities p_i.

For the variable Y

$$\text{Var}(Y) = \sum (y_i - \mu_Y)^2 p_i$$
$$= \sum ((ax_i + b) - (a\mu_X + b))^2 p_i$$
$$= \sum (a(x_i - \mu_X))^2 p_i$$
$$= \sum a^2 (x_i - \mu_X)^2 p_i = a^2 \sum (x_i - \mu_X)^2 p_i$$
$$= a^2 \text{Var}(X).$$

Since $Y = aX + b$, $\text{Var}(Y) = \text{Var}(aX + b)$; it follows that $\text{Var}(aX + b) = a^2 \text{Var}(X)$.

The proof of Equation 2.2 for a continuous random variable is in Exercise 2A Question 10.

For any random variable X,

$$E(aX + b) = aE(X) + b,$$

$$\text{Var}(aX + b) = a^2 \text{Var}(X),$$

where a and b are constants.

2.2 Linear combinations of more than one random variable

Situations often arise in which you know the expected value and variance of each of several random variables and would like to find the expected value and variance of a linear combination. For example, you might know the expected value and variance of the thickness of the sheets which make up a laminated windscreen and wish to find the expected value and variance of the total thickness of the windscreen.

In order investigate any possible relations between expected values and variances you could start by considering two discrete random variables, X and Y. Table 2.1 gives the probability distributions of two such random variables.

x	1	2	3
$P(X = x)$	$\frac{1}{2}$	$\frac{1}{3}$	$\frac{1}{6}$

y	2	4
$P(Y = y)$	$\frac{1}{3}$	$\frac{2}{3}$

Table 2.1. Probability distributions of two discrete random variables.

It is left as an exercise for you to show that $E(X) = \frac{5}{3}$, $Var(X) = \frac{5}{9}$, $E(Y) = \frac{10}{3}$ and $Var(Y) = \frac{8}{9}$. (You will find it more convenient to use the second form of the formula for variance in your calculations.)

Table 2.2 gives the probability distribution of S, the sum of X and Y. (The fractions have been left uncancelled to show the shape of the distribution.) Again check that you can obtain this probability distribution for yourself.

s	3	4	5	6	7
$P(S = s)$	$\frac{3}{18}$	$\frac{2}{18}$	$\frac{7}{18}$	$\frac{4}{18}$	$\frac{2}{18}$

Table 2.2. Probability distribution of S where $S=X+Y$.

Now check that $E(S) = 5$ and $Var(S) = \frac{13}{9}$. You should be able to spot that the relation between the expected values is $E(S) = E(X) + E(Y)$ and between the variances is $Var(S) = Var(X) + Var(Y)$. These are particular instances of general results which hold for both discrete and continuous random variables. However, it is important to appreciate that while the relation between expected values is true for *all* random variables the relation between the variances is only true for *independent* random variables.

When the variables are not independent the relation between the variances becomes $Var(S) = Var(X) + Var(Y) + 2\,Cov(X,Y)$, where $Cov(X,Y)$ stands for 'the covariance of X and Y' and measures the joint variability of X and Y. Covariance is discussed in more detail in S4 Chapter 6.

The relations $E(S) = E(X) + E(Y)$ and $Var(S) = Var(X) + Var(Y)$ can be extended to situations in which there are more than two random variables.

Example 2.2.1

My journey to work is made up of four stages: a walk to the bus-stop, a wait for the bus, a bus journey and a walk at the other end. The times taken for these four stages are independent random variables U, V, W and X with expected values (in minutes) of 4.7, 5.6, 21.6 and 3.7 respectively and standard deviations of 1.1, 1.2, 3.1 and 0.8 respectively. What is the expected time and standard deviation for the total journey?

The expected time for the whole journey is

$$E(U + V + W + X) = E(U) + E(V) + E(W) + E(X)$$
$$= 4.7 + 5.6 + 21.6 + 3.7 = 35.6.$$

Since the variables U, V, W and X are independent

$$\text{Var}(U + V + W + X) = \text{Var}(U) + \text{Var}(V) + \text{Var}(W) + \text{Var}(X)$$
$$= 1.1^2 + 1.2^2 + 3.1^2 + 0.8^2 = 12.9,$$

so the standard deviation for the whole journey is $\sqrt{12.9} = 3.59$, correct to 3 significant figures.

The relations between expected values and variances can also be generalised to the situation where $S = aX + bY$ and a and b are constants. Then

$$E(S) = E(aX + bY) = E(aX) + E(bY)$$
$$= aE(X) + bE(Y), \qquad \text{(using Equation 2.1)}$$

and for independent X and Y

$$\text{Var}(S) = \text{Var}(aX + bY) = \text{Var}(aX) + \text{Var}(bY)$$
$$= a^2 \text{Var}(X) + b^2 \text{Var}(Y). \qquad \text{(using Equation 2.2)}$$

Example 2.2.2

The length, L (in cm), of the boxes produced by a machine is a random variable with mean 26 and variance 4 and the width, B (in cm), is a random variable with mean 14 and variance 1. The variables L and B are independent. What are the expected value and variance of

(a) the perimeter of the boxes,

(b) the difference between the length and the width?

(a) The perimeter is $2L + 2B$, so

$$E(2L + 2B) = 2E(L) + 2E(B) = 2 \times 26 + 2 \times 14 = 80,$$

$$\text{Var}(2L + 2B) = 2^2 \text{Var}(L) + 2^2 \text{Var}(B) = 4 \times 4 + 4 \times 1 = 20.$$

(b) The difference between length and width is $L - B$, so

$$E(L - B) = E(L) - E(B) = 26 - 14 = 12,$$

$$\text{Var}(L - B) = 1^2 \text{Var}(L) + (-1)^2 \text{Var}(B) = 1 \times 4 + 1 \times 1 = 5.$$

The result for the variance is an example of a general rule which applies when variances are combined, namely that they are always added.

For any random variables X, Y, U, V etc.,

$$E(aX + bY + cU + dV + ...) = aE(X) + bE(Y) + cE(U) + dE(V) + ... \quad (2.3)$$

For *independent* random variables X, Y, U, V etc.,

$$Var(aX + bY + cU + dV + ...)$$
$$= a^2 Var(X) + b^2 Var(Y) + c^2 Var(U) + d^2 Var(V) + ... \quad (2.4)$$

2.3 Linear relations involving more than one observation of a random variable

Equations 2.3 and 2.4 can be applied to repeated observations of a single random variable. Suppose, for example, you make two observations of a random variable X where $E(X) = 3$ and $Var(X) = 4$. Denote these observations by X_1 and X_2. Then the expected values and variances of X_1 and X_2 will be equal to the corresponding values for X. It follows that

$$E(X_1 + X_2) = E(X_1) + E(X_2) = E(X) + E(X) = 3 + 3 = 6,$$

and, providing the observations are independent, that

$$Var(X_1 + X_2) = Var(X_1) + Var(X_2) = Var(X) + Var(X) = 4 + 4 = 8.$$

It is instructive to compare these results with the values for $E(2X)$ and $Var(2X)$ obtained using Equations 2.1 and 2.2:

$$E(2X) = 2E(X) = 2 \times 3 = 6, \quad \text{and} \quad Var(2X) = 2^2 Var(X) = 2^2 \times 4 = 16.$$

The expected values for $X_1 + X_2$ and $2X$ are the same. This is not surprising since $2X = X + X$ and so $E(2X) = E(X) + E(X) = 6$. Why then do the variances of $X_1 + X_2$ and $2X$ differ? The answer is that it is not true to say that $Var(2X) = Var(X) + Var(X)$, because the variables X and X are not independent: they refer to the *same* observation of the same variable. This means that it is important to distinguish clearly between situations in which a single observation is multiplied by a constant and those in which several different observations of the same random variable are added.

Exercise 2A

1 The random variable X is the number of even numbers obtained when two ordinary fair dice are thrown. The random variable Y is the number of even numbers obtained when two fair pentagonal spinners, each numbered 1, 2, 3, 4, 5, are spun simultaneously.

Copy and complete the following probability distributions.

x	0	1	2
p	0.25		

y	0	1	2
p	0.36		

$x + y$	0	1	2	3	4
p	0.09				

Find $E(X)$, $Var(X)$, $E(Y)$, $Var(Y)$, $E(X + Y)$, $Var(X + Y)$ by using the probability distributions.

Verify that $E(X + Y) = E(X) + E(Y)$ and $Var(X + Y) = Var(X) + Var(Y)$.

2 X and Y are independent random variables with probability distributions as shown.

x	1	2	3
p	0.4	0.2	0.4

y	0	1	2
p	0.3	0.5	0.2

You are given that $E(X) = 2$, $Var(X) = 0.8$, $E(Y) = 0.9$ and $Var(Y) = 0.49$.

The random variable T is defined as $2X - Y$. Find $E(T)$ and $Var(T)$ using Equations 2.3 and 2.4.

Check your answers by completing the following probability distribution and calculating $E(T)$ and $Var(T)$ directly.

t	0	1	2	3	4	5	6
p	0.08						0.12

3 The independent random variables W, X and Y have means 10, 8 and 6 respectively and variances 4, 5 and 3 respectively.

Find $E(W + X + Y)$, $Var(W + X + Y)$, $E(2W - X - Y)$ and $Var(2W - X - Y)$.

4 A piece of laminated plywood consists of three pieces of wood of type A and two pieces of type B. The thickness of A has mean 2 mm and variance 0.04 mm^2. The thickness of B has mean 1 mm and variance 0.01 mm^2. Find the mean and variance of the thickness of the laminated plywood.

5 The random variable S is the score when an ordinary fair dice is thrown. The random variable T is the number of tails obtained when a fair coin is tossed once.

Find $E(S)$, $Var(S)$, $E(6T)$, $Var(6T)$, $E(S + 6T)$ and $Var(S + 6T)$.

6 The random variable X has the probability distribution shown in the table.

x	1	2	3	4
$P(X = x)$	$\frac{3}{8}$	$\frac{1}{4}$	$\frac{1}{4}$	$\frac{1}{8}$

Find the mean and variance of the distribution of the sum of three independent observations of X.

7 In American football, the quarterback's rating, Q, is calculated using the formula

$Q = \frac{5}{6}(C + 5Y + 2.5 + 4T - 5I)$, where C, Y, T and I are variables which can be considered independent with means and variances as shown in the table.

Variable	C	Y	T	I
Mean	60.0	6.8	4.5	3.1
Variance	68.5	2.3	9.0	7.1

C, T and I are the percentage completions, touchdown passes and interceptions per pass attempt. Y is the number of yards gained divided by the passes attempted.

Find $E(Q)$ and $Var(Q)$.

8 The random variable Y which can only take the values 0 and 1 is called the Bernoulli distribution. Given that $P(1) = p$, show that $E(Y) = p$ and $Var(Y) = p(1-p)$.

The binomial distribution can be considered to be a series of Bernoulli trials. That is,

$$X = Y_1 + Y_2 + \ldots + Y_n.$$

Show that $E(X) = np$ and $Var(X) = np(1-p)$.

9 Let X_1, X_2, $\ldots$, X_n be a random sample of size n taken from any population, which can be considered infinite, with mean μ and variance σ^2.

By considering $\overline{X} = \dfrac{X_1 + X_2 + \ldots + X_n}{n}$, show that $E(\overline{X}) = \mu$ and $Var(\overline{X}) = \dfrac{\sigma^2}{n}$.

10 Prove that Equation 2.2 is true for a continuous variable. Start by defining $Var(Y) = \displaystyle\int_{-\infty}^{\infty} (y - \mu_Y)^2 f(y) \, dy$. From Equation 1.4, this can be written as

$Var(Y) = E\left((Y - \mu_Y)^2\right)$. Now let $Y = aX + b$. Substitute for Y and μ_Y in the expression for $Var(Y)$, and hence obtain Equation 2.2.

2.4 Linear functions and combinations of normally distributed random variables

A normally distributed random variable has the useful and interesting property that a linear function of it is also normally distributed. In addition, linear combinations of independent normal variables are also normally distributed.

> If a continuous random variable X is distributed normally, then $aX + b$ (where a and b are constants) is also distributed normally.
>
> If continuous random variables X, Y, $\ldots$ have independent normal distributions, then $aX + bY + \ldots$ (where a, b, $\ldots$ are constants) is also distributed normally.

You have already met an application of this result in S2, where you used the fact that the mean of a random sample of independent observations taken from a normal population also has a normal distribution. This result follows from the second statement in the shaded box above since the mean is given by $\overline{X} = \dfrac{1}{n}(X_1 + X_2 + \ldots + X_n)$, which is a linear combination of X_1, X_2, $\ldots$, X_n.

The following two examples illustrate other applications of these important properties.

Example 2.4.1

The mass of an empty lift cage is 210 kg. If the masses (in kg) of adults are distributed as $N(70, 950)$, what is the probability that the mass of the lift cage containing 10 adults chosen at random exceeds 1000 kg?

Let the mass in kg of an adult chosen at random be X. Then $X \sim N(70, 950)$.

Let the mass of the cage containing 10 adults be M. Then

$$M = 210 + X_1 + X_2 + \ldots + X_{10}.$$

Assuming that the masses of the adults are independent, M will be normally distributed with mean and variance given by

$$\begin{aligned}
\mathrm{E}(M) &= \mathrm{E}(210 + X_1 + X_2 + \ldots + X_{10}) \\
&= 210 + \mathrm{E}(X_1) + \mathrm{E}(X_2) + \ldots + \mathrm{E}(X_{10}) \\
&= 210 + 10 \times \mathrm{E}(X) \\
&= 210 + 10 \times 70 = 910,
\end{aligned}$$

and $\quad \begin{aligned}[t]
\mathrm{Var}(M) &= \mathrm{Var}(210 + X_1 + X_2 + \ldots + X_{10}) \\
&= \mathrm{Var}(X_1) + \mathrm{Var}(X_2) + \ldots + \mathrm{Var}(X_{10}) \\
&= 10 \times \mathrm{Var}(X) \\
&= 10 \times 950 = 9500.
\end{aligned}$

So $\quad M \sim \mathrm{N}(910, 9500)$.

As the masses of the adults are for 10 different adults, $M \neq 210 + 10X$.
So $\mathrm{Var}(M) \neq 10^2 \, \mathrm{Var}(X)$.

$$\begin{aligned}
\mathrm{P}(M > 1000) &= \mathrm{P}\left(Z > \frac{1000 - 910}{\sqrt{9500}}\right) = \mathrm{P}(Z > 0.923) \\
&= 1 - \Phi(0.923) \\
&= 1 - 0.8220 = 0.1780.
\end{aligned}$$

The probability that the mass of the lift cage with 10 adults exceeds 1000 kg is 0.178, correct to 3 significant figures.

Example 2.4.2

An engineering company buys steel rods and steel tubes. Without heating the tubes so that they expand, an insufficient proportion of the rods will fit inside the tubes. Measured in centimetres, the internal diameter at room temperature of a randomly chosen tube is denoted by T, and the diameter at room temperature of a randomly chosen rod is denoted by R. It is given that $T \sim \mathrm{N}(4.00, 0.10^2)$, that $R \sim \mathrm{N}(4.02, 0.10^2)$, and that T and R are independent. Find the probability that a randomly chosen rod would fit inside a randomly chosen tube, without heating the tube.

The tubes are heated so that the internal diameter of each tube increases by 5%. Find the probability that a randomly chosen rod fits inside a randomly chosen tube, after the tube has been heated.   (OCR)

In order for a randomly chosen rod to fit inside a randomly chosen tube it is necessary that $T > R$. This inequality can also be expressed as $T - R > 0$, so the problem can be solved by considering the distribution of $T - R$. Since T and R are independent, $T - R$ is normally distributed with

$$\mathrm{E}(T - R) = \mathrm{E}(T) - \mathrm{E}(R) = 4.00 - 4.02 = -0.02,$$

and

$$\text{Var}(T - R) = 1^2 \times \text{Var}(T) + (-1)^2 \times \text{Var}(R)$$
$$= (0.10)^2 + (0.10)^2 = 0.02.$$

So $T - R \sim N(-0.02, 0.02)$.

A randomly chosen rod will fit inside a randomly chosen tube if $T - R > 0$.

$$P(T - R > 0) = P\left(Z > \frac{0 - (-0.02)}{\sqrt{0.02}}\right) = P(Z > 0.141)$$
$$= 1 - \Phi(0.141)$$
$$= 1 - 0.5561 = 0.4439.$$

When the tubes have been heated, their diameter is given by $1.05T$. A rod will now fit inside a tube provided that $1.05T - R > 0$.

$$E(1.05T - R) = 1.05E(T) - E(R)$$
$$= 1.05 \times 4.00 - 4.02 = 0.18.$$

$$\text{Var}(1.05T - R) = (1.05)^2 \text{Var}(T) + (-1)^2 \text{Var}(R)$$
$$= (1.05)^2 \times 0.1^2 + 0.1^2 = 0.021\,025.$$

Thus $1.05T - R \sim N(0.18, 0.021\,025)$.

$$P(1.05T - R > 0) = P\left(Z > \frac{0 - 0.18}{\sqrt{0.021\,025}}\right) = P(Z > 1.241)$$
$$= \Phi(1.241) = 0.8927.$$

The probability that a randomly chosen rod fits inside a randomly chosen tube after the tube has been heated is 0.893, correct to 3 significant figures.

2.5 The distribution of the sum of two independent Poisson variables

Suppose you have two Poisson variables, $X \sim \text{Po}(\lambda_X)$ and $Y \sim \text{Po}(\lambda_Y)$.

Then

$$E(X + Y) = E(X) + E(Y) = \lambda_X + \lambda_Y.$$

Since X and Y are Poisson variables, their variances are equal to their corresponding means. Thus, provided that X and Y are independent,

$$\text{Var}(X + Y) = \text{Var}(X) + \text{Var}(Y) = \lambda_X + \lambda_Y.$$

Thus the mean and variance of $X + Y$ are also equal. This means that it is *possible* for $X + Y$ to have a Poisson distribution. In fact, it can be *proved* that $X + Y$ has a Poisson distribution, provided that X and Y are independent, but a proof will not be given here. (See S4 Exercise 3C Question 5 for a proof.)

Note that a linear combination of independent Poisson variables of the form $aX + bY$ (where a and b take values other than 1) cannot have a Poisson distribution since in that case the mean $(a\lambda_X + b\lambda_Y)$ is not equal to the variance $(a^2\lambda_X + b^2\lambda_Y)$.

Example 2.5.1

The numbers of emissions per minute from two radioactive sources are modelled by independent random variables X and Y which have Poisson distributions with means 5 and 8 respectively. Calculate the probability that in any minute the total number of emissions from the two sources is less than 6.

> The total number of emissions, $X + Y$, has a Poisson distribution with mean $5 + 8 = 13$.

> Note first that $P(X < 6) = P(X \leqslant 5)$. Then, from the cumulative Poisson probability tables, $P(X \leqslant 5) = 0.0107$.

> The probability that in any minute the total number of emissions from the two sources is less than 6 is 0.0107, correct to 3 significant figures.

Since $X + Y$ has a normal distribution when X and Y have independent normal distributions and $X + Y$ has a Poisson distribution when X and Y have independent Poisson distributions you may be wondering whether these are particular instances of a general rule. This is not the case. If two independent random variables follow the same type of distribution, it is not necessarily true that their sum also follows this type of distribution.

For example, if X and Y have binomial distributions with different values of p, $X + Y$ does not have a binomial distribution; if X and Y have uniform distributions, $X + Y$ does not have a uniform distribution.

Exercise 2B

1 The heights of a population of male students are distributed normally with mean 178 cm and standard deviation 5 cm. The heights of a population of female students are distributed normally with mean 168 cm and standard deviation 4 cm. Find the probability that a randomly chosen female is taller than a randomly chosen male.

2 W is the mass of wine in a fully filled bottle, B is the mass of the bottle and C is the mass of the crate into which 12 filled bottles are placed for transportation, all in grams. It is given that $W \sim N(825, 15^2)$, $B \sim N(400, 10^2)$ and $C \sim N(1500, 20^2)$. Find the probability that a fully filled crate weighs less than 16.1 kg.

3 The times of four athletes for the 400 m are each distributed normally with mean 47 seconds and standard deviation 2 seconds. The four athletes are to compete in a 4×400 m relay race. Find the probability that their total time is less than 3 minutes.

4 The capacities of small bottles of perfume are distributed normally with mean 50 ml and standard deviation 3 ml. The capacities of large bottles of the same perfume are distributed normally with mean 80 ml and standard deviation 5 ml. Find the probability that the total capacity of 3 small bottles is greater than the total capacity of 2 large bottles.

5 The diameters of a consignment of bolts are distributed normally with mean 1.05 cm and standard deviation 0.1 cm. The diameters of a consignment of nuts are distributed normally with mean 1.1 cm and standard deviation 0.1 cm. Find the probability that a randomly chosen bolt will not fit inside a randomly chosen nut.

6 The amount of black coffee dispensed by a drinks machine is normally distributed with mean 200 ml and standard deviation 5 ml. If a customer requires white coffee, milk is also dispensed. The amount of milk is distributed normally with mean 20 ml and standard deviation 2 ml. Find the probability that the total amount of liquid dispensed when a customer chooses white coffee is less than 210 ml.

7 Given that $X \sim N(\mu, 10)$, $Y \sim N(12, \sigma^2)$ and $3X - 4Y \sim N(0, 234)$, find μ and σ^2.

8 You are given that $X \sim Po(3)$ and $Y \sim Po(2)$. Find the mean and variance of
(a) $X + Y$,   (b) $X - Y$,   (c) $3X + 2$.
Which of (a), (b) and (c) has a Poisson distribution?

9 The number of vehicles travelling on a particular road towards a town centre has a Poisson distribution with mean 10 per minute. The number of vehicles travelling away from the town centre on the same road at the same time of day has a Poisson distribution with mean 3 per minute. Find the probability that the total number of vehicles seen passing a given point in a 1-minute period is greater than 16.

10 The number of goals scored per match by a football team during a season has a Poisson distribution with mean 1.5. The number of goals conceded per match by the same team during the same season has a Poisson distribution with mean 1. Find the probability that a match involving the team produced more than 3 goals.

Miscellaneous exercise 2

1 The random variable X has mean 0 and variance $\frac{4}{5}$. $Y = aX + b$. It is given that $E(Y) = 50$ and $Var(Y) = 80$. Find a and b. (OCR)

2 During winter a family requests 4 bottles of milk every day, and these are left on the doorstep. Three of the bottles have silver tops and the fourth has a gold top. A thirsty blue-tit attempts to remove the tops from these bottles. The probability distribution of X, the number of silver tops removed by the blue-tit, is the same each day and is given by
$$P(X = 0) = \tfrac{5}{15}, \quad P(X = 1) = \tfrac{6}{15}, \quad P(X = 2) = \tfrac{3}{15}, \quad P(X = 3) = \tfrac{1}{15}.$$
The blue-tit finds the gold top particularly attractive, and the probability that this top is removed is $\frac{3}{5}$, independent of the number of silver tops removed. Determine the expectation and variance of
(a) the number of silver tops removed in a day,
(b) the number of gold tops removed in a day,
(c) the total number of tops (silver and gold) removed in 7 days. (OCR)

3   Alan and his younger brother Bill play a game each day. Alan throws three darts at a
    dartboard and for each dart that scores a bull (which happens with probability p) Bill gives
    him a penny, while for each dart which misses the bull (which happens with probability
    $1-p$) Alan gives Bill two pence. By considering all possible outcomes for the three
    throws, or otherwise, find the distribution of the number of pence (positive or negative) that
    Bill receives each day. Show that when $p = \frac{1}{3}$, the mean is 3 and the variance 6.

    The game takes place on 150 days. What are the mean and standard deviation of Bill's
    winnings when $p = \frac{1}{3}$? (OCR)

4   The random variable X takes values –2, 0, 2 with probabilities $\frac{1}{4}, \frac{1}{2}, \frac{1}{4}$ respectively. Find
    $\mathrm{Var}(X)$ and $\mathrm{E}(|X|)$.

    The random variable Y is defined by $Y = X_1 + X_2$, where X_1 and X_2 are two independent
    observations of X. Find $\mathrm{Var}(Y)$ and $\mathrm{E}(Y+3)$. (OCR)

5   The probability of there being X unusable matches in a full box of Surelite matches is
    given by

    $$P(X=0) = 8k, \quad P(X=1) = 5k, \quad P(X=2) = P(X=3) = k, \quad P(X \geqslant 4) = 0.$$

    Determine the constant k and the expectation and variance of X. Two full boxes of
    Surelite matches are chosen at random and the total number Y of unusable matches is
    determined. State the values of the expectation and variance of Y. (OCR)

6   In a packaging factory, the empty containers for a certain product have a mean weight of
    400 g with a standard deviation of 10 g. The mean weight of the contents of a full container
    is 800 g with a standard deviation of 15 g. Find the expected total weight of 10 full
    containers and the standard deviation of this weight, assuming that the weights of
    containers and contents are independent.

    Assuming further that these weights are normally distributed random variables, find the
    proportion of batches of 10 full containers which weigh more than 12.1 kg.

    If 1% of the containers are found to be holding weights of product which are less than the
    guaranteed minimum amount, deduce this minimum weight. (OCR)

7   Telephone calls reach a secretary independently and at random, internal ones at a mean rate
    of 2 in any 5-minute period, and external ones at a mean rate of 1 in any 5-minute period.
    Calculate the probability that there will be more than 2 calls in any period of 2 minutes.
    (OCR)

8   During a weekday, heavy lorries pass a census point P on a village high street
    independently and at random times. The mean rate for westward travelling lorries is 2 in
    any 30-minute period, and for eastward travelling lorries is 3 in any 30-minute period.

    Find the probability

    (a) that there will be no lorries passing P in a given 10-minute period,

    (b) that at least one lorry from each direction will pass P in a given 10-minute period,

    (c) that there will be exactly 4 lorries passing P in a given 20-minute period. (OCR)

9 The mass of tea in Supacuppa tea-bags has a normal distribution with mean 4.1 g and standard deviation 0.12 g. The mass of tea in Bumpacuppa tea-bags has a normal distribution with mean 5.2 g and standard deviation 0.15 g.

    (a) Find the probability that five randomly chosen Supacuppa tea-bags contain a total of more that 20.8 g of tea.

    (b) Find the probability that the total mass of tea in five randomly chosen Supacuppa tea-bags is more than the total mass of tea in four randomly chosen Bumpacuppa tea-bags.   (OCR)

10 The independent random variables R and S each have normal distributions. The means of R and S are 10 and 12 respectively, and the variances are 9 and 16 respectively. Find the following probabilities, giving your answer correct to 3 significant figures.

    (a) $P(R < S)$

    (b) $P(2R > S_1 + S_2)$, where S_1 and S_2 are two independent observations of S (OCR)

11 Small packets of nails are advertised as having average weight 500 g, and large packets as having average weight 1000 g. Assume that the packet weights are distributed normally with means as advertised, and standard deviations of 10 g for a small packet and 15 g for a large packet. Giving your answers correct to 3 decimal places,

    (a) find the probability that two randomly chosen small packets have a total weight between 990 g and 1020 g,

    (b) find the probability that the weight of one randomly chosen large packet exceeds the total weight of two randomly chosen small packets by at least 25 g,

    (c) find the probability that one half of the weight of one randomly chosen large packet exceeds the weight of one randomly chosen small packet by at least 12.5 g.   (OCR)

12 The random variable X has a normal distribution with mean 3 and variance 4. The random variable S is the sum of 100 independent observations of X, and the random variable T is the sum of a further 300 independent observations of X. Giving your answers to 3 decimal places, find

    (a) $P(S > 310)$,   (b) $P(3S > 50 + T)$.

The random variable N is the sum of n independent observations of X. State the approximate value of $P(N > 3.5n)$ as n becomes very large, justifying your answer.

                                                                   (OCR)

3 Confidence intervals and the *t* distribution

This chapter introduces the idea of a confidence interval. It also introduces the
t distribution, which is used in the context of small samples. When you have completed
the chapter you should be able to

- determine a confidence interval for the population mean in the context of a sample
  drawn from a normal population of known variance
- determine a confidence interval for the population mean in the context of a large sample
  drawn from any population
- determine, from a large sample, an approximate confidence interval for a population
  proportion
- use a *t* distribution, in the context of a small sample drawn from a normal population, to
  determine a confidence interval of the population mean
- use a *t* distribution, in the context of a small sample drawn from a normal population, to
  carry out a hypothesis test of the population mean.

3.1 The concept of a confidence interval

In S2 Section 4.7 you learnt that the mean, $\overline{X}$, of a random sample is an unbiased
estimator of the population mean, μ. For example, to estimate the mean amount of
pocket money received by all the children in a primary school you could take a random
sample of the children and ask each child how much pocket money he or she receives.
Suppose you find that $\sum x = 111.50$ for a random sample of 50 children, where x is
measured in £. Then an unbiased estimate of the population mean, μ, is given by

$$\overline{x} = \frac{\sum x}{n} = \frac{111.50}{50} = 2.23.$$

Such a value is called a **point estimate** because it gives an estimate of the population
mean in the form of a single value or 'point' on a number line. Such values are useful,
for example, in comparing populations. However, since $\overline{X}$ is a random variable, the
value which it takes will vary from sample to sample. As a result you have no idea how
close to the actual population mean a point estimate is likely to be. The purpose of a
'confidence interval' is to give an estimate in a form which also indicates the estimate's
likely accuracy. A **confidence interval of the mean** is a range of values which has a
given probability of 'trapping' the population mean. It is usually taken to be
symmetrical about the sample mean. So, if the sample mean takes the value $\overline{x}$, the
associated confidence interval would be $[\overline{x} - c, \overline{x} + c]$ where c is a number whose value
has yet to be found.

*Notice the notation for an interval which is being used. The interval $[\overline{x} - c, \overline{x} + c]$ means
the real numbers from $\overline{x} - c$ to $\overline{x} + c$, including the end-points. For example, $[-2.1, 6.8]$
means real numbers y such that $-2.1 \leqslant y \leqslant 6.8$.*

In Fig. 3.1 the sample mean $\overline{X}$ takes a value $\bar{x}_1$ and the confidence interval covers the range of values $[\bar{x}_1 - c, \bar{x}_1 + c]$. In this case the confidence interval traps the population mean, μ. For a different sample, with a different sample mean, $\bar{x}_2$, the confidence interval might not trap μ. This situation is illustrated in Fig. 3.2.

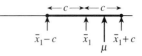

Fig. 3.1. Confidence interval which traps the population mean μ.

The end-points of the confidence interval are themselves random variables since they vary from sample to sample. They can be written as $\overline{X} - c$ and $\overline{X} + c$. You can see from Fig. 3.1 and Fig. 3.2 that the confidence interval will trap μ if the difference between the sample mean and the population mean is less than or equal to c. Expressed algebraically this condition is $|\overline{X} - \mu| \leqslant c$.

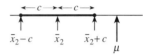

Fig. 3.2. Confidence interval which does not trap the population mean μ.

The next section explains how the value of c is chosen so as to give a specified probability that the confidence interval traps μ.

3.2 Calculating a confidence interval

Consider the following situation. The masses of tablets produced by a machine are known to be distributed normally with a standard deviation of 0.012 g. The mean mass of the tablets produced is monitored at regular intervals by taking a sample of 25 tablets and calculating the sample mean, $\overline{X}$.

Suppose you wish to find an interval which has a 95% probability of trapping the population mean, μ. The mass, X (in grams), of a single tablet is distributed normally with unknown mean μ and standard deviation 0.012; that is, $X \sim \text{N}(\mu, 0.012^2)$. So, for a sample of size 25, $\overline{X} \sim \text{N}\left(\mu, \dfrac{0.012^2}{25}\right)$ (see S2 Section 4.6).

Using the notation of the previous section, the population mean is trapped in the interval $[\overline{X} - c, \overline{X} + c]$, where c is a constant, if $|\overline{X} - \mu| \leqslant c$. The interval has a probability of 95% of trapping the population mean if, and only if, $\text{P}(|\overline{X} - \mu| \leqslant c) = 0.95$.

Fig. 3.3 shows the sampling distribution of $\overline{X}$ with this probability indicated. The value of c is found by standardising $|\overline{X} - \mu|$ to give

$$Z = \frac{\overline{X} - \mu}{\sqrt{\dfrac{0.012^2}{25}}} \text{ where } Z \sim \text{N}(0,1).$$

Fig. 3.4 shows the distribution of Z with the probability of 0.95 indicated. The value of z in this diagram is given by $\Phi^{-1}(0.975) = 1.96$.

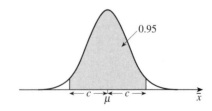

Fig. 3.3. Diagram to illustrate $\text{P}((\overline{X} - \mu) \leqslant c) = 0.95$.

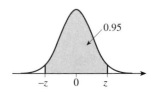

Fig. 3.4. Standardisation of Fig. 3.3.

Thus $1.96 = \dfrac{\overline{X} - \mu}{\sqrt{\dfrac{0.012^2}{25}}} = \dfrac{\overline{X} - \mu}{\dfrac{0.012}{\sqrt{25}}}$. But $\overline{X} - \mu = c$, so

$$1.96 = \frac{c}{\dfrac{0.012}{\sqrt{25}}} \qquad (3.1)$$

giving $c = 1.96 \dfrac{0.012}{\sqrt{25}} = 0.004\ 70$, to 3 significant figures.

So the interval which has a 95% probability of trapping μ is $\left[\overline{X} - 0.0047, \overline{X} + 0.0047 \right]$.

Suppose that you took a sample of 25 tablets and found that the mean mass was, for example, 0.5642 g. This sample mean would give a value for the interval of $[0.5642 - 0.0047, 0.5642 + 0.0047]$, which is $[0.5595, 0.5689]$. Such an interval is called a **95% confidence interval of the population mean**.

It is important to realise that such a confidence interval may or may not trap μ, depending on the value of $\overline{X}$. Suppose, for a moment, that you know the value of μ and you take a number of different samples of 25 tablets. Fig. 3.5 shows confidence intervals calculated in the way described above for 30 different samples of 25 tablets. The majority of the confidence intervals trap μ but a few (marked *) do not. On average, the proportion of 95% confidence intervals which trap μ is 95%. In practice, of course, you do not know μ and would usually take only one sample and from it calculate one confidence interval. In this situation, you cannot *know* whether your particular confidence interval does include μ: all you can say is that, on average, 95 times out of 100 it will contain μ.

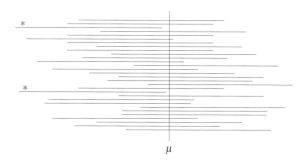

Fig. 3.5. 95% confidence intervals calculated from 30 random samples.

The method which has been described for finding a 95% confidence interval of the mean can be generalised to a sample of size n from a normal population with standard deviation σ. Replacing 25 by n and 0.012 by σ in Equation 3.1 gives

$$1.96 = \frac{c}{\dfrac{\sigma}{\sqrt{n}}},$$

which, on rearranging, gives $c = 1.96 \dfrac{\sigma}{\sqrt{n}}$.

Given a sample of size n from a normal population with variance σ^2, a 95% confidence interval for the population mean is given by

$$\left[\bar{x} - 1.96 \frac{\sigma}{\sqrt{n}}, \bar{x} + 1.96 \frac{\sigma}{\sqrt{n}} \right], \qquad (3.2)$$

where $\bar{x}$ is the sample mean.

Computer activity

Make a spreadsheet containing 500 samples of size 25 from a population which is distributed as $N(0.56, 0.012^2)$. Using the facilities of the spreadsheet, calculate the 95% confidence interval of the mean for each sample. How many of these confidence intervals trap the population mean, 0.56? (Your answer should be reasonably close to 475. Why?) Explain why your answer need not necessarily be 475 exactly.

Example 3.2.1

The lengths of nails produced by a machine are known to be distributed normally with mean μ mm and standard deviation 0.7 mm. The lengths, in mm, of a random sample of 5 nails are 107.29, 106.56, 105.94, 106.99, 106.47.

(a) Calculate a symmetric 95% confidence interval for μ, giving the end-points correct to 1 decimal place.

(b) Two hundred random samples of 5 nails are taken and a symmetric 95% confidence interval for μ is calculated for each sample. Find the expected number of intervals which do not contain μ.

(a) The mean of the sample is given by

$$\bar{x} = \frac{107.29 + 106.56 + 105.94 + 106.99 + 106.47}{5} = 106.65.$$

Substituting this value of $\bar{x}$ together with $\sigma = 0.7$ and $n = 5$ into Equation 3.2 gives a symmetric 95% confidence interval for μ of

$$\left[106.65 - 1.96 \frac{0.7}{\sqrt{5}}, 106.65 + 1.96 \frac{0.7}{\sqrt{5}} \right],$$

which, on simplifying, gives $[106.036\ldots, 107.263\ldots]$. So, to 1 decimal place, the symmetric 95% confidence interval for μ, measured in mm, is $[106.0, 107.3]$.

(b) On average, 95% of the confidence intervals should include μ. This means that 5% will not include μ. So out of 200 confidence intervals you would expect $200 \times 5\% = 10$ not to include μ.

Example 3.2.2

For a method of measuring the velocity of sound in air, the results of repeated experiments are known to be distributed normally with standard deviation $6\ \mathrm{m\,s^{-1}}$. A number of measurements are made using this method, and from these measurements a symmetric 95% confidence interval for the velocity of sound in air is calculated. Find the width of this confidence interval for   (a) 4,   (b) 36 measurements.

A symmetric 95% confidence interval extends from $\bar{x} - 1.96 \dfrac{\sigma}{\sqrt{n}}$ to $\bar{x} + 1.96 \dfrac{\sigma}{\sqrt{n}}$,

so its width is $\bar{x} + 1.96 \dfrac{\sigma}{\sqrt{n}} - \left(\bar{x} - 1.96 \dfrac{\sigma}{\sqrt{n}} \right) = 2 \times 1.96 \dfrac{\sigma}{\sqrt{n}}$.

In this example $\sigma = 6$, so the width of the confidence interval is $2 \times 1.96 \dfrac{6}{\sqrt{n}} = \dfrac{23.52}{\sqrt{n}}$.

(a) For $n = 4$, the width of the confidence interval is $\dfrac{23.52}{\sqrt{4}} = 11.76$.

(b) For $n = 36$, the width of the confidence interval is $\dfrac{23.52}{\sqrt{36}} = 3.92$.

Note that nine times as many measurements are required to reduce the width of the confidence interval by a factor of three.

3.3 Different levels of confidence

As Example 3.2.1 makes clear, there is a probability of 5 in 100 that a 95% confidence interval does not include μ. There are circumstances in which you may wish to be more certain that the confidence interval which you have calculated does include μ. For example, you may wish to be 99% certain. Fig. 3.6 is the diagram corresponding to Fig. 3.3 for this situation. The only difference in the calculation of the confidence interval is that a different value of z is needed. In this case $\Phi(z) = 0.995$, giving $z = 2.576$, so that the 99% confidence interval of the mean is given by

$$\left[\bar{x} - 2.576 \frac{\sigma}{\sqrt{n}}, \bar{x} + 2.576 \frac{\sigma}{\sqrt{n}} \right].$$

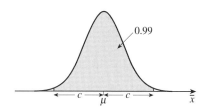

Note that this 99% confidence interval is wider than the 95% confidence interval: this is to be expected since the former is more likely to trap μ than the latter. You can see that there is a balance between precision and certainty: if you increase one you decrease the other. This is

Fig. 3.6. Diagram to illustrate $P\big((\bar{X} - \mu) \leqslant c \big) = 0.99$.

similar to the balance between Type I and Type II errors in hypothesis testing, which you met in S2 Chapter 7. The only way of decreasing the probabilities of both types of error simultaneously is to increase the sample size. In the same way, to increase both the precision and the certainty of a confidence interval you have to increase the sample size.

If you want a 90% confidence interval, then the appropriate value of z is that value for which $\Phi(z) = 0.95$ giving $z = 1.465$. You may have spotted that the values of z used in confidence intervals correspond to those used in hypothesis testing. To generalise, the critical value of z for a two-tail test at the $100\alpha\%$ significance level is the same as the value of z used to calculate a symmetric $100(1 - \alpha)\%$ confidence interval (see Fig. 3.7). The critical value of z for a two-tail test at the $100\alpha\%$ level is also the same as the critical value of z for a one-tail test at the $\frac{1}{2} \times 100\alpha\%$ level. These values are given in the table at the bottom of page 270, where the probabilities refer to the acceptance region.

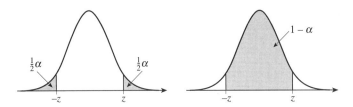

Fig. 3.7. Diagram to illustrate the relation between critical values and confidence intervals.

A $100(1-\alpha)\%$ confidence interval of the population mean for a sample of size n taken from a normal population with variance σ^2 is given by

$$\left[\bar{x} - z\frac{\sigma}{\sqrt{n}}, \bar{x} + z\frac{\sigma}{\sqrt{n}} \right], \qquad (3.3)$$

where $\bar{x}$ is the sample mean and the value of z is such that $\Phi(z) = 1 - \frac{1}{2}\alpha$.

Example 3.3.1

The measurement error made in measuring the concentration in parts per million (ppm) of nitrate ions in water by a particular method is known to be distributed normally with mean 0 and standard deviation 0.05.

(a) If 10 measurements on a specimen gave $\sum x = 11.37$ ppm, determine a symmetric 99.5% confidence interval for the true concentration, μ, of nitrate ions in the specimen, giving the end-points of the interval correct to 2 decimal places.

(b) How many measurements would be required in order to reduce the width of this interval to 0.03 ppm at most?

    (a) The measured value, X, of the nitrate ion concentration is equal to $\mu + Y$ where Y is the measurement error. Thus

$$\mathrm{E}(X) = \mathrm{E}(\mu + Y) = \mu + \mathrm{E}(Y) = \mu + 0 = \mu \qquad \text{(using Equation 2.1)}$$

$$\text{and} \quad \mathrm{Var}(X) = \mathrm{Var}(\mu + Y) = \mathrm{Var}(\mu) + \mathrm{Var}(Y) \qquad \text{(using Equation 2.2)}$$

$$= 0 + 0.05^2 = 0.05^2.$$

This means that $X \sim \mathrm{N}(\mu, 0.05^2)$. For a 99.5% confidence interval, $1 - \alpha = 0.995$, so $\alpha = 0.005$ and $\frac{1}{2}\alpha = 0.0025$. Thus $\Phi(z) = 1 - \frac{1}{2}\alpha = 1 - 0.0025 = 0.9975$. For $p = 0.9975$ the table at the bottom of page 270 gives $z = 2.807$. So a 99.5% confidence interval for μ is

$$\left[\bar{x} - 2.807\frac{\sigma}{\sqrt{n}}, \bar{x} + 2.807\frac{\sigma}{\sqrt{n}} \right] = \left[\frac{11.37}{10} - 2.807\frac{0.05}{\sqrt{10}}, \frac{11.37}{10} + 2.807\frac{0.05}{\sqrt{10}} \right]$$

$$= [1.092\ldots, 1.181\ldots]$$

$$= [1.09, 1.18], \quad \text{correct to 2 decimal places.}$$

(b) The width of the 99.5% confidence interval for a sample of size n is

$$2 \times 2.807 \frac{0.05}{\sqrt{n}}.$$

For this width to be at most 0.03, $2 \times 2.807 \dfrac{0.05}{\sqrt{n}} \leqslant 0.03$.

Rearranging gives

$$\sqrt{n} \geqslant \frac{2 \times 2.807 \times 0.05}{0.03}, \qquad \text{so} \qquad n \geqslant 87.5\ldots.$$

Since n must be an integer, 88 or more measurements are required to give a confidence interval of width 0.03 ppm at most.

Exercise 3A

1   Bags of sugar have masses which are distributed normally with mean μ grams and standard deviation 4.6 grams. The sugar in each of a random sample of 5 bags taken from a production line is weighed, with the following results, in grams.

   498.2   501.3   503.7   496.8   502.5

Calculate a symmetric 95% confidence interval for μ.

If a 95% symmetric confidence interval for μ was calculated for each of the 200 samples of 5 bags, how many of the confidence intervals would be expected to contain μ?

2   The volume of milk in litre cartons filled by a machine has a normal distribution with mean μ litres and standard deviation 0.05 litres. A random sample of 25 cartons was selected and the contents, x litres, measured. The results are summarised by $\sum x = 25.11$. Calculate

   (a) a symmetric 98% confidence interval for μ,

   (b) the width of a symmetric 90% confidence interval for μ based on the volume of milk in a random sample of 50 cartons.

3   The random variable X has a normal distribution with mean μ and variance σ^2. A symmetric 90% confidence interval for μ based on a random sample of 16 observations of X has width 4.24. Find

   (a) the value of σ,

   (b) the width of a symmetric 90% confidence interval for μ based on a random sample of 4 observations of X,

   (c) the width of a symmetric 95% confidence interval for μ based on a random sample of 4 observations of X.

4   The heights of fully-grown British males may be modelled by a normal distribution with mean 178 cm and standard deviation 7.5 cm. The 11 male (fully-grown) biology students present at a university seminar had a mean height of 175.2 cm. Assuming a standard deviation of 7.5 cm, and stating any further assumption, calculate a symmetric 99% confidence interval for the mean height of all fully-grown male biology students.

Does the confidence interval suggest that fully-grown male biology students have a different mean height from 178 cm?

5 A machine is designed to produce metal rods of length 5 cm. In fact, the lengths are distributed normally with mean 5.00 cm and standard deviation 0.032 cm. The machine is moved to a new site and, in order to check whether or not the mean length has altered, the lengths of a random sample of 8 rods are measured. The results, in cm, are as follows.

> 5.07 4.95 4.98 5.06 5.13 5.05 4.98 5.06

(a) Assuming that the standard deviation is unchanged, calculate a symmetric 95% confidence interval for the mean length of the rods produced by the machine in its new position.

(b) State, giving a reason, whether you consider that the mean length has changed.

6 A method used to determine the percentage of nitrogen in a fertiliser has an error which is distributed normally with zero mean and standard deviation 0.34%. Ten independent determinations of the percentage of nitrogen gave a mean value of 15.92%.

(a) Calculate a symmetric 98% confidence interval for the percentage of nitrogen in the fertiliser.

(b) Find the smallest number of extra independent determinations that would reduce the width of the symmetric 98% confidence interval to at most 0.4%.

3.4 Confidence interval for a large sample

In the examples considered so far it has been assumed that the samples are drawn from a normal distribution and that the variance of this distribution is known. In practice you will not always be sure that the population is normal and you may or may not have accurate information about its variance. However, the method of calculating a confidence interval which has been described in this chapter can still be applied provided that the sample is large.

Consider first the distribution from which the sample is taken. Although this may not be normal, the central limit theorem (see S2 Section 4.4) tells you that the sample mean, $\overline{X}$, is distributed approximately normally provided that the sample is large.

Next, consider the population variance. An unbiased estimate of this can be calculated from the sample using the equation

$$s^2 = \frac{1}{n-1}\sum(x-\overline{x})^2 = \frac{n}{n-1}\left(\frac{\sum x^2}{n} - \overline{x}^2\right).$$

This estimate will vary from sample to sample, but for large samples the variation is so small that s can be treated as though it is constant and be used in place of σ in Equation 3.3. A rule of thumb is that 'large' means a sample size of 30 or more.

You may remember that you encountered a similar situation in S2 Chapter 5 in the context of hypothesis testing. There a method of hypothesis testing was derived for samples from normal populations of known variance. The method was then extended (for large samples) to include situations where the population was not necessarily normal and the population variance may or may not have been known.

Given a *large* sample $(n \geqslant 30)$ from any population, a $100(1-\alpha)\%$ confidence interval for the population mean is given by

$$\left[\bar{x} - z\frac{s}{\sqrt{n}}, \bar{x} + z\frac{s}{\sqrt{n}} \right] \qquad (3.4)$$

where $\bar{x}$ is the sample mean, the value of z is such that $\Phi(z) = 1 - \frac{1}{2}\alpha$ and

$$s^2 = \frac{n}{n-1}\left(\frac{\sum x^2}{n} - \bar{x}^2 \right).$$

Example 3.4.1

On 1 January 100 new Eternity light bulbs were installed in a certain building, together with a device which records how long each light bulb is used. By 1 March all 100 bulbs had failed. The data for the recorded lifetimes, t (in hours of use), are summarised by $\sum t = 10\,500$, $\sum t^2 = 1\,712\,500$. Assuming that the bulbs constituted a random sample of Eternity light bulbs, obtain a symmetric 99% confidence interval for the mean lifetime of Eternity light bulbs, giving your answer correct to the nearest hour.

(OCR, adapted)

In this example neither the distribution of the population of lifetimes nor the population variance are known. However, the sample size is much larger than 30, so Equation 3.4 can be used. First it is necessary to calculate $\bar{t}$ and s^2.

$$\bar{t} = \frac{\sum t}{n} = \frac{10500}{100} = 105.$$

$$s^2 = \frac{n}{n-1}\left(\frac{\sum t^2}{n} - \bar{t}^2 \right) = \frac{100}{100-1}\left[\frac{1\,712\,500}{100} - 105^2 \right]$$

$$= 6161.6\ldots.$$

Thus $s = 78.49\ldots$.

For a 99% confidence interval, $1 - \alpha = 0.99$, so $\alpha = 0.01$ and $\frac{1}{2}\alpha = 0.005$.

Thus $\Phi(z) = 1 - \frac{1}{2}\alpha = 1 - 0.005 = 0.995$.

From the table at the bottom of page 270, taking $p = 0.995$ gives $z = 2.576$.

So, substituting into Equation 3.4 gives a 99% confidence of the population mean as

$$\left[105 - 2.576\frac{78.49\ldots}{\sqrt{100}}, 105 + 2.576\frac{78.49\ldots}{100} \right]$$

$$= [85, 125], \text{ to the nearest hour.}$$

<hr>

Exercise 3B

1 During one year, a squash player bought 72 balls of a certain brand and recorded for each the time, x hours, before failing. The results are summarised by $\sum x = 372.4$ and $\sum x^2 = 2301.32$.

   (a) Find a symmetric 90% confidence interval for the mean life of that brand of squash ball.

   (b) State, and justify, any approximation used in your calculation.

2 The contents of 140 bags of flour selected randomly from a large batch delivered to a store are weighed and the results, w grams, summarised by $\sum(w - 500) = -266$ and $\sum(w - 500)^2 = 1178$.

   (a) Calculate unbiased estimates of the batch mean and variance of the mass of flour in a bag.

   (b) Calculate a symmetric 95% confidence interval for the batch mean mass.

   The manager of the store believes that the confidence interval indicates a mean less than 500 g and considers the batch to be sub-standard. She has all of the bags in the batch weighed and finds that the batch mean mass is 501.1 g. How can this be reconciled with the confidence interval calculated in part (b)?

3 An environmental science student carried out a study of the incidence of lichens on a stone wall in Derbyshire. She selected, at random, 100 one-metre lengths of wall, all of the same height. The number of lichens in each section was counted and the results are summarised in the following frequency table.

Number of lichens	0	1	2	3	4	5	6
Number of sections	8	22	27	19	13	8	3

   (a) Calculate the sample mean and an unbiased estimate of the population variance of the number of lichens per metre length of the wall.

   (b) Calculate a symmetric 90% confidence interval for the mean number of lichens per metre length of the wall.

4 The depth of water in a lake was measured at 50 randomly chosen points on a particular day. The depths, d metres, are summarised by $\sum d = 366.45$ and $\sum d^2 = 2978.16$.

   (a) Calculate an unbiased estimate of the variance of the depth of the lake.

   (b) Calculate a symmetric 99% confidence interval for the mean depth of the lake.

   The three months after the depths were obtained were very hot and dry and the water level in the lake dropped by 1.34 m. Based on readings taken at the same 50 points as before, which were all greater than 1.34 m, what will be a symmetric 99% confidence interval for the new mean depth?

5 The pulse rates of 90 eight-year-old children chosen randomly from different schools in a city gave a sample mean of $\bar{x} = 86.6$ beats per minute and an estimate of population variance of $s^2 = 106.09$.

  (a) Calculate a symmetric 98% confidence interval for the mean pulse rate of all eight-year-old children in the city.

  (b) If, in fact, the 90 children were chosen randomly from those attending a hospital clinic, comment on how this information affects the interpretation of the confidence interval found in part (a).

6 C60 audio cassette tapes of a particular brand are claimed by the manufacturer to give, on average, at least 60 minutes of playing time. After receiving some complaints, the manufacturer's quality control manager obtains a random sample of 64 tapes and measures the playing time, t minutes, of each. The results are summarised by $\sum t = 3953.28$ and $\sum t^2 = 244\,557.00$.

  (a) Calculate a symmetric 99% confidence interval for the population mean playing time of this brand of C60 tape.

  (b) Does the confidence interval support the customers' complaints? Give a reason for your answer.

3.5 Confidence interval for a proportion

Many statistical investigations are concerned with finding the proportion of a population which has a specified attribute. Suppose you were a manufacturer of a version of an appliance designed for left-handed people. In order to assess the potential market you would be interested in the proportion of left-handed people in the population. It would be impossible to ask everybody and so you would have to rely on a sample. Suppose that you were able to obtain information from a random sample of 500 people and you found that 60 of them were left-handed. It would seem reasonable to estimate that the proportion, p, of the population who are left-handed is $\frac{60}{500} = 0.12$, or 12%. However, you need to be certain that this method gives you an unbiased estimate of p.

Consider the more general situation where a random sample of n people are questioned. Provided that n is much smaller than the population size the distribution of X, the number of people in a sample of size n who are left-handed, will be $B(n, p)$ since

- there are a fixed number of trials (n people asked)
- each trial has two possible outcomes (left-handed or right-handed)
- the outcomes are mutually exclusive (assuming that no one is ambidextrous)
- the probability of a person being left-handed is constant
- the trials are independent.

Let P_s be the random variable 'the proportion of people in the sample who are left-handed'. Then $P_s = \dfrac{X}{n}$. The expected value of P_s is

$$E(P_s) = E\left(\frac{X}{n}\right) = \frac{1}{n}E(X) \qquad \text{(using Equation 2.1)}$$

$$= \frac{1}{n} \times np \qquad \text{(since the mean of a binomial distribution is } np)$$

$$= p.$$

Thus the proportion in the sample does provide an unbiased point estimate of the population proportion.

It would be more useful, however, to find a confidence interval for p since this gives an idea of the precision of the estimate. In order to do this you need to consider the distribution of P_s. For a large sample, X will be distributed approximately normally and so P_s will also be distributed approximately normally (see Section 2.4). In order to calculate a confidence interval you also need the variance of P_s. This can be found as follows.

$$\text{Var}(P_s) = \text{Var}\left(\frac{X}{n}\right) = \frac{1}{n^2} \times \text{Var}(X) \qquad \text{(using Equation 2.2)}$$

$$= \frac{1}{n^2} \times npq \qquad \text{(since the variance of a binomial distribution is } npq)$$

$$= \frac{pq}{n}.$$

If $X \sim B(n, p)$, then the sample proportion P_s,

where $P_s = \dfrac{X}{n}$, is distributed approximately as $N\left(p, \dfrac{pq}{n}\right)$

when n is large enough that $np > 5$ and $nq > 5$.

In practice, this will be achieved if there are more than 5 successes and 5 failures in n trials.

In Section 3.3 you saw that for the sampling distribution $\overline{X} \sim N\left(\mu, \dfrac{\sigma^2}{n}\right)$, a confidence interval for μ is given by $\left[\overline{x} - z\dfrac{\sigma}{\sqrt{n}}, \overline{x} + z\dfrac{\sigma}{\sqrt{n}}\right]$. By analogy a confidence interval for p is found by replacing $\overline{x}$ by p_s, where $p_s = \dfrac{x}{n}$, and $\dfrac{\sigma}{\sqrt{n}}$ by $\sqrt{\dfrac{pq}{n}}$ to give an approximate confidence interval of $\left[p_s - z\sqrt{\dfrac{pq}{n}}, p_s + z\sqrt{\dfrac{pq}{n}}\right]$, where values of z are obtained as before.

This confidence interval is expressed in terms of p and q, which are not known (otherwise a confidence interval would not be required!). However, again similar to finding a confidence interval for the mean, these unknown quantities can be replaced by their estimates from the sample provided that the sample is large. The result is the interval

$$\left[p_s - z\sqrt{\frac{p_s q_s}{n}}, p_s + z\sqrt{\frac{p_s q_s}{n}}\right], \text{ where } q_s = 1 - p_s = 1 - \frac{x}{n}.$$

Strictly speaking, since a discrete distribution has been replaced by a continuous one in this calculation, a continuity correction should be applied. However, this is usually ignored when calculating a confidence interval for a proportion and it will be ignored here. Also, strictly speaking, an unbiased estimate of the population variance, given by $\frac{n}{n-1}\left(\frac{p_s q_s}{n}\right)$ rather than $\frac{p_s q_s}{n}$, should be used. The term $\frac{n}{n-1}$ is an adjustment similar to that in the formula for s^2. When n is large this adjustment makes little difference, and it will be ignored here.

Given a large random sample, size n, from a population in which a proportion of members, p, has a particular attribute, an approximate $100(1-\alpha)\%$ confidence interval for p is

$$\left[p_s - z\sqrt{\frac{p_s q_s}{n}}, p_s + z\sqrt{\frac{p_s q_s}{n}}\right], \qquad (3.5)$$

where p_s is the sample proportion with this attribute, $q_s = 1 - p_s$ and the value of z is such that $\Phi(z) = 1 - \frac{1}{2}\alpha$.

This confidence interval is approximate because

- a discrete distribution has been approximated by a continuous one
- a continuity correction has not been applied
- the population variance is estimated from the sample and the estimate used is biased
- the distribution of P_s is only approximately normal.

Equation 3.5 can now be used to calculate a confidence interval for the proportion of left-handers in the population. For the sample taken, $n = 500$, $p_s = 0.12$ and $q_s = 0.88$, and for a 95% confidence interval, $z = 1.96$. This gives a 95% confidence interval

$$\left[0.12 - 1.96\sqrt{\frac{0.12 \times 0.88}{500}}, 0.12 + 1.96\sqrt{\frac{0.12 \times 0.88}{500}}\right] = [0.092, 0.148]$$

where the answers have been given to 3 decimal places.

The same answer is obtained if a continuity correction is made and an unbiased estimate of variance is used.

It is interesting to note that the answer does not depend on the size of the population, only the size of the sample. This will always be true if the sample size is much less than the population size so that the value of p is effectively constant. This fact can be used to calculate the sample size required to give a confidence interval of specified width as illustrated in the following example.

Example 3.5.1

An opinion poll is to be carried out to estimate the proportion of the electorate of a country who will vote 'yes' in a forthcoming referendum. In a trial run a random sample of 100 were questioned; 42 people said they would vote 'yes'. Estimate the random sample size required to give a 99% confidence interval of the proportion with a width of 0.02.

For a 99% confidence interval, z takes the value 2.576 in Equation 3.5, so the width of this interval is $2 \times 2.576 \sqrt{\dfrac{p_s q_s}{n}}$, where p_s and q_s are used to estimate p and q.

The trial run gives $p_s = 0.42$ and hence $q_s = 0.58$. Thus the required value of n is

$$2 \times 2.576 \sqrt{\frac{0.42 \times 0.58}{n}} = 0.02.$$

Rearranging and solving for n gives 16 165 to the nearest integer. This answer will only be approximate, for all four of the reasons in the shaded box.

It is interesting to think that if this example referred to the UK, where the size of the electorate is about 44 million, then the sample required is only about 0.04% of the electorate. The problem lies in obtaining a random sample. In practice opinion polls do not rely on random samples but use sophisticated techniques which are meant to ensure representative samples.

Exercise 3C

1 For the following sample sizes, n, and sample proportions, p_s, determine whether Equation 3.5 may be applied to find a valid confidence interval for the population proportion, p. Check whether the sample size is large enough.

   (a) $n = 60,\ p_s = 0.1$ (b) $n = 100,\ p_s = 0.04$ (c) $n = 14,\ p_s = 0.5$

2 For those cases in Question 1 where Equation 3.5 is suitable, calculate symmetric 95% confidence intervals of p.

3 In a study of computer usage a random sample of 200 private households in a particular town was selected and the number that own at least one computer was found to be 68. Calculate a symmetric 90% confidence interval of the percentage of households in the town that own at least one computer.

4 Of 500 cars passing under a road bridge on the M1 motorway 92 were found to be red.

   (a) Find a symmetric 98% confidence interval of the population proportion of red cars.

   (b) State any assumption required for the validity of the interval.

   (c) Describe a suitable population to which the interval applies.

   (d) If 50 students carried out this experiment, what is the expected number of confidence intervals which would contain the population proportion of red cars?

5 A biased dice was thrown 600 times and resulted in 224 sixes. Calculate a symmetric 99% confidence interval of p, the probability of obtaining a six in a single throw of the dice.

   Estimate the smallest number of times the dice should be thrown for the width of the symmetric 99% confidence interval of p to be at most 0.08.

   Give two reasons for the previous answer being only an estimate.

6 Two machines, machine 1 and machine 2, produce shirt buttons. Random samples of 80 buttons are selected from the output of each machine and each button is inspected for faults. The sample from machine 1 produced 8 faulty buttons and that from machine 2 produced 19 faulty buttons.

   (a) Calculate symmetric 90% confidence intervals for the proportion, p_1 and p_2, of faulty buttons produced by each machine.

   (b) State, giving a reason, what the confidence intervals indicate about the relative sizes of p_1 and p_2.

3.6   Confidence interval for a small sample from a normal population

The derivation of a confidence interval for the population mean μ of a normal population which was given in Section 3.2 relied on the fact that $\dfrac{\overline{X}-\mu}{\sqrt{\dfrac{\sigma^2}{n}}}$ is distributed as $N(0,1)$.

If σ is unknown it can be replaced by s for *large* samples since s is likely to be close to σ and so is effectively constant from sample to sample: this method was used in Section 3.4. For *small* samples from a normal population, however, the variation in the estimator s^2 can no longer be ignored. In order to calculate a confidence interval it is necessary to know the probability distribution of the variable T, where

$$T = \frac{\overline{X}-\mu}{\sqrt{\dfrac{S^2}{n}}} \qquad (3.6)$$

In this equation the standard deviation is denoted by a capital letter since it is a variable.

The distribution of T was studied by the British statistician W. S. Gosset (1876–1937) who wrote under the pen-name 'Student'. Much of Gosset's statistical work was done while he was employed at the Guinness brewery in Dublin. He found that Equation 3.6 determines a whole 'family' of distributions, whose shape depends on the sample size n through a term in $n-1$. Some of these distributions are shown in Fig. 3.8. For large n they are similar in shape to the distribution $N(0,1)$, which is also shown, but they spread out as n decreases. This family of distributions is known as **Student's *t* distribution**, or just the *t* **distribution**. A convenient way of identifying which member of the family you are considering is to write t_{n-1}. The quantity $n-1$ is known as the number of **degrees of freedom** and is given the symbol ν.

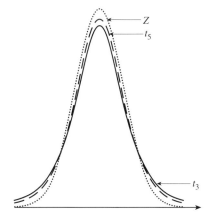

Fig. 3.8. A comparison of t_3, t_5 and $Z \sim N(0,1)$.

The letter ν, pronounced 'nu', is the Greek letter 'n'.

The term 'degrees of freedom' refers to the number of *independent* values which are used in the calculation of T. Although a sample of size n contains n data values, these values are not independent because $\sum(x_i - \bar{x}) = 0$. This means that once $n-1$ values have been used in the calculation of T, the last value is fixed. The condition $\sum(x_i - \bar{x}) = 0$ is known as a **constraint**. In general,

number of degrees of freedom = number of values – number of constraints.

For a random sample from a normal population with mean μ the variable $\dfrac{\overline{X} - \mu}{\sqrt{\dfrac{S^2}{n}}}$

has a t distribution with ν degrees of freedom, where $\nu = n-1$.

That is, $\dfrac{\overline{X} - \mu}{\sqrt{\dfrac{S^2}{n}}} \sim t_{n-1}$.

Because n can take any value the tables for the t distribution are not given in the form of a cumulative distribution function. Instead they are given in the form shown on page 271. For pairs of values of probability, p, and degrees of freedom, ν, this table gives the value of t such that $P(T \leqslant t) = p$. For example, if $p = 0.95$ and $\nu = 6$, $P(T \leqslant 1.943) = 0.95$.

The last line of the table, labelled ∞, gives the probabilities for a normal distribution. For example, the value of z such that $P(Z \leqslant z) = 0.95$ is 1.645.

Some calculators will give cumulative probabilities for a t distribution.

With knowledge of the t distribution it is possible even from a small sample to calculate a confidence interval for the mean of a normal population of unknown variance. If σ is replaced by s in Equation 3.3, then z will need to be replaced by the value of t such that $P(T \leqslant t) = 1 - \frac{1}{2}\alpha$ for ν degrees of freedom.

Given a sample of size n from a normal population of unknown variance, a $100(1-\alpha)\%$ confidence interval for the population mean is given by

$$\left[\bar{x} - t\frac{s}{\sqrt{n}}, \bar{x} + t\frac{s}{\sqrt{n}} \right], \qquad (3.7)$$

where $\bar{x}$ is the sample mean and the value of t is such that $P(T \leqslant t) = 1 - \frac{1}{2}\alpha$ for ν degrees of freedom.

When the sample is large the value of t will be very similar to that of z in Equation 3.3. You can see this by comparing the bottom two lines of the table on page 271: the last line gives the value of z and the line above gives t for 120 degrees of freedom. In this situation Equations 3.7 and 3.3 will give similar results and Equation 3.3 is sometimes used for convenience.

Computer activity

Use a spreadsheet to generate 1000 samples of size $n = 3$ from a $N(0,1)$ distribution.

For each sample calculate (a) $z = \dfrac{\bar{x}}{\sqrt{\dfrac{1^2}{n}}}$, (b) $t = \dfrac{\bar{x}}{\sqrt{\dfrac{s^2}{n}}}$.

Compare the values of the range and the interquartile range for the two variables z and t and comment on any differences which you observe. Repeat for different sample sizes.

Example 3.6.1

Ten measurements of the zero error on an ammeter yielded the results $+0.13$, -0.09, $+0.06$, $+0.15$, -0.02, $+0.03$, $+0.01$, -0.02, -0.07, $+0.05$. (The zero error is the reading when no electric current is passing through the ammeter.) Assuming that these measurements come from a normal population, calculate a 95% confidence interval for the mean zero error.

First it is necessary to calculate the sample mean and an unbiased estimate of the population variance from these results.

$$\bar{x} = \frac{\sum x}{n} = \frac{0.23}{10} = 0.023, \quad \text{and} \quad s^2 = \frac{n}{n-1}\left(\frac{\sum x^2}{n} - \bar{x}^2\right) \text{ so } s = 0.078\,18\ldots$$

For a 95% confidence interval, $\alpha = 0.05$, so $P(T \leqslant t) = 1 - \frac{1}{2} \times 0.05 = 0.975$ for $v = n - 1 = 9$ degrees of freedom. From the table on page 271, the value of t is 2.262; so from Equation 3.7 a 95% confidence interval for the population mean is

$$\left[0.023 - 2.262\,\frac{0.078\,18\ldots}{\sqrt{10}}, 0.023 + 2.262\,\frac{0.078\,18\ldots}{\sqrt{10}}\right] = \left[-0.0329, 0.0789\right],$$

where the answers have been given to 3 significant figures.

Exercise 3D

1 A symmetric $c\%$ confidence interval for a population mean is to be calculated using a random sample of n observations of the normal random variable X, which has unknown mean and unknown variance. State the values of t used in the following cases.

(a) $c = 90$, $n = 12$ (b) $c = 95$, $n = 10$ (c) $c = 98$, $n = 25$ (d) $c = 99.5$, $n = 100$

2 Bottles of El Bombero 1999, a Spanish red wine, were advertised as having 'an incredible 15%' alcohol content. Wine from a random sample of six bottles was analysed and gave percentage alcohol contents of 14.6, 15.1, 14.7, 15.3, 14.9, 15.0.

Stating any required assumption, calculate a symmetric 95% confidence interval for the mean percentage alcohol content in all bottles of El Bombero 1999.

3 The number of calls made in May 2000 to each of 20 randomly chosen ambulance stations in the UK was monitored. The resulting sample mean was 2846.6 and an unbiased estimate of the population variance was 312.4^2. Calculate a symmetric 90% confidence interval for the mean number of calls made to all ambulance stations in the UK in May 2000.

At the end of the year, the monthly figures for all the ambulance stations were obtained and the mean for May was found to lie outside the interval. How might this be explained?

4   The times, t minutes, taken by 18 children in an infant reception class to complete a jig-
    saw puzzle were measured. The results are summarised by $\sum t = 75.6$ and $\sum t^2 = 338.1$.

    (a) Stating your assumptions, calculate a symmetric 95% confidence interval for the
         population mean time for children to complete the puzzle.

    (b) The manufacturers of the puzzle indicate a mean completion time of 5 minutes. What
         conclusion might be made about the children in the class?

5   The acceleration due to gravity, g, is determined experimentally. In 5 independent
    determinations the values, in m s^{-2}, are 9.79, 9.82, 9.80, 9.78, 9.84. It may be assumed that
    these values are observations from a normal distribution whose mean is g.

    (a) Obtain a point estimate for g based on the 5 values.

    (b) Calculate a symmetric 99% confidence interval for g, giving end-points to 3 decimal
         places.

    (c) State whether or not, apart from rounding errors, the confidence interval found is
         exact.

6   A random sample of 12 fully-grown swallows (*Hirundo rustica*) were captured and
    released after their lengths, from tip of tail to tip of beak, were measured. The results,
    x cm, are summarised by $\sum x = 229.2$ and $\sum x^2 = 4389.16$.

    (a) Assuming that the lengths are distributed normally, calculate a symmetric 98%
         confidence interval for the mean length of all fully-grown swallows.

    (b) A thirteenth swallow was caught and found to have a length of 15.9 cm. Assuming
         that the mean and variance of the lengths of fully-grown swallows are approximated
         well by the sample estimates, is it likely that this swallow is fully grown?

3.7   Hypothesis test of the population mean for a small sample from a normal population

In S2 Chapter 5 you saw how to carry out hypothesis tests on the population mean for
(a) samples of any size from normal populations of known variance
(b) large samples from populations which are not distributed normally and whose
     variance may or may not be unknown.

The method involves taking the null hypothesis $H_0 : \mu = \mu_0$ and calculating the value of

the test statistic $\dfrac{\overline{X} - \mu_0}{\sqrt{\dfrac{\sigma^2}{n}}}$ in the case of (a) above and $\dfrac{\overline{X} - \mu_0}{\sqrt{\dfrac{S^2}{n}}}$ in the case of (b).

The rejection region is found by using the fact that, in the circumstances described in (a)
and (b), the test statistic is distributed as $N(0, 1)$.

With a knowledge of the t distribution it is possible to extend hypothesis tests on the
population mean to the situation in which a small sample is taken from a normal

population of unknown variance. In this situation the test statistic $\dfrac{\overline{X} - \mu_0}{\sqrt{\dfrac{S^2}{n}}}$ is distributed as t_{n-1} and the rejection region is found by using this distribution. The following examples illustrate how rejection regions are found for one- and two-tail tests.

Example 3.7.1

In the past the mean lifetime, X (in hours), of a certain electrical component has been 10.4. A new manufacturing process is introduced which is designed to increase the lifetime. Experimental data collected from a random sample of components manufactured by the new process are summarised by $\sum x = 139.7$, $\sum x^2 = 1858.1$, $n = 11$. Making a suitable assumption, which you should state, test whether there is evidence at the 10% significance level that the new process has increased the lifetime.

This is a one-tail test looking for an increase. The null and alternative hypotheses are $H_0: \mu = 10.4$, $H_1: \mu \geqslant 10.4$.

The sample mean is $\bar{x} = \dfrac{\sum x}{n} = \dfrac{139.7}{11} = 12.7$,

and an unbiased estimate of the population variance is

$$s^2 = \frac{n}{n-1}\left(\frac{\sum x^2}{n} - \bar{x}^2\right)$$

$$= \frac{11}{10}\left(\frac{1858.1}{11} - 12.7^2\right) = 8.391\ldots.$$

The value of the test statistic is

$$t = \frac{\bar{x} - \mu_0}{\sqrt{\dfrac{s^2}{n}}} = \frac{12.7 - 10.4}{\sqrt{\dfrac{8.391\ldots}{11}}} = 2.633\ldots.$$

Fig. 3.9 shows the rejection and acceptance regions for this test. The critical value is found from the table on page 271. It is that value of t for which $P(T \leqslant t) = 0.90$ with, in this case, 10 degrees of freedom. From the table this is $t = 1.372$. Thus the rejection region is $T \geqslant 1.372$. The observed value of T does lie in the rejection region and so the null hypothesis is rejected: there is evidence at the 10% significance level that the mean lifetime has increased. The test which has been carried out assumes that the data are drawn from a normal population.

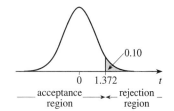

Fig. 3.9. Acceptance and rejection regions for Example 3.7.1.

In S2 Section 5.6 you were introduced to another method of significance testing. In this method the probability of the test statistic taking the observed (or a more extreme) value was calculated. This p-value was then compared with the significance level. The table on page 271 does not allow you to use this method for the test statistic T. However, statistical software often gives the result of a significance test using the t distribution in the form of a p-value.

Example 3.7.2

A student titrates 10 ml of 0.1 M acid against 0.1 M alkali five times and obtains the following results for the volume in ml of alkali.

   9.88   10.18   10.23   10.39   10.25

Assuming that the volume of alkali used has a normal distribution, test at the 5% significance level whether these results show bias from the expected value of 10 ml.

   Since the bias can be in either direction a two-tail test is appropriate. The null and alternative hypotheses are $H_0: \mu = 10$, $H_1: \mu \neq 10$.

The sample mean is $\bar{x} = \dfrac{\sum x}{n} = \dfrac{50.93}{5} = 10.186\ldots$,

and an unbiased estimate of the population variance is

$$s^2 = \frac{n}{n-1}\left(\frac{\sum x^2}{n} - \bar{x}^2\right) = \frac{5}{4}\left(\frac{518.9143}{5} - 10.186\ldots^2\right) = 0.035\,33\ldots.$$

The value of the test statistic is $t = \dfrac{\bar{x} - \mu_0}{\sqrt{\dfrac{s^2}{n}}} = \dfrac{10.186\ldots - 10}{\sqrt{\dfrac{0.035\,33\ldots}{5}}} = 2.2127\ldots.$

A two-tail test at the 5% significance level has a rejection region divided into two parts, each corresponding to a probability of $2\frac{1}{2}\%$. The rejection and acceptance regions are shown in Fig. 3.10. The upper critical value is given by $P(T \leqslant t) = 0.975$ for 4 degrees of freedom. From the table on page 271, $t = 2.776$ and so the rejection region for this test is $|T| \geqslant 2.776$. The observed

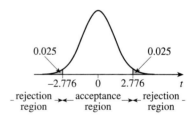

0.025   0.025

−2.776   0   2.776   t

rejection → ← acceptance → ← rejection
region   region   region

Fig. 3.10. Acceptance and rejection regions for Example 3.7.2.

value of T does not lie in the rejection region and so the null hypothesis is not rejected. The null hypothesis that the student's results do not show bias is accepted.

Example 3.7.3

The weights of packets of a certain brand of breakfast cereal are known to be distributed normally. It is claimed that the net weight of the contents is 450 g. The weights of the contents of seven packets are

   445, 453, 447, 451, 440, 460, 449.

Is there any evidence at the 5% level that the population mean is less than 450 g? What assumption must be made to carry out this test?

The sample mean is $\bar{x} = \dfrac{\sum x}{n} = \dfrac{3145}{7} = 449.28\ldots$, and an unbiased estimate of the population variance is

$$s^2 = \frac{n}{n-1}\left(\frac{\sum x^2}{n} - \bar{x}^2\right) = \frac{7}{6}\left(\frac{1\,413\,245}{7} - 449.28\ldots^2\right) = 40.238\ldots.$$

The null and alternative hypotheses are $H_0: \mu = 450$, $H_1: \mu < 450$.

The value of the test statistic is $t = \dfrac{\bar{x} - \mu_0}{\sqrt{\dfrac{s^2}{n}}} = \dfrac{449.28\ldots - 450}{\sqrt{\dfrac{40.238\ldots}{7}}} = -0.297\ldots.$

Fig. 3.11 shows the rejection and acceptance regions for this test. In this case the critical value is negative and has to be found using symmetry. Consider first a one-tail test for an *increase* at the 5% level. This requires $P(T \leqslant t) = 0.95$ with, in this case, 6 degrees of freedom. The corresponding rejection region is $T \geqslant 1.943$. Thus the rejection region for a *decrease*, as shown in Fig. 3.11, is $T \leqslant -1.943$. The observed value

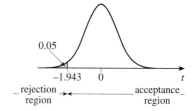

Fig. 3.11. Acceptance and rejection regions for Example 3.7.3.

of T is not in the rejection region and so the null hypothesis is not rejected. There is not evidence, at the 5% level, to say that the population mean is less than 450 g.

The assumption which has been made in carrying out this test is that the seven packets of cereal are randomly chosen.

Here is the generalisation of the method used in the examples above.

If a random sample of size n is drawn from a normal population of unknown variance, then the null hypothesis $H_0: \mu = \mu_0$ can be tested using the test statistic T. The value of T is given by

$$t = \frac{\bar{x} - \mu_0}{\sqrt{\dfrac{s^2}{n}}}, \text{ where } s^2 = \frac{n}{n-1}\left(\frac{\sum x^2}{n} - \bar{x}^2\right).$$

The rejection region for T depends on the form of the alternative hypothesis, H_1, the significance level and the number of degrees of freedom, $v = n - 1$.

- For a two-tail test at the $100\alpha\%$ significance level, the rejection region is given by $|T| \geqslant t$ where $P(T \leqslant t) = 1 - \frac{1}{2}\alpha$.

- For a one-tail test for an increase at the $100\alpha\%$ significance level, the rejection region is given by $T \geqslant t$ where $P(T \leqslant t) = 1 - \alpha$.

- For a one-tail test for a decrease at the $100\alpha\%$ significance level, the rejection region is given by $T \leqslant -t$ where $P(T \leqslant t) = 1 - \alpha$.

3.8 Practical activities

1 Simulating an opinion poll   The 'population' for this activity consists of the first digits of random numbers generated by a calculator or computer. A first digit of 0, 1, 2 or 3 represents a person who would answer 'yes' to a particular question in an opinion poll while a first digit of 4, 5, 6, 7, 8, or 9 represents a person who would answer 'no'. Each member of the class takes a sample of size 30, notes the number of 'people' who would vote 'yes' and then calculates a 95% confidence interval for the proportion of people in the population who would vote 'yes'. The confidence intervals for the class should be displayed on a diagram like that in Fig. 3.5. This diagram should also show the exact value for the proportion of people in the population who would vote 'yes', which in this case is 0.4. Comment on the results.

This activity can be repeated with different values for the proportion who would vote 'yes', with different confidence intervals and with different sizes of samples.

2 How long is a 'foot'?   Measure the foot length in cm of at least 30 adult male subjects in (a) socks and (b) shoes. Use your results to calculate a confidence interval for the population mean for each set of measurements. Compare your results with those obtained by other members of the class. Do any of the students' confidence intervals contain the value for the imperial unit of length of 1 foot which is equal to 30.48 cm? Discuss: to what extent was your sample a random one from a well-defined population?

Exercise 3E

1   A new method for determining the pH value of soil has been developed and is used on a random sample of 15 specimens taken from an area whose pH value has a mean of 6.32. The 15 values give a sample mean of $\bar{x} = 6.14$ and an estimated population variance of $s^2 = 1.10$. Assuming that the pH values in the area have a normal distribution, test, at the 5% significance level, whether the mean pH value as determined by the new method differs from 6.32.

2   The time taken for a machine to produce a certain plastic bowl has a normal distribution with mean 4.8 seconds. An adjustment is made to the machine which is intended to reduce the mean, and in order to test that it is successful, the times taken to produce 8 bowls are measured. The results, t seconds, are as follows.

   4.2   4.5   4.9   4.3   4.5   4.7   4.6   4.4

   Test, at the $2\frac{1}{2}\%$ significance level, whether or not the adjustment had the desired effect.

3   The plate glass used in a construction project is required to have a mean thickness greater than 5 mm in order to be acceptable. The thickness of each of 25 samples of a certain kind of plate glass is measured, giving a sample mean of 5.14 mm and estimated population variance of 0.29^2 mm^2.

   (a)   Assuming that the thickness of the glass is distributed normally, carry out a test, at the 5% significance level, to decide whether or not the sampled kind of plate glass is acceptable.

   (b)   Use the table of critical values of the t distribution to give limits for the p-value of the test.

4   The number of minutes late that a Number 38 bus arrives at a city centre stop has a mean of 5.7 during the 'rush hour'. After a reorganisation of the traffic lights in the city, the times of arrival of six Number 38 buses at the city centre bus stop were noted. The number of minutes late were as follows, a negative value indicating that the bus was early.

   2.3   5.6   –1.8   4.3   –1.1   3.2

   Assuming that these times comprise a random sample selected from a normal distribution, test, at the 1% significance level, whether or not the new mean is less than 5.7.

5   Haemoglobin levels in females may be modelled by a normal distribution with mean 14.2 (grams per decilitre). As part of a health study, 10 randomly chosen female students from a college had their haemoglobin levels, h, measured. Results summaries are $\sum h = 147.9$ and $\sum h^2 = 2203.19$. Test, at the 5% significance level, whether the mean haemoglobin level of female students in the college differs from the mean level of all females.

6   The mean birth weights of 20 babies born during April 2001 in a London hospital maternity department was 3.207 kg and gave an unbiased estimate of the population variance of $s^2 = 0.461^2 \text{ kg}^2$. It may be assumed that these babies form a random sample of all those born in London hospitals during 2001, whose birth weights are distributed normally with mean μ kg. A test of the null hypothesis $\mu = \mu_0$ against the alternative hypothesis $\mu \neq \mu_0$ is carried out at the 10% significance level. Find the set of values of μ_0 for which the null hypothesis is accepted. What is another description of this set of values?

Miscellaneous exercise 3

1   A youth club has a large number of members (referred to as the population later on in the question). In order to find the weekly distribution of pocket money of the members, a random sample of 10 is questioned. The sample produced the following amounts, £ x.

   6.20   5.40   4.00   3.00   3.30   8.50   6.00   7.50   5.80   6.70

   (a)   Describe a method by which the random sample of members may have been produced.

   (b)   Estimate the mean and variance of the weekly pocket money.

   (c)   Find a symmetric 95% confidence interval for the population mean. State any assumption on which your method is based.

   (d)   If 100 random samples were collected and a 95% confidence interval was calculated from each sample, what is the expected number of confidence intervals which would contain the population mean?   (OCR, adapted)

2   The mean of a random sample of n observations of the random variable X, where $X \sim N(\mu, \sigma^2)$, is denoted by $\overline{X}$. In the following cases, find the value of $b - a$ in terms of n and σ.

   (a) $P(\overline{X} < a) = 0.03$, $P(\overline{X} > b) = 0.07$

   (b) $P(\overline{X} < a) = 0.04$, $P(\overline{X} > b) = 0.06$

   (c) $P(\overline{X} < a) = 0.05$, $P(\overline{X} > b) = 0.05$

   What do these results confirm about the width of a symmetric confidence interval for μ?

3 The mass of a certain brand of chocolate bar has a normal distribution with mean μ grams and standard deviation σ grams. The masses, in grams, of 5 randomly chosen bars are

124.31, 125.14, 124.23, 125.41, 125.76.

Calculate a symmetric 95% confidence interval for the mean mass of the population

(a) assuming that $\sigma = 0.85$,   (b) without assuming that $\sigma = 0.85$.   (OCR, adapted)

4 The lengths of times, x hours, for which cars were parked in a town centre carpark were measured for a random sample of 200 cars, and it was found that $\sum x = 358.2$ and $\sum x^2 = 773.18$. Denoting the population mean and variance of the parking times by μ and σ^2 respectively, calculate

(a) unbiased estimates of μ and σ^2,   (b) a symmetric 90% confidence interval for μ.

It was also found that 39 of the 200 cars stayed in the carpark for more than $2\frac{1}{2}$ hours. Calculate a symmetric 90% confidence interval for the population proportion of cars staying for longer than $2\frac{1}{2}$ hours, giving the end-points to 3 decimal places.

The manager of the carpark believes that only 10% of all cars stay for longer than $2\frac{1}{2}$ hours. Is this supported by your calculations?   (OCR, adapted)

5 The mass of vitamin E in a capsule manufactured by a certain drug company was measured in a random sample of 12 capsules. The sample mean was 5.14 mg and an unbiased estimate of the population variance was 0.0021 mg^2. Assuming that the mass of vitamin E in a capsule has a normal distribution, calculate a symmetric 95% confidence interval for the population mean mass of vitamin E in a capsule.

Assuming the same estimate of the population variance, estimate the width of a 95% symmetric confidence interval for the mean mass of vitamin E, based on a random sample of 20 capsules.   (OCR, adapted)

6 The volume of paint dispensed into litre cans was measured for 100 randomly chosen cans and the results, x litres, are summarised by $\sum x = 104.0$ and $\sum x^2 = 110.06$.

(a) Calculate unbiased estimates of the mean and variance of the volumes dispensed into the cans.

(b) Calculate a symmetric 90% confidence interval for the mean volume, giving the end-points to a suitable degree of accuracy.

(c) Estimate the smallest sample size required to give a symmetric 90% confidence interval of width at most 0.02 litres.   (OCR, adapted)

7 Brilliant fireworks are intended to burn for 40 seconds. A random sample of 15 Brilliant fireworks is selected. Each firework in the sample is ignited and the burning time, x seconds, is measured. The results are summarised by $\sum(x-40) = -18$ and $\sum(x-40)^2 = 90$.

(a) Stating an assumption on which your method is based, calculate a symmetric 95% confidence interval for the mean burning time of all Brilliant fireworks.

(b) Test, at the 5% significance level, whether or not the mean burning time is less than 40 seconds.

Comment on the conclusion of the test in relation to the confidence interval.

          (OCR, adapted)

8 A particular brand of petrol was used in 80 randomly chosen cars of the same model and age. The petrol consumption, x miles per gallon, was obtained for each car. The results are summarised by $\sum x = 1896$ and $\sum x^2 = 45\,959$. Calculate an approximate symmetric 98% confidence interval for the mean petrol consumption of all cars of this model and age.

Give a reason why the interval is approximate.   (OCR, adapted)

9 The board of trustees of a charitable trust wishes to make a change to the trust's constitution. In order for this to happen at least two-thirds of the members must vote for the change. Before the vote is taken, the secretary consults a random sample of 60 members and finds that 75% of them will vote for the change. Calculate a symmetric 95% confidence interval for the proportion of all members who will vote for the change.

Nearer the time at which the vote is to be taken, the secretary consults a random sample of n members and finds, again, that 75% of them will vote for the change. Using this figure, he calculates a symmetric 99% confidence interval for the proportion of members who will vote for the change. This interval does not include the value two-thirds. Find the smallest possible value of n.   (OCR)

10 The random variable X has a normal distribution with unknown mean μ and known variance σ^2. A symmetric 98% confidence interval for μ, based on a random sample of 25 observations of X, is $[12.4, 12.6]$. Find

(a) the value of σ,

(b) the size of a random sample that will give a symmetric 95% confidence interval for μ of width as close as possible to 0.8.

11 A random sample of 200 fish was collected from a pond containing a large number of fish. Each was marked and returned to the pond. A day later, 400 fish were collected and 22 were found to be marked. These were also returned to the pond.

(a) Obtain a symmetric 90% confidence interval for the proportion of marked fish in the pond.

(b) Assuming that the number of marked fish is still 200, what can be said about the size of the population of fish in the pond?

12 The quality control manager of the poultry department of a supermarket states that for a delivery of a large batch of fresh chickens to be acceptable the mean weight should be at least 3 kg. In order to decide whether or not to accept a batch she selects a random sample of 12 chickens and finds that the sample mean weight is 2.84 kg and an unbiased estimate of the population variance is 0.21^2 kg^2.

Stating any assumption, carry out a suitable test, at the 5% significance level, and advise the manager whether or not to accept the batch.

13 A slimming regime, consisting of a mixture of diet and exercise, is claimed by the designer to decrease the weight of people using the regime by an average of 4 kg over a three-month period. To support the claim, the designer measures the weight losses of 16 randomly chosen people who used the regime for three months. The results, w kg, are summarised by $\sum w = 46.44$ and $\sum w^2 = 180.5$.

 (a) Test, at the 10% significance level, the null hypothesis that the population mean weight loss is 4 kg against the alternative hypothesis that it is not 4 kg. Weight loss may be assumed to be distributed normally.

 (b) Find the set of values of the population mean weight loss for which the null hypothesis would be rejected in a two-tail test at the 5% significance level using the above data.

14 The compiler of crossword puzzles classifies a puzzle as 'easy' if 60% or more people attempting the puzzle can complete it correctly within 20 minutes. It is classified as 'hard' if fewer than 30% of people can complete it correctly within 20 minutes. All other puzzles are classified as 'average'. A particular puzzle was given to 150 competitors in a contest and 74 completed it correctly within 20 minutes. The compiler wishes to be 90% confident of correctly classifying the puzzle.

 (a) How should she classify the puzzle?

 (b) Can she be 95% confident that her classification is correct?

15 A certain type of melon sold by a supermarket chain is intended to have a mean weight of 750 grams. A random sample of 8 melons selected from a large batch are each weighed and the results, m grams, are summarised by $\sum (m - 750) = -68.8$ and $\sum (m - 750)^2 = 1263.68$.

 (a) Assuming that the weights have a normal distribution, test, at the 1% significance level, whether or not the mean weight of melons in the batch is less than 750 grams.

 (b) Comment on the assumption made in part (a).

16 A television viewer notices that many TV programmes start a few minutes later than the advertised time. For a random sample of 120 programmes, unbiased estimates of the mean and variance of the delay times are 1.75 minutes and 2.46 minutes^2 respectively, each correct to 3 significant figures. Use these estimates to calculate a symmetric 99% confidence interval for the population mean delay.

The viewer considers a normal distribution $N(1.75, 2.46)$ as a model for the delay, in minutes, at the start of a randomly chosen TV programme. Show that this model is not consistent with the viewer's observation that TV programmes almost never start before the advertised time.

Does the fact that the distribution of the delay times may not be normal affect the validity of the calculation of the confidence interval for the mean delay? Give a reason for your answer.   (OCR)

4 Testing for differences between populations

This chapter develops the concepts of hypothesis testing and confidence intervals to cover situations in which there are two populations. When you have completed it you should be able to

- understand the difference between a two-sample test and a paired-sample test, and select the appropriate form of test in solving problems
- formulate hypotheses and carry out a test for a difference of population means or population proportions using a normal distribution, and appreciate the conditions necessary for the test to be valid
- calculate a pooled estimate of variance based on the data from two samples
- formulate hypotheses and carry out either a two-sample t-test or a paired-sample t-test, as appropriate, for a difference of population means, and appreciate the conditions necessary for these tests to be valid
- calculate a confidence interval for a difference between population means, using a normal distribution or a t distribution, as appropriate.

4.1 Testing for a difference between the means of two populations

The confidence intervals and hypothesis tests which you have met so far have been concerned with only one population. For example in S2 and in the previous chapter of this book you carried out tests on the mean of a single population and the null hypothesis took the form $H_0: \mu = \mu_0$. However, in many situations two populations must be compared. For example:

(a) Do two different fertilisers give the same crop yield?
(b) Are the lengths of stay in hospital the same for male and female patients?
(c) Do people in their twenties take the same number of driving tests before they pass as people under twenty?
(d) Do two different brands of light bulb have the same lifetime?

To discuss these problems it is helpful to use the following notation for the two populations.

	Population 1	Population 2
Population mean	μ_x	μ_y
Population variance	σ_x^2	σ_y^2
Sample size	n_x	n_y
Sample mean	$\overline{x}$	$\overline{y}$
Unbiased estimate of population variance	s_x^2	s_y^2

In this and the following section it will be assumed that the samples are chosen randomly and independently from the two populations.

For each of questions (a) to (d) posed above the null hypothesis theorises no difference between the means of the populations. This can be expressed as $H_0: \mu_x = \mu_y$, which can also be written as $H_0: \mu_x - \mu_y = 0$. This null hypothesis can be tested by looking at the difference between the means of the two samples, that is $\bar{x} - \bar{y}$. If the population means are equal, then you would expect $\bar{x} - \bar{y}$ to be close to zero. It will not necessarily be equal to zero since the sample means will not necessarily equal the population means. The larger $\bar{x} - \bar{y}$ becomes, the less likely it is that the population means are equal. In order to decide whether $\bar{x} - \bar{y}$ differs significantly from zero you need to consider the sampling distribution of the random variable $\bar{X} - \bar{Y}$.

As in previous discussions of hypothesis tests and confidence intervals, it is helpful to start by assuming that both populations are normal, that is $X \sim N(\mu_x, \sigma_x^2)$ and $Y \sim N(\mu_y, \sigma_y^2)$. Then the sample means will be distributed as $\bar{X} \sim N\left(\mu_x, \dfrac{\sigma_x^2}{n_x}\right)$ and $\bar{Y} \sim N\left(\mu_y, \dfrac{\sigma_y^2}{n_y}\right)$. The difference between the means, $\bar{X} - \bar{Y}$, will also be distributed normally (see Section 2.4). The mean of this distribution is

$$E(\bar{X} - \bar{Y}) = E(\bar{X}) - E(\bar{Y}) \qquad \text{(from Equation 2.3)}$$
$$= \mu_x - \mu_y,$$

and the variance is

$$\text{Var}(\bar{X} - \bar{Y}) = \text{Var}(\bar{X}) + \text{Var}(\bar{Y}) \qquad \text{(from Equation 2.4)}$$
$$= \frac{\sigma_x^2}{n_x} + \frac{\sigma_y^2}{n_y}.$$

Thus $\bar{X} - \bar{Y} \sim N\left(\mu_x - \mu_y, \dfrac{\sigma_x^2}{n_x} + \dfrac{\sigma_y^2}{n_y}\right)$.

If a random sample of size n_x is taken from the population $X \sim N(\mu_x, \sigma_x^2)$ and an independent random sample of size n_y is taken from the population $Y \sim N(\mu_y, \sigma_y^2)$, then $\bar{X} - \bar{Y} \sim N\left(\mu_x - \mu_y, \dfrac{\sigma_x^2}{n_x} + \dfrac{\sigma_y^2}{n_y}\right)$.

Standardising the random variable $\bar{X} - \bar{Y}$ gives

$$Z = \frac{(\bar{X} - \bar{Y}) - (\mu_x - \mu_y)}{\sqrt{\dfrac{\sigma_x^2}{n_x} + \dfrac{\sigma_y^2}{n_y}}}$$

where $Z \sim N(0,1)$. This statistic can be used to test the null hypothesis $H_0: \mu_x - \mu_y = 0$.

Under H_0,

$$Z = \frac{(\overline{X} - \overline{Y}) - 0}{\sqrt{\dfrac{\sigma_x^2}{n_x} + \dfrac{\sigma_y^2}{n_y}}} = \frac{\overline{X} - \overline{Y}}{\sqrt{\dfrac{\sigma_x^2}{n_x} + \dfrac{\sigma_y^2}{n_y}}}. \qquad (4.1)$$

As with previous hypothesis tests, the form of the alternative hypothesis will depend on the nature of the problem. The rejection regions are found in the same way as they were for one-sample tests.

Example 4.1.1

For a test of whether the means of two normally distributed populations are equal or not, a random sample is taken from each population. The sample from the first population has size 8 and the sample mean is 19.9. The sample from the second population has size 10 and the sample mean is 16.7. The population variances are known to be 2.8 and 2.9 respectively. Calculate an appropriate test statistic and decide, at the 1% significance level, whether to reject the hypothesis that the means of the two populations are equal.   (OCR)

The null hypothesis is $H_0 : \mu_x = \mu_y$, which is equivalent to $H_0 : \mu_x - \mu_y = 0$, where μ_x and μ_y are the means of the two populations. No indication is given of the direction in which μ_x and μ_y might differ from each other, so the alternative hypothesis is $H_1 : \mu_x \neq \mu_y$, or $H_1 : \mu_x - \mu_y \neq 0$.

The test statistic is $Z = \dfrac{\overline{X} - \overline{Y}}{\sqrt{\dfrac{\sigma_x^2}{n_x} + \dfrac{\sigma_y^2}{n_y}}}$.

For the given samples it takes the value

$$z = \frac{\overline{x} - \overline{y}}{\sqrt{\dfrac{\sigma_x^2}{n_x} + \dfrac{\sigma_y^2}{n_y}}} = \frac{19.9 - 16.7}{\sqrt{\dfrac{2.8}{8} + \dfrac{2.9}{10}}} = 4.$$

For a two-tail test at the 1% significance level the rejection region is $|Z| \geqslant 2.576$. The observed value of Z lies in the rejection region and so the null hypothesis that the means of the two populations are equal is rejected.

In practice you may not know the population variances, and there are circumstances in which the populations are not distributed normally. It should come as no surprise, however, that the method which has been derived will still be valid provided that the samples are large: in this case σ_x^2 and σ_y^2 can be replaced by their unbiased estimates s_x^2 and s_y^2 and the central limit theorem will ensure that $\overline{X} - \overline{Y}$ is distributed approximately normally As before, 'large' is assumed to refer to samples of size 30 or more.

Example 4.1.2

It is often claimed that women with children take more time off from work than those without children. A manager of a large company decides to test this claim by taking random samples of company employees who fall into the two groups. In the previous year she found that the mean number of days absent for 50 women with children was 5.9 with an estimated population variance of 2.6^2 days^2 whereas the mean number of days absent for 60 women without children was 5.3 with an estimated population variance of 3.1^2 days^2. Test, at the 5% significance level, whether there is evidence that the population mean for women with children is greater than that for women without children.

The null hypothesis is $H_0 : \mu_x = \mu_y$, or $H_0 : \mu_x - \mu_y = 0$, where μ_x and μ_y are the population means for women with and without children respectively. It was thought, before the data were collected, that μ_x might be greater than μ_y, so the appropriate alternative hypothesis is $H_1 : \mu_x > \mu_y$, or $H_1 : \mu_x - \mu_y > 0$.

In this example the variable 'number of days absent' is discrete and so it cannot be distributed normally. However, the samples are large, so, according to the central limit theorem, the sample means are distributed approximately normally. No knowledge of the population variances is available, but they can be replaced by unbiased estimates, again since the samples are large. The value of the test statistic Z is

$$z = \frac{\bar{x} - \bar{y}}{\sqrt{\dfrac{s_x^2}{n_x} + \dfrac{s_y^2}{n_y}}} = \frac{5.9 - 5.3}{\sqrt{\dfrac{2.6^2}{50} + \dfrac{3.1^2}{60}}} = 1.104\ldots .$$

The rejection region for Z for a one-tail test for an increase at the 5% significance level is $Z \geqslant 1.645$. The calculated value of Z is not in the rejection region and so the null hypothesis of equal population means is not rejected: there is insufficient evidence to say that the mean number of absences is greater for women with children than it is for women without children.

You can also perform a test of a null hypothesis that the difference between two population means takes a specified value other than zero, that is $H_0 : \mu_x - \mu_y = c$ where c is a constant.

Example 4.1.3

Manufacturer Y claims that a certain type of electronic component which it produces lasts at least 10 hours longer than the corresponding component produced by manufacturer X. A customer tests samples of size 50 of each type of component. The results can be summarised as follows:

$$\sum x = 2091, \qquad \sum x^2 = 221\,829, \qquad \sum y = 2332, \qquad \sum y^2 = 206\,389.$$

Assuming that the customer's samples are random, test, at the 5% significance level, whether these results support manufacturer Y's claim.

First calculate the sample mean and unbiased estimate of population variance for each manufacturer. For manufacturer X,

$$\bar{x} = \frac{\sum x}{n} = \frac{2091}{50} = 41.82,$$

and

$$s_x^2 = \frac{n}{n-1}\left[\frac{\sum x^2}{n} - \bar{x}^2\right] = \frac{50}{49}\left[\frac{221\,829}{50} - 41.82^2\right] = 2742.517\ldots.$$

Similarly, for manufacturer Y, $\bar{y} = 46.64$ and $s_y^2 = 1992.337\ldots$.

The null and alternative hypotheses are $H_0: \mu_y - \mu_x = 10$ and $H_1: \mu_y - \mu_x < 10$ respectively. Under H_0,

$$\bar{Y} - \bar{X} \sim N\left(\mu_y - \mu_x, \frac{\sigma_x^2}{n_x} + \frac{\sigma_y^2}{n_y}\right) = N\left(10, \frac{2742.517\ldots}{50} + \frac{1992.337\ldots}{50}\right)$$

where the population variances have been replaced by unbiased estimates. The value of the test statistic is

$$z = \frac{(\bar{y} - \bar{x}) - c}{\sqrt{\dfrac{s_x^2}{n_x} + \dfrac{s_y^2}{n_y}}} = \frac{46.64 - 41.82 - 10}{\sqrt{\dfrac{2742.517\ldots}{50} + \dfrac{1992.337\ldots}{50}}} = -0.532\ldots.$$

The rejection region for Z for a one-tail test for a decrease at the 5% significance level is $Z \leqslant -1.645$. The calculated value of Z is not in the rejection region and so the null hypothesis that the mean for manufacturer Y exceeds the mean for manufacturer X by at least 10 is not rejected. The results support manufacturer Y's claim.

If independent random samples of sizes n_x and n_y are drawn from populations $X \sim N(\mu_x, \sigma_x^2)$ and $Y \sim N(\mu_y, \sigma_y^2)$ respectively, then the null hypothesis $H_0: \mu_x - \mu_y = c$ can be tested using the test statistic Z. The value of Z is given by

$$z = \frac{(\bar{x} - \bar{y}) - c}{\sqrt{\dfrac{s_x^2}{n_x} + \dfrac{s_y^2}{n_y}}}.$$

The rejection region for Z depends on the form of the alternative hypothesis, H_1. For a test at the $100\alpha\%$ significance level,

- with $H_1: \mu_x - \mu_y \neq c$, the rejection region is $|Z| \geqslant z$ where $\Phi(z) = 1 - \frac{1}{2}\alpha$
- with $H_1: \mu_x - \mu_y > c$, the rejection region is $Z \geqslant z$ where $\Phi(z) = 1 - \alpha$
- with $H_1: \mu_x - \mu_y < c$, the rejection region is $Z \leqslant -z$ where $\Phi(z) = 1 - \alpha$.

If the samples are *large*, this test statistic may also be used when

- the populations are not normal or
- the population variances are unknown and have been replaced by their unbiased estimates s_x^2 and s_y^2.

Exercise 4A

1   The independent random variables X and Y, where $X \sim N(\mu_x, 24)$ and $Y \sim N(\mu_y, 32)$, have different means and it is believed that $\mu_x > \mu_y$. In order to test this belief, random samples of 5 were taken of each of X and Y, giving $\bar{x} = 32.4$ and $\bar{y} = 30.9$. Carry out a suitable test at the 5% significance level.

2   Batteries which are claimed to be identical are manufactured in two factories A and B. As part of a monitoring procedure, random samples of 50 batteries made at factory A and 60 made at factory B were tested and the sample means and unbiased estimates of the population variances were calculated, with the following results.

	Sample size	Sample mean (hours)	Unbiased estimate of population variance ($hours^2$)
Factory A	50	42.75	1.98
Factory B	60	42.15	1.82

Test, at the 5% significance level, whether there is a difference between the mean lives of the batteries manufactured at the two factories.

State, giving a reason, whether it is necessary for the lives to have normal distributions for your test to be valid.

3   Two machines are intended to dispense 500 grams of washing powder into cartons. Previous tests have indicated that the amounts dispensed are distributed normally, from machine 1 with standard deviation 10.8 grams and from machine 2 with standard deviation 9.4 grams. A test is carried out to decide whether the mean amounts dispensed by the two machines differ significantly. Ten cartons filled by each machine are selected at random and their contents weighed. The sample means are 498.3 grams and 501.2 grams.

(a)   Find the p-value of the test.

(b)   What is the conclusion of the test at the 5% significance level?

4   A study was carried out of the sales of a newly published technical book to determine whether there is a 'North-South divide'. The sales, x_S and x_N, at 50 randomly selected book-shops situated in the UK south of Watford and 50 situated north of Watford were obtained for a particular month. The results are summarised by

$$\sum x_S = 3991, \qquad \sum x_S^2 = 325\,269, \qquad \sum x_N = 3745, \qquad \sum x_N^2 = 299\,803.$$

(a)   Test, at the 5% significance level, whether the mean number of sales south of Watford exceeds the mean north of Watford in that month.

(b)   State what further information would be required in order to judge whether the total sales of the book were greater south of Watford than north of Watford.

5 A machine produces components whose lengths are distributed normally with standard deviation 0.42 cm. A random sample of 25 components had a sample mean length of 12.94 cm. After the machine had been serviced, a random sample of 40 components was selected and each one measured. Their lengths, y cm, are summarised by $\sum y = 524.4$ and $\sum y^2 = 6877.94$. Test, at the 10% significance level, whether the mean length has changed,

(a) assuming that, after the service, the standard deviation is still 0.42 cm,

(b) without assuming that the standard deviation is 0.42 cm.

Which test do you consider to be more reliable?

6 A particular drug was used on rats to determine its effect on their maze-solving ability. The maze used in the test contained a 'reward' of food at its end. It was believed that the number of errors made in the maze by rats given the drug (the experimental group) would exceed those by the rats not given the drug (the control group). In total 66 rats were used, 36 in the experimental group and 30 in the control group. The numbers of errors, x_E and x_C, made by rats in the experimental and control groups respectively are summarised by

$$\bar{x}_E = 20.5, \qquad s_E^2 = 30.3, \qquad \bar{x}_C = 16.6, \qquad s_C^2 = 21.2.$$

(a) Test, at the 1% significance level, whether rats given the drug make more errors, on average, than rats not given the drug.

(b) One researcher hypothesised that the mean number of errors made by rats given the drug exceeds the mean number made by rats not given the drug by more than 2. Test this hypothesis at the 10% significance level.

4.2 The two-sample *t*-test

In the previous section you learnt how to test for a difference between population means, even when the population variances are unknown, provided that the samples are large. But what about the situation when the samples are small? This section develops a method which is applicable to samples of any size, provided that two conditions are met. These are that

(a) the populations are normal and
(b) the populations have equal (although unknown) variances.

You know from the previous section that the null hypothesis $H_0: \mu_x - \mu_y = c$ can be tested for samples from normal populations by using the test statistic

$$Z = \frac{(\bar{X} - \bar{Y}) - c}{\sqrt{\dfrac{\sigma_x^2}{n_x} + \dfrac{\sigma_y^2}{n_y}}}.$$

If you assume that the two populations have equal variances then σ_x^2 and σ_y^2 can be replaced in this equation by their common value σ^2 to give

$$Z = \frac{(\overline{X} - \overline{Y}) - c}{\sqrt{\sigma^2 \left(\dfrac{1}{n_x} + \dfrac{1}{n_y} \right)}}. \qquad (4.2)$$

If σ^2 were known, then it could be substituted into this equation to give a value of Z and a hypothesis test could be carried out as in Section 4.1. Here, however, it is the situation where σ^2 is not known which is of interest.

Samples from each population give unbiased estimates of the common population variance, σ^2. These estimators, S_x^2 and S_y^2, need to be combined, or 'pooled', in some way in order to give an overall estimate of σ^2. One way of doing this would be to average them, but this takes no account of the relative sizes of the samples. The larger sample gives the better estimate, so it is more sensible to weight the two estimators in a way which reflects the respective sample sizes. In fact it can be shown that the best way to weight them is according to $n - 1$. The pooled estimator, S_p^2, of the common population variance, σ^2, is given by

$$S_p^2 = \frac{(n_x - 1)S_x^2 + (n_y - 1)S_y^2}{(n_x - 1) + (n_y - 1)} = \frac{(n_x - 1)S_x^2 + (n_y - 1)S_y^2}{n_x + n_y - 2}.$$

This estimator is unbiased; that is, $E(S_p^2) = \sigma^2$. It is also the best unbiased estimator. This means that the variance of S_p^2 has the smallest possible value so that the estimates are clustered as closely as possible about the true value, σ^2. More about unbiased estimators can be found in S4 Chapter 5.

The estimator S_p^2 can then be substituted in Equation 4.2 to give the random variable

$$\frac{(\overline{X} - \overline{Y}) - c}{\sqrt{S_p^2 \left(\dfrac{1}{n_x} + \dfrac{1}{n_y} \right)}}.$$

This variable no longer has a standard normal distribution because σ^2 has been replaced by its estimate. However, it has a distribution with which you are already familiar, that is the t distribution. The number of degrees of freedom of this t distribution is $n_x + n_y - 2$. The reason for this is that the variable $\dfrac{(\overline{X} - \overline{Y}) - c}{\sqrt{S_p^2 \left(\dfrac{1}{n_x} + \dfrac{1}{n_y} \right)}}$ is calculated from $n_x + n_y$ data values but there are two constraints, namely $\sum (x - \overline{x}) = 0$ and $\sum (y - \overline{y}) = 0$. Thus

number of degrees of freedom, v = number of values − number of constraints

$$= n_x + n_y - 2.$$

If independent random samples of sizes n_x and n_y are drawn from populations $X \sim N(\mu_x, \sigma^2)$ and $Y \sim N(\mu_y, \sigma^2)$ respectively (where the common variance is unknown), then the null hypothesis $H_0: \mu_x - \mu_y = c$ can be tested using the test statistic T. The value of T is given by

$$t = \frac{(\bar{x} - \bar{y}) - c}{\sqrt{s_p^2 \left(\frac{1}{n_x} + \frac{1}{n_y} \right)}}. \qquad (4.3)$$

The pooled estimate, s_p^2, of the common population variance, σ^2, is given by

$$s_p^2 = \frac{(n_x - 1)s_x^2 + (n_y - 1)s_y^2}{n_x + n_y - 2}, \qquad (4.4)$$

where s_x^2 and s_y^2 are unbiased estimates of the population variances and n_x and n_y are the corresponding sample sizes.

This test is called the **two-sample t-test**.

The rejection region for T depends on the form of the alternative hypothesis, H_1, the significance level and the number of degrees of freedom, $v = n_x + n_y - 2$.

For a test at the $100\alpha\%$ significance level,

- with $H_1: \mu_x - \mu_y \neq c$, the rejection region is $|T| \geqslant t$ where $P(T \leqslant t) = 1 - \frac{1}{2}\alpha$
- with $H_1: \mu_x - \mu_y > c$, the rejection region is $T \geqslant t$ where $P(T \leqslant t) = 1 - \alpha$
- with $H_1: \mu_x - \mu_y < c$, the rejection region is $T \leqslant -t$ where $P(T \leqslant t) = 1 - \alpha$.

In some books the two-sample t-test is referred to as the independent sample t-test.

Example 4.2.1

In an experiment 22 mice were divided into two groups, one of which was given a special diet which was designed to give faster mass gain. After an interval the gains in mass (measured in grams) of the mice were measured, with the results given below.

	Sample size	Mean (grams)	Unbiased estimate of population variance ($grams^2$)
Special diet	10	20.6	4.51
Usual diet	12	18.2	3.17

The mass gains for each group may be assumed to be distributed normally with the same variance. Calculate an estimate of this common variance from the combined results of both groups. Test, at the 5% significance level, whether the special diet produced a greater increase in mass than the usual diet.

What additional assumption must be made to carry out this test?   (OCR, adapted)

The null hypothesis is $H_0: \mu_x = \mu_y$, or $H_0: \mu_x - \mu_y = 0$, where μ_x and μ_y are the means of the populations fed on the special diet and the usual diet respectively. Since the special diet is expected to produce the greater gain in mass the alternative hypothesis is $H_1: \mu_x > \mu_y$, or $H_1: \mu_x - \mu_y > 0$.

From Equation 4.4 an estimate of the common variance is

$$s_p^2 = \frac{(n_x - 1)s_x^2 + (n_y - 1)s_y^2}{n_x + n_y - 2} = \frac{(10 - 1) \times 4.51 + (12 - 1) \times 3.17}{10 + 12 - 2} = 3.773.$$

Using Equation 4.3 gives

$$t = \frac{(\bar{x} - \bar{y}) - c}{\sqrt{s_p^2 \left(\frac{1}{n_x} + \frac{1}{n_y} \right)}} = \frac{(20.6 - 18.2) - 0}{\sqrt{3.773 \left(\frac{1}{10} + \frac{1}{12} \right)}} = 2.88 \ldots .$$

The test statistic T has a t distribution with $v = n_x + n_y - 2 = 10 + 12 - 2 = 20$ degrees of freedom. For a one-tail test at the 5% significance level the critical region is $T \geqslant 1.725$. The observed value of T lies in the rejection region. The null hypothesis is rejected: there is evidence at the 5% significance level that the special diet produces a greater mass gain than the usual diet.

The additional assumption which has been made is that the samples of mice which were fed the two different diets were chosen at random.

Example 4.2.2

Two different types of nylon fibre were tested for the amount of stretching under tension. Ten random samples of each fibre, of the same length and diameter, were stretched by applying a standard load. For fibre 1 the increases in length, x mm, were as follows.

12.84 14.26 13.23 14.75 15.13 14.15 13.37 12.96 15.02 14.38

$$\left(\sum x = 140.09, \quad \sum x^2 = 1969.0513 \right)$$

For fibre 2 the increases in length, y mm, were as follows.

14.27 13.25 14.17 13.11 14.92 12.12 14.21 13.68 15.14 14.81

$$\left(\sum y = 139.68, \quad \sum y^2 = 1958.9794 \right)$$

Test whether the mean increase in length of the two types of fibre is different, stating any conditions necessary for your test to hold. Use a 10% significance level.   (OCR, adapted)

Since the population variances are unknown and the samples are small, the test statistic Z cannot be used. The appropriate test to use is the two-sample t-test: the conditions necessary for this to hold are that the populations are normal and the population variances are equal.

The null hypothesis is $H_0: \mu_x = \mu_y$, or $H_0: \mu_x - \mu_y = 0$, where μ_x and μ_y are the population means for the amounts stretched by fibres 1 and 2 respectively. No indication is given of the direction in which μ_x and μ_y might differ from each other, so the alternative hypothesis is $H_1: \mu_x \neq \mu_y$, or $H_1: \mu_x - \mu_y \neq 0$.

First the sample means and unbiased estimates of the population variances must be calculated. For fibre 1

$$\bar{x} = \frac{\sum x}{n} = \frac{140.09}{10} = 14.009,$$

$$s_x^2 = \frac{n}{n-1}\left(\frac{\sum x^2}{n} - \bar{x}^2\right) = \frac{10}{9}\left(\frac{1969.0513}{10} - 14.009^2\right) = 0.725\,61.$$

Similarly, for fibre 2, $\bar{y} = 13.968$, $s_y^2 = 0.881\,01....$

The pooled estimate of σ^2 is

$$s_p^2 = \frac{(n_x - 1)s_x^2 + (n_y - 1)s_y^2}{n_x + n_y - 2}$$

$$= \frac{(10-1) \times 0.725\,61... + (10-1) \times 0.881\,01...}{10 + 10 - 2} = 0.803\,31....$$

$$t = \frac{(\bar{x} - \bar{y}) - c}{\sqrt{s_p^2\left(\dfrac{1}{n_x} + \dfrac{1}{n_y}\right)}} = \frac{(14.009 - 13.968) - 0}{\sqrt{0.803\,31...\left(\dfrac{1}{10} + \dfrac{1}{10}\right)}} = 0.102....$$

The test statistic T has a t distribution with $v = n_x + n_y - 2 = 10 + 10 - 2 = 18$ degrees of freedom. For a two-tail test at the 10% significance level the critical region is $|T| \geq 1.734$. The observed value of T does not lie in the rejection region. The null hypothesis is not rejected: there is no evidence at the 10% significance level that the mean increase in length differs for the two types of fibre.

You may wonder how a hypothesis test of $H_0: \mu_x = \mu_y$ is carried out for small samples if the conditions

(a) the populations are normal and
(b) the populations have equal (although unknown) variances

are not met. If condition (a) is met but (b) is not, then there is an approximate method based on the statistic T: this is beyond the scope of this book. If condition (a) is not met, then so-called non-parametric tests are used. Some of these are described later in this book in Chapter 2 of S4.

Large samples: pooled versus non-pooled tests

Suppose you have two large independent random samples from different populations and you wish to test for the equality of population means. In these circumstances, two tests are possible. If you can assume that the population variances are equal, then you can use the two-sample t-test as in Example 4.2.1 (where the critical value of T will be close to the corresponding value of Z since the number of degrees of freedom will be large); if you can make no assumptions about the equality of the population variances, then you will have to use the test statistic Z as in Example 4.1.2. In examination questions the method to use will be made explicit, but what about data which you collect yourself?

It might seem that the safest course would be always to assume that the population variances are not equal since in that way you can never be wrong. In fact it can be shown that if the assumption of equal variances is valid, then the two-sample t-test has a slightly smaller probability of a Type II error (that is of accepting a false H_0). Thus when the assumption of equal variances is a safe one the pooled test is the preferred method. (There is a statistical test for equality of variance, but it will not be described here.)

Exercise 4B

1 Independent random samples are taken of X and Y, where $X \sim N(\mu_x, \sigma^2)$ and $Y \sim N(\mu_y, \sigma^2)$. The sample statistics are given in the following table.

	n	Sample mean	Unbiased estimate of population variance
From X	10	42.5	4.8
From Y	12	41.4	6.2

(a) Find an unbiased estimate of σ^2.

(b) Test, at the 5% significance level, the null hypothesis $H_0: \mu_x = \mu_y$ against the alternative hypothesis $H_1: \mu_x \neq \mu_y$.

2 To test the engine performance of two similar cars produced by manufacturers A and B, 15 cars were selected at random from each manufacturer. They were all driven over the same distance and the number of kilometres travelled per litre of petrol used was calculated for each car. The results, x_A km l^{-1} and x_B km l^{-1} for cars from manufacturers A and B respectively, are summarised as follows:

$$\sum x_A = 122.6, \qquad \sum x_A^2 = 1022.33, \qquad \sum x_B = 137.0, \qquad \sum x_B^2 = 1275.32.$$

Assuming that the populations are normal with a common variance, find the p-value of a test of whether cars from manufacturer A have greater petrol consumption on average than those from manufacturer B.

3 A botanist believes that the moisture content of the soil in the northern half of a large field is significantly different from that in the southern half. To test this belief he measures the moisture content at five randomly chosen points in the northern half of the field and four randomly chosen points in the southern half. The results are as follows.

Northern half (%)	8.7	9.3	10.1	9.0	10.3
Southern half (%)	7.4	9.1	8.6	8.2	

Stating your assumptions, test, at the 5% significance level, whether the mean moisture content of the southern half of the field is less than that of the northern half.

4 Kapil believes that the carrots he grows in his garden are heavier, on average, than those grown by his friend Jack. To confirm his belief they both select 8 carrots, chosen at random from their crops, whose weights x_K grams and x_J grams are summarised by

$$\sum x_K = 1510, \qquad \sum x_K^2 = 285\,351, \qquad \sum x_J = 1406, \qquad \sum x_J^2 = 247\,512.$$

(a) Stating your assumptions, show that there is strong evidence that Kapil's carrots weigh more, on average, than Jack's. The strength of the evidence should be indicated by a suitable significance level.

(b) Test, at the 5% significance level, whether Kapil's carrots are heavier, on average, than Jack's by more than 10 grams.

5 Two groups of children in an unstreamed school were taught by different teachers for a GCSE examination. The marks obtained by the 15 children taught by Mrs Green and the 19 taught by Mr Jones are summarised by

$$\sum x_G = 876, \qquad \sum x_G^2 = 52\,409, \qquad \sum x_J = 1028, \qquad \sum x_J^2 = 57\,042.$$

The marks may be considered to have normal distributions.

(a) Describe populations from which the two groups could be considered to be random samples.

(b) Calculate unbiased estimates of the two population variances.

(c) Assuming that the two populations have the same variance, calculate an unbiased estimate of this variance.

(d) Test, at the 5% significance level, whether there is a difference in the population mean marks of students taught by Mrs Green and by Mr Jones.

6 An archaeologist wishes to compare the sizes of ears of corn found at two archaeological sites of the same period. She believes that those grown at site 1 are larger than those grown at site 2. The sizes, in cm, of samples found at the two sites are as follows.

Site 1	9.2	11.3	13.0	15.2	6.9	14.3		
Site 2	7.6	9.4	10.3	14.8	8.2	6.5	9.8	7.8

(a) Find unbiased estimates of the population means and variances of the sizes of ears of corn grown at the two sites.

(b) Assuming that the sizes have normal distributions with a common variance, find limits to the p-value of a test of the archaeologist's belief.

4.3   The paired *t*-test

Suppose you want to see whether the time taken to complete a simple task decreases with practice. One way of investigating this would be to take a random sample of people and measure the time which each person takes to complete the task. Then for another, different, random sample allow each person to perform the task twice and measure the time they take on the second attempt. The two samples are independent and so their means can be compared using one of the tests described so far in this chapter (assuming that the necessary conditions for the application of the test hold). The null hypothesis would take the form $H_0 : \mu_x - \mu_y = 0$ where μ_x is the mean time taken by all people on their first attempt and μ_y is the mean time taken by all people on their second attempt. The alternative hypothesis would take the form $H_1 : \mu_x - \mu_y > 0$ since it is to be expected that people might improve with practice.

Another, perhaps more obvious, method would be to choose one random sample of people and measure the times which each person takes to perform the task on their first and second attempts. An example of such data is shown in Table 4.1.

Person	A	B	C	D	E	F	G	H
First attempt	6.3	3.5	7.1	3.7	8.4	3.9	4.7	5.2
Second attempt	5.1	3.4	6.2	4.5	7.3	4.0	3.6	5.1
Difference, *d*	1.2	0.1	0.9	−0.8	1.1	−0.1	1.1	0.1

Table 4.1. Times (in minutes) taken by 8 people on their first and second attempts at a simple task.

The null hypothesis is again $H_0 : \mu_x - \mu_y = 0$, where μ_x is the mean time taken by all people on their first attempt and μ_y is the mean time taken by all people on their second attempt. However, the method of analysis is different because you no longer have two independent samples. Instead the data collected takes the form of pairs of values, one pair for each person. You can see that there is quite a lot of variation between different people. For example, B is fast on both attempts whereas E is slow. However, it is not the variation between individuals which is of interest but their improvement with practice. If practice does decrease the time taken, then you would expect the first value to be greater than the second. This means that the improvement can be measured by the difference, d, between the first and the second values. The values of these differences are given in the last line of the table. You can check that the average difference, $\bar{d}$, is 0.45 minutes. The question which now needs to be answered is whether this value indicates that the second time is significantly lower than the first. In order to do this you need to consider the distribution of $D = X - Y$, where X is the time on the first attempt and Y is the time on the second attempt.

The mean, μ_d, of the sampling distribution of D is given by

$$\mu_d = \mathrm{E}(D) = \mathrm{E}(X - Y) = \mathrm{E}(X) - \mathrm{E}(Y) = \mu_x - \mu_y.$$

The null hypothesis $H_0: \mu_x - \mu_y = 0$ is thus equivalent to $H_0: \mu_d = 0$. This is just the form of the null hypothesis for a single sample which you met in Section 3.7. So, provided that D has a normal distribution, this null hypothesis can be tested using the statistic T with $n-1$ degrees of freedom. The variance of the sampling distribution of D is not known, but it can be estimated by S_d^2, where S_d^2 is the unbiased estimator. For the data in Table 4.1 the unbiased estimate of the variance of the differences is $s_d^2 = 0.531\ldots$. Using Equation 3.6

$$t = \frac{\bar{d} - 0}{\sqrt{\dfrac{s_d^2}{n}}} = \frac{0.45 - 0}{\sqrt{\dfrac{0.531\ldots}{8}}} = 1.745\ldots .$$

The alternative hypothesis is $H_1: \mu_x > \mu_y$, or $H_1: \mu_x - \mu_y > 0$. For a one-tail test at the 10% level with $\nu = 7$, the rejection region is $T \geqslant 1.415$. Since the observed value of T lies in the rejection region, the alternative hypothesis that people take less time with practice is accepted.

Students sometimes find it difficult to decide whether data are paired when the samples are the same size. If you are not sure, consider whether it would be possible to alter the order of one set of values without altering the meaning of the data. For example in Table 4.1, could you swap the values 6.3 and 3.5 for the 'first attempt' without altering the meaning of the data? The answer is 'no' because you would then have a set of data in which the times for A's first and second attempts are recorded as 3.5 and 5.1 minutes respectively rather than 6.3 and 5.1 minutes.

Two possible methods were suggested above for testing whether people get faster with practice. In this situation using pairs of values is better because the analysis removes any variation between individuals: it is not how slow or fast each person is which matters but the change in his or her performance from one attempt to the next. Taking a difference removes a source of variation which is not of interest. As a result the test is more effective at detecting a difference between the population means, if such a difference exists, than an unpaired method. Sometimes, however, it is not possible to collect data so that they are paired. In Example 4.2.1 the same mice could not be given both the special and the usual diets.

For large samples the condition that D is distributed normally is no longer necessary since the central limit theorem ensures that $\overline{D}$ is distributed approximately normally. In this case the test statistic $Z = \dfrac{\overline{D}}{\sqrt{\dfrac{S_d^2}{n}}}$, where Z is distributed approximately as $N(0,1)$, is used. Such a situation is illustrated in the following example.

Example 4.3.1

To investigate the difference in wear on front and rear tyres of motorcycles, 50 motorcycles of the same model were fitted with new tyres of the same brand. After the motorcycles had been driven for 2000 miles the depths of tread on the front and rear tyres were measured in mm. For each motorcycle the value of d = (depth of front tread – depth of rear tread) was calculated. The results can be summarised by $\sum d = 4.7$ and $\sum d^2 = 0.79$. Test at the 5% significance level, whether there is a difference in wear on the front and rear tyres.

This is an example of an experiment where the data are collected in pairs. The null hypothesis is $H_0: \mu_x = \mu_y$ where μ_x is the population mean for front tyres and μ_y the population mean for rear tyres. The alternative hypothesis is $H_1: \mu_x \neq \mu_y$. The mean and variance of the paired differences are 0.094 and 0.007 10…. The value of the test statistic Z is $\dfrac{0.94}{\sqrt{\dfrac{0.007\,10\ldots}{50}}} = 7.88\ldots$. The rejection region is $|Z| \geqslant 1.96$. Thus H_0 is rejected and H_1, that there is different wear on the front and rear tyres, is accepted.

A paired test can also be used to test whether the mean of paired differences is some constant value, expressed by the null hypothesis $H_0: \mu_x - \mu_y = c$. In this case the test statistic would be $\dfrac{\overline{D} - c}{\sqrt{\dfrac{S_d^2}{n}}}$.

Here is a summary of tests for paired data.

If n pairs of data are drawn from two populations with means μ_x and μ_y respectively, then the null hypothesis $H_0: \mu_x - \mu_y = c$ can be tested using the test statistic T with $n-1$ degrees of freedom. The value of T is given by

$$t = \frac{\overline{d} - c}{\sqrt{\dfrac{s_d^2}{n}}} \qquad (4.5)$$

where d is equal to $x - y$, the difference between the pairs of values, $\overline{d}$ is the sample mean of these differences and s_d^2 is an unbiased estimate of the variance of the population of the differences. The critical values of T are found in the same way as they are for a one-sample t-test; see page 271.

This test assumes that differences between the paired values are normally distributed.

When n is large the test statistic $Z = \dfrac{\overline{D} - c}{\sqrt{\dfrac{S_d^2}{n}}}$ may be used even if the differences are not distributed normally.

Exercise 4C

1 Some psychologists believe that the IQ of the first-born child in a family is significantly greater than the IQ of the last born. In order to investigate this belief, a random sample of 8 families with more than one child agreed to allow their children's IQs to be measured, with the following results.

Family	1	2	3	4	5	6	7	8
IQ of first born	97	121	89	112	138	125	104	114
IQ of last born	101	116	97	108	130	121	101	105

Assuming that the differences have a normal distribution test the psychologists' belief using a 5% significance level.

2 A person's systolic blood pressure is a measure of the pressure exerted by the heart when it contracts and pushes blood around the body. When the heart has just ceased to contract and is dilating ready for the next contraction, the blood pressure drops and is called the diastolic pressure.

The following table gives the systolic and diastolic blood pressures (measured in mm of mercury) of 6 randomly chosen people with diabetes.

Patient	1	2	3	4	5	6
Systolic pressure	141	129	117	115	93	101
Diastolic pressure	83	76	71	59	51	64

Let D denote the amount by which the systolic pressure exceeds the diastolic pressure of a randomly chosen person with diabetes, and let μ_D denote the mean of D. Assuming that D has a normal distribution, test the hypothesis $\mu_D > 40$ at the 5% significance level.

3 Blood pressure data were obtained from a larger set of 97 people with diabetes. The values of D are summarised by $\sum d = 4092$ and $\sum d^2 = 187\,948$. Find the p-value of a test of the hypothesis $\mu_D > 40$ which does not rely on D having a normal distribution.

4 The reaction times taken by 10 motorists to apply the brakes of their cars were measured when the motorists had not drunk any alcohol, and after they had drunk a measured amount of alcohol. The reaction times, in hundredths of a second, are given in the following table.

Motorist	1	2	3	4	5	6	7	8	9	10
Without alcohol	40	25	19	23	38	37	28	37	41	27
With alcohol	50	37	35	34	52	50	40	46	53	38

Assuming that the population of differences has a normal distribution, test, at the 1% significance level, whether the drinking of alcohol increases the mean reaction time by more than 0.1 s.

5 An experiment was carried out to compare the difference in the effects of organic and chemical fertilisers on potato yields. Eleven plots of land were selected and two seed potatoes were grown on each plot at a distance of 10 m apart. On one potato an organic fertiliser was used, and on the other, a chemical fertiliser. The choice of which to use was decided by tossing a coin. The differences in yields, d grams, where d = (mass of organic crop − mass of chemical crop), are summarised by

$$\sum d = -310 \quad \text{and} \quad \sum d^2 = 208\ 702.$$

Assuming that the differences have a normal distribution, test, at the 5% significance level, whether there is a difference between the population mean yields.

6 A study of the effect of vitamins on attention span was carried out on 40 sets of identical twins of the same age. One twin was randomly chosen to have the vitamin pill and the other was given a placebo (a pill with no vitamin). Each twin was given a puzzle to solve and the time, in minutes, that each twin remained with the puzzle was measured. The summary statistics for the difference in time, d minutes, where d = (vitamin time − placebo time), are summarised by $\bar{d} = 2.92$ and $s_d^2 = 141.23$.

Without assuming that the differences are distributed normally, test, at the 5% significance level, whether the vitamins increase attention span.

What would be the conclusion of the test if it could be assumed that the differences are distributed normally?

4.4 Testing for a difference between two population proportions

Just as tests on the population mean can be extended to situations in which there are two populations, so can tests on the population proportion. Here are some examples of questions which might be addressed.

(a) Does the proportion of patients who recover from a disease differ for two different kinds of treatment?
(b) Does the proportion of televisions which break down in the first year of use differ for two different brands?
(c) Does the proportion of children receiving free school meals differ between two areas of a city?

Only large samples will be considered here. The following notation will be helpful.

	Population 1	Population 2
Population proportion	p_x	p_y
Sample size	n_x	n_y
Number of successes	x	y
Sample proportion	$p_{sx} = \dfrac{x}{n_x}$	$p_{sy} = \dfrac{y}{n_y}$

The null hypothesis for each of questions (a) to (c) above is $H_0: p_x = p_y$, which can also be written $H_0: p_x - p_y = 0$. This hypothesis can be tested by considering the distribution of the random variable $P_{sx} - P_{sy}$, the difference between the sample proportions. Provided that both n_x and n_y are large, the sample proportions will be distributed

normally with $P_{sx} \sim N\left(p_x, \dfrac{p_x q_x}{n_x}\right)$ and $P_{sy} \sim N\left(p_y, \dfrac{p_y q_y}{n_y}\right)$ (see Section 3.5). Thus the

difference between the proportions is distributed

$$P_{sx} - P_{sy} \sim N\left(p_x - p_y, \frac{p_x q_x}{n_x} + \frac{p_y q_y}{n_y}\right).$$

According to H_0, the two population proportions are equal. Suppose that their common value is p, so $p_x = p_y = p$ and $q_x = q_y = q = 1 - p$. Then the expression for the distribution

of $P_{sx} - P_{sy}$ becomes $P_{sx} - P_{sy} \sim N\left(p - p, \dfrac{pq}{n_x} + \dfrac{pq}{n_y}\right)$, that is $P_{sx} - P_{sy} \sim N\left(0, pq\left(\dfrac{1}{n_x} + \dfrac{1}{n_y}\right)\right)$.

This variable can be standardised to give the test statistic

$$Z = \frac{P_{sx} - P_{sy}}{\sqrt{pq\left(\dfrac{1}{n_x} + \dfrac{1}{n_y}\right)}}$$

where $Z \sim N(0,1)$.

In order to calculate a value for Z a value of the common population proportion, p, is required. This can be estimated from the samples. Combining the information from both samples gives $x + y$ successes in $n_x + n_y$ trials, so the estimate of p is $\dfrac{x + y}{n_x + n_y}$.

Example 4.4.1

An ecologist collected random samples of a particular species of crab from two different beaches and counted the number of females in each sample (the remainder were males). The results are shown below.

Beach	1	2
Number of females	44	96
Total number in sample	100	200

Test, at the 5% significance level, whether the proportion of females differs significantly between the two beaches. (OCR, adapted)

The null hypothesis is $H_0: p_x = p_y$ where p_x and p_y are the population proportions of females on beach 1 and beach 2 respectively. The test is a two-tail one as there is no indication of the way in which the proportions might differ. Thus the alternative hypothesis is $H_1: p_x \neq p_y$. The sample proportions of females for beach 1 and beach 2 are $\dfrac{44}{100} = 0.44$ and $\dfrac{96}{200} = 0.48$ respectively. The estimate of p, the common proportion of females, is $\dfrac{44 + 96}{100 + 200} = 0.466\ldots$, giving $q = 1 - 0.466\ldots = 0.533\ldots$. Substituting these values into the expression for Z gives the value of

$$z = \frac{p_{sx} - p_{sy}}{\sqrt{pq\left(\dfrac{1}{n_x} + \dfrac{1}{n_y}\right)}} = \frac{0.44 - 0.48}{\sqrt{0.466\ldots \times 0.533\ldots\left(\dfrac{1}{100} + \dfrac{1}{200}\right)}} = 0.654\ldots.$$

For a two-tail test at the 5% significance level the rejection region is $|Z| \geqslant 1.96$. Since the observed value of Z is in the acceptance region, the null hypothesis that the proportions of females on the two beaches are equal is accepted.

It is also possible to test a null hypothesis of the type $H_0 : p_x - p_y = c$ where c is a constant. In this case it is not appropriate to calculate a pooled estimate p, and the test statistic will be $Z = \dfrac{\left(P_{sx} - P_{sy}\right) - c}{\sqrt{\left(\dfrac{P_{sx}q_{sx}}{n_x} + \dfrac{P_{sy}q_{sy}}{n_y}\right)}}$.

Here is a summary of the method.

If large, independent samples of sizes n_x and n_y are drawn from two populations, then the null hypothesis $H_0 : p_x = p_y$ where p_x and p_y are the population proportions can be tested using the test statistic Z. The value of Z is given by

$$z = \frac{p_{sx} - p_{sy}}{\sqrt{pq\left(\dfrac{1}{n_x} + \dfrac{1}{n_y}\right)}}, \qquad (4.6)$$

where p_{sx} and p_{sy} are the sample proportions, the value of the common population proportion, p, is estimated as $p = \dfrac{x + y}{n_x + n_y}$, and $q = 1 - p$.

In order to test $H_0 : p_x - p_y = c$ the test statistic $Z = \dfrac{\left(P_{sx} - P_{sy}\right) - c}{\sqrt{\left(\dfrac{P_{sx}q_{sx}}{n_x} + \dfrac{P_{sy}q_{sy}}{n_y}\right)}}$ is used.

The critical values of Z are found in the same way as they are for a test of the difference between two population means (see Section 4.1).

Exercise 4D

1   The manufacturer of a new electronic calculator claims that the percentage of faulty calculators is less than that of a rival brand of similar calculator. Evidence for the claim was obtained by testing 100 new calculators and 60 of the rival brand; 8 of the new calculators were found to be faulty compared with 10 of the rival brand. Test, at the 5% significance level, whether the manufacturer's claim is supported.

2   Two weeks before a city council held elections the agent for a particular candidate carried out a survey of a random sample of 250 voters, 87 of whom said they would vote for the candidate. In order to increase the candidate's chances she undertook a vigorous campaign during the following week. The agent then carried out another survey, this time of 200 voters. Of these, 92 said that they would vote for the candidate. Carry out a test, at the 10% significance level, to decide whether the proportion of voters in the city who will vote for the candidate has increased.

Test whether it can be concluded, at the 10% significance level, that after the campaign the proportion of voters supporting the candidate increased by more than 5%.

3   The makers of Luxibrite washing powder wished to find out whether the percentage of households in London using Luxibrite differs from that in Birmingham. Random samples of 800 London households and 500 Birmingham households were selected and the proportions of these households using Luxibrite were 35% and 39% respectively. Test, at the 5% significance level, whether the proportions of households using Luxibrite in London and Birmingham differ.

4   There is concern at some airports regarding the numbers of articles of luggage that are damaged whilst in transit. In airport A, out of 987 articles handled on three randomly chosen flights there were 41 claims for damage. In airport B, out of 738 articles handled on three randomly chosen flights there were 36 claims for damage. Do these figures indicate, at the 10% significance level, a difference between the claim rates at the two airports?

5   Researchers wish to discover whether two universities have different drop-out rates, that is the proportion of enrolled students who fail to complete their courses. A random sample of 200 students was chosen at each university, and their records were examined. It was found that the numbers who dropped out were 59 and 66. Find an approximation to the p-value of a test of whether the drop-out rates are different for the two universities.

What can be concluded about the drop-out rates at the two universities?

Give a reason why (apart from rounding) the value is approximate.

6   A drug company is testing a new headache pill which it will market only if its success rate is more than 10% greater than the success rate of the company's current headache pill. A random sample of 220 headache sufferers were selected, 100 of whom were given the new pills and 120 the current pills. Of those given the new pills, 92 claimed fast relief, whereas, of the others, 84 claimed fast relief. By carrying out a test at the 2% significance level, advise the company as to whether it should market the new pill.

4.5 Confidence intervals for a difference of population means

In some cases, particularly when two populations have been shown to have significantly different means, it may be of interest to calculate a confidence interval for the difference between the means. Such a confidence interval may be found by analogy with the method used in Chapter 3 for a single population. There a confidence interval for the mean of a single population was derived using the fact that $\overline{X} \sim N\left(\mu, \dfrac{\sigma^2}{n}\right)$ for a sample

of size n from a population $X \sim N(\mu, \sigma^2)$. The confidence interval takes the form

$\left(\overline{x} - z\dfrac{\sigma}{\sqrt{n}}, \overline{x} + z\dfrac{\sigma}{\sqrt{n}}\right)$ (see Equation 3.3). For samples of sizes n_x and n_y taken from

populations $N\left(\mu_x, \sigma_x^2\right)$ and $N\left(\mu_y, \sigma_y^2\right)$ respectively, $\overline{X} - \overline{Y} \sim N\left(\mu_x - \mu_y, \dfrac{\sigma_x^2}{n_x} + \dfrac{\sigma_y^2}{n_y}\right)$.

So, by analogy, a confidence interval for the difference between the population means, $\mu_x - \mu_y$, is

$$\left[\overline{x} - \overline{y} - z\sqrt{\dfrac{\sigma_x^2}{n_x} + \dfrac{\sigma_y^2}{n_y}}, \ \overline{x} - \overline{y} + z\sqrt{\dfrac{\sigma_x^2}{n_x} + \dfrac{\sigma_y^2}{n_y}}\right]. \qquad (4.7)$$

As before the value of z depends on the confidence level required.

Example 4.5.1

Random samples are taken from two different populations. The sample from the first population has size 8 and mean 19.9. The sample from the second population has size 10 and mean 16.7. The population variances are known to be 2.8 and 2.9 respectively. Calculate a 99% confidence interval for the difference between the population means.

The appropriate values to substitute into Equation 4.7 are

$$\overline{x} = 19.9, \quad \overline{y} = 16.7, \quad \sigma_x^2 = 2.8, \quad \sigma_y^2 = 2.9, \quad n_x = 8, \quad n_y = 10.$$

For a 99% confidence interval $z = 2.576$ (see Section 3.3). This gives a 99% confidence interval for $\mu_x - \mu_y$ of

$$\left[19.9 - 16.7 - 2.576\sqrt{\dfrac{2.8}{8} + \dfrac{2.9}{10}}, \ 19.9 - 16.7 + 2.576\sqrt{\dfrac{2.8}{8} + \dfrac{2.9}{10}}\right],$$

which is $[1.14, 5.26]$, correct to 3 significant figures.

You may have noticed that this example is similar to Example 4.1.1, where the same data were used to test for a significant difference between the population means. This has been done deliberately in order to illustrate the equivalence between symmetric confidence intervals and two-tail tests. In Example 4.1.1 it was found that there was a significant difference between the population means at the 1% level. When you carry out a test at the 1% level there is a probability of 1% that you will conclude the means are different when, in fact, they are the same (that is make a Type I error). Looking at the 99% symmetric confidence interval in Example 4.5.1 you can see that it does not contain the value zero. If the population means were equal, you would expect the confidence interval to trap the value zero with a probability of 99%. Since it does not you can conclude, with 99% certainty, that the population means are not equal. Again there is a probability of 1% that you will conclude the means are different when, in fact, they are the same. Thus both the confidence interval and the hypothesis test lead you to the same conclusion with the same risk of making a Type I error. If the 99% confidence interval *had* trapped zero, then a two-tail test at the 1% level would not have given a significant result. In general a two-tail test at the $\alpha\%$ significance level and a $(1-\alpha)\%$ confidence interval are equivalent.

Just as hypothesis tests can be developed to deal with circumstances in which the populations are not normal or the population variances are not known, so can the calculation of confidence intervals. Recognising the equivalence between hypothesis tests and confidence intervals will help you to decide on the correct form for the latter. If, for example, the samples are large, then the condition of normality is no longer necessary since the sample means will be distributed approximately normally and also, if the population variances are unknown, they can be replaced by values estimated from the samples.

Example 4.5.2

Data were collected for the mass (in grams) of tomatoes of a particular species grown under glass and outdoors. The results can be summarised as follows.

Under glass: $\quad \sum x = 9568.5$, $\quad \sum x^2 = 918\,141.55$, $\quad n_x = 100$.

Outdoors: $\quad \sum y = 9012.1$, $\quad \sum y^2 = 814\,725.65$, $\quad n_y = 100$.

Assuming that the data can be treated as independent random samples, calculate a 95% confidence interval for the difference in population masses for tomatoes grown under glass and outdoors.

The sample means are $\bar{x} = 95.685$ and $\bar{y} = 90.121$. Unbiased estimates of the population variances can be calculated from the samples. You can check that the values for these are $s_x^2 = 26.05\ldots$ and $s_y^2 = 25.71\ldots$. For a 95% confidence interval $z = 1.96$.

Let μ_x be the population mean for tomatoes grown under glass and μ_y the population mean for tomatoes grown outdoors. Substitution into Equation 4.7 gives a 95% confidence interval for $\mu_x - \mu_y$ of

$$\left[95.685 - 90.121 - 1.96\sqrt{\frac{26.05\ldots}{100} + \frac{25.71\ldots}{100}}, \right.$$
$$\left. 95.685 - 90.121 + 1.96\sqrt{\frac{26.05\ldots}{100} + \frac{25.71\ldots}{100}} \right]$$

which on simplifying gives $[4.15, 6.97]$, correct to 3 significant figures.

This confidence interval does not include zero, so you can conclude that, at the 5% significance level, the tomatoes grown under the two conditions differ in mass.

For small samples from normal populations with equal but unknown variances a pooled estimate of variance can be made using Equation 4.4. Then the confidence interval will have the form

$$\left[\bar{x} - \bar{y} - t s_p \sqrt{\frac{1}{n_x} + \frac{1}{n_y}}, \ \bar{x} - \bar{y} + t s_p \sqrt{\frac{1}{n_x} + \frac{1}{n_y}} \right], \qquad (4.8)$$

where s_p^2 is the estimate of the common population variance σ^2 and t is the critical value for the t distribution with $v = n_x + n_y - 2$ degrees of freedom.

Example 4.5.3

A maths teacher at a large school wishes to find a confidence interval for the difference in performance at a mental arithmetic test between students in Year 9 and students in Year 11. He takes random samples of size 15 from each year and obtains the following results for the scores, measured out of 100.

Year	Sample mean	Unbiased estimate of population variance
9	62.1	4.58^2
11	66.4	5.24^2

Find a 98% confidence interval for the difference between the population means for the two years. You may assume that the scores are distributed normally and that the variances for the two years are equal.

Using Equation 4.4 gives a pooled estimate of variance of

$$s_p^2 = \frac{(15-1) \times 5.24^2 + (15-1) \times 4.58^2}{15+15-2} = 24.217.$$

The number of degrees of freedom is $v = n_x + n_y - 2 = 28$. For a 98% confidence interval the corresponding value of t is 2.467. Let μ_x be the population mean for Year 11 and μ_y the population mean for Year 9.

Substitution into Equation 4.8 gives a 98% confidence interval of $\mu_x - \mu_y$ equal to

$$\left[66.4 - 62.1 - 2.467 \sqrt{24.217} \sqrt{\frac{1}{15} + \frac{1}{15}}, \right.$$
$$\left. 66.4 - 62.1 + 2.467 \sqrt{24.217} \sqrt{\frac{1}{15} + \frac{1}{15}} \right],$$

which, on simplifying gives $[-0.13, 8.73]$, correct to 2 decimal places.

Here is a summary of the methods for calculating a confidence interval for the difference between population means.

A $100(1-\alpha)\%$ confidence interval for the difference between two population means, $\mu_x - \mu_y$, is given by the following expressions:

(1) $$\left[\bar{x} - \bar{y} - z\sqrt{\frac{\sigma_x^2}{n_x} + \frac{\sigma_y^2}{n_y}}, \bar{x} - \bar{y} + z\sqrt{\frac{\sigma_x^2}{n_x} + \frac{\sigma_y^2}{n_y}}\right]$$

for samples from normal distributions of known variance. The value of z is such that $\Phi(z) = 1 - \frac{1}{2}\alpha$.

If the samples are *large* this expression may also be used when

- the populations are not normal or
- the population variances are unknown and have been replaced by their unbiased estimates s_x^2 and s_y^2.

(2) $$\left[\bar{x} - \bar{y} - ts_p\sqrt{\frac{1}{n_x} + \frac{1}{n_y}}, \bar{x} - \bar{y} + ts_p\sqrt{\frac{1}{n_x} + \frac{1}{n_y}}\right]$$

for samples of any size from normal populations of equal, but unknown, variance where s_p^2 is the estimate of the common population variance σ^2 and t has $v = n_x + n_y - 2$ degrees of freedom. The value of t is such that $P(T \leq t) = 1 - \frac{1}{2}\alpha$.

Exercise 4E

1 Metal castings are manufactured on two production lines, A and B. Their masses are distributed normally with means μ_A and μ_B and standard deviations 0.18 kg and 0.21 kg respectively. A random sample of 8 castings from production line A has mean mass 5.43 kg and a random sample of 12 castings from production line B has mean mass 5.58 kg.

(a) Calculate a symmetric 98% confidence interval for $\mu_A - \mu_B$.

(b) State, giving a reason, whether there is evidence of a difference between the means at the 2% significance level.

2 Ball-bearings are produced on two different machines. To investigate whether the machines produce ball-bearings which differ significantly, the diameters of random samples of 75 ball-bearings from each machine are measured. The sample statistics for machine 1 are $\bar{x}_1 = 17.52$ mm and $s_1^2 = 0.38$ mm^2 and for machine 2 $\bar{x}_2 = 17.41$ mm and $s_2^2 = 0.44$ mm^2. The mean diameters of the ball-bearings produced by the machines are μ_1 mm and μ_2 mm. Find a symmetric 95% confidence interval for $\mu_1 - \mu_2$.

3 A random sample of six US women had their blood cholesterol levels measured, with the following results, in grams per litre.

   1.9   3.1   2.2   2.6   2.9   1.5

The corresponding results for a random sample of five English women were as follows.

   1.6   3.0   2.9   1.8   1.4

Assuming normal distributions with a common variance, find

(a) an unbiased estimate of the common variance,

(b) a symmetric 80% confidence interval for the difference in the population mean cholesterol levels.

4 Each of a group of six rats were each introduced to a maze at the end of which was placed some food. They were subsequently given two further attempts at the maze, one when they were satiated with food and the other when they were deprived of food. The times, in seconds, taken for the rats to complete the maze were as follows.

Rat	1	2	3	4	5	6
Food satiated	25	19	8	21	13	6
Food deprived	10	9	8	14	5	9

Assuming that the differences in times follow a normal distribution, calculate a symmetric 99% confidence interval for the difference in population mean completion times.

5 The effects on yields resulting from two catalysts in a chemical reaction were observed in 10 identical experiments using each catalyst. The yields, x_1 grams and x_2 grams, resulting from catalysts 1 and 2 respectively are summarised by

$$\sum x_1 = 423.1, \qquad \sum x_1^2 = 18\,101.55, \qquad \sum x_2 = 381.8, \qquad \sum x_2^2 = 14\,877.23.$$

Assuming normal populations with a common variance, calculate a symmetric 90% confidence interval for $\mu_1 - \mu_2$, the difference in the population mean yields.

Can it be concluded that catalyst 1 gives a greater mean yield than catalyst 2? Explain your answer.

6 The difference in heights between a man and his eldest (or only) fully-grown son is measured for 150 randomly chosen pairs. The amount by which the height of the son exceeds the height of the father is denoted by d cm, and the results are summarised by

$$\sum d = 152 \quad \text{and} \quad \sum d^2 = 1518.$$

Find a symmetric 99% confidence interval for μ_d.

What does your interval show about the relative heights of fathers and their eldest sons?

4.6   Confidence intervals for a difference of population proportions

A method analogous to that of the previous section can be used to calculate a confidence interval for a difference between two proportions. You saw in Section 4.4 that, if the samples are large, the difference between two proportions is distributed as

$$P_{sx} - P_{sy} \sim N\left(p_x - p_y, \frac{p_x q_x}{n_x} + \frac{p_y q_y}{n_y}\right).$$

Thus a $(100 - \alpha)\%$ confidence interval for $p_x - p_y$ is given by

$$\left[P_{sx} - P_{sy} - z\sqrt{\frac{p_x q_x}{n_x} + \frac{p_y q_y}{n_y}}, \, P_{sx} - P_{sy} + z\sqrt{\frac{p_x q_x}{n_x} + \frac{p_y q_y}{n_y}}\right].$$

However, p_x, q_x, p_y and q_y are unknown and so must be replaced by their estimates P_{sx}, q_{sx}, P_{sy} and q_{sy}.

If large random samples of sizes n_x and n_y are drawn from two populations with population proportions p_x and p_y, then a $(100 - \alpha)\%$ confidence interval for the difference between the two population proportions, $p_x - p_y$, is given by

$$\left[P_{sx} - P_{sy} - z\sqrt{\frac{p_{sx} q_{sx}}{n_x} + \frac{p_{sy} q_{sy}}{n_y}}, \, P_{sx} - P_{sy} + z\sqrt{\frac{p_{sx} q_{sx}}{n_x} + \frac{p_{sy} q_{sy}}{n_y}}\right] \qquad (4.9)$$

where the value of z is such that $\Phi(z) = 1 - \frac{1}{2}\alpha$, P_{sx} and P_{sy} are the sample proportions and $q_{sx} = 1 - p_{sx}$, $q_{sy} = 1 - p_{sy}$.

Example 4.6.1

Random samples of pupils were taken from two schools in a large city. At school C, in the city centre, it was found that 69 children out of a sample of 110 were eligible for free school meals, whereas at school S, in the suburbs, 24 children out of a sample of 90 were eligible for free school meals. Calculate a 95% confidence interval for the difference between the proportions of children at the two schools who are eligible for free school meals.

The following quantities can be calculated from the given information:

$$P_{sx} = \frac{69}{110}, \quad q_{sx} = \frac{41}{110}, \quad P_{sy} = \frac{24}{90}, \quad q_{sy} = \frac{66}{90}.$$

For a 95% confidence interval $z = 1.96$.

Substituting these values into Equation 4.9 gives a 95% confidence interval for the difference in the proportions of children receiving free school meals at school C and school S of

$$\left[\frac{69}{110} - \frac{24}{90} - 1.96\sqrt{\frac{\frac{69}{110} \times \frac{41}{110}}{110} + \frac{\frac{24}{90} \times \frac{66}{90}}{90}}, \, \frac{69}{110} - \frac{24}{90} + 1.96\sqrt{\frac{\frac{69}{110} \times \frac{41}{110}}{110} + \frac{\frac{24}{90} \times \frac{66}{90}}{90}}\right],$$

which is $[0.232, 0.489]$, correct to 3 significant figures.

Since this interval does not include zero the difference in proportions is significant at the 5% level.

Exercise 4F

1   A survey was carried out for a restaurant owner in a town to find out how many people in the town were familiar with the name of the restaurant. It was found that out of a random sample of size 100, 43 people had heard of the restaurant. Following an advertising campaign for the restaurant in the local paper another survey was carried out. This showed that 59 people out of a random sample of size 100 were now familiar with the name of the restaurant. Calculate a 90% symmetric confidence interval for the difference between proportions of people in the town familiar with the name of the restaurant after and before the advertising campaign.

2   In order to investigate the effectiveness of a new cream for acne a random sample of 90 patients were asked to try the cream. Of these 63 found the cream effective. Another random sample of 80 patients were given a cream identical to the new cream but without the active ingredient. Of these 40 reported that the cream which they had been given was effective. Calculate a 95% symmetric confidence interval for the difference between the proportions of patients who found the two creams effective.

3   A gardener wishes to compare the quality of seeds from two different suppliers. Out of a packet of 113 seeds from the first supplier, 98 germinate, whereas 103 out of 120 seeds from the second supplier germinate. Calculate a 99% confidence interval for the difference between the proportions of seeds which germinate for the two populations.

Is there any difference, at the 1% significance level, between the germination rates for seeds from the two suppliers?

4.7   Practical activities

1 Left-handedness   Does the proportion of left-handers differ in different generations? During the course of the last century attitudes to left-handedness changed. At one time children were made to write with their right hands, even when they showed a tendency to be left-handed, but gradually this rigid attitude was relaxed. Is this reflected in the proportions of people who are left-handed in different generations? Record the writing hand for at least 50 people of your own age (or younger) and also for at least 50 people aged sixty or over. Test whether the proportion of left-handers is higher for the first group than for the second.

You could compare other groups, for example males and females or 'scientists' and 'artists'.

2 Sentence length   Do different authors use significantly different sentence lengths? Choose two authors who interest you. For each author take a random sample of 50 sentences and record the sentence lengths. (Devise a method for selecting a random sample by using random numbers.) Test for a significant difference between sentence lengths.

This activity could also be used to compare two newspapers. You may already have collected the relevant data in Activity 3 of S1 Section 2.10.

3 Does 'practice make perfect'?   Choose a simple task, such as doing a small jigsaw puzzle or some kind of sorting activity. Ask 30 subjects to carry out the task twice and record the times which they take on their first and second attempts. Carry out a test of whether the time taken decreases with practice.

4 Do teams play better at home? Choose a football team and find the scores for their last 50 home matches and last 50 away matches. Test whether their mean home score is significantly greater than their mean away score.

This could also be done with paired data, by looking at the difference between home and away scores when the team plays the same opponent.

Miscellaneous exercise 4

1 Two random samples, x_1, x_2, ... , x_n and y_1, y_2, ... , y_n, of equal size are taken from normal distributions with means and variances μ_x, σ_x^2 and μ_y, σ_y^2 respectively. It is required to test a hypothesis concerning $\mu_x - \mu_y$. State under what circumstances it would be correct to use

(a) the two-sample t-test, (b) a t-test applied to the differences $x_i - y_i$.

In order to test two mixtures, X and Y, of unleaded petrol, 10 new cars were randomly selected and divided randomly into two groups of 5. One group was given a measured amount of mixture X and the other group the same amount of mixture Y. All cars were driven under similar conditions until the petrol ran out and the distances, in miles, travelled were recorded. The results were as follows.

Mixture X	18.2	17.2	15.4	16.4	17.3
Mixture Y	19.1	16.4	19.4	16.0	18.7

Stating your assumptions, test, at the 5% significance level, whether mixture Y gives a better performance, on average, than mixture X.

Using the same 10 cars, describe a better way of testing whether mixture Y gives a better performance than mixture X. State why this method is better than the one used above.

(OCR, adapted)

2 An experiment is performed to compare the effectiveness of two treatments which are designed to improve the resistance of a certain metal against corrosion. Eight sheets of the metal are each divided into two equal-sized pieces which are weighed. One piece from each pair, chosen at random, is assigned to treatment 1 and the second piece to treatment 2. After treatment the pieces are immersed in acid for a fixed time, and then are removed and weighed. The loss of mass, in grams, for each piece, is given in the following table.

Treatment 1	3.1	2.8	2.9	3.2	3.3	3.2	2.6	3.0
Treatment 2	3.1	3.2	3.4	3.5	2.8	3.5	2.7	3.2

Stating suitable assumptions, calculate a symmetric 95% confidence interval for the mean difference in losses between the two treatments. Give the end-points correct to 2 decimal places.

(OCR, adapted)

3 An estimate of a population proportion p is given by $P_s = \dfrac{X}{n}$, where X is the number of 'successes' in a random sample of size n. State what you can about the distribution of P_s for large values of n. In particular, state the mean and variance of P_s.

A study investigated the incidence of a particular disease. A random sample of 1000 hospital patients, aged 21 or over, was selected; of the 580 women in the sample, 18 suffered from the disease, whereas of the 420 men, 26 suffered from the disease. Find the p-value of a test of whether there is a difference in the proportions of men and women who suffer from this disease. What can be concluded at the 1% significance level?

Calculate a 95% confidence interval for the difference between the proportions of men and women who suffer from the disease. (OCR, adapted)

4 The mean numbers of letters delivered to a school office and to the principal's office were recorded over varying periods of time. The number of days recorded, n, the mean number of letters, $\bar{x}$, and s^2, an unbiased estimate of the population variance, are given in the following table.

	n	$\bar{x}$	s^2
School office	63	48.1	6.24^2
Principal's office	52	44.6	8.56^2

Test, at the 5% significance level, whether the principal's office receives fewer letters, on average, than does the school office. (OCR, adapted)

5 At the beginning of the spring term 2000, a school cafeteria supervisor was concerned that a sandwich shop which had opened during the Christmas holidays would reduce the cafeteria's takings. She recorded the takings on 8 randomly chosen days during the spring term 2000 and compared them with the takings on 9 randomly chosen days of the corresponding period of the previous year. With the daily takings in 2000 denoted by £x and those in 1999 by £y, the summarised results were

$$n_x = 8, \quad \sum x = 3209, \quad \sum (x - \bar{x})^2 = 3480, \quad n_y = 9, \quad \sum y = 3792, \quad \sum (y - \bar{y})^2 = 3302.$$

Stating suitable assumptions, test, at the 5% significance level, whether the average daily takings had decreased. (OCR, adapted)

6 A manufacturer of vitamin pills claimed that they could improve children's IQ scores. To test this claim, an experiment was carried out in which a random sample of 15 children from a class of ten-year-olds took the recommended pill over a period of two years. A random sample of 15 children taken from a similar class took a placebo (a pill that contains no vitamins) for two years. At the end of the two years all children took an IQ test. With the IQ scores of those who took the vitamins denoted by x and of those who took the placebo denoted by y, the summarised results were

$$\sum x = 1622, \quad \sum x^2 = 179\,744, \quad \sum y = 1490, \quad \sum y^2 = 151\,816.$$

Stating your assumptions, test, at the 5% significance level, whether children taking the vitamins achieved a higher mean score than children taking the placebo.

Suggest a change to the experiment which might lead to a better test of the manufacturer's claim. (OCR, adapted)

7 In 1978 the Borsetshire County Council tree officer did a survey of a random sample of 64 separate areas, each 1 km square, and found an average of 19.5 diseased trees per square. The next year, to test if the disease had spread, she took a new random sample of 36 separate areas, each 1 km square, and found an average of 21.7 diseased trees per square.

(a) Assume that, in both years, the number of diseased trees per 1 km square had a normal distribution with variance 18.2. Test, at the 1% significance level, the hypothesis that the mean number of diseased trees per 1 km square in 1979 was the same as in 1978, against the hypothesis that the mean number had increased.

(b) Further evidence suggests that the number of diseased trees per 1 km square is not distributed normally. State what changes you would have to make, if any, to the test you have carried out, explaining the reasons for your answer. Do not carry out any further test. (OCR)

8 A machine produces circular metal discs. A sample of 100 discs was taken and their radii were measured. The sample mean radius was 10.40 cm. The cutting edge of the machine was subsequently changed, and a second sample of 100 discs was taken. The mean radius of this sample was 10.33 cm.

(a) Assume that, before the cutting edge was changed, the population variance of the radii of the discs was $0.022\,30$ cm^2.

(i) State two further assumptions which must be made in order to apply a test, using the normal distribution, for a decrease in the population mean radius.

(ii) Given that the assumptions are valid, carry out the test at the 10% significance level.

(b) Assume, instead, that no information about the population variance is available. For the data below, r_1 is the radius of a disc before the cutting edge was changed and r_2 the radius after the cutting edge was changed:

$$\sum r_1 = 1040.0, \qquad \sum r_1^2 = 10\,818.22, \qquad \sum r_2 = 1033, \qquad \sum r_2^2 = 10\,675.14.$$

Use the data to obtain a symmetric 90% confidence interval for the difference in population mean radii $r_1 - r_2$. (OCR, adapted)

9 An advertisement in a newspaper offered a correspondence course which, it was claimed, would 'improve memory'. A psychologist investigated this claim by selecting a random sample of 9 people to take the course. They were given a memory test before taking the course and another one afterwards. Their scores on the tests, out of 100, were as follows.

Person	1	2	3	4	5	6	7	8	9
Before	35	39	47	48	57	59	64	69	80
After	39	53	46	58	52	71	70	77	78

It may be assumed that the differences in scores comprise a random sample from a normal distribution.

Find an approximation to the p-value of a test of whether the course does, on average, improve people's memory.

What is the conclusion of the test at the $2\frac{1}{2}$% significance level? (OCR, adapted)

10 A doctor made a comparison of ointment A and ointment B for the cure of a skin disease. He chose, at random, which ointment to use for each patient and assessed the results after two weeks. Of the 95 patients receiving ointment A, 82 were cured, while of the 105 patients receiving ointment B, 78 were cured. Is there any evidence, at the 5% significance level, that one ointment is better than the other?

Suppose that ointment A had been used by Doctor C on his patients and ointment B had been used by Doctor D on her patients, and the same number of patients and cures had resulted as before. Would this affect the interpretation of the data? (OCR, adapted)

11 In a random sample of 400 people living in Manchester it was found that 285 had surnames beginning with a letter between A and M. For a random sample of 300 people living in Leeds the corresponding number was 191. The population proportions in Manchester and Leeds are p_1 and p_2 respectively.

(a) Test, at the $2\frac{1}{2}$% significance level, the hypothesis $p_1 > p_2$.

(b) Calculate a symmetric 95% confidence interval for $p_1 - p_2$.

12 The drug sodium aurothiomalate is sometimes used to treat rheumatoid arthritis. Twenty patients were treated with this drug, and of these, twelve suffered an adverse reaction, whilst eight did not. The ages, in years, of the two groups were as follows.

Adverse reaction (x yr)	53	63	53	29	53	67	54	57	51	68	38	44
No adverse reaction (y yr)	44	51	64	33	39	37	41	72				

$$\sum x = 630, \quad \sum x^2 = 34\,496, \quad \sum y = 381, \quad \sum y^2 = 19\,477.$$

Assuming that the populations have normal distributions with a common variance, calculate a symmetric 95% confidence interval for the difference in population mean ages.

Does this interval indicate a difference in the mean ages? Explain your answer. (OCR, adapted)

13 The amounts of orange juice in litre cartons of two brands were investigated by a quality control inspector. She used 60 randomly selected cartons of each brand. The quantities a litres in a carton of brand A and b litres in a carton of brand B are summarised by

$$\sum (a-1) = 1.23, \quad \sum (a-1)^2 = 0.3226, \quad \sum (b-1) = 1.08, \quad \sum (b-1)^2 = 0.2414.$$

Calculate a symmetric 90% confidence interval for $\mu_A - \mu_B$ without assuming that the contents have a normal distribution.

Justify the use of the normal distribution in the calculation.

The inspector noted that 7 of the 60 brand A cartons contained less than 1.01 litres of juice and 11 of the 60 brand B cartons contained less than 1.01 litres of juice. Estimate the p-value of a test of whether a smaller proportion of brand A cartons than of brand B cartons contains less than 1.01 litres of juice. (OCR, adapted)

14 Ten students were asked to perform a simple task and the times, in seconds, that they took to complete the task were recorded. The next day, the students were asked to perform the same task and the times taken on the second attempt were recorded. A researcher was interested to know whether the practice in the first attempt led to a reduction in time at the second attempt. The times are given in the following table.

Student	1	2	3	4	5	6	7	8	9	10
First attempt	16.3	54.2	63.2	42.0	38.7	48.3	11.2	41.3	52.1	44.9
Second attempt	13.2	57.1	50.1	40.0	36.0	30.2	9.6	44.0	40.3	23.8

(a) Stating your assumptions, use a suitable test, at the 5% significance level, to advise the researcher as to whether there is a reduction in time at the second attempt.

(b) Calculate a 95% confidence interval for the population mean reduction in time for the two attempts. (OCR, adapted)

15 In a newspaper article it was claimed that, for the age group 14–18, girls spend more on their clothes each month, on average, than boys do. In order to test the truth of this claim, a sample of 12 girls and 11 boys who attended a sixth form college were each asked how much, to the nearest £1, they had spent on clothes the previous month. The results are summarised by

$$\sum g = 306, \qquad \sum g^2 = 8508, \qquad \sum b = 198, \qquad \sum b^2 = 3895,$$

where £g and £b are the amounts spent by a girl and a boy respectively.

(a) Assuming that the samples may be considered to be random samples of all girls and boys in that age range, test the article's claim at the 5% significance level. State any further assumption needed for your test to be valid.

(b) The mean amounts spent each month by girls and boys are denoted by £μ_g and £μ_b respectively. Find the largest value of a, correct to the nearest integer, for which it would be accepted, at the 10% significance level, that £μ_g exceeds £μ_b by more than a.

(c) Give a reason why the assumption of randomness in part (a) may not be valid.

5 Chi-squared tests

This chapter introduces a method of testing whether observed frequencies are consistent with a given hypothesis. When you have completed it you should be able to

- fit a theoretical distribution, as prescribed by a given hypothesis, to given data
- use a χ^2 test with the appropriate number of degrees of freedom to carry out the corresponding goodness of fit test
- use a χ^2 test with the appropriate number of degrees of freedom to test for independence in a contingency table
- use Yates' correction in the case of a 2×2 contingency table.

5.1 Comparing observed and expected frequencies

Table 5.1 shows the results obtained when a dice was thrown 120 times.

Score	1	2	3	4	5	6
Frequency	18	24	21	19	17	21

Table 5.1. Results of an experiment in which a dice is thrown 120 times.

How would you set about deciding whether these results indicate that the dice is a fair one? A start would be to compare these observed frequencies with the theoretical frequencies which you would expect if the dice is fair. The theoretical frequency for each score is found by multiplying the total frequency by the corresponding probability. In this case, the probability of each possible score is $\frac{1}{6}$ and so all the theoretical frequencies are equal to $120 \times \frac{1}{6} = 20$. These theoretical frequencies are usually known as **expected frequencies** and the process of calculating them is called 'fitting a theoretical distribution'. The equation defining expected frequency is

$$\text{Expected frequency of a value} = \text{Total frequency} \times \text{Probability of that value} \quad (5.1)$$

The second and third columns of Table 5.2 give the observed frequencies and the expected frequencies for the results of the dice experiment, where the observed and expected frequencies for the ith class are denoted by O_i and E_i respectively.

You can see that the agreement between the observed and expected frequencies is not exact for all the classes. This is what you would expect since the frequencies for each class are random variables: they vary each time the experiment is carried out. What the expected frequency tells you is the mean (or expected value) of each of these random variables.

The fourth column of Table 5.2 gives the difference $O_i - E_i$ for each class. If the agreement between experiment and theory is a good one, then you would expect these differences to be small. A logical measure of the total discrepancy between the observed and expected frequencies would be the total of this column, $\sum (O_i - E_i)$.

Score	O_i	E_i	$O_i - E_i$	$(O_i - E_i)^2/E_i$
1	18	20	−2	0.2
2	24	20	4	0.8
3	21	20	1	0.05
4	19	20	−1	0.05
5	17	20	−3	0.45
6	21	20	1	0.05
Total	120	120	0	$X^2 = 1.6$

Table 5.2. Comparing observed and expected frequencies for the dice experiment.

However, you can see from the table that this total is zero, even though the observed and expected frequencies do not all agree. In fact, this quantity will always equal zero (because the sums of the observed and expected frequencies are both equal to the total frequency) and so it is no use as a measure of discrepancy. This problem could be overcome by squaring the differences and calculating $\sum(O_i - E_i)^2$.

However, this measure of the discrepancy is still not satisfactory because it makes no allowance for the size of the difference relative to the size of the expected frequencies. For example, the difference between an observed frequency of 11 and expected frequency of 10 would give the same contribution to this sum as the difference between an observed frequency of 101 and expected frequency of 100, even though the percentage difference between the two values is 10% in the first instance and 1% in the second. The measure of discrepancy which is actually used is $\sum\dfrac{(O_i - E_i)^2}{E_i}$. It is given the symbol X^2. The square emphasises that this is always a positive quantity. Thus:

$$X^2 = \sum\frac{(O_i - E_i)^2}{E_i} \qquad (5.2)$$

The statistic X^2 gives a measure of the **goodness of fit** of the model, that is how well the observed and theoretical frequencies agree. For perfect agreement it takes the value zero, and it increases as the differences between the observed and expected frequencies increase. The value of X^2 for the dice data is calculated in the last column of Table 5.2 and is equal to 1.6.

If you repeated the experiment with the same dice, different values of O_i and hence a different value of X^2 would be obtained. In other words, X^2 is also a random variable. In order to decide whether the value 1.6 indicates a significant difference between the observed and expected frequencies it is necessary to study the probability distribution of X^2. This distribution is different from any of the distributions which you have already met. It is approximately related to a new family of continuous distributions which is introduced in the next section.

5.2 The chi-squared (χ^2) family of distributions

Fig. 5.3 shows some of the members of the χ^2 family of distributions. The symbol χ is a Greek letter whose name 'chi' is pronounced as the 'ki' in 'kite'. Thus χ^2 is read as 'chi-squared'. The shape of each member of the family is determined by a single parameter, v, which is known as the **number of degrees of freedom**. You write χ_v^2 to indicate the member of the family with v degrees of freedom. The mean and variance of a χ_v^2 distribution are v and $2v$ respectively. This means that as v increases the location of the distribution shifts to the right and the spread of the distribution increases. You can see this effect in Fig. 5.3, which shows χ_2^2, χ_4^2 and χ_8^2.

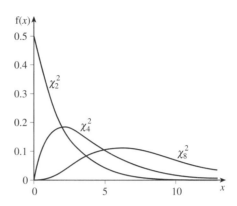

Fig. 5.3. Some of the family of χ^2 distributions.

The table on page 272 gives information about the probability distribution of χ^2. The lay-out of this table is similar to that in the table for the t distribution. For example, if $v = 5$, then $P(\chi_5^2 \leqslant 9.236) = 0.90$ and thus $P(\chi_5^2 > 9.236) = 0.10$.

In order to decide which member of the χ^2 family gives an approximation to the distribution of X^2 you need to know the value of v. As for the t distribution, this is given by the number of independent values, in this case expected frequencies (or equivalently classes), which are used in the calculation of X^2. There are 6 expected frequencies in Table 5.2. Since the total of the expected frequencies must equal 120, there is 1 constraint. Thus

number of degrees of freedom = number of classes − number of constraints
$$= 6 - 1 = 5,$$

and the distribution of X^2 for this experiment can be approximated by the χ_5^2 distribution.

A useful way of thinking of a constraint in the context of χ^2 tests is as a piece of information which is obtained from the observed frequencies and then used in the calculation of the expected frequencies. In this example the total observed frequency of 120 was multiplied by the probabilities to find the expected frequencies. This gave one constraint. Later in this chapter you will see examples where there is more than one constraint.

A χ^2 distribution (which is continuous) can be used as an approximation to the distribution of X^2 (which is discrete) only if none of the expected frequencies falls below 5. This condition is obviously satisfied for the data in Table 5.2.

If this condition is not met, then classes are combined in order to make all the expected frequencies greater than 5. You will meet examples of this later in the chapter.

5.3 Carrying out a χ^2 goodness of fit test

For the dice data it was found that $X^2 = 1.6$. This value is based on expected frequencies which assume that the dice is fair and so this assumption forms the null hypothesis. The alternative is that the dice is not fair:

H_0: the dice is fair; H_1: the dice is not fair.

As explained above the distribution of X^2 can be approximated by χ_5^2. If H_0 is true, then the expected and observed frequencies should be similar and so the value of X^2 will be low. A high value of X^2 is unlikely and would lead you to reject H_0. The rejection region thus takes the form $X^2 > c$ where the critical value, c, depends on the significance level.

For a test at the 5% significance level you need to know the value of c such that $P(X^2 > c) = 0.05$. From the table on page 272, $P(\chi_5^2 > 11.07) = 0.05$ so $c = 11.07$.

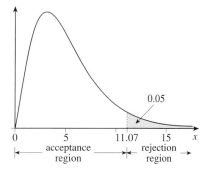

Fig. 5.4 shows the distribution of X^2 and the acceptance and rejection regions. Since the calculated value of X^2 (1.6) is less than the critical value (11.07), the null hypothesis that the dice is a fair one is accepted.

Fig. 5.4. Acceptance and rejection regions for a χ^2 test at the 5% level.

Although in a χ^2 test you ask whether X^2 exceeds a critical value, very low values of X^2 should be treated with suspicion since they are very unlikely. For example, the table on page 272 shows that there is only a 5% probability that X^2 is less than or equal to 1.145. A value of X^2 lower than 1.145 is almost too good to be true. It may indicate that the sample is not random or that the data are fictitious.

The following example illustrates a χ^2 goodness of fit test in a situation in which the expected frequencies are not all the same.

Example 5.3.1

In genetic work it is predicted that the children with both parents of blood group AB will fall into blood groups AB, A and B in the ratio 2:1:1. Of a random sample of 100 such children 55 were blood group AB, 27 blood group A and 18 blood group B. Test at the 10% significance level whether the observed results agree with the theoretical prediction.

Take

H_0: the offspring fall into groups AB, A and B in the ratio 2:1:1;
H_1: the offspring do not fall into groups in the ratio 2:1:1.

The probabilities of falling into the groups AB, A and B are $\frac{1}{2}$, $\frac{1}{4}$ and $\frac{1}{4}$ respectively. The expected frequencies are found by multiplying these probabilities by the total frequency of 100, giving 50, 25 and 25. None of these is less than 5, so the distribution of X^2 can be approximated by a χ^2 distribution.

Table 5.5 shows the calculation of X^2.

Blood group	O_i	E_i	$O_i - E_i$	$(O_i - E_i)^2 / E_i$
AB	55	50	+5	0.5
A	27	25	+2	0.16
B	18	25	−7	1.96
Total	100	100	0	$X^2 = 2.62$

Table 5.5. Calculation of X^2 for Example 5.3.1.

In this example there are 3 classes. There is 1 constraint because the total observed frequency of 100 was used in the calculation of the expected frequencies. Thus

$$\nu = \text{number of classes} - \text{number of constraints} = 3 - 1 = 2.$$

The critical value, c, is such that $P\left(\chi_2^2 > c\right) = 0.1$. From page 272, $c = 4.605$ so the rejection region is $X^2 > 4.605$. Since 2.62 does not lie in the rejection region, the null hypothesis is accepted. The offspring fall into the groups AB, A and B in the ratio 2:1:1 as predicted by genetic theory.

5.4   The relationship between the χ^2 family and the normal distribution

If $Z_1, Z_2, \ldots, Z_\nu$ are ν independent variables, each with a $N(0,1)$ distribution, then the sum of their squares, that is $\sum Z_i^2$, has a χ_ν^2 distribution. In this chapter you have used the result that the statistic $\sum \dfrac{(O_i - E_i)^2}{E_i}$ has a distribution which is approximately χ_ν^2

where there are ν degrees of freedom. It is fairly simple to show that this is true for the particular case in which there is one degree of freedom. In this case $\sum \dfrac{(O_i - E_i)^2}{E_i} \sim \chi_1^2$,

so $\sum \dfrac{(O_i - E_i)^2}{E_i} = Z^2$.

Consider the situation in which the results fall into one of two classes. Suppose the null hypothesis is that the values are divided between the two classes in the ratio $p:(1-p)$. If the observed frequencies are O_1 and O_2, then the total frequency, n, is given by $n = O_1 + O_2$. The corresponding expected frequencies are np and $n(1-p)$. Then

$$\sum \frac{(O_i - E_i)^2}{E_i} = \frac{(O_1 - np)^2}{np} + \frac{(O_2 - n(1-p))^2}{n(1-p)}$$

$$= \frac{(O_1 - np)^2}{np} + \frac{(n - O_1 - n + np)^2}{n(1-p)} \qquad (\text{since } O_2 = n - O_1)$$

$$= \frac{(O_1 - np)^2}{np} + \frac{(np - O_1)^2}{n(1-p)}$$

$$= \frac{(O_1 - np)^2}{n}\left(\frac{1}{p} + \frac{1}{1-p}\right) = \frac{(O_1 - np)^2}{n}\left(\frac{1-p+p}{p(1-p)}\right)$$

$$= \frac{(O_1 - np)^2}{np(1-p)}.$$

Now O_1 is distributed as $B(n, p)$ since there are n trials and the probability for a result in the first class is p. If n is such that np and $n(1-p)$ are both at least 5, then this binomial distribution can be approximated by $N(np, np(1-p))$. Thus $O_1 \sim N(np, np(1-p))$ approximately. Standardising this distribution gives

$$Z = \frac{O_i - np}{\sqrt{np(1-p)}} \sim N(0,1).$$

Squaring gives $Z^2 = \frac{(O_1 - np)^2}{np(1-p)}$. It was shown above that $\sum \frac{(O_i - E_i)^2}{E_i} = \frac{(O_1 - np)^2}{np(1-p)}$

so, in this case, $\sum \frac{(O_i - E_i)^2}{E_i} = Z^2$, approximately.

This result is consistent with the rule for calculating the number of degrees of freedom since there are 2 classes and 1 constraint; that is, that the total observed frequency n is used in the calculation of the expected frequencies.

5.5 Testing the goodness of fit of a binomial model

Table 5.6 shows the results of an experiment in which four coins were thrown 160 times. The results are divided into groups according to the number of heads obtained each time.

Number of heads	0	1	2	3	4
Frequency	15	46	54	35	10

Table 5.6. Frequency distribution of the number of heads when four coins are thrown.

Assuming that the coins are fair you would expect the binomial distribution $B\left(4, \frac{1}{2}\right)$ to be a suitable model for the variable 'the number of heads' since

- there are a fixed number of trials (four coins are thrown each time)
- the trials are independent
- the probability of a head is fixed and equal to $\frac{1}{2}$.

Example 5.5.1

(a) Fit a binomial distribution $B\left(4, \frac{1}{2}\right)$ to the data in Table 5.6.
(b) Test the goodness of fit of the model $B\left(4, \frac{1}{2}\right)$ using a χ^2 test at the 5% significance level.

(a) The third column of Table 5.7 gives the expected frequencies for the model $B\left(4,\frac{1}{2}\right)$. These are found by multiplying the binomial probability for each class by the total frequency, 160.

Number of heads	Observed frequency, O_i	Expected frequency, E_i
0	15	$\binom{4}{0}\left(\frac{1}{2}\right)^0\left(\frac{1}{2}\right)^4 \times 160 = 10$
1	46	$\binom{4}{1}\left(\frac{1}{2}\right)^1\left(\frac{1}{2}\right)^3 \times 160 = 40$
2	54	$\binom{4}{2}\left(\frac{1}{2}\right)^2\left(\frac{1}{2}\right)^2 \times 160 = 60$
3	35	$\binom{4}{3}\left(\frac{1}{2}\right)^3\left(\frac{1}{2}\right)^1 \times 160 = 40$
4	10	$\binom{4}{4}\left(\frac{1}{2}\right)^4\left(\frac{1}{2}\right)^0 \times 160 = 10$
Total	160	160

Table 5.7. Observed and expected frequencies when four coins are thrown 160 times.

(b) The null and alternative hypotheses are

H_0: the data can be modelled by $B\left(4,\frac{1}{2}\right)$;

H_1: the data cannot be modelled by $B\left(4,\frac{1}{2}\right)$.

Table 5.8 shows the calculation of X^2.

Number of heads	O_i	E_i	$O_i - E_i$	$(O_i - E_i)^2/E_i$
0	15	10	+5	2.5
1	46	40	+6	0.9
2	54	60	−6	0.6
3	35	40	−5	0.625
4	10	10	0	0
Total	160	160	0	$X^2 = 4.625$

Table 5.8. Calculation of X^2 for data in Table 5.7.

There are 5 classes and 1 constraint since the total observed frequency of 160 was used in the calculation of the expected frequencies. Thus $v = 5 - 1 = 4$. From the table on page 272, the rejection region is $X^2 > 9.488$. Since 4.625 does not lie in the rejection region, the null hypothesis is accepted. The model $B\left(4,\frac{1}{2}\right)$ gives a good fit to the data.

In some cases a binomial distribution may appear to be a suitable model, but a value of p is not known at the start. In this case it is estimated from the data. The mean, μ, of a binomial distribution is given by $\mu = np$. Hence $p = \dfrac{\mu}{n}$. Taking $\bar{x}$ as an estimate of μ gives $p = \dfrac{\bar{x}}{n}$.

> In testing the goodness of fit of a binomial distribution, where p is unknown at the start, an estimate of p is given by
>
> $$p = \frac{\bar{x}}{n}.$$

Example 5.5.2

In routine tests of germination rates, parsley seeds are planted in rows of 5 and the number of seeds which have germinated in each row after a fixed time interval is counted. Table 5.9 shows the results for 100 such rows.

Number of seeds germinated (x)	0	1	2	3	4	5
Number of rows (f)	0	0	8	23	43	26

Table 5.9. Frequency distribution of number of seeds germinating.

(a) Use the data to estimate a value for p, the probability that a seed germinates.
(b) Calculate the expected frequencies for the model $B(5, p)$.
(c) Use a χ^2 goodness of fit test at the 5% significance level to test the suitability of the model $B(5, p)$.

(a) For the data in Table 5.9, $\sum fx = 387$, so $\bar{x} = 3.87$. Thus the estimate of p is $\frac{1}{5} \times 3.87 = 0.774$.

(b) The null and alternative hypotheses are

H_0: the data can be modelled by $B(5, 0.774)$;
H_1: the data cannot be modelled by $B(5, 0.774)$.

The expected frequencies are found by multiplying the binomial probabilities by the total observed frequency of 100. For example

$$\text{expected frequency for 2 seeds germinating} = \binom{5}{2}(0.774)^2(0.226)^3 \times 100 = 6.92,$$

correct to 2 decimal places. The third column of Table 5.10 gives the remaining values of E_i, which you can verify for yourself. (All these values are given correct to 2 decimal places, which is sufficient for the calculation of X^2.) Two of the expected frequencies are less than 5, so it is necessary to combine classes. This is usually done by taking adjacent classes as indicated by the brackets in Table 5.10. The calculation of X^2 then proceeds as before using the combined values.

Number germinated	O_i	E_i	$O_i - E_i$	$(O_i - E_i)^2 / E_i$
0	$\left.\begin{array}{c} 0 \\ 0 \\ 8 \end{array}\right\} = 8$	$\left.\begin{array}{c} 0.06 \\ 1.01 \\ 6.92 \end{array}\right\} = 7.99$	+0.01	0.00
1				
2				
3	23	23.68	−0.68	0.02
4	43	40.55	+2.45	0.15
5	26	27.78	−1.78	0.11
Total	100	100	0	$X^2 = 0.28$

Table 5.10. Calculation of X^2 for the data in Table 5.9.

The number of classes after combination, in this case 4, is used in the calculation of the degrees of freedom. There are 2 constraints because two pieces of information have been obtained from the observed frequencies in order to calculate the expected frequencies: these are the total frequency (100) and the value of p (0.774). Thus $\nu = 4 - 2 = 2$.

From the table on page 272, the rejection region for a 5% significance level is $X^2 > 5.991$. Since 0.28 does not lie in the rejection region, the null hypothesis is accepted. The data can be modelled by a binomial distribution $B(5, 0.774)$.

If you combine classes when you do not have to, then you increase the probability of making a Type II error, that is keeping a false null hypothesis.

You may have noticed that the alternative hypothesis for a χ^2 goodness of fit test does not specify the way in which the null hypothesis might be incorrect. If the null hypothesis is rejected, it could be either because the value of the parameter which was used was incorrect or because the conditions for the distribution to be a suitable model are not met. This point is explored further in some of the exercises.

5.6 Testing the goodness of fit of a geometric model

In S2 Section 4.2 you met random numbers as a device for selecting random samples. Below is the start of a list of digits obtained by using the random number generator on a calculator. If such a list is random, then each digit is equally likely to appear in any position in the list. As a result odd and even digits are also equally likely to appear in any position on the list.

6 3 3 0 4 5 3 2 1 4 1 3 2 1 2 7 2 2 5 1 1 1 4 1 2 5 3...

One way of testing for the property of randomness is to look at the intervals separating the odd digits. The list is repeated below with a line placed after each odd digit. This has the effect of breaking the sequence up into 'runs', consisting of even digits, until the last digit, which is odd. The lengths of the runs below are 2, 1, 3, 1, 2, 2, etc.

6 3|3|0 4 5|3|2 1|4 1|3|2 1|2 7|2 2 5|1|1|1|4 1|2 5|3|...

If the digits are random, then the length, Y, of a run will have a geometric distribution. You can see this by considering an even number as a 'failure' and an odd number as a 'success'. In this case $p = q = \frac{1}{2}$, so $Y \sim \text{Geo}\left(\frac{1}{2}\right)$. Table 5.11 gives the frequency distribution of run length for 50 runs.

Length of run	1	2	3	4	5	6	7	> 7
Frequency	21	18	5	2	3	0	1	0

Table 5.11. Frequency distribution of 'runs' of even digits.

A χ^2 goodness of fit test can be used to test whether the data in Table 5.11 can be modelled by the distribution $\text{Geo}\left(\frac{1}{2}\right)$. The null and alternative hypotheses are

H_0: the data can be modelled by $\text{Geo}\left(\frac{1}{2}\right)$;
H_1: the data cannot be modelled by $\text{Geo}\left(\frac{1}{2}\right)$.

The geometric probabilities are given by $P(Y = y) = \left(\frac{1}{2}\right)^{y-1}\left(\frac{1}{2}\right) = \left(\frac{1}{2}\right)^y$ and the expected frequencies are found by multiplying these probabilities by the total observed frequency of 50. For example, the expected frequency for a run length of 2 is equal to $\left(\frac{1}{2}\right)^2 \times 50 = 12.5$.

Unlike the binomial distribution there is no upper limit on the value of Y. Although the longest run length in Table 5.11 is 7, greater run lengths are possible. For this reason a table of the expected and observed frequencies must also include a class for values greater than 7. The expected frequency for this class must be such that the total expected frequency is 100 and so its value (in this case 0.39) can be found by subtraction. Table 5.12 shows the calculation of X^2. Classes have been combined where necessary to make all expected frequencies at least 5.

Run length	O_i	E_i	$O_i - E_i$	$(O_i - E_i)^2/E_i$
1	21	25	−4	0.64
2	18	12.5	+5.5	2.42
3	5	6.25	−1.25	0.25
4	2 ⎫	3.13 ⎫		
5	3 ⎪	1.56 ⎪		
6	0 ⎬ = 6	0.78 ⎬ = 6.25	−0.25	0.01
7	1 ⎪	0.39 ⎪		
> 7	0 ⎭	0.39 ⎭		
Total	50	50	0	$X^2 = 3.32$

Table 5.12. Calculation of X^2 for the data in Table 5.11.

There are 4 classes after combination and 1 constraint as the total observed frequency of 50 has been used to calculate the expected frequencies. So $v = 4 - 1 = 3$. From the table on page 272, the rejection region for a 5% significance level is $X^2 > 7.815$. Since 3.32 is not in the rejection region, the null hypothesis that the model $\text{Geo}\left(\frac{1}{2}\right)$ is suitable is accepted.

5.7   Testing the goodness of fit of a Poisson model

The Poisson probability formula was introduced in S2 Chapter 3 by using data relating to the number of calls arriving at a switchboard in time intervals of 5 minutes. These data are reproduced in Table 5.13.

Number of calls	0	1	2	3	4 or more
Frequency	71	23	4	2	0

Table 5.13.   Frequency distribution of number of telephone calls in 5-minute intervals.

A χ^2 goodness of fit test can now be applied to these data. The value of the parameter, λ, the population mean, is not known and so it is estimated by the sample mean. You can check that the sample mean is 0.37. So the null and alternative hypotheses for a goodness of fit test are

H_0: the data can be modelled by $Po(0.37)$;
H_1: the data cannot be modelled by $Po(0.37)$.

The expected frequencies are found by multiplying the Poisson probabilities by the total observed frequency, 100. For example, the expected frequency for 3 calls is

$e^{-0.37} \dfrac{0.37^3}{3!} \times 100 = 0.58$. You can check that you agree with the other expected

frequencies in Table 5.14. As for the geometric distribution there is no theoretical upper limit on the number of calls and so the expected frequency for 4 or more is found by subtracting the sum of the expected frequencies for $x = 0$, 1, 2 and 3 from the total frequency of 100. Table 5.14 shows the calculation of X^2, where classes have been combined to make all expected frequencies at least 5.

Number of calls	O_i	E_i	$O_i - E_i$	$(O_i - E_i)^2 / E_i$
0	71	69.07	+1.93	0.05
1	23	25.56	−2.56	0.26
2 3 $\geqslant 4$	$\left.\begin{matrix}4\\2\\0\end{matrix}\right\} = 6$	$\left.\begin{matrix}4.73\\0.58\\0.06\end{matrix}\right\} = 5.37$	+0.63	0.07
Total	100	100	0	$X^2 = 0.38$

Table 5.14. Calculation of X^2 for data in Table 5.13.

There are 3 classes after combination and 2 constraints since the mean (0.37) and the total frequency (100) were both obtained from the observed values, so $v = 3 - 2 = 1$. From the table on page 272, the rejection region for a 5% significance level is $X^2 > 3.841$. Since 0.38 is not in the rejection region, the null hypothesis that the model $Po(0.37)$ is a suitable one is accepted.

If the value of the mean, λ, is known or given, this value would be used in the calculation of the expected frequencies and the number of constraints would be 1 rather than 2.

Exercise 5A

1   A dice is rolled 60 times. The results are shown in the table.

Score	1	2	3	4	5	6
Frequency	10	11	9	6	10	14

Use a χ^2 test at the 5% significance level to test the hypotheses

H_0: the dice is fair;
H_1: the dice is not fair.

2   In experiments on the breeding of flowers a researcher obtained 95 magenta flowers with a green stigma, 32 magenta flowers with a red stigma, 26 red flowers with a green stigma and 7 red flowers with a red stigma. Genetic theory predicts that flowers of these types should occur in the ratios 9:3:3:1. Carry out a χ^2 test at the 1% significance level to see if the experimental results are in line with the theory.

3   When a tetrahedral dice is thrown the number landing face down counts as the score. Four such dice are thrown 200 times and the numbers of fours obtained are shown.

Number of fours	0	1	2	3	4
Frequency	20	47	83	41	9

(a) Use a χ^2 test at the 5% level to test whether the dice are fair, that is that a $B\left(4,\frac{1}{4}\right)$ model is appropriate.

(b) Use the data to estimate a value for p, the probability that the score is 4. Test at the 5% level whether a $B(4, p)$ model is appropriate.

4   Sixty samples of size 6 are taken after a manufacturing process. The number of defective items in each sample is recorded and the results are shown in the table.

Number of defectives	0	1	2	3	4	5	6
Number of samples	8	24	14	11	1	1	1

Calculate the mean of the frequency distribution and hence find an estimate of p, the probability that an individual item is defective. Using your estimate calculate the expected frequencies corresponding to a binomial distribution and perform a χ^2 goodness of fit test at the 1% level of significance.

5   I wish to investigate the efficiency of the random number generating function on my new calculator, using the method of Section 5.6. A 10% level is to be used.

The results obtained were the following.

Length of run	1	2	3	4	5	6	7 or more
Frequency	26	13	8	2	0	1	0

Carry out the test and state your conclusion.

6 Despite the result of the test in Question 5, I am not convinced of the randomness of the numbers generated. The digits generated while obtaining the 50 runs yielded the following probability distribution.

Digit	0	1	2	3	4	5	6	7	8	9
Frequency	11	13	5	7	12	6	6	7	6	17

Conduct a χ^2 goodness of fit test at the 10% level using the method of Section 5.1.

7 The number of phone calls I received each day during the first three months of 2001 are recorded in the table.

Number of calls	0	1	2	3	4
Number of days	44	24	14	6	2

It is suspected that they follow a Poisson distribution. Calculate the mean of the frequency distribution and use it to calculate the expected frequencies for $x = 0, 1, 2, 3, 4$ or more. Hence carry out a χ^2 test of goodness of fit at the 5% level.

8 The first 100 draws in the National Lottery produced the following results. (Six balls are drawn each time.)

Ball numbers	1–7	8–14	15–21	22–28	29–35	36–42	43–49
Frequency	88	80	80	91	87	78	96

Carry out a χ^2 goodness of fit test at the 5% level to test the null hypothesis
$$P(1–7) = P(8–14) = \ldots = P(43–49) = \tfrac{1}{7}.$$

9 The results of Question 8 could also be grouped according to the colours of the balls used in the draws.

Colour	White	Blue	Pink	Green	Yellow
Ball numbers	1–9	10–19	20–29	30–39	40–49
Frequency	107	125	116	114	138

Carry out a χ^2 goodness of fit test at the 10% level to test the null hypothesis
$$P(W) = \tfrac{9}{49}, \ P(B) = P(P) = P(G) = P(Y) = \tfrac{10}{49}.$$

10 Five drawing pins are thrown onto a table. The number landing point up is recorded. The experiment is conducted 50 times in all, resulting in the following frequency distribution.

Number landing point up	0	1	2	3	4	5
Frequency	3	9	20	15	3	0

Calculate the mean of the frequency distribution, estimate p, the probability of a pin landing point up, and carry out a goodness of fit test at the 5% significance level.

11 The goals scored in each match by a football team during two successive seasons are shown in the table.

Number of goals	0	1	2	3	4	5	6	7
Number of matches	14	32	21	12	3	1	0	1

It is suspected that a Poisson distribution is appropriate.

(a) In the season previous to these two seasons, the mean number of goals scored per match was 1. Carry out a χ^2 goodness of fit test of the model Po(1). Use a 5% significance level.

(b) Calculate the mean of the frequency distribution in the table. Test whether a Poisson distribution with this mean gives a better fit to the data. Use a 5% significance level.

12 The number of accidents occurring on a busy road each week is recorded for one year. The results are shown in the table.

Number of accidents (x)	0	1	2	3	4	5
Number of weeks	26	12	10	3	1	0

It is suspected that a Poisson distribution is appropriate. Calculate $\bar{x}$, and use it to find the expected frequencies for $x = 0, 1, 2, 3$ or more. Conduct a χ^2 goodness of fit test at the 2.5% level of significance.

5.8 Testing the goodness of fit of a normal model

So far the goodness of fit tests which have been carried out have been applied to models for discrete variables. It is also possible to apply the method to continuous data which have been grouped into suitable class intervals. Here is an example of testing the goodness of fit of the normal distribution.

Example 5.8.1

The height, in centimetres, gained by a conifer in its first year after planting is denoted by the random variable H. The value of H is measured for a random sample of 86 conifers and the results obtained are summarised in the table.

H	< 35	35–45	45–55	55–65	> 65
Observed frequency	10	18	28	18	12

(a) Assuming that the random variable is modelled by a $N(50, 15^2)$ distribution, calculate the expected frequencies for each of the five classes.

(b) Carry out a χ^2 goodness of fit analysis to test, at the 5% level, the hypothesis that H can be modelled as in part (a). (OCR)

(a) If $H \sim N(50, 15^2)$ then $Z \sim N(0, 1)$ where $Z = \dfrac{H - 50}{15}$.

The values of Z corresponding to the class boundaries of 35, 45, 55 and 65 are -1, $-0.333...$, $0.333...$ and 1 respectively.

Expected frequency for the first class $= P(Z < -1) \times 86 = \Phi(-1) \times 86$
$$= (1 - 0.8413) \times 86 = 13.65.$$

Expected frequency for the second class $= P(-1 < Z < -0.333...) \times 86$
$$= \left(\Phi(-0.333...) - \Phi(-1)\right) \times 86$$
$$= (0.6304 - (1 - 0.8413)) \times 86 = 18.14.$$

Expected frequency for the third class $= P(-0.333... < Z < 0.333...) \times 86$
$$= \left(\Phi(0.333...) - \Phi(-0.333...)\right) \times 86$$
$$= (0.6304 - (1 - 0.6304)) \times 86 = 22.43.$$

By symmetry, the expected frequencies for the fourth and fifth classes are 18.14 and 13.65. All the expected frequencies are greater than 5, so no combination of classes is necessary.

(b) The null and alternative hypotheses are

H_0: H is $N(50, 15^2)$; H_1: H is not $N(50, 15^2)$.

Table 5.15 gives the calculation of X^2. The total of the expected frequencies is not exactly equal to 86 because of rounding errors.

Class boundaries	O_i	E_i	$O_i - E_i$	$(O_i - E_i)^2 / E_i$
< 35	10	13.65	−3.65	0.98
35–45	18	18.14	−0.14	0.00
45–55	28	22.43	5.57	1.38
55–65	18	18.14	−0.14	0.00
> 65	12	13.65	−1.65	0.20
Total	86	86.01	−0.01	$X^2 = 2.56$

Table 5.15. Calculation of X^2 for Example 5.8.1.

There are 5 classes and 1 constraint (use of the total observed frequency) so $\nu = 5 - 1 = 4$. From the table on page 272, the rejection region for a 5% significance level is $X^2 > 9.488$. Since 2.56 is not in the rejection region, the null hypothesis that H can be modelled by $N(50, 15^2)$ is accepted.

In order to calculate expected frequencies for a normal distribution you need values of μ and σ^2. In the example above these values were given. If either or both of μ and σ^2 are not given, then the unbiased estimates $\bar{x}$ and s^2 respectively are used instead.

(These estimates should be calculated from the grouped frequency table.) For each estimate used another constraint is added. For example, if both μ and σ^2 are estimated there will be 3 constraints in total.

Note that the normal model allows values of the variable from $-\infty$ to $+\infty$ and so the classes for the expected frequencies must also cover this range. Suppose that you wish to fit a normal model to the data in Table 5.16, which relates to the lifetimes of 50 light bulbs.

Lifetime (h)	Frequency
650–659	1
660–669	3
670–679	3
680–689	7
690–699	15
700–709	7
710–719	7
720–729	4
730–739	3

Table 5.16. Frequency distribution of lifetimes of a sample of 50 light bulbs.

Then you would have to calculate expected frequencies for classes with the boundaries <649.5, 649.5–659.5, 659.5–669.5 and so on up to 729.5–739.5 and >739.5. The goodness of fit of a normal distribution to these data is tested in Exercise 5B Question 2.

5.9 Practical activities

1 Birth month Are birthdays spread uniformly throughout the year? Record the month of birth for a sample of at least 70 people. Assuming that birthdays occur uniformly throughout the year, calculate the expected frequencies for each month. You will need to allow for the fact that the lengths of months are not all the same and decide how to tackle February with its leap day. Carry out a χ^2 goodness of fit test of the model.

2 Is the National Lottery fair? Articles frequently appear in the national press claiming that the National Lottery is not fair because some numbers are more popular than others. Obtain data (the Internet is a possible source) which will allow you to test the null hypothesis that all numbers are equally probable.

3 Traffic flow Investigate whether the Poisson distribution is a suitable model for the number of cars passing a given point on a road in a given time interval. Choose a time interval so that the average number of cars in this interval is about 2. You could study traffic flow under a variety of conditions, for example (a) freely flowing, (b) near a set of traffic lights, (c) in a busy street. Carry out a χ^2 goodness of fit test of the Poisson model in each case. Comment on whether the results agree with what you would expect theoretically.

4 Football goals Carry out a hypothesis test of whether the number of goals scored in football matches in the FA Premiership and Nationwide First, Second and Third divisions in one particular week can be modelled by the Poisson distribution. Do you think that the variable 'number of goals scored by each team' satisfies the conditions required for the Poisson distribution to be a suitable model? Comment on the results of your hypothesis test.

5 Waste paper   Select a student and ask her or him to try to throw a ball of waste paper into a waste paper bin 2 to 3 metres away. Repeat 5 more times and record the number of successful attempts. Repeat this experiment with about 50 students. Discuss whether the variable 'the number of successful attempts' meets the conditions required for the binomial distribution to be a suitable model. Carry out a χ^2 goodness of fit test of whether the number of attempts can be modelled by a binomial distribution and comment on the result.

6 Just a minute!   Ask at least 50 people (age 16 or above) to estimate a time interval of one minute. You will need to decide on a standard procedure for doing this. Record their estimates to the nearest second. Carry out a χ^2 goodness of fit test of the hypothesis that the time estimate can be modelled by a normal distribution.

Exercise 5B

1   It is thought that the random variable Y is distributed as $N(50,100)$. One hundred observations of Y are made and result in the given frequency distribution. Carry out a goodness of fit test as outlined in Example 5.8.1 at the 2.5% level of significance to confirm that Y is indeed distributed normally with the given parameters.

Observations of Y	< 30	30–	40–	50–	60–	> 70
Frequency	3	14	30	35	14	4

2   (a) Calculate unbiased estimates of the population mean and variance for the data in Table 5.16, which refers to the lifetimes of a sample of light bulbs.

(b) Fit a normal distribution with this mean and variance.

(c) Carry out a χ^2 goodness of fit test, at the 5% level, of the hypothesis that the lifetime of these light bulbs can be modelled by a normal distribution.

3   Human intelligence is often measured by calculating the Intelligence Quotient (IQ) of an individual, where $IQ \sim N(100,15^2)$. Three hundred new entrants to a school have IQ scores distributed according to the table.

IQ score	⩽ 55	–70	–85	–100	–115	–130	–145	–160	> 160
Frequency	0	10	50	125	82	30	2	1	0

(a) Are the IQs of these new entrants typical of the population at large? Use a χ^2 test at the 5% level.

(b) Instead of taking $\mu = 100$, obtain an estimate of μ from the data. Test whether a normal distribution with this mean and $\sigma = 15$ gives a better fit to the data.

4 The heights of 50 male students aged 18 were recorded correct to the nearest centimetre. The results are summarised in the table.

Heights	156–160	161–165	166–170	171–175	176–180	181–185	186–190
Frequency	2	7	12	14	9	3	3

Find the sample mean and an unbiased estimate of population variance and use them to conduct a goodness of fit test at the 5% level, to see whether height is distributed normally.

5 The durations (in minutes) of 100 phone calls were recorded, resulting in the frequency distribution below.

Duration of calls	0–	1–	2–	3–	4–	5–	10–	> 20
Frequency		7	18	34	25	13	2	1	0

Are the data normally distributed? Conduct a goodness of fit test at 0.1% level of significance.

6 The amounts of meat eaten per week in a sample of 100 families of four is shown in the table.

Amount of meat (kg)	0–	2–	4–	6–	8–10
Number of families	2	10	20	50	18

It is thought that the amount of meat eaten per week by such families can be modelled by the probability density function $f(w) = 0.0002w^3(10 - w)$, for $0 \leqslant w \leqslant 10$, and zero elsewhere.

Calculate the expected frequencies for the intervals in the table and conduct a goodness of fit test at the 10% level.

5.10 Contingency tables

This section turns to a different kind of significance test which makes use of the χ^2 distribution. It is concerned with whether two attributes of a population tend to be associated, that is to occur together, or whether they occur independently of each other.

Table 5.17 gives some data relating to the income level and the method of getting to work for a random sample of people. The income level is described as 'small' (less than £10 000), 'average' (£10 000 to £20 000), or 'large' (greater than £20 000) and the way of getting to work as 'car' (travelling by car either as driver or passenger), 'public' (using public transport) or 'self' (either cycling or walking). Thus the two attributes are income level and method of transport. A table like this, in which the total frequency has been divided into rows and columns according to the values taken by two attributes, is called a **contingency table**.

		Method of transport			
		Car	Public	Self	Total
	Small	58	21	36	115
Income	Average	199	49	64	312
level	Large	205	32	29	266
	Total	462	102	129	693

Table 5.17. Contingency table giving income level and method of transport to work for a random sample of people.
[Data adapted from *Statistical News* (ONS), no. 125, Autumn 1999]

The row and column totals allow you to estimate probabilities of the values for the different attributes. For example, $\text{P(small)} = \frac{115}{693}$ and $\text{P(public)} = \frac{102}{693}$.

Are the variables 'income level' and 'method of transport' independent of each other? This question can be tested by calculating the frequencies which you would expect if the variables *are* independent and then carrying out a χ^2 test. The null and alternative hypotheses are

H_0: the variables 'income level' and 'method of transport' are independent;
H_1: the variables 'income level' and 'method of transport' are not independent.

Suppose you want to find the expected frequency for the group of people with small income who travel by public transport. In order to do this you need an estimate of P(small and public). If H_0 is true and the variables are independent, then

$$\text{P(small and public)} = \text{P(small)} \times \text{P(public)} = \frac{115}{693} \times \frac{102}{693}.$$

Since the total sample size is 693, the corresponding expected frequency is equal to $693 \times \frac{115}{693} \times \frac{102}{693} = 16.93$, correct to 2 decimal places.

The other expected frequencies can be found in a similar fashion. For example,

$$\text{P(large and self)} = \text{P(large)} \times \text{P(self)} = \frac{226}{693} \times \frac{129}{693},$$

so the expected frequency is $693 \times \frac{226}{693} \times \frac{129}{693} = 49.52$, correct to 2 decimal places.

There is a quicker way of calculating the expected frequencies. Look at $693 \times \frac{115}{693} \times \frac{102}{693}$, which is the expression for the expected frequency for people with small income travelling by public transport. Two of the 693s cancel to give $\dfrac{115 \times 102}{693}$. The numerator of this fraction is the product of the row total for small income and the column total for public transport, while the denominator is the total sample size, usually called the 'grand total'. This is an example of a general rule for finding expected frequencies.

Expected frequencies for a contingency table are given by

$$\text{expected frequency} = \frac{\text{row total} \times \text{column total}}{\text{grand total}}.$$

Table 5.18 shows the calculation of the expected frequencies using this formula.

		Method of transport			
		Car	Public	Self	Total
Income level	Small	$\frac{115 \times 462}{693} = 76.67$	$\frac{115 \times 102}{693} = 16.93$	$\frac{115 \times 129}{693} = 21.41$	115
	Average	$\frac{312 \times 462}{693} = 208.00$	$\frac{312 \times 102}{693} = 45.92$	$\frac{312 \times 129}{693} = 58.08$	312
	Large	$\frac{266 \times 462}{693} = 177.33$	$\frac{266 \times 102}{693} = 39.15$	$\frac{266 \times 129}{693} = 49.52$	266
	Total	462	102	129	693

Table 5.18. Calculation of expected frequencies for Table 5.17.

A value of X^2 can now be calculated from the observed and expected frequencies as shown in Table 5.19. The total of the expected frequencies is not equal to 693 exactly because of rounding errors.

Income - Transport pairs	O_i	E_i	$O_i - E_i$	$(O_i - E_i)^2 / E_i$
Small - Car	58	76.67	−18.67	4.55
Small - Public	21	16.93	+4.07	0.98
Small - Self	36	21.41	+14.59	9.94
Average - Car	199	208.00	−9.00	0.39
Average - Public	49	45.92	+3.08	0.21
Average - Self	64	58.08	+5.92	0.60
Large - Car	205	177.33	+27.67	4.32
Large - Public	32	39.15	−7.15	1.31
Large - Self	29	49.52	−20.52	8.50
Total	693	693.1	− 0.01	$X^2 = 30.8$

Table 5.19. Calculation of X^2 for data in Table 5.17.

In order to find a critical value for the test statistic you need to know the number of degrees of freedom of the χ^2 distribution which will approximate the distribution of X^2. As for goodness of fit tests this is calculated from

ν = number of classes − number of constraints.

There are 9 classes, but how many constraints are there? Look at Table 5.18 again. In this table all three column totals, all three row totals and the grand total were used to calculate the expected frequencies. However, the calculation could have been done with fewer pieces of information as shown in Table 5.20. The missing row and column totals in this table can be found by subtraction and then the expected frequencies calculated as before (check that you agree with this statement). So this table shows that there are 5 constraints, because 5 pieces of information from the observed contingency table are needed in order to calculate the expected frequencies. Thus $\nu = 9 - 5 = 4$.

		Method of transport			
		Car	Public	Self	Total
	Small				115
Income	Average				312
level	Large				
	Total	462	102		693

Table 5.20. Demonstration of number of degrees of freedom of Table 5.18.

From the table on page 272, $P(\chi_4^2 > 18.47) = 0.001$. Thus the null hypothesis that the two variables are independent can be rejected at any reasonable significance level: there is evidence that income size and method of transport are related.

Having found that income level and method of transport are not independent it is interesting to see if there is any obvious reason for this. If you look at Table 5.19 you will see that large contributions to the value of X^2 are made by the first, third, seventh and ninth classes. If you then compare the observed and expected frequencies for these classes you will see that among people with small incomes fewer than expected travel to work by car and more than expected walk or cycle. Among people with large incomes the opposite is true.

5.11 Degrees of freedom of a contingency table

The method used in the previous section to find the number of degrees of freedom of a contingency table can be generalised. If there are h rows and k columns, then the number of classes is hk. Provided you are given all but one of the column totals, all but one of the row totals and the grand total, you can find all the expected frequencies, using subtraction where appropriate. So the number of constraints is equal to $(h-1)+(k-1)+1 = h+k-1$. Thus

$$v = \text{number of classes} - \text{number of constraints}$$
$$= hk - (h+k-1) = hk - h - k + 1$$
$$= (h-1)(k-1).$$

> The number of degrees of freedom of a contingency table is given by
>
> $$v = (\text{number of rows} - 1) \times (\text{number of columns} - 1).$$

Applying this rule to the example in Section 5.10, where $h = k = 3$, gives $v = (3-1) \times (3-1) = 4$, as before.

5.12 Combining rows and columns

As for goodness of fit tests, each expected frequency must be at least 5 in order to carry out a χ^2 test for independence of the two attributes. If necessary, rows or columns in the contingency table can be combined in order to meet the second condition. Note that individual classes should not be combined.

Example 5.12.1

A university sociology department believes that students with a good grade in A level General Studies tend to do well on sociology degree courses. To check this it collected information on a random sample of 100 students who had just graduated and had also taken General Studies at A level. The students' performance in General Studies was divided into two categories, those with grade A or B and 'others'. Their degree classes were recorded as Class I, Class II, Class III and Fail. The data are given in the table below.

	Class I	Class II	Class III	Fail	Total
Grade A or B	11	22	6	1	40
Others	4	28	24	4	60
Total	15	50	30	5	100

Use these data to test, at the 1% significance level, the hypothesis that degree class is independent of General Studies A level performance. State your conclusion clearly.

(OCR, adapted)

Take

H_0: degree class is independent of General Studies A level performance;

H_1: degree class is not independent of General Studies A level performance.

Table 5.21 shows the calculation of the expected frequencies, assuming independence.

	Class I	Class II	Class III	Fail	Total
Grade A or B	$\frac{40\times15}{100}=6$	$\frac{40\times50}{100}=20$	$\frac{40\times30}{100}=12$	$\frac{40\times5}{100}=2$	40
Others	$\frac{60\times15}{100}=9$	$\frac{60\times50}{100}=30$	$\frac{60\times30}{100}=18$	$\frac{60\times5}{100}=3$	60
Total	15	50	30	5	100

Table 5.21. Calculation of expected frequencies for Example 5.12.1.

Minimum expected frequencies of 5 can be achieved by combining the columns for Class III and Fail, that is, in each row, adding the frequencies for Class III and Fail.

This combination is logical because it groups 'weak' students together. It would not be sensible, for example, to combine Class I with Class III. Note also that in this example it would be pointless to combine rows since there would then only be one category for General Studies grade. In general, the combination of rows and columns should always be done on the basis of common sense.

Table 5.22 gives the observed and expected frequencies after combination. The values in brackets are the expected frequencies.

	Class I	Class II	Class III and Fail
Grade A or B	11(6)	22(20)	7(14)
Others	4(9)	28(30)	28(21)

Table 5.22. Observed and expected frequencies for Example 5.12.1 after the combination of columns.

Table 5.23 gives the calculation of X^2.

Grade - Class pair	O_i	E_i	$O_i - E_i$	$(O_i - E_i)^2/E_i$
A/B - I	11	6	5	4.17
A/B - II	22	20	2	0.20
A/B - III/Fail	7	14	-7	3.50
Others - I	4	9	-5	2.78
Others - II	28	30	-2	0.13
Others - III/Fail	28	21	7	2.33
Total	100	100	0	$X^2 = 13.11$

Table 5.23. Calculation of X^2 for Example 5.12.1.

The number of degrees of freedom is calculated after any combination of rows or columns has been made in the contingency table. So it is calculated on the basis of Table 5.22:

$$v = (\text{number of rows} - 1) \times (\text{number of columns} - 1)$$
$$= (2-1)(3-1) = 2.$$

From page 272, the rejection region for a 1% significance level is $X^2 > 9.210$. Since 13.11 is in the rejection region, the null hypothesis that degree class is independent of General Studies A level performance is rejected.

Inspection of Table 5.23 suggests that Class I degree results tend to be associated with grade A or B in General Studies while Class III degrees tend to be associated with lower grades in General Studies.

5.13 Yates' correction

The distribution of X^2 is not continuous while that of χ^2, which is used to approximate it, is. In the case of a 2×2 contingency table, for which $v = 1$, the agreement between the two distributions can be improved by applying a continuity correction called **Yates' correction**. This involves reducing each value of $|O_i - E_i|$ by 0.5. The following example illustrates the method.

Example 5.13.1

A random sample of 930 companies quoted on the stock exchange revealed the information summarised in the table below, which shows the distribution of these companies, classified according to two attributes. In this table, D indicates that the company has diversified its product range during the previous financial year, and P indicates that there has been a significant rise in profits during the previous financial year.

	D	Not D
P	148	106
Not P	299	377

The null hypothesis that the attributes D and P are independent is to be tested against the alternative hypothesis that they are not independent. Show that the null hypothesis can be rejected at all reasonable significance levels. (OCR, adapted)

Table 5.24 shows the row, column and grand totals and the calculation of the expected frequencies assuming that the attributes D and P are independent.

	D	Not D	Total
P	$\dfrac{254\times447}{930}=122.08$	$\dfrac{254\times483}{930}=131.92$	254
Not P	$\dfrac{676\times447}{930}=324.92$	$\dfrac{676\times483}{930}=351.08$	676
Total	447	483	930

Table 5.24. Calculation of expected frequencies for Example 5.13.1.

Table 5.25 gives the calculation of X^2.

P - D pair	O_i	E_i	$O_i - E_i$	$|O_i - E_i|$	$|O_i - E_i| - 0.5$	$(|O_i - E_i| - 0.5)^2/E_i$
P - D	148	122.08	25.92	25.92	25.42	5.29
P - Not D	106	131.92	-25.92	25.92	25.42	4.90
Not P - D	299	324.92	-25.92	25.92	25.42	1.99
Not P - Not D	377	351.08	25.92	25.92	25.42	1.84
Total	930	930	0			$X^2 = 14.02$

Table 5.25. Calculation of X^2 showing the application of Yates' correction.

For $v = 1$, $P(\chi^2 > 10.83) < 0.001$. Thus the null hypothesis that the attributes P and D are independent can be rejected at all reasonable significance levels.

The hypothesis that P and D are independent is equivalent to saying that the likelihood that a company's profits have increased is the same whether or not the company has diversified its product range. In other words, the proportion of companies for which profits have increased is the same among those companies that have diversified as among those that have not. Thus Example 5.13.1 can also be tackled by testing for a difference between population proportions using the method of Section 4.4. You can check that this method gives $z = 3.83$. Since $P(Z > 3.83)$ is about 0.0001, the null hypothesis can be rejected at all reasonable significance levels as before.

5.14 Practical activities

1 Sporting interests   Do males and females have similar sporting interests? Choose three popular sports. Ask at least 50 people of each gender to indicate which sport, if any, is their favourite. Assemble your results into a contingency table as shown below and test whether or not 'favourite sport' is dependent on gender.

		Favourite sport			
		A	B	C	None of these
Gender	Male				
	Female				

2 Part-time jobs   Are male and female students equally likely to have part-time jobs? For at least 50 males and at least 50 females of your own age record whether or not they have a part-time job. Test whether having a part-time job is independent of gender.

Exercise 5C

1   The table below gives some data which were obtained from a random sample of men in the course of a study into heart disease. Each man was classified according to his income level and his level of physical activity. The amount of exercise is described as 'Low', 'Medium' or 'High' and the income level as 'Small', 'Average' or 'Large'

		Level of physical activity		
		Low	Medium	High
Income	Small	143	56	108
level	Average	134	130	188
	Large	53	82	106

Use these data to test, at the 1% significance level, the hypothesis that level of physical activity and income level are independent.

2   The milk yield from two breeds of cows is classified as 'High', 'Medium' or 'Low'. The yields of 100 cows were classified as in the table.

	Yield		
	High	Medium	Low
Breed A	30	20	18
Breed B	18	10	4

Use these data to test, at the 2.5% level of significance, whether breed of cow and milk yield are independent.

3 Six hundred individuals were classified according to their hair colour and eye colour.

		Brown	Eye colour Green/Grey	Blue
	Black	95	56	44
Hair	Brown	78	64	90
colour	Fair	37	35	61
	Ginger	10	10	20

Conduct a χ^2 test at the 0.1% significance level to test the hypothesis that hair colour and eye colour are independent.

4 One hundred and thirty people in London were asked to identify their favourite brand of soap from among Brand X, Brand Y and Brand Z. Seventy people in Manchester were asked the same question. The results of the surveys are shown in the table.

	Brand X	Brand Y	Brand Z
London	35	70	25
Manchester	15	35	20

Is there any association between the city and the brand of soap preferred? Use a 5% level of significance.

5 The grades achieved at GCSE in maths and English of 500 students are summarised in the table.

		A or A*	Maths grade B	C or worse
English	A or A*	15	30	15
grade	B	33	105	102
	C or worse	27	65	108

Conduct a χ^2 test at the 5% significance level to test the hypothesis that the grades achieved in maths and English are independent.

6 The number of seats won at the 1983 General Election in Great Britain are classified according to party and region.

	Wales	Region/Country Scotland	N. England	S. England
Conservative	14	21	134	228
Labour	20	41	120	28
Others	4	10	6	7

Is the number of seats won by each party independent of the region? Use a 0.1% significance level.

7 The results of a group of students are classified according to gender and success/failure in the examination for which they were studying.

	Pass	Fail
Male	32	8
Female	25	9

Is there an association between gender and success in examinations? Use a χ^2 test at the 5% significance level.

8 One thousand patients suffering from shingles are classified according to whether or not they received a new treatment and whether or not they made a full recovery.

	Full recovery	Not full recovery
Received new treatment	415	145
Did not receive new treatment	294	146

Is there evidence, at the 5% level, that the new treatment is effective?

Miscellaneous exercise 5

If no significance level is given in the question, use 5%.

1 In a table of random sampling numbers it is stated that each digit in the table is an independent sample from a population in which each of the digits 0 to 9 is equally likely. A sample of 80 digits yielded the following frequencies.

Digit	0	1	2	3	4	5	6	7	8	9
Frequency	5	9	5	6	6	8	9	10	16	6

Perform a χ^2 test, at the 10% significance level, that each digit is equally likely. (OCR)

2 According to genetic theory the number of colour strains red, yellow, blue and white in a certain plant should appear in proportions 4:12:5:4. Observed frequencies of red, yellow, blue and white strains amongst 800 plants were 110, 410, 150, 130 respectively. Are these differences from the expected frequencies significant at the 5% level? If the number of plants had been 1600 and the observed frequencies 220, 820, 300, 260, would the difference have been significant at the 5% level? (OCR)

3 A six-sided dice with faces numbered as usual from 1 to 6 was thrown 5 times and the number of sixes was recorded. The experiment was repeated 200 times, with these results.

x	0	1	2	3	4	5
Frequency	66	82	40	10	2	0

(a) Test the goodness of fit of the model $B\left(5, \frac{1}{6}\right)$ at the 5% level.

(b) Estimate a value of p, the probability of getting a six, from the data and test the goodness of fit of the model $B(5, p)$ at the 5% level. (OCR)

4 A gardener sows 4 seeds in each of 100 plant pots. The number of pots in which r of the 4 seeds germinate is given in the table below.

Number of seeds germinating (r)	0	1	2	3	4
Number of pots	21	27	27	21	4

Estimate the probability, p, of an individual seed germinating. Fit a binomial distribution and test for goodness of fit at the 1% level. (OCR)

5 In a test of car components in which the failure rate is thought to be constant, the numbers of failures in a series of 100-mile intervals are recorded in the following table.

Number of failures	0	1	2	3	4	5	6	7
Frequency	25	30	26	18	9	5	6	1

Calculate the mean number of failures per interval and the expected distribution of failures for the 120 intervals that would be given by a Poisson distribution with this mean.

A good fit between the sets of observed and expected frequencies is taken as evidence of the constancy of the failure rate. Use a χ^2 test to test the goodness of fit. (OCR)

6 A sample of 200 values of the discrete random variable Y is summarised in the table.

y	1	2	3	4	5	6	7 or more
Frequency	140	35	17	3	3	2	0

Find the sample mean $\bar{y}$ of these 200 values.

It is believed that Y has a geometric distribution with parameter p. Using $\dfrac{1}{\bar{y}}$ as an estimate of p complete the table of expected frequencies given below.

y	1	2	3	4	5	6	7 or more
Frequency					1.6	0.5	0.3

Test, at the 10% significance level, whether this sample supports this belief. (OCR)

7 The data below relate to the daily coke yield (%) of a coke oven plant over a period of 260 days.

Daily coke yield (%, to nearest unit)	67	68	69	70	71	72	73
Number of days	7	23	61	87	56	19	7

Calculate the mean daily coke yield (%) for the period and also the standard deviation of the yield.

Calculate the expected frequencies for the above classes, using a normal distribution with mean and variance found above. Conduct a χ^2 goodness of fit test at the 5% level. (MEI)

8 Describe how the number of degrees of freedom is calculated in a χ^2 goodness of fit test. The following set of grouped data from 100 observations has mean 1.03. The data are thought to come from a normal distribution with variance 1 but unknown mean. Using an appropriate χ^2 distribution, test this hypothesis at the 1% significance level.

Lower value of grouping interval	$-\infty$	-2.0	-1.5	-1.0	-0.5	0.0	0.5
Number of observations	0	1	0	6	10	12	15

Lower value of grouping interval	1.0	1.5	2.0	2.5	3.0	3.5	
Number of observations	23	16	13	3	1	0	(OCR)

9 A meteorologist conjectures that, at a certain location, the rainfall (x mm) on June 30th may be regarded as an observation from the exponential distribution with probability density function given by $f(x) = \lambda e^{-\lambda x}, \quad 0 \le x \le \infty$. Show that $E(X) = \dfrac{1}{\lambda}$.

It is known that during the 25-year period 1936 to 1960 a total of 260 mm of rain fell on June 30th. Use this information to provide an estimate of λ. Hence show that the probability that more than 20 mm of rain will fall at this location on June 30th, 1989, is 0.146, correct to 3 significant figures.

The individual rainfall measurements on June 30th for the period from 1961 to 1985 are summarised in the table.

Rainfall (x mm)	Number of days
$x \le 4$	10
$4 < x \le 9$	5
$9 < x \le 16$	6
$x > 16$	4

Using your estimate of λ obtained above, test the conjecture of the meteorologist, using a 5% significance level and showing your working clearly.   (OCR)

10 In 1988 the number of new cases of insulin-dependent diabetes in children under the age of 15 years was 1495. The table below breaks down this figure according to age and sex.

	Age (yrs)			
	0–4	5–9	10–14	Total
Boys	205	248	328	781
Girls	182	251	281	714
Total	387	499	609	1495

Perform a suitable test, at the 5% significance level, to determine whether age and sex are independent factors.   (OCR)

11 A random sample of 100 housewives were asked by a market research team whether or not they used Sudso Soap; 58 said yes and 42 said no. In a second random sample of 80 housewives, 62 said yes and 18 said no. By considering a suitable 2×2 contingency table, test whether these two samples are consistent with each other.   (OCR)

Revision exercise 1

1 In the winter, the monthly demand, in tonnes, for solid fuel from a coal merchant may be modelled by the continuous random variable X with probability density function given by

$$f(x) = \begin{cases} \frac{1}{30}x & 0 \leqslant x < 6, \\ \frac{1}{180}(12-x)^2 & 6 \leqslant x \leqslant 12, \\ 0 & \text{otherwise.} \end{cases}$$

(a) Sketch a graph of $y = f(x)$.

(b) State, giving a reason, whether the median demand is less than 6 tonnes.

(c) Calculate the mean monthly demand.   (d) Show that $P(X \geqslant 8) = \frac{16}{135}$.

The coal merchant has sufficient storage for 8 tonnes of solid fuel and this is replenished each month. Find the expected amount of solid fuel sold each month.

The coal merchant is considering extending the storage of the solid fuel to 12 tonnes, at a cost of £800. The profit on each tonne of solid fuel sold is £60.

(e) Calculate the expected increase in monthly profit if the extension were to be built.

(f) Advise the coal merchant whether she should have the extension built.

2 Drops of water falling onto a smooth horizontal surface form circles and the radius, R cm, of a randomly chosen circle may be modelled by a random variable with cumulative density function given by

$$F(r) = \begin{cases} 0 & r < 0, \\ kr^2 - r^4 & 0 \leqslant r < 1, \\ 1 & r \geqslant 1, \end{cases}$$

where k is a positive constant. Find

(a) the value of k,

(b) the cumulative density function of A, where $A = \pi r^2$,

(c) the probability density function of A,   (d) $E(A)$ and $\text{Var}(A)$.

Let S cm^2 be the sum of the areas of 36 of these circles, randomly chosen. Find $P(S > 20)$.

3 The total number of units of electricity that Anne uses over the period April to June in any year has a normal distribution with mean 920 and standard deviation 95. The supplier has two methods of payment. In method 1, there is a fixed charge of £10 together with a charge of 6.45p per unit of electricity used. Method 2 has no fixed charge but each unit of electricity used costs 7.88p. Calculate the probability that, over the same period next year, Anne would pay more using method 1 than using method 2.

Over the same period, the units of electricity that Baz uses have a normal distribution with mean 750 and standard deviation 64. Given that Baz uses method 2 and Anne uses method 1, calculate the probability that, over the period April to June next year Baz's electricity bill will be greater than Anne's. Assume that the charges are unchanged, that the amounts of electricity used follow the same distributions as before and that the amounts of electricity used by Anne and Baz are independent.

4 In an experiment, a variety of potato was grown in two types of soil. From the crops, two random samples of 100 potatoes were washed and weighed. The results, in grams, are summarised in the box and whisker diagrams shown below.

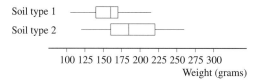

Soil type 1

Soil type 2

100 125 150 175 200 225 250 275 300

Weight (grams)

(a) State, giving your reasons, whether these diagrams confirm that the weights of potatoes from each soil have normal distributions.

(b) The weights, x_1 grams and x_2 grams, of the 100 potatoes grown in type 1 soil and the 100 in type 2 soil respectively are summarised by

$$\sum x_1 = 15\,829, \quad \sum x_1^2 = 2\,542\,324, \quad \sum x_2 = 17\,749, \quad \sum x_2^2 = 3\,248\,951.$$

The population mean weights are denoted by μ_1 and μ_2. Show that, at any reasonable significance level, the null hypothesis $\mu_2 = \mu_1$ can be rejected in favour of the alternative hypothesis $\mu_2 > \mu_1$.

(c) Calculate a symmetric 99% confidence interval for $\mu_2 - \mu_1$.

(d) State, giving a reason, whether it is necessary for the two populations to be distributed normally for your calculations to be valid.

5 The germination rate of nasturtium seeds marketed by Daley's Seeds is monitored by growing a random sample of 200 seeds in 50 rows of 4. The numbers of seeds that germinated in the rows are summarised in the following table.

Number germinating	0	1	2	3	4
Number of rows	1	10	14	20	5

(a) Show that an estimate of the probability that a randomly chosen seed germinates is 0.59.

(b) Test, at the 10% significance level, whether a binomial distribution fits the data.

(c) State, giving a reason, whether there is evidence to suggest that seeds do not germinate independently.

6 In a study of the use by university students of the Internet, a random sample of 500 students was selected in the UK and 184 were found to spend longer than 3 hours each week using the Internet. Calculate a symmetric 95% confidence interval for the proportion of all UK university students who spend longer than 3 hours each week using the Internet.

As part of the study, a random sample of 400 French university students was selected and 168 of these were found to spend longer than 3 hours each week using the Internet. Test, at the 10% significance level, whether there is a difference between the proportions of UK and French university students who spend longer than 3 hours each week using the Internet.

7 A body mass index (BMI) is often used as a measure of obesity. The BMIs of a random sample of 8 people attending a line dancing class were measured at the beginning and at the end of a ten-week course. The results are shown in the following table.

Person	1	2	3	4	5	6	7	8
BMI at beginning	18.79	16.83	15.80	16.39	21.13	21.47	22.50	25.27
BMI at end	18.01	16.14	15.81	16.02	20.10	20.86	22.62	24.09

Stating any required distributional assumption, test, at the 5% significance level, whether the data support the claim that line dancing reduces (on average) the BMI.

What type of error might have been made in the test carried out? State when this error

(a) will not occur,   (b) will occur.

8 A computer-generated table of 'random' numbers consists of digits 0 to 9 which are intended to be equally likely to appear. The digits are printed in blocks of four. Assuming that each digit is equally likely, calculate the probability that the digits in a randomly chosen block of four will all be different.

The printed table contains 250 blocks of four digits and, of these, 118 blocks have all their digits different. Calculate a symmetric 95% confidence interval for the proportion of blocks in all such tables whose digits are all different.

Is there reason to doubt that the digits are random? Explain your answer.

If the digits were random, and were read in consecutive pairs, then it would be expected that the pairs 00, 11, 22 , ... , 99 would occur with equal frequency. There are 98 of these pairs in the table and their frequencies are given below.

Digit pair	00	11	22	33	44	55	66	77	88	99
Frequency	10	9	11	15	13	7	6	11	8	8

Test, at the 5% significance level, whether these digit pairs are equally likely to occur in the table.

9 A machine produces metal studs which are required by the manufacturer to have a mean length of at least 3.80 mm. The quality is monitored by examining a random sample of 25 studs and measuring their lengths, x mm. The results are summarised by

$$\sum x = 94.5 \quad \text{and} \quad \sum x^2 = 357.31.$$

Assume that the lengths of all studs produced by the machine have a normal distribution.

Test, at the 10% significance level, whether the manufacturer's requirement is being met.

The factory making the studs closes for a week, for electrical maintenance, during which all production ceases. After production re-starts a random sample of 30 studs is selected and the lengths, y mm, of each measured. The results are summarised by

$$\sum y = 114.5 \quad \text{and} \quad \sum y^2 = 437.19.$$

Assuming a common variance of the lengths of the studs produced before and after the closure, test, at the 5% significance level, whether the mean length has changed.

10 A clinical trial was carried out to compare the effects of two drugs on patients suffering from arthritis. The trial involved 300 patients and each was given one of the drugs selected by tossing a coin. After a week of taking the drug, the patients were asked to choose one of the responses No Change, Improved, or Much Improved that they thought best described the drug's effect. The results are given in the following contingency table.

	Response			
	No Change	Improved	Much Improved	Total
Drug *A*	64	69	8	141
Drug *B*	52	105	2	159
Total	116	174	10	300

A test is carried out of whether patient response depended on which drug was used.

(a) State suitable hypotheses for the test.

(b) Calculate expected values appropriate to the test.

(c) Give a reason why two categories should be combined.

(d) Using Yates' correction, carry out the test at the $2\frac{1}{2}\%$ significance level.

(e) Why was Yates' correction critical in this case?

Mock examination 1 for S3

Time 1 hour 20 minutes

Answer all the questions.
You are permitted to use a graphic calculator in this paper.

1 An accident and emergency department at a city hospital monitors the numbers of cases arriving between the hours of 22.00 and 23.00 throughout the week. These numbers, each day, have a Poisson distribution with mean 4.3 from Monday to Friday and mean 6.2 on Saturday and Sunday.

  (i) State the probability distribution of T, the total number of cases that arrive at the hospital between 22.00 and 23.00, over a randomly chosen week. [1]

  (ii) Find the mean of T. [2]

  (iii) Write down, without evaluating, an expression for $P(T = 40)$. [1]

2 The random variable X has cumulative distribution function given by

$$F(x) = \begin{cases} 0 & x < 1, \\ \frac{1}{3}(x-1) & 1 \leqslant x \leqslant 4, \\ 0 & x > 4. \end{cases}$$

Find the cumulative density function of Y, where $Y = \ln X$ and hence find the probability density function of Y. [4]

3 As part of a study of reading skills, an education student gave a group of 10 eight-year-old children the same passage to read. The times, x seconds, for each child to read the passage were as follows.

  43   58   41   63   39   50   52   60   49   55
  $\sum x = 510, \quad \sum x^2 = 26\ 614.$

It may be assumed that the data are a random sample taken from a normal distribution with mean μ seconds.

  (i) Calculate a symmetric 99% confidence interval for μ. [5]

  (ii) State why the normality assumption is necessary and where it is used in the calculation. [2]

4 A company employs 190 male and 210 female staff. The weights, in kg, of the males may be modelled by $N(73.1, 39)$ and the females by $N(56.8, 21)$. There are 5 male and 4 female staff in one of the company lifts. At the next stop no passenger leaves, but one of indeterminate sex enters the lift. Calculate the probability that the total weight of these 10 passengers does not exceed the maximum safe load of 700 kg. [7]

State one assumption made in your calculation and comment on its validity. [2]

5 The lifetimes of an item of electrical equipment are monitored by testing to failure a random sample of 120. The results are summarised in the grouped frequency table below.

Lifetime (hours)	4–5	5–6	6–7	7–8	> 8
Frequency	75	35	6	3	1

It was suggested that the probability density of the lifetimes, t hours, may be modelled by

$$f(t) = \begin{cases} \dfrac{5120}{t^6} & t \geqslant 4, \\ 0 & \text{otherwise.} \end{cases}$$

Some of the expected frequencies (correct to 2 decimal places) conforming to this model are given in the following table.

Lifetime (hours)	4–5	5–6	6–7	7–8	> 8
Expected frequency	80.68	23.52			3.75

Find the two remaining expected frequencies and carry out a goodness of fit test at the 10% significance level.   [9]

6 A factory making electric ovens has two eight-hour shifts, one during the day and one at night. The numbers of defective ovens produced on the two shifts were monitored over equal numbers of day and night shifts chosen at random. Of the 181 ovens made on the day shift, 9 were defective, and of the 168 ovens made on the night shift, 13 were defective.

(i)   Test, at the 5% significance level, whether the proportion of defective ovens is greater on night shifts than on day shifts.   [6]

(ii) Calculate a symmetric 95% confidence interval for the proportion of defective ovens made in the factory.   [7]

7 The random variable X has probability density function given by

$$f(x) = \begin{cases} k(x-1)^2 & 1 \leqslant x < 3, \\ k(5-x)^2 & 3 \leqslant x \leqslant 5, \\ 0 & \text{otherwise,} \end{cases}$$

where k is a positive constant. Show that $k = \frac{3}{16}$.   [3]

(i)   Sketch the graph of $f(x)$ and write down the value of $E(X)$.   [3]

(ii) Calculate $P(|X - E(X)| > 1)$.   [3]

The random variable Y is given by $Y = \dfrac{a}{(X-1)^2(5-X)^2}$, where a is a constant.

(iii) Find the value of a for which $E(Y) = E(X)$.   [5]

Mock examination 2 for S3

Time 1 hour 20 minutes

Answer all the questions.
You are permitted to use a graphic calculator in this paper.

1 Along a particular stretch of motorway, vehicle breakdowns occur over time at an
average rate of 3.2 per day on the northbound carriageway and 2.8 per day along the
southbound carriageway. Calculate the probability that a total of between 20 and 25
(inclusive) breakdowns occur along this stretch of motorway over a randomly chosen
period of three days. [5]

2 The cumulative density function of the random variable X is given by

$$F(x) = \begin{cases} 0 & x < 1, \\ \dfrac{2x - 2}{x + 3} & 1 \leqslant x \leqslant 5, \\ 1 & x > 5. \end{cases}$$

   (i) Find and simplify the cumulative density function of Y, where $Y = 2X - 3$. [4]

   (ii) Calculate the 40th percentile of Y. [2]

3 A multiple choice test consists of 50 questions each with 5 possible responses, only one of
which is correct. A correct response receives a score of $+5$ and an incorrect response
receives a score of $-a$. A particular candidate has not revised and does not know any of
the answers for certain and so chooses a response at random for the 50 questions. The
number of the candidate's correct responses is denoted by X and the total score for the
paper by Y.

   (i) State the distribution of X. [1]

   (ii) Show that $Y = (5 + a)X - 50a$. [2]

   (iii) Find the value of a for which the expected score is 10 for a candidate who chooses
   all responses at random. [4]

4 Smith and Jones are athletes who specialise in the long jump. Currently, the lengths of their jumps may be modelled by normal distributions with means and variances as follows.

	Mean (m)	Variance (m^2)
Smith	8.13	0.24
Jones	8.49	0.21

They both compete in an athletics competition in which they each have three jumps. Assuming that their jumps are independent, calculate

   (i)   the probability that their first jumps differ by more than 1 m,   [5]

  (ii)   the probability that the sum of Smith's three jumps exceeds the sum of Jones' three jumps.   [4]

State where in the calculations the assumption of independence is required.   [1]

5 In a random sample of 250 families who watched TV last Thursday, the percentage who watched 'Treble Your Money' is denoted by p_s. For all such random samples state, giving a reason, whether the random variable P_s is discrete or continuous.

For a particular sample $p_s = 34\%$.

   (i)   Calculate a symmetric 95% confidence interval for p, the percentage of all viewing families who watched 'Treble Your Money' last Thursday.   [4]

  (ii)   Give a reason, apart from rounding, why your interval is approximate.   [1]

A further random sample of families who watched TV last Thursday was selected. Estimate the sample size for which a symmetric 99% confidence interval for p_s would have a width of 5%.   [2]

What can be said about the accuracy of p_s, found using the calculated sample size, as an estimate of p?   [1]

6 A sociologist wished to test his belief that married couples tended to choose their partners with similar hair colour. He chose a random sample of 200 married couples and classified each partner's hair as Dark, Fair or Red. The results are given in the following table.

| | | Wife | | | |
		Dark	Fair	Red	Total
	Dark	20	25	7	52
Husband	Fair	33	80	9	122
	Red	9	10	7	26
	Total	62	115	23	200

(i) State hypotheses suitable for the sociologist's test. [1]

The expected frequencies under the null hypotheses are given in the following table.

| | | Wife | | |
		Dark	Fair	Red
	Dark	16.12	29.90	5.98
Husband	Fair	37.82	70.15	14.03
	Red	8.06	14.95	2.99

(ii) Show how the value of 37.82 has been obtained. [1]

(iii) State why two rows or columns should be combined in a χ^2 test. [1]

(iv) Combine the categories Fair and Red for both husbands and wives and carry out a test of the sociologist's belief at the 5% significance level. [8]

(Continued on the next page)

7　Two random samples, each of size n, are drawn from the independent random variables X_1 and X_2, where $X_1 \sim N(\mu_1, \sigma^2)$ and $X_2 \sim N(\mu_2, \sigma^2)$. Unbiased estimates of σ^2 calculated from the samples are s_1^2 and s_2^2 respectively. Show that the pooled estimate s_p^2 of σ^2 is $\frac{1}{2}\left(s_1^2 + s_2^2\right)$ and state the number of degrees of freedom associated with this estimate. [3]

Tara, an environmentalist, wished to investigate the effects of water discharged from a power station into a nearby river. As part of the study she collected 16 specimens of river water, 8 of which were obtained at random times from points 5 km downstream and 8 from points 5 km upstream of the power station. The alkalinity of the water was measured and the results, x_1 mg l^{-1} and x_2 mg l^{-1}, are summarised by

$$\bar{x}_1 = 70.97, \quad s_1^2 = 10.90, \quad \bar{x}_2 = 146.91, \quad s_2^2 = 19.14.$$

It may be assumed that the values are samples from normal distributions with a common variance.

To compare the upstream and downstream values Tara decided to calculate a symmetric 90% confidence interval for $\mu_2 - \mu_1$, the difference in mean alkalinity in the two areas where the samples were taken.

(i)　Why should Tara use a t distribution rather than a normal distribution to calculate the interval? [1]

(ii)　Calculate the confidence interval. [5]

Find the smallest value of d for which the null hypothesis $\mu_2 - \mu_1 = d$ is rejected in favour of the alternative hypothesis $\mu_2 - \mu_1 < d$ at the 10% significance level. [4]

Module S4

Statistics 4

1 Probability

This chapter gives a formal description of probability theory in terms of set notation. When you have completed it you should be able to

- use the notation $P(A)$ for the probability of event A, and the notations $P(A \cap B)$, $P(A \cup B)$ and $P(A \mid B)$ relating to probabilities involving two events
- understand and use the result $P(A \cup B) = P(A) + P(B) - P(A \cap B)$, and know how to extend it to deal with situations involving the union of three events
- use the formula $P(A \cap B) = P(A)P(B \mid A) = P(B)P(A \mid B)$ and the ideas underlying Bayes' theorem to solve problems involving conditional probability.

1.1 Set notation

In S1 Section 4.1 you met the concept of a **sample space**. A sample space is the list of possible outcomes of an experiment and is often denoted by the letter S. For example, if you toss a coin twice, then the list of possible outcomes is (H,H), (H,T), (T,H) and (T,T) where H denotes a head and T a tail. You can summarise this information by writing $S = \{(H,H),(H,T),(T,H),(T,T)\}$. Note how the list is enclosed in curly brackets. Curly brackets are used in a branch of mathematics called 'set theory' to denote a **set**. A set is a collection of objects, called **elements**; in this case the elements are all the possible outcomes of the experiment. Probability theory is usually developed in terms of set notation because this notation provides an exact and concise way of expressing probabilities. This is the method which will be used in this chapter. It builds naturally on the notation which was introduced in S1 Section 4.1.

In addition to identifying all possible outcomes of an experiment you want to be able to specify outcomes which satisfy particular conditions. Consider an experiment in which a dice is thrown once and the number on the top face is recorded. The sample space S is therefore $S = \{1,2,3,4,5,6\}$. Now suppose that you are interested in outcomes which are multiples of 3. The list of outcomes in which you are interested is called an **event**, and it is a **subset** of S. An event is denoted by a capital letter. Thus if A denotes the event 'obtaining a multiple of 3', then $A = \{3,6\}$.

A convenient way of illustrating sets is on a **Venn diagram**. These diagrams were developed by the English logician turned historian, John Venn (1834–1923). Fig. 1.1 shows a Venn diagram of the sample space S and the event A. The rectangular box contains all the outcomes in the sample space S and the outcomes contained in A are enclosed by a closed curve, here a circle.

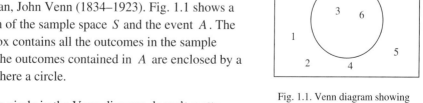

Fig. 1.1. Venn diagram showing the sample space S and an event A.

The size of the circle in the Venn diagram doesn't matter. What does matter is that it contains the outcomes 3 and 6, and does not contain the outcomes 1, 2, 4 and 5. Another possible event when a dice is thrown is 'obtaining a 1'. If this event is denoted by B, then $B = \{1\}$.

Fig. 1.2 is a Venn diagram showing the events A and B. These two events have no outcomes in common: they are said to be **mutually exclusive**. This is indicated on the Venn diagram by drawing the circles for A and B so that they do not intersect.

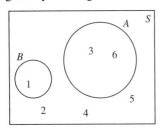

Fig. 1.2. Two mutually exclusive events.

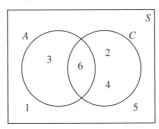

Fig. 1.3. Two events which are not mutually exclusive.

Another possible event when a dice is thrown is 'obtaining a multiple of 2'. If this event is denoted by C, then $C = \{2,4,6\}$. The events A and C are not mutually exclusive since they have the outcome 6 in common. Fig. 1.3 is a Venn diagram illustrating the events A and C. In this case the circles for A and C must intersect because the events are not mutually exclusive.

The notation for the set of outcomes common to the two events A and C is $A \cap C$, which is read as 'A **intersection** C'. In this example $A \cap C = \{6\}$. This is the set of outcomes which are multiples of 2 *and* of 3.

Looking back to Fig. 1.2 you can see that the event $A \cap B$ has no members; that is, it is an **empty set**. This can be indicated by writing $A \cap B = \{\ \}$. $A \cap B = \{\ \}$ if and only if the events A and B are mutually exclusive.

Other notations are sometimes used for the empty set. You may see $\varnothing$ or ϕ in other books.

There is also a notation for the set of outcomes which contribute to either or both of two events. For example, the set of outcomes in A or C or both is written $A \cup C$, which is read as 'A **union** C'. Looking at Fig. 1.3 you can see that $A \cup C = \{2,3,4,6\}$. This is the set of outcomes which are multiples of 2 *or* of 3. Similarly, from Fig. 1.2, $A \cup B = \{1,3,6\}$. This is the set of outcomes which are equal to 1 or are multiples of 3.

The notation A' denotes the set of outcomes which are in S but not in A. This set is called the **complement** of A. For the dice example $A' = \{1,2,4,5\}$. The event $A' \cap C$ is the set of outcomes which are not in A but are in C. Since $A' = \{1,2,4,5\}$ and $C = \{2,4,6\}$, $A' \cap C = \{2,4\}$. This is the set of outcomes which are multiples of 2 but not of 3. In Fig. 1.4 the regions corresponding to the events A' and C have been shaded. The event $A' \cap C$

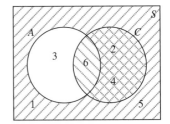

Fig. 1.4. Venn diagram showing $A' \cap C$.

corresponds to the region where the shadings overlap. Also $A' \cup C = \{1,2,4,5,6\}$. This set corresponds to the whole of the region in Fig. 1.4 which is shaded. When working with events, brackets perform their usual function. The notation $(A \cup C)'$ means that you first find the event $A \cup C$ and then find its complement. Since $A \cup C = \{2,3,4,6\}$ it follows that $(A \cup C)' = \{1,5\}$.

Other books may denote the complement of A by $\overline{A}$ or by $\sim A$.

Example 1.1.1

A sample space S is given as $\{1,2,3,4,5,6,7,8,9,10\}$. Three events in this sample space are $A = \{2,4,6,8,10\}$, $B = \{1,2,3,4,5\}$ and $C = \{4,5,6,8,9\}$.

Find   (a) $A \cap B$,   (b) $B \cup C$,   (c) $A' \cup B$,   (d) $A \cap B'$,   (e) $(A \cap C)'$.

(a) $A \cap B$ is the set of outcomes common to A and B, so $A \cap B = \{2,4\}$.

(b) $B \cup C$ is the set of outcomes in B or C or both, so $B \cup C = \{1,2,3,4,5,6,8,9\}$.

(c) $A' \cup B$ is the set of outcomes in A' or B or both. $A' = \{1,3,5,7,9\}$, so $A' \cup B = \{1,2,3,4,5,7,9\}$.

(d) $A \cap B'$ is the set of outcomes common to A and B'. $B' = \{6,7,8,9,10\}$, so $A \cap B' = \{6,8,10\}$.

(e) $(A \cap C)'$ is the set of outcomes not in $A \cap C$. Since $A \cap C$ is the set of outcomes common to A and C, $A \cap C = \{4,6,8\}$. It follows that $(A \cap C)' = \{1,2,3,5,7,9,10\}$

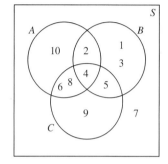

Fig. 1.5. Venn diagram for Example 1.1.1.

All the sets in Example 1.1.1 are shown on the Venn diagram in Fig. 1.5.

The notation for union and intersection can be extended to more than two events. For example, $A \cup B \cup C$ is the set of outcomes which are in the event A or B or C (or any two, or all three of them). In Example 1.1.1, $A \cup B \cup C = \{1,2,3,4,5,6,8,9,10\}$. The region corresponding to this event is shaded in Fig. 1.6a. Similarly $A \cap B \cap C$ is the set of outcomes which are common to all of the events A, B and C. In Example 1.1.1 $A \cap B \cap C = \{4\}$. The region corresponding to this event is shaded in Fig. 1.6b.

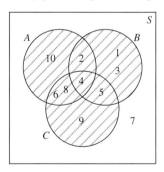

Fig. 1.6a. $A \cup B \cup C$ from Example 1.1.1.

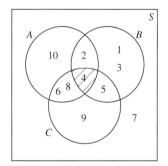

Fig. 1.6b. $A \cap B \cap C$ from Example 1.1.1.

Strictly speaking you should show that $A \cup (B \cup C) = (A \cup B) \cup C$ and that $A \cap (B \cap C) = (A \cap B) \cap C$ before you can talk about $A \cup B \cup C$ and $A \cap B \cap C$ without ambiguity. However, these properties are obvious from the definition.

With three events it is possible to have expressions containing both $\cup$ and $\cap$. In such cases brackets are necessary to make the meaning clear. For example, $(A \cap B) \cup C$ is the set formed from the union of the events C and $A \cap B$. In Fig. 1.7 the regions corresponding to the events C and $A \cap B$ are shaded. Thus the event $(A \cap B) \cup C$ is represented by the region which is shaded in this diagram.

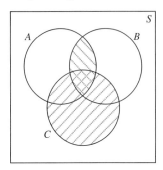

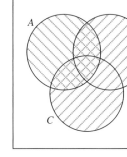

Fig. 1.7. $(A \cap B) \cup C$.   Fig. 1.8. $A \cap (B \cup C)$.

Contrast this with $A \cap (B \cup C)$ which is the intersection of the sets A and $B \cup C$. These two events correspond to regions which are shaded in Fig. 1.8. The set $A \cap (B \cup C)$ is represented by the region where the shadings overlap. You can see that this is very different from the region corresponding to the event $(A \cap B) \cup C$, shown in Fig. 1.7.

Example 1.1.2

For the sample space and events defined in Example 1.1.1 ($S = \{1, 2, 3, 4, 5, 6, 7, 8, 9, 10\}$, $A = \{2, 4, 6, 8, 10\}$, $B = \{1, 2, 3, 4, 5\}$ and $C = \{4, 5, 6, 8, 9\}$) write down the members of the sets

(a) $(A \cap B) \cup C$,   (b) $A \cap (B \cup C)$.

(a) $A \cap B = \{2, 4\}$ and $C = \{4, 5, 6, 8, 9\}$, so $(A \cap B) \cup C = \{2, 4, 5, 6, 8, 9\}$.

(b) $A = \{2, 4, 6, 8, 10\}$ and $B \cup C = \{1, 2, 3, 4, 5, 6, 8, 9\}$, so $A \cap (B \cup C) = \{2, 4, 6, 8\}$.

Exercise 1A

1   A sample space, S, is defined by $S = \{1, 2, 3, 4, 5, 6\}$. Two events in this sample space are defined by $C = \{1, 2, 3\}$ and $D = \{3, 4, 5\}$. Write down the outcomes in each of the following events.

(a) C' (b) D' (c) $C \cap D$ (d) $C' \cap D$

(e) $C' \cap D'$ (f) $C' \cup D'$ (g) $(C \cap D)'$ (h) $(C \cup D)'$

2   Draw a Venn diagram for each part of Question 1 and shade the region which corresponds to the event found.

What do you notice about your diagrams for parts (e) and (h)? And for parts (f) and (g)?

3   (a) Draw Venn diagrams to show that $A \cap B = B \cap A$.

(b) Draw Venn diagrams to show that $A \cup B = B \cup A$.

(These properties will be used, without reference, throughout the chapter.)

4 A random number generator produces the digits 0, 1, 2, 3, 4, 5, 6, 7, 8, 9. If the experiment consists of producing one digit with this random number generator, then the sample space is $S = \{0, 1, 2, 3, 4, 5, 6, 7, 8, 9\}$. Events A, B, C and D are defined as follows. A is the event that the digit is odd, B is the event that the digit is even (including 0), C is the event that the digit is a prime and D is the event that the digit is a multiple of 3.

  (a) List the outcomes in the events A, B, C and D and state which two events are mutually exclusive.

  (b) List the outcomes in the events A', B', C' and D'.

  (c) List the outcomes in

     (i) $A \cup C$,   (ii) $B \cup D'$,   (iii) $A' \cup B'$,   (iv) $(A \cup D)'$.

  (d) List the outcomes in

     (i) $A \cap C$,   (ii) $B \cap D'$,   (iii) $A' \cap B$,   (iv) $(C' \cap D')'$.

  (e) List the outcomes in

     (i) $A \cap C \cap D$,   (ii) $A \cup D \cup C$,   (iii) $D \cap B \cap C$.

5 A coin is tossed 7 times and the number of heads obtained is recorded.

  (a) List the outcomes in the sample space, S.

The following events are defined. E is the event that the numbers of heads is a multiple of 2, F is the event that the number of heads is a multiple of 3 and G is the event that the number of heads is a multiple of 4.

  (b) Write down the outcomes in the events E, F and G.

  (c) Write down the outcomes in the events

     (i) $E \cap F \cap G$,   (ii) $E \cup F \cup G$,   (iii) $(E \cap F) \cup G$,   (iv) $E \cap (F \cup G)$,

     (v) $E \cup (F \cap G)$,   (vi) $(E \cup F) \cap G$,   (vii) $E' \cap F' \cap G'$.

1.2 Probabilities of events

Each of the outcomes in a sample space has a probability assigned to it. An event A, which is a set of outcomes, has a probability associated with it denoted by $P(A)$. This probability is the sum of the probabilities of the set of outcomes in the event A.

These probabilities have to satisfy certain basic assumptions which you have already met in S1 Sections 4.1 and 4.2. In set language they are as follows.

If S is a sample space, then probabilities assigned to outcomes must satisfy

- $0 \leqslant P(A) \leqslant 1$ for every event A;

- if A_1, A_2 A_3, ... have no outcomes in common, then
  $P(A_1 \cup A_2 \cup A_3 \cup ...) = P(A_1) + P(A_2) + P(A_3) + ... $;

- the sum of all the probabilities assigned must equal 1, that is $P(S) = 1$.

The second result in the shaded box is called the **addition law for mutually exclusive events**. When you met it before $P(A_1 \cup A_2 \cup A_3 \cup \dots)$ was written using words rather than set notation as $P(A_1 \text{ or } A_2 \text{ or } A_3 \text{ or } \dots)$ but the meaning is the same. If the events A_1, A_2, A_3, ... have no outcomes in common, then the circles representing them on a Venn diagram do not intersect, as shown in Fig. 1.9, and $A_1 \cup A_2 \cup A_3 \cup \dots$ is the event whose members are members of the event A_1 or A_2 or ... as indicated by the shaded region in Fig. 1.9.

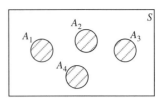

Fig. 1.9. Four events representing mutually exclusive events.

You can make one important deduction immediately from the rules in the shaded box.

Consider the events A and A'. Together $A \cup A' = S$ by definition, so $P(A \cup A') = P(S) = 1$. But also by definition A and A' are mutually exclusive, so $P(A \cup A') = P(A) + P(A')$. Thus $P(A) + P(A') = 1$, so $P(A') = 1 - P(A)$.

For any event A, $P(A') = 1 - P(A)$.

Example 1.2.1
Three fair coins are spun. List the outcomes in the sample space, S. What is the probability of each of these outcomes?

If R is the event that two heads and one tail are obtained (in any order) and Q is the event that three heads are obtained, find
(a) $P(Q)$ and $P(Q')$,   (b) $P(R)$,   (c) $P(R \cup Q)$.

The sample space is
$S = \{TTT, HTT, THT, TTH, THH, HTH, HHT, HHH\}$.
By symmetry the probability of each of these outcomes is $\frac{1}{8}$.

(a) The only outcome in the event Q is HHH, so
$P(Q) = \frac{1}{8}$.

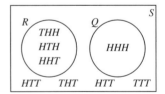

Fig. 1.10. Venn diagram for Example 1.2.1.

Using the result in the shaded box above,
$P(Q') = 1 - P(Q) = \frac{7}{8}$.

(b) Now $R = \{THH, HTH, HHT\}$. Since each of these outcomes has probability $\frac{1}{8}$,
$P(R) = \frac{3}{8}$.

(c) Since R and Q are mutually exclusive, $P(R \cup Q) = P(R) + P(Q) = \frac{3}{8} + \frac{1}{8} = \frac{1}{2}$.

Fig. 1.10 shows the events S, R and Q on a Venn diagram.

Example 1.2.2

A playing card is drawn from a well-shuffled pack. Let A be the event that the card is a king and B be the event that the card is a heart. Find

(a) $P(A)$,   (b) $P(B)$,   (c) $P(A \cup B)$.

(a) This experiment has 52 equally likely different outcomes: AH, KH, QH and so on. The event A is $A = \{KH, KD, KS, KC\}$, so $P(A) = \frac{4}{52}$.

(b) The event B is $B = \{AH, KH, \ldots, 2H\}$, so $P(B) = \frac{13}{52}$.

(c) Since A and B are not mutually exclusive $P(A \cup B)$ must be found by enumerating the outcomes which make up $A \cup B$, that is
$A \cup B = \{AH, KH, \ldots 2H, KD, KS, KC\}$, so $P(A \cup B) = \frac{16}{52}$.

In Example 1.2.2, where the events A and B are not mutually exclusive, $P(A \cup B) \neq P(A) + P(B)$. The reason is clear from Fig. 1.11, which shows the events S, A and B on a Venn diagram. When $P(A) + P(B)$ is calculated the probability that the card is the king of hearts is included twice. This probability can be denoted by $P(A \cap B)$, that is the probability that the outcome is included in both event A (a king) and event B (a heart). To allow for the fact that outcomes in the intersection are counted twice the addition law is modified to

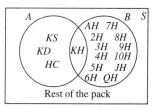

Fig. 1.11. Venn diagram for Example 1.2.2.

$$P(A \cup B) = P(A) + P(B) - P(A \cap B).$$

This result is true for all pairs of events, whether they are mutually exclusive or not.

To prove the result $P(A \cup B) = P(A) + P(B) - P(A \cap B)$ using the properties listed at the beginning of this section, let A and B be two events in a sample space, and define the events C_1, C_2 and C_3 by

$$C_1 = A \cap B, \qquad C_2 = A \cap B' \quad \text{and} \quad C_3 = A' \cap B.$$

Fig. 1.12 is a Venn diagram illustrating the events A, B, C_1, C_2 and C_3. It shows that C_2 and C_3, C_3 and C_1, and C_2 and C_3 are mutually exclusive. Therefore

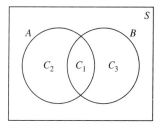

Fig. 1.12. Venn diagram illustrating $A \cap B$, $A \cap B'$ and $A' \cap B$.

$$P(C_1 \cup C_2 \cup C_3) = P(C_1) + P(C_2) + P(C_3),$$

$$P(C_2 \cup C_3) = P(C_2) + P(C_3) \quad \text{and so on.}$$

Now $C_1 \cup C_2 \cup C_3 = A \cup B$, $C_1 \cup C_2 = A$ and $C_1 \cup C_3 = B$, so from the equation $P(C_1 \cup C_2 \cup C_3) = P(C_1) + P(C_2) + P(C_3)$,

$$P(C_1 \cup C_2 \cup C_3) + P(C_1) = \big(P(C_1) + P(C_2)\big) + \big(P(C_1) + P(C_3)\big),$$

which gives $P(A \cup B) + P(A \cap B) = P(C_1 \cup C_2) + P(C_1 \cup C_3) = P(A) + P(B)$.

So $P(A \cup B) = P(A) + P(B) - P(A \cap B)$.

The **addition law** for any two events A and B is

$$P(A \cup B) = P(A) + P(B) - P(A \cap B). \qquad (1.1)$$

Another useful result has been proved at the same time.

As $C_1 \cup C_2 = A$, and C_1 and C_2 are mutually exclusive,

$$P(A) = P(C_1 \cup C_2) = P(C_1) + P(C_2)$$
$$= P(A \cap B) + P(A \cap B').$$

If A and B are any two events,

$$P(A) = P(A \cap B) + P(A \cap B'). \qquad (1.2)$$

If a collection of events is such that one of them must happen, the events are said to be exhaustive. For example, if you roll an ordinary dice and define the events A, B and C by $A = \{\text{odd numbers}\}$, $B = \{\text{even numbers}\}$ and $C = \{\text{multiples of 3}\}$, then A, B and C are exhaustive; A and B are also exhaustive. Since one of A, B and C is bound to happen, then $P(A \cup B \cup C) = 1$; similarly $P(A \cup B) = 1$.

Thus A_1, A_2, ... are **exhaustive** if and only if $P(A_1 \cup A_2 \cup ...) = 1$.

Example 1.2.3
Two events C and D are such that $P(C) = 0.5$, $P(D) = 0.8$ and $P(C \cap D) = 0.3$. Show that the events C and D are exhaustive.

From Equation 1.1, $P(C \cup D) = P(C) + P(D) - P(C \cap D)$, so

$$P(C \cup D) = 0.5 + 0.8 - 0.3 = 1.$$

So, from the definition, the events C and D are exhaustive.

Example 1.2.4
Given that $P(A) = 0.3$, $P(B) = 0.4$ and $P(A \cap B') = 0.2$, find
(a) $P(A \cup B)$,   (b) $P(A' \cap B)$,   (c) $P(A' \cup B)$.

(a) From Equation 1.2, $P(A) = P(A \cap B) + P(A \cap B')$, so

$$P(A \cap B) = P(A) - P(A \cap B') = 0.3 - 0.2 = 0.1.$$

From Equation 1.1, $P(A \cup B) = P(A) + P(B) - P(A \cap B)$, so

$$P(A \cup B) = 0.3 + 0.4 - 0.1 = 0.6.$$

(b) From Equation 1.2, with A and B interchanged, $P(B) = P(B \cap A) + P(B \cap A')$, so

$$P(B \cap A') = P(B) - P(B \cap A) = 0.4 - 0.1 = 0.3.$$

Since $P(X \cap Y) = P(Y \cap X)$ (Exercise 1A Question 3), $P(A' \cap B) = 0.3$.

(c) From Equation 1.1, with A' in place of A,

$$P(A' \cup B) = P(A') + P(B) - P(A' \cap B)$$
$$= (1 - P(A)) + P(B) - P(A' \cap B)$$
$$= (1 - 0.3) + 0.4 - 0.3 = 0.8.$$

The Venn diagram in Fig. 1.13, where the probabilities for each separate region are given, provides a helpful way of checking the preceding calculations. Outcomes in non-overlapping regions of the diagram are mutually exclusive and so the probability of an event that corresponds to more than one region can be found simply by adding the appropriate probabilities. The region for $A' \cup B$ has been shaded in this diagram and you can see that $P(A' \cup B) = 0.1 + 0.3 + 0.4 = 0.8$.

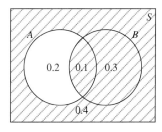

Fig. 1.13. Venn diagram for Example 1.2.4.

1.3 The addition law for three events

The addition law for two events, $P(A \cup B) = P(A) + P(B) - P(A \cap B)$, can be extended to the situation in which there are three events A, B and C.

> The addition law for three events A, B and C is
>
> $$P(A \cup B \cup C) = P(A) + P(B) + P(C)$$
> $$- P(B \cap C) - P(C \cap A) - P(A \cap B)$$
> $$+ P(A \cap B \cap C). \qquad (1.3)$$

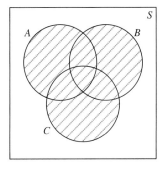

Fig. 1.14a. $A \cup B \cup C$.

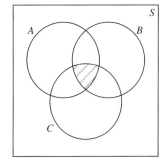

Fig. 1.14b. $A \cap B \cap C$.

Fig. 1.14a shows a Venn diagram for three intersecting events A, B and C with the region corresponding to $A \cup B \cup C$, the union of the three events, shaded. $A \cap B \cap C$ is the event consisting of outcomes common to all three events A, B and C. This corresponds to the region which is shaded in Fig. 1.14b. You can see intuitively why the addition law for three events takes the form it does by looking at Fig. 1.14a and Fig. 1.14b. If you write down $P(A) + P(B) + P(C)$, then the outcomes in each of the intersections $B \cap C$, $C \cap A$, and $A \cap B$ are counted twice. This is why the probabilities for these events are subtracted in Equation 1.3. However, this means that the outcomes in $A \cap B \cap C$ are counted three times and then subtracted three times with the net result that they are not accounted for at all. This is why the term $P(A \cap B \cap C)$ is added in Equation 1.3.

Example 1.3.1

A café serves a basic breakfast of bacon and eggs. Customers may choose any combination of mushrooms, beans and tomatoes as optional extras if they wish. The probability that a customer chooses at least one of these is 0.88. The probability that a customer chooses beans or tomatoes or both is 0.74, beans or mushrooms or both 0.63, tomatoes or mushrooms or both 0.81, tomatoes 0.57, beans 0.40 and mushrooms 0.38.

Find the probability that a customer
(a) chooses all three of beans, mushrooms and tomatoes,
(b) chooses tomatoes but not beans or mushrooms.

(a) If B, M and T are the events that a customer chooses beans, mushrooms and tomatoes respectively, then you want to find $P(B \cap M \cap T)$. The following information is given:

$$P(B \cup T) = 0.74, \ P(B \cup M) = 0.63, \ P(M \cup T) = 0.81, \ P(T) = 0.57,$$
$$P(B) = 0.40, \ P(M) = 0.38, \ P(B \cup M \cup T) = 0.88.$$

The addition law for two events can be used to find $P(B \cap M)$.

From Equation 1.1, $P(B \cup M) = P(B) + P(M) - P(B \cap M)$, so

$$0.63 = 0.40 + 0.38 - P(B \cap M), \quad \text{giving} \quad P(B \cap M) = 0.15.$$

By a similar method you can obtain $P(T \cap B) = 0.23$ and $P(M \cap T) = 0.14$.

Using the addition law for three events (Equation 1.3) gives

$$P(B \cup M \cup T) = P(B) + P(M) + P(T)$$
$$- P(M \cap T) - P(T \cap B) - P(B \cap M) + P(B \cap M \cap T).$$

Substituting gives

$$0.88 = 0.40 + 0.38 + 0.57 - 0.14 - 0.23 - 0.15 + P(B \cap M \cap T),$$

so $P(B \cap M \cap T) = 0.05$.

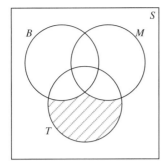

Fig. 1.15. $T \cap (B \cup M)'$ from Example 1.3.1.

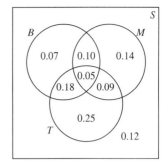

Fig. 1.16. Venn diagram for Example 1.3.1.

(b) When it seems difficult to use formulae to solve a problem it can be extremely helpful to draw a Venn diagram, which may enable you to pose the same problem in a different form.

Fig. 1.15 shows the region corresponding to the event 'chooses tomatoes but not beans or mushrooms', which can be expressed as $T \cap (B \cup M)'$. By looking at this diagram you can see that

$$P\left(T \cap (B \cup M)'\right) = P(T \cup B \cup M) - P(B \cup M)$$
$$= 0.88 - 0.63 = 0.25.$$

Fig. 1.16 is a Venn diagram which shows the probabilities corresponding to each event in Example 1.3.1. Check that you can obtain these values for yourself. This diagram allows you to write down any other probability which you might require. For example, the probability that a customer chooses beans and mushrooms but not tomatoes is 0.10. Drawing such a diagram is often the easiest method of solving complicated probability problems.

Exercise 1B

1 A and B are two events such that $P(A) = 0.5$, $P(B) = 0.7$ and $P(A \cap B) = 0.3$. Find the values of

(a) $P(A \cup B)$,   (b) $P(A \cap B')$.

2 C and D are two events such that $P(C) = 0.1$, $P(D) = 0.2$ and $P(C \cup D) = 0.3$. Are C and D mutually exclusive events? Justify your answer.

Find the values of

(a) $P(C')$,   (b) $P(C' \cap D')$.

3 E and F are events such that $P(E) = 0.7$, $P(F) = 0.6$ and $P(E \cap F) = 0.4$. Find

(a) $P(E \cup F)$,   (b) $P(E' \cap F)$,   (c) $P(E' \cap F')$,

(d) $P(E$ or F but not both occurs$)$.

4 In a group of 50 students, 30 study either or both of chemistry and biology. The number of students studying chemistry is 20 and the number studying biology is 15. A student is chosen at random from the group. Let B be the event that the student studies biology and C be the event that they study chemistry. Write down the values of $P(B)$, $P(C)$ and $P(B \cup C)$.

Hence find the probability that a student chosen at random studies

(a) both chemistry and biology, (b) biology but not chemistry,

(c) neither chemistry nor biology, (d) chemistry or biology but not both.

5 Three events A, B and C are such that $P(A) = 0.39$, $P(B) = 0.57$, $P(C) = 0.53$, $P(A \cap B) = 0.21$, $P(B \cap C) = 0.19$, $P(C \cap A) = 0.16$ and $P(A \cap B \cap C) = 0.07$. Find

(a) $P(A \cup B)$, (b) $P(A \cup B \cup C)$, (c) P(only one of A, B or C occurs),

(d) P(exactly two out of three of A, B or C occur).

6 In the Mediterranean town of Journale the probability that a person chosen at random buys a national daily paper is 0.36, the probability that they buy a local daily paper is 0.29, the probability that they buy a local weekly paper is 0.52, the probability that they buy none of these is 0.14, the probability that they buy all three is 0.03, the probability that they buy both a local daily and a local weekly paper is 0.10 and the probability they buy a local daily paper but not a weekly or national paper is 0.14. Find the probability that they buy both a local weekly paper and a daily national paper.

1.4 Conditional probability and the multiplication law

Some events are related in such a way that knowing whether one event has occurred tells you something about the likelihood of the other event. This relation is made precise in the idea of conditional probability. You have met conditional probability in S1 Section 4.4, and it may be helpful to recall the example which was used to introduce the concept.

Consider a class of 30 pupils, of whom 17 are girls and 13 are boys. Suppose that five of the girls and six of the boys are left-handed, and all the remaining pupils are right-handed. If a pupil is selected at random from the whole class, then the probability that he or she is left-handed is $\dfrac{6+5}{30} = \dfrac{11}{30}$. If, however, you are told that the pupil who has been selected at random is a girl, then this information alters the probability that the pupil is left-handed. The probability that this girl will be left-handed is $\frac{5}{17}$. This is an example of a **conditional probability**.

If G is the event that the pupil chosen is a girl and L is the event that the pupil is left-handed, then $P(L \mid G)$ denotes the conditional probability that the pupil is left-handed given that the pupil is a girl. In this case $P(L \mid G) = \frac{5}{17}$, while $P(L) = \frac{11}{30}$. Looking at these numbers more carefully will suggest a way to define the conditional probability in general.

If you divide the numerator and denominator of $P(L \mid G)$ by 30 you obtain $P(L \mid G) = \dfrac{\frac{5}{30}}{\frac{17}{30}}$.
The numerator is equal to the probability of choosing a left-handed girl from the whole class; expressed in set notation this is $P(L \cap G)$. The denominator is the probability of choosing a girl from the whole class, that is $P(G)$. So in this example

$$P(L \mid G) = \frac{P(L \cap G)}{P(G)}.$$

This expression is taken as the *definition* of conditional probability.

> If A and B are any two events, and if $P(A) \neq 0$, then the **conditional probability** of B given A is
> $$P(B \mid A) = \frac{P(A \cap B)}{P(A)}. \qquad (1.4)$$

Multiplying both sides of this equation by $P(A)$ gives

$$P(A \cap B) = P(A)\,P(B \mid A).$$

Since $P(A \mid B) = \dfrac{P(B \cap A)}{P(B)} = \dfrac{P(A \cap B)}{P(B)}$, provided $P(B) \neq 0$, it also follows that

$$P(A \cap B) = P(B)\,P(A \mid B).$$

> If A and B are any two events, then
> $$P(A \cap B) = P(A)\,P(B \mid A) \quad \text{and} \quad P(A \cap B) = P(B)\,P(A \mid B). \qquad (1.5)$$
>
> This is called the **multiplication law of probability**.

Since these equations are not written in terms of fractions the restrictions $P(A) \neq 0$ and $P(B) \neq 0$ are no longer needed.

Suppose now that $P(A \mid B)$ is equal to $P(A)$. In this case the probability of A is the same whether B has taken place or not. This relation between A and B is what you would like to express by saying that A and B are independent.

If $P(A \mid B) = P(A)$, then, using Equation 1.4 with A and B interchanged,

$$P(A) = P(A \mid B) = \frac{P(B \cap A)}{P(B)}, \qquad \text{giving} \qquad P(A \cap B) = P(A)\,P(B).$$

This is now taken as the *definition* of independence of A and B.

> Two events A and B are said to be **independent** if
> $$P(A \cap B) = P(A)\,P(B). \qquad (1.6)$$

You met these results in S1 Section 4.4 but with $P(A \cap B)$ expressed in words as $P(A \text{ and } B)$.

Example 1.4.1

Students in a maths class were given two problems to solve. The second problem was harder than the first. Within the class $\frac{5}{6}$ of the students got the first problem correct and $\frac{7}{12}$ got the second one correct. Of those students who got the first problem correct, $\frac{3}{5}$ got the second one correct. A student is chosen at random from the class. C is the event that this student got the first problem correct and D is the event that the student got the second question correct. Find

(a) $P(C \cap D)$,   (b) $P(C \cup D)$,   (c) $P(C' \cap D')$,   (d) $P(C \mid D)$.

Express each of these probabilities in words.

The information given is $P(C) = \frac{5}{6}$, $P(D) = \frac{7}{12}$ and $P(D \mid C) = \frac{3}{5}$.

(a) From Equation 1.5,

$$P(C \cap D) = P(C)P(D \mid C) = \frac{5}{6} \times \frac{3}{5} = \frac{1}{2}.$$

This is the probability that the student got both questions correct.

(b) From Equation 1.1,

$$P(C \cup D) = P(C) + P(D) - P(C \cap D) = \frac{5}{6} + \frac{7}{12} - \frac{1}{2} = \frac{11}{12}.$$

This is the probability that the student got either or both of the questions correct.

(c) The set $C' \cap D'$ corresponds to the region in Fig. 1.17 where the shadings overlap. You can see that it is equivalent to $(C \cup D)'$. Thus

$$P(C' \cap D') = P\big((C \cup D)'\big) = 1 - P(C \cup D)$$

$$= 1 - \frac{11}{12} = \frac{1}{12}.$$

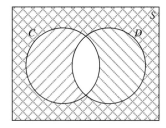

This is the probability that the student got neither of the questions correct.

Fig. 1.17. $C' \cap D'$ from Example 1.4.1.

(d) From Equation 1.4,

$$P(C \mid D) = \frac{P(C \cap D)}{P(D)} = \frac{\frac{1}{2}}{\frac{7}{12}} = \frac{6}{7}.$$

This is the probability that the student got the first question correct given that he or she got the second one correct.

Example 1.4.2

Events A and B are independent, events A and C are independent and events B and C are mutually exclusive. If $P(A) = \frac{1}{2}$, $P(B) = \frac{1}{3}$ and $P(C) = \frac{1}{4}$, find

(a) $P(A \cap B)$,   (b) $P(C \cap B)$,   (c) $P(A \cup B)$,

(d) $P(A \cup B \cup C)$,   (e) $P(C \mid B')$,   (f) $P(C' \mid A \cup B)$.

(a) Since A and B are independent, from Equation 1.6

$$P(A \cap B) = P(A)P(B) = \tfrac{1}{2} \times \tfrac{1}{3} = \tfrac{1}{6}.$$

(b) Since B and C are mutually exclusive, $P(C \cap B) = 0$.

(c) From Equation 1.1, $P(A \cup B) = P(A) + P(B) - P(A \cap B) = \tfrac{1}{2} + \tfrac{1}{3} - \tfrac{1}{6} = \tfrac{2}{3}$.

(d) From Equation 1.3,

$$P(A \cup B \cup C) = P(A) + P(B) + P(C)$$
$$- P(B \cap C) - P(C \cap A) - P(A \cap B) + P(A \cap B \cap C).$$

You know the probabilities of A, B and C. Since B and C are mutually exclusive, $B \cap C = \{\ \}$. It follows that $A \cap B \cap C = \{\ \}$. Thus $P(B \cap C) = P(A \cap B \cap C) = 0$. Alternatively, you could draw the Venn diagram in Fig. 1.18, to illustrate the situation.

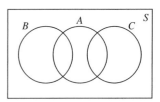

Fig. 1.18. Venn diagram for Example 1.4.2.

As A and C are independent,

$$P(C \cap A) = P(C)P(A) = \tfrac{1}{4} \times \tfrac{1}{2} = \tfrac{1}{8}.$$

Substituting all these values gives

$$P(A \cup B \cup C) = \tfrac{1}{2} + \tfrac{1}{3} + \tfrac{1}{4} - \tfrac{1}{6} - 0 - \tfrac{1}{8} + 0 = \tfrac{19}{24}.$$

(e) From Equation 1.4, $P(C \mid B') = \dfrac{P(C \cap B')}{P(B')}$.

From Equation 1.2, $P(C \cap B') = P(C) - P(C \cap B) = \tfrac{1}{4} - 0 = \tfrac{1}{4}$.

Also, $P(B') = 1 - P(B) = 1 - \tfrac{1}{3} = \tfrac{2}{3}$; so $P(C \mid B') = \dfrac{\tfrac{1}{4}}{\tfrac{2}{3}} = \tfrac{3}{8}$.

(f) From Equation 1.4, $P(C \mid A \cup B) = \dfrac{P(C' \cap (A \cup B))}{P(A \cup B)}$.

In Fig. 1.19 the regions corresponding to the events C' and $A \cup B$ have been shaded. The event $C' \cap (A \cup B)$ corresponds to the region where these shadings overlap. From this diagram you can see that

$$P(C' \cap (A \cup B)) = P(A \cup B) - P(A \cap C)$$
$$= \tfrac{2}{3} - \tfrac{1}{8} = \tfrac{13}{24}.$$

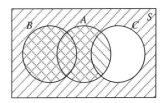

Fig. 1.19. Venn diagram for Example 1.4.2(e).

So $P(C' \mid (A \cup B)) = \dfrac{\tfrac{13}{24}}{\tfrac{2}{3}} = \tfrac{13}{16}$.

Exercise 1C

1 Two independent events, C and D, are such that $P(C) = 0.2$ and $P(D) = 0.3$. Find

(a) $P(C \cup D)$,   (b) $P(C$ or D but not both$)$.

2 Two events, A and B, have probabilities $P(A) = 0.2$ and $P(B) = 0.5$. Given the conditional probability $P(A \mid B) = 0.15$, determine the probabilities

(a) $P(A \cap B)$,   (b) $P(B \mid A)$.   (OCR)

3 A person is selected at random from among the members of a social club. The probability that the person plays golf is $\frac{1}{10}$. The probability that the person plays bridge if he or she plays golf is $\frac{14}{15}$. The probability that the person plays golf if he or she plays bridge is $\frac{3}{10}$. Find the probability that a person chosen at random from the club plays bridge.

4 The events A and B are such that $P(A) = \frac{1}{2}$, $P(B) = \frac{1}{4}$ and $P(A$ or B but not both$) = \frac{1}{3}$. Calculate

(a) (i) $P(A \cap B)$,   (ii) $P(A' \cap B)$,   (iii) $P(A \mid B)$,   (iv) $P(B \mid A')$.

(b) State, giving reasons, whether A and B are

  (i) independent,   (ii) mutually exclusive.   (OCR, adapted)

5 The probability of event A occurring is $P(A) = \frac{13}{25}$. The probability of event B occurring is $P(B) = \frac{9}{25}$. The conditional probability of A occurring given that B has occurred is $P(A \mid B) = \frac{5}{9}$.

Determine the following probabilities:

(a) $P(A \cap B)$,   (b) $P(B \mid A)$,   (c) $P(A \cup B)$,   (d) $P(A' \cap B')$,

(e) $P(A \cap B')$.   (OCR, adapted)

6 The probability that an event A occurs is $P(A) = 0.3$. The event B is independent of A and $P(B) = 0.4$.

(a) Calculate $P(A \cup B)$.

Event C is defined to be the event that neither A nor B occurs.

(b) Calculate $P(C \mid A')$ where A' is the event that A does not occur.   (OCR)

7 E, F and G are three independent events such that $P(E) = \frac{1}{2}$, $P(F) = \frac{1}{4}$ and $P(G) = \frac{1}{8}$. Find the probability that

(a) E, F and G all occur,   (b) none of E, F or G occurs.

8 B, C and D are three events such that $P(B) = \frac{1}{3}$, $P(C) = \frac{1}{4}$ and $P(D) = \frac{1}{2}$. Given that B and C are independent, C and D are independent and B and D are mutually exclusive, show that $P(B \cup C \cup D) = \frac{7}{8}$. Find

(a) $P(C \cap (B \cup D))$,   (b) $P(B' \cap C \cap D)$

1.5 Tree diagrams

You may have noticed in Section 1.4 that, although Venn diagrams can help you to organise the information needed to calculate conditional probabilities, they can't represent the idea itself of one event being conditional on another. Fortunately you already know about a kind of diagram which can represent this relation between events: tree diagrams (S1 Section 4.4).

The multiplication laws of probability, namely

$$P(A \cap B) = P(A) P(B \mid A) \quad \text{and} \quad P(A \cap B) = P(B) P(A \mid B),$$

justify using tree diagrams to solve problems involving conditional probabilities.

Suppose that you have a situation in which two events A and B are occurring, which may or may not be independent, and suppose that it is convenient to consider the event A first.

Then, either A happens, or it does not, in which case A' happens, and these events take place with probability $P(A)$ and $P(A')$. These are shown by drawing the first two branches of a tree diagram, as shown in Fig. 1.20.

Fig. 1.20. Tree diagram.

The probability of the event occurring at the end of the branch of the tree is written along the branch.

Now consider the event B. Either B occurs, or it doesn't, but you have to take into account the fact that A has already occurred. So, on the branches leading from A in Fig. 1.21, the relevant probabilities are $P(B \mid A)$ and $P(B' \mid A)$. And, at the end of the top branch both A and B have taken place, so the relevant event is $A \cap B$, while at the end of the second branch the relevant event is $A \cap B'$.

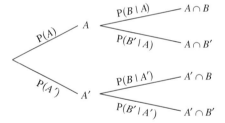

Fig. 1.21. A tree diagram showing two events A and B.

The multiplication law $P(A \cap B) = P(B) P(A \mid B)$ tells you that to find the probability of the event which occurs at the end of the branch, you multiply the probabilities along the branches. Notice also, that if the events A and B are independent, then $P(B \mid A) = P(B)$, so the multiplication principle is still valid.

There is another important aspect to tree diagrams, which will be stated but not proved. At every stage, events which are at the ends of different branches are mutually exclusive.

You are very probably familiar with using tree diagrams, which are an effective way of solving problems on probability. You should continue to use them, even if you only use them as a way of organising your information.

1.6 Bayes' theorem

In dealing with conditional probabilities you were able to use Equation 1.4 to find either $P(A \mid B)$ or $P(B \mid A)$, depending on how you chose to plug in A and B.

Imagine the end of your day at school. Suppose A is the event 'stops at the post office to buy stamps' and B is the event 'arrives at home by 4 p.m.' The probability $P(B \mid A)$ addresses a straightforward question: If you stop at the post office to buy stamps, are you likely to be home by 4 p.m.? The probability $P(A \mid B)$ addresses a more interesting question (from the point of view of the person who asked you to buy stamps): Given that you reach home by 4 p.m., did you or did you not remember to stop at the post office? It was the Reverend Thomas Bayes (c.1701–1761) of Tunbridge Wells who first realised that conditional probabilities could be turned around in this way to make inferences based on observations.

Consider the following situation. A hardware store purchases light bulbs from three different manufacturers A_1, A_2 and A_3. Of the bulbs, 30% come from A_1, 45% from A_2 and 25% from A_3. This means that if a bulb is picked at random from stock $P(A_1) = 0.30$, $P(A_2) = 0.45$ and $P(A_3) = 0.25$ (where A_1 is the event that the bulb came from manufacturer A_1 and so on). In the past it has been found that 1% of bulbs from each of manufacturers A_1 and A_2 are faulty whereas 2% of manufacturer A_3's bulbs are faulty. If a bulb chosen at random is found to be faulty what is the probability that it was produced by manufacturer A_3?

The probability will be greater than $P(A_3)$ (= 0.25) since A_3 is more likely to produce a faulty bulb than are the other two manufacturers. If F is the event that the bulb chosen is faulty, then the probability required is $P(A_3 \mid F)$. The information which is given is

$$P(A_1) = 0.30, \qquad\qquad P(A_2) = 0.45, \qquad\qquad P(A_3) = 0.25,$$

$$P(F \mid A_1) = 0.01, \qquad\qquad P(F \mid A_2) = 0.01, \qquad\qquad P(F \mid A_3) = 0.02.$$

This information is summarised in the tree diagram in Fig. 1.22.

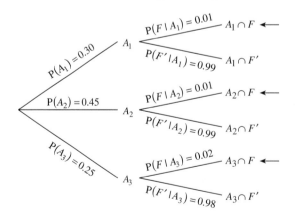

Fig. 1.22. Tree diagram illustrating Bayes' theorem.

From Equation 1.4, $P(A_3 \mid F) = \dfrac{P(A_3 \cap F)}{P(F)}$.

To find the denominator of this expression, you need to identify the events in F. These are $A_1 \cap F$, $A_2 \cap F$ and $A_3 \cap F$, which are indicated by arrows in the tree diagram. As they are mutually exclusive,

$$P(F) = P(A_1 \cap F) + P(A_2 \cap F) + P(A_3 \cap F).$$

Using Equation 1.5,

$$P(A_1 \cap F) = P(A_1)P(F \mid A_1) = 0.30 \times 0.01 = 0.003,$$
$$P(A_2 \cap F) = P(A_2)P(F \mid A_2) = 0.45 \times 0.01 = 0.0045,$$
$$P(A_3 \cap F) = P(A_3)P(F \mid A_3) = 0.25 \times 0.02 = 0.005.$$

Thus $P(F) = 0.003 + 0.0045 + 0.005 = 0.0125,$

and $P(A_3 \mid F) = \dfrac{P(A_3 \cap F)}{P(F)} = \dfrac{0.005}{0.0125} = 0.4.$

Written completely in terms of conditional probabilities the expression for $P(A_3 \mid F)$ is

$$P(A_3 \mid F) = \frac{P(A_3)P(F \mid A_3)}{P(F)}.$$

This expression is a particular case of **Bayes' theorem** which may be stated as follows.

If A_1, A_2, ... , A_n are n mutually exclusive and exhaustive events in a sample space S and B is another event in S, then

$$P(A_j \mid B) = \frac{P(A_j)P(B \mid A_j)}{P(B)} = \frac{P(A_j)P(B \mid A_j)}{\sum_i P(A_i)P(B \mid A_i)}.$$

The sum in the denominator of this expression generalises the sum of the terms indicated by the arrows in Fig. 1.22.

In practice you will probably find it easier to solve problems of this type by drawing a tree diagram rather than applying the theorem directly. It is left as an exercise for you to check that for the light bulb example $P(A_1 \mid F) = 0.24$ and $P(A_2 \mid F) = 0.36$.

Exercise 1D

1   A shop stocks tinned pet food for cats and dogs in two sizes, large and small. Of the stock of tins, 70% is dog food and 30% cat food. Of the tins of dog food 30% are of small size, whereas of the tins of cat food 40% are of small size.

(a) Find the probability that a tin chosen at random from the stock will be of small size.

The shop is flooded and the tins lose their labels.

(b) A small tin is chosen at random. Find the probability that it contains cat food.

2 A certain rare genetic condition affects 0.01% of the population. A test has been developed which can detect the condition, if it is present, with a probability of 95%. Unfortunately, when the condition is not present, there is a probability of 0.05% that the test will still give a positive result. Calculate the probability to 2 decimal places that a person has the condition given that the test gives a positive result.

Comment on the usefulness of the test in light of your answer.

3 I try to catch the bus to work but if I miss it I have to walk. Sometimes, when I walk, a friend overtakes me and gives me a lift. The probability that I catch the bus is 0.7 and if I catch the bus the probability that I arrive on time at my desk is 0.98. The probability that I get a lift from a friend is 0.1 and in this case the probability that I arrive on time is 0.92. If I walk the probability that I arrive on time falls to 0.84. My boss sees me arriving late at my desk one day. What is the probability that I had walked?

4 A quality control system is designed to monitor the mean mass of the population of aspirin tablets coming off a production line. This is done by measuring the mean mass of a sample of 5 tablets at 20-minute intervals. If the mass of this sample lies outside certain specified limits, the production line is stopped. There is a probability of 0.05 of stopping the line when in fact the system is under control (a Type I error) and a probability of 0.10 of failing to stop the line when the system is not under control (a Type II error). The probability that the system is under control is 0.9.

Given that the production line has been stopped, what is the probability that the correct action has been taken?

5 An accused prisoner is on trial. The defence lawyer asserts that, on the basis of the evidence so far produced, there is a probability of 1 in a million that the prisoner is guilty. At this point the prosecution produces further evidence. The prosecution claims that if the prisoner is guilty the probability of obtaining this evidence is 0.99 but if the prisoner is not guilty the probability of obtaining this evidence is 0.01. Assuming that all the probabilities are correct, calculate the probability that the prisoner is guilty now that this further evidence has been revealed. Comment on your answer.

6 Geological surveys can be used to indicate the presence of oil-wells but they are not infallible. There is a probability of 0.92 that an oil-well is present when such a survey gives a positive result and a probability of 0.96 that an oil-well is absent when such a survey gives a negative result.

Suppose an oil-well is present in $100p\%$ of the surveys which are carried out. Find, in terms of p, the probability that an oil-well is present given that a positive result has been obtained from a survey.

The profit from sinking a well correctly is 100 times the loss from sinking a well incorrectly. Show that a prospector who only sinks a well when the result of a survey is positive will make a profit in the long run provided that $p > \frac{1}{2301}$.

(Assume that the cost of a survey can be ignored in comparison with the cost of sinking a well.)

Miscellaneous exercise 1

1 The event that Melanie goes to a disco is M and the event that Gita goes to the same disco is G. Given that $P(G' \cap M') = \frac{1}{5}$ and $P(M) + P(G) = \frac{21}{25}$, find the probability that both Melanie and Gita go to the disco.

2 If $P(A \cap B) = \frac{1}{4}$ and $P(A) = P(B) + \frac{1}{5}$, find $P(A)$ if A and B are exhaustive events.

3 If $P(A) = \frac{3}{4}$ and $P(B) = \frac{2}{3}$, find the maximum and minimum values of $P(A \cap B)$. In each case state the value of $P(A \cup B)$.

4 (a) The probability that an event A occurs is $P(A) = 0.4$. B is an event independent of A and $P(A \cup B) = 0.7$. Find $P(B)$.

   (b) C and D are two events such that $P(D \mid C) = \frac{1}{5}$ and $P(C \mid D) = \frac{1}{4}$. Given that $P(C \cap D) = p$, express $P(C)$ and $P(D)$ in terms of p.

   (c) Given also that $P(C \cup D) = \frac{1}{5}$, find the value of p. (OCR, adapted)

5 Three identical boxes each contain two balls. The balls are identical apart from their colour. One box contains two gold balls, the second two silver balls and the third one gold and one silver ball. A box is chosen at random and one ball is removed at random. If the ball is gold, what is the probability that the second ball in the box is also gold?

6 A lecturer uses a statistical technique to judge the true reception given to her lectures. She asks each student in the lecture-room to toss two coins in the air and note whether or not they land showing two heads. She then tells the students to raise their right arm if one of the following two conditions apply:

   I both coins land heads and the student enjoyed the lecture;

   II the coins do not land showing two heads and the student did not enjoy the lecture.

   Let A denote the event that a randomly selected student obtains two heads, and let B denote the event that a randomly chosen student raises his or her right arm.

   (a) Describe in words the complement, A', of the event A described above.

   (b) If the proportion of students who enjoyed the lecture is p, what are the following probabilities?

   (i) $P(A)$ (ii) $P(B \mid A)$ (iii) $P(A \cap B)$ (iv) $P(A' \cap B)$

   (c) Hence, or otherwise, demonstrate that $P(B) = \frac{1}{4}(3 - 2p)$.

   (d) What conclusion would you draw if it turned out that 36 out of an audience of 100 raised their right arms? (OCR, adapted)

7 It is estimated that one-quarter of the drivers on the road between 11 p.m. and midnight have been drinking during the evening. If a driver has not been drinking, the probability that he or she will have an accident at that time of night is 0.004%; if the driver has been drinking, the probability of an accident goes up to 0.1%. What is the probability that a car selected at random at that time of night will have an accident?

A policeman on patrol at 11.30 p.m. sees a car run into a lamp-post and concludes that the driver has been drinking. What is the probability that he is right? (OCR, adapted)

8 Two events C and D are such that $P(C) = 0.2$, $P(C \mid D) = 0.3$ and $P(C \cup D) = 0.6$. Find

 (a) $P(D)$ (b) $P(D' \mid C')$.

9 My son enjoys skiing on a dry-ski slope. He attempts to carry out two types of turn: a snowplough turn and a parallel turn; he is not always successful. The table below gives the probabilities that he falls as a result of using these turns and also the probabilities that he uses these turns.

Type of turn	Probability	
	Falling	Using
Snowplough	0.1	0.4
Parallel	0.2	0.6

Let S and L be the events that he uses a snowplough and a parallel turn respectively, and let F be the event that he falls.

 (a) Calculate

   (i) $P(S \cap F)$,   (ii) $P(L \cap F)$,   (iii) $P(F)$.

 (b) One day I arrive at the ski slope to collect my son and see that he has fallen. Assuming that he fell while making a turn, calculate the probability that he had been trying to carry out a parallel turn.   (OCR, adapted).

10 Events A and B are such that $P(A) = \frac{1}{2}$, $P(B) = \frac{1}{3}$, $P(A \cup B) = \frac{3}{4}$.

 (a) Determine, giving your reasons, whether A and B are

   (i) mutually exclusive,   (ii) independent.

 (b) Find the values of

   (i) $P(A \mid B)$,   (ii) $P(A \mid B')$.   (OCR, adapted)

11 Three production lines A, B and C produce 25%, 25% and 50% respectively of the output of a factory manufacturing steering-locks for cars. A sample of three articles is selected at random from the total output. Find the probabilities that

 (a) they are all from C,   (b) at least two are from B.

 Of the articles produced by A, B and C, 1%, 2% and 5% respectively are defective. An article is examined and found to be defective.

 (c) What is the probability that it was produced by C?   (OCR, adapted)

12 An experiment is performed with a six-sided dice and two packs of cards. The dice is thrown and if it shows 1, 2, 3 or 4 a card is drawn at random from the first pack, which contains the usual 52 cards; if the score on the dice is 5 or 6 a card is drawn from the second pack, which contains only 39 cards, all the clubs having been removed. X denotes the event 'the first pack with 52 cards is used', and Y denotes the event 'the card drawn is a diamond'. Calculate the probabilities

 (a) $P(X)$,   (b) $P(X \cap Y)$,   (c) $P(Y)$,

 (d) $P(Y \mid X)$,   (e) $P(X \mid Y)$.   (OCR)

13 Three events A, B and C are such that $P(A) = 0.3$, $P(B) = 0.2$, $P(C) = 0.5$ and $P(A \cap B \cap C) = 0$. The events A and B are independent and the events B and C are independent. What is the value of $P(A \cup B \cup C)$ when A and C are

(a) independent,   (b) mutually exclusive?

Find the value of $P(A \mid B \cup C)$ for each of the situations in (a) and (b).

14 A box contains six coins. Two of the coins are fair and each of the other four coins are biased so that the probability of obtaining a 'head' when tossed is $\frac{1}{4}$.

    (a) One coin is selected at random from the box and tossed twice. Given that A_i denotes the event that a 'head' is obtained on the ith toss ($i = 1, 2$):

        (i) show that $P(A_1) = \frac{1}{3}$;

        (ii) calculate $P(A_2)$ and $P(A_1 \cap A_2)$;

        (iii) state, with a reason, whether or not A_1 and A_2 are independent.

    (b) Two coins now are selected at random from the six coins in the box and tossed simultaneously.

        (i) Calculate the probability that one 'head' and one 'tail' are obtained.

        (ii) Given that one 'head' and one 'tail' are obtained, calculate the probability that at least one of the two coins selected was fair.   (OCR)

2 Non-parametric tests

This chapter introduces hypothesis tests which do not assume that the population distribution is of a given type, for example normal. Such tests are called non-parametric tests. When you have completed this chapter you should

- understand what is meant by a non-parametric test, appreciate situations where such tests are useful and be able to select an appropriate test
- understand the basis of the sign test, the Wilcoxon signed-rank test and the Wilcoxon rank-sum test, and be able to use normal approximations, where appropriate, in these tests
- be able to test a hypothesis concerning a population median using a single-sample sign test and a single-sample Wilcoxon signed-rank test
- be able to test for identity of populations using a paired-sample sign test, a Wilcoxon matched-pairs signed-rank test and, for unpaired samples, a Wilcoxon rank-sum test.

This chapter can be tackled between Chapters 3 and 4, or between Chapters 4 and 5.

2.1 The need for non-parametric tests

In S3 Chapters 3 and 4 you met hypothesis tests applicable to small samples which assumed that the populations from which the samples were drawn were distributed normally. These tests were the single-sample t-test, the paired-sample t-test and the two-sample t-test. Such tests are often called **parametric tests**. However, there are often situations in which you want to carry out a hypothesis test on the basis of a small sample but you cannot be certain how the population from which the sample is drawn is distributed. The so-called **non-parametric tests,** or, more descriptively, **distribution-free tests,** were developed in order to cover such situations. This chapter introduces some of these tests for both single-sample and two-sample situations.

Some of these tests are concerned with the median rather than the mean. You should recall from S3 Section 1.3 that the median, by definition, divides the probability distribution for a continuous variable in such a way that the probability of a value chosen at random falling on or below the median and the probability of a value chosen at random falling on or above the median are both equal to $\frac{1}{2}$.

The next section introduces the simplest non-parametric test.

2.2 Sign tests

The data below give the lifetimes, in hours, of a random sample of fuses made by a certain manufacturer.

133   14   60   315   98   44   147   389   106   238   10   80

The manufacturer claims that the fuses it produces have a median lifetime of 200 hours whereas a user suspects that the median is less than this. The appropriate null and alternative hypotheses are H_0: median = 200 and H_1: median < 200 respectively. How can the null hypothesis be tested?

Fig. 2.1 shows these values plotted on a number line.

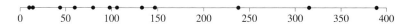

Fig. 2.1. Lifetimes of a random sample of fuses plotted on a number line.

Although the evidence is limited, this diagram suggests that the distribution of the lifetimes is far from symmetrical and so it cannot be normal. Thus a hypothesis test cannot be carried out using a t-test. Consider instead how each value deviates from the proposed median of 200. The deviations are

$$-67 \quad -186 \quad -140 \quad +115 \quad -102 \quad -156 \quad -53 \quad +189 \quad -94 \quad +38 \quad -190 \quad -120.$$

Now consider just the signs of these deviations. These are

$$- \quad - \quad - \quad + \quad - \quad - \quad - \quad + \quad - \quad + \quad - \quad -.$$

There are fewer plus signs (3) than minus signs (9). This is what you might expect if the manufacturer is overestimating the median lifetime, but are there so few + signs that the manufacturer's claim should be rejected?

If the proposed value of 200 for the median is correct, then the probability of a + sign and the probability of a − sign in the list of signs above are both $\frac{1}{2}$. Thus X, the number of + signs, should have a distribution which is $B(12, \frac{1}{2})$. From the cumulative binomial probability tables $P(X \leqslant 3) = 0.0730$. For a test at the 5% significance level this result would not be significant since $0.0730 > 0.05$. Thus at the 5% significance level the null hypothesis that the median is equal to 200 cannot be rejected. The test which has just been carried out is called a **single-sample (binomial) sign test**.

If there had been more + signs than − signs in this example, then there would be no point in performing a significance test since then the fuses last, on average, longer than 200 hours.

The following example illustrates a two-tail sign test.

Example 2.2.1
A machine is designed to produce rods whose median length is 2 cm. After the machine has been moved to a new position in the factory the lengths of the first nine rods produced are measured in order to test whether the setting for the median length has altered. If the lengths, in cm, are 1.89, 1.92, 2.05, 1.88, 1.96, 1.97, 2.01, 1.94, 1.90, test, at the 10% significance level, whether the median setting differs from 2 cm.

Take H_0: median = 2, H_1: median ≠ 2.

The deviations from the hypothesised median of 2 are −0.11, −0.08, +0.05, −0.12, −0.04, −0.03, +0.01, −0.06, −0.10. In this list there are 2 plus signs and 7 minus signs. Under H_0, X, the number of pluses, is $B(9, \frac{1}{2})$. From the cumulative binomial probability tables $P(X \leqslant 2) = 0.0898$. For a two-tail test at the 10% significance level, this probability must be compared with 0.05. Since $0.0898 > 0.05$, the result is not significant at the 5% level and the null hypothesis that the median is still 2 cm is accepted.

Alternatively you could have calculated $P(X \geqslant 7)$ *which, by symmetry, is equal to* 0.0898.

When the data are paired the sign test can be used to test whether the two samples come from identical populations. This version of the test is called the **paired-sample (binomial) sign test**. It provides a non-parametric alternative to the paired-sample t-test. The following example illustrates the method.

Example 2.2.2
The table below shows the times taken by a random sample of people to perform a simple task on their first and second attempts. Test, at the 10% significance level, whether most people take less time on the second attempt than on the first attempt.

Person	A	B	C	D	E	F	G	H
First attempt	6.3	3.5	7.1	3.7	8.4	3.9	4.7	5.2
Second attempt	5.1	3.4	6.2	4.5	7.3	4.0	3.6	5.1

The null and alternative hypotheses are

H_0: the time taken on the second attempt is the same as that on the first attempt;
H_1: the time taken on the second attempt is lower than that on the first attempt.

The differences between the times taken on the first and second attempts are $+1.2$, $+0.1$, $+0.9$, -0.8, $+1.1$, -0.1, $+1.1$, $+0.1$. There are 2 minus and 6 plus signs. Under H_0, X, the number of $-$ signs, is distributed as $B\left(8, \frac{1}{2}\right)$; thus $P(X \leqslant 2) = 0.1445$. The test is one-tail, so 0.1445 is compared with 0.10. Since $0.1445 > 0.10$, this result is not significant at the 10% level and the null hypothesis of no difference in times is accepted.

The data analysed in Example 2.2.2 are the same as the data which were used in S3 Section 4.3 to illustrate the paired t-test. Unlike the paired-sample sign test, the paired t-test gave a significant result and the null hypothesis was rejected. It may seem puzzling that two tests can give different results for the same data. However, you must remember that the assumptions made about the data in order to apply the tests are not the same.

The sign test makes only a very weak assumption about the population distributions, that you can tell whether each piece of data lies above or below the median, so you can be certain that it is valid for the data in Example 2.2.2. However, the sign test has the disadvantage that it only uses a limited amount of the information available from the sample since it considers the sign of the deviations but not their size. As a result the probability of making a Type II error (that is, keeping a false null hypothesis) is high when a sign test is used.

By contrast the paired t-test, which assumes that the deviations are normally distributed, has a lower probability of giving a Type II error. This is the reason why the t-test can give a significant result when the sign test does not. If you can be certain that the t-test is valid, then it is the better test to use.

The paired-sample sign test and the paired t-test are also trying to detect slightly different things. The paired t-test is trying to detect whether the mean difference is greater than zero. Since this test assumes that the differences are distributed normally, this is equivalent to saying that the median difference is greater than zero. The paired-sample sign test is trying to detect only whether the median difference is greater than zero. It says nothing about the mean difference.

By making an assumption about symmetry it is possible to develop a non-parametric test which gives a lower probability of a Type II error than the sign test, and this is described in the next section.

The **sign test** can be used to test

(a) the null hypothesis that a sample comes from a population with a given median (the single-sample sign test);

(b) the null hypothesis that paired data are drawn from the same population (the paired-sample sign test).

The sign test is based on the signs of differences: in case (a) the differences between the observed values and the hypothesised median, in case (b) between the pairs of values.

If there are n differences, the number of $-$ signs and the number of $+$ signs are both distributed as $B\left(n, \frac{1}{2}\right)$ if the null hypothesis is true.

To test for significance the probability, p, of the observed (or a more extreme value) of the observed number of $-$ signs (or alternatively $+$ signs) is calculated assuming that the null hypothesis is true. For a test at the $\alpha\%$ significance level, the null hypothesis is rejected if $100p < \alpha$ for a one-tail test or $100p < \frac{1}{2}\alpha$ for a two-tail test.

The sign test makes no assumptions about the population distribution other than that the data can be said to be either above or below the median.

2.3 The Wilcoxon signed-rank test

The **Wilcoxon signed-rank test** is a non-parametric test which takes into account the sizes of the deviations from the median as well as their signs. It can be used provided that you can assume that the population has a symmetrical (although not necessarily normal) distribution. A consequence of this assumption is that mean and median are equal and so the null hypothesis can refer to either of these parameters.

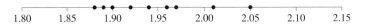

Fig. 2.2. Lengths of nine rods plotted on a number line.

Consider again the data from Example 2.2.1 (1.89, 1.92, 2.05, 1.88, 1.96, 1.97, 2.01, 1.94, 1.90). These values are plotted on a number line in Fig. 2.2. This diagram suggests that you would be justified in assuming that the lengths of the rods are distributed symmetrically, although not necessarily about the value 2. The deviations from the median of 2 are shown in the first line of Table 2.3. The second line of the table shows the deviations without their signs, that is $|\text{deviation}|$. The third line shows the ranks of the values in the second line. The bottom line shows the ranks with the signs of the original values restored. These are the **signed ranks**.

Deviation	−0.11	−0.88	+0.05	−0.12	−0.04	−0.03	+0.01	−0.06	−0.10
$\lvert\text{Deviation}\rvert$	0.11	0.08	0.05	0.12	0.04	0.03	0.01	0.06	0.10
Rank	8	6	4	9	3	2	1	5	7
Signed rank	−8	−6	+4	−9	−3	−2	+1	−5	−7

Table 2.3. Finding signed ranks for the deviations in Example 2.2.1.

Now consider P, the sum of the positive ranks, and Q, the sum of the negative ranks. In this case $P = 5$ and $Q = 40$. If H_0 is correct, then you would expect each rank to be equally likely to be preceded by a + sign or a − sign and so you would expect the values of P and Q to be similar.

In this example the sum of all the ranks is $1 + 2 + 3 + \ldots + 9 = 45$, so if H_0 were true you would expect P and Q to be roughly equal to $\frac{1}{2} \times 45 = 22.5$. In fact, P is considerably less than this and Q is correspondingly greater.

In order to decide whether this imbalance between P and Q is significant, you take as the test statistic the smaller of P and Q. This statistic is given the symbol T; in this example $T = 5$. The rejection region for T can be found from the table on page 273. This gives the *largest* value of T for which H_0 is rejected. For a two-tail test at the 10% significance level with n (sample size) $= 9$, the rejection region is $T \leqslant 8$. Since the calculated value of $T\,(= 5)$ falls in the rejection region, the null hypothesis that the median equals 2 is rejected.

Note that this result is the opposite of that obtained in Example 2.2.1. This is because the Wilcoxon signed-rank test uses aspects of the data which the sign test ignores and is thus a more discriminating test. It gives a lower probability of a Type II error; that is, it is better at detecting a false null hypothesis.

The critical values in the table on page 273 are obtained by considering the sampling distributions of P and Q and hence the sampling distribution of T. To understand how this would work consider the situation in which the sample size is $n = 3$ and hence there are three ranks. If the population is symmetrical, then, under H_0, these ranks are equally likely to be plus or minus.

Table 2.4 shows all 8 possible arrangements of the signed ranks and the resulting values of P, Q and T. Assuming that the null hypothesis is true each arrangement is equally likely.

Signed ranks			P	Q	T
+1	+2	+3	6	0	0
−1	+2	+3	5	1	1
+1	−2	+3	4	2	2
+1	+2	−3	3	3	3
−1	−2	+3	3	3	3
−1	+2	−3	2	4	2
+1	−2	−3	1	5	1
−1	−2	−3	0	6	0

Table 2.4. Possible values of signed ranks for a sample of size $n = 3$.

Table 2.4 shows why there is no entry for $n = 3$ in the table on page 273. For a two-tail test you are interested in an imbalance between P and Q in either direction. In this case the probability that $T = 0$ is $\frac{2}{8} = \frac{1}{4}$. Thus the lowest significance level for which it is possible to give a critical value for a two-tail test is 25%, when the rejection region is $T = 0$.

For a one-tail test you are interested in an imbalance between P and Q in one direction only, say $P > Q$. Thus the lowest significance level for which it is possible to give a critical value for a one-tail test is $\frac{1}{8} = 12.5\%$, when the rejection region is $T = 0$.

Table 2.4 also shows that the distribution of T is discrete. As a consequence the significance levels given in the table on page 273 are only approximate and are not equal to $P(\text{Type I error})$. You met a similar situation in S2 Chapter 7 in connection with significance tests involving the binomial and Poisson distributions.

For values of n greater than 20 the distributions of P and Q (when H_0 is true) are approximately normal with mean $\frac{1}{4}n(n+1)$ and variance $\frac{1}{24}n(n+1)(2n+1)$. Thus the significance of a large value of T can be tested by standardising to give a value of the standard normal variable, Z. Since T is a discrete variable, and it is being approximated by a continuous variable, a continuity correction is required.

Suppose, for example, you obtain $T = 104$ for a sample of size $n = 23$ and wish to carry out a one-tail test at the 5% significance level in a situation where the alternative hypothesis suggests that $P > Q$. Under H_0, P and Q are both distributed normally with

$$\text{mean} = \tfrac{1}{4}n(n+1) = \tfrac{1}{4} \times 23 \times 24 = 138,$$

$$\text{variance} = \tfrac{1}{24}n(n+1)(2n+1) = \tfrac{1}{24} \times 23 \times 24 \times 47 = 1081.$$

You are interested in low values of T which arise because of low values of Q. Using a continuity correction in going from Q to Z,

$$P(T \leqslant 104) = P(Q \leqslant 104) \approx P\left(Z \leqslant \frac{104.5 - 138}{\sqrt{1081}} \right)$$

$$= P(Z \leqslant -1.0189\ldots) = 1 - \Phi(1.019) = 0.1541.$$

For a one-tail test at the 5% level this probability is compared with 0.05. Since $0.1541 > 0.05$ the result is not significant at the 5% level and the null hypothesis would be accepted. Alternatively you can calculate the value of Z and see whether it lies in the rejection region, which is $Z \leqslant -1.645$ for a one-tail test at the 5% significance level.

For a two-tail test at the 5% level the probability which is calculated would be compared with 0.025. Alternatively you can see whether the value of Z lies in the rejection region, which is $|Z| \geqslant 1.96$ for a two-tail test at the 5% significance level.

When the data are paired the Wilcoxon signed-rank test can be used to test whether two samples come from identical populations. This test is called the **Wilcoxon matched-pairs signed-rank test**, or **paired-sample signed-rank test**. It does not require any assumptions to be made about the shape of the population distributions, but it is necessary for the distribution of the differences between matched pairs to be symmetrical. Unlike the paired t-test, however, it does not require that the distribution of the differences between matched pairs is normal.

It can be shown that, under H_0, *the distribution of the differences between the matched pairs will be symmetrical, whatever the shape of the common population distribution.*

Example 2.3.1
Ten people enrolled on a new slimming course for six months. Their weights in kilograms before and after the course are shown in the table below.

Person	1	2	3	4	5	6	7	8	9	10
Before	75.4	78.1	79.7	70.3	72.0	74.1	78.5	74.9	70.3	72.9
After	70.9	71.3	69.5	73.2	72.1	72.0	71.6	73.1	70.8	71.6

Test at the 5% level whether the course is effective.

The differences between the initial and final weights (in kilograms) are given below with their signed ranks beneath them.

Difference	4.5	6.8	10.2	–2.9	–0.1	2.1	6.9	1.8	–0.5	1.3
Signed rank	7	8	10	–6	–1	5	9	4	–2	3

The null and alternative hypotheses are

H_0: median difference $= 0$;
H_1: median difference < 0.

The sum of the positive ranks is $P = 46$, and the sum of the negative ranks is $Q = 9$. Thus the test statistic, T, takes the value 9. In this case the test is a one-tail test. For $n = 10$, the rejection region for a test at the 5% level is $T \leqslant 10$ (from page 273). Since the calculated value of T lies in the rejection region H_0 is rejected. There is evidence at the 5% significance level that the course is effective.

Note that in this example, if H_0 is false, you would expect the sum of the negative ranks to be low and the sum of the positive ranks to be high. If the reverse had been the case and the results gave a higher value for Q than for P, then the course would obviously not be having the desired effect and a formal hypothesis test would not be appropriate.

In carrying out the tests described in Sections 2.2 and 2.3 it is possible that a difference of zero could have been obtained. Although zero can be ranked, it does not have a sign and so such values are ignored in carrying out these tests.

The **Wilcoxon signed-rank test** can be used to test

(a) the null hypothesis that a sample comes from a population with a given median (the single-sample signed-rank test);

(b) the null hypothesis that paired data are drawn from the same population (the matched-pairs signed-rank test).

The steps in a signed-rank test are:

Step 1 Calculate differences: in case (a) between the observed values and the hypothesised median, in case (b) between the pairs of values.

Step 2 Ignoring the signs of the differences, assign ranks to the differences in order of increasing size.

Step 3 Give each rank the same sign as the original value.

Step 4 Find P, the sum of the positive ranks, and Q, the sum of the negative ranks.

Step 5 Take the smaller of P and Q as the test statistic, T.

Step 6 For small samples find the rejection region from the table on page 273 and reject H_0 if the calculated value of T lies in the rejection region.

For large samples calculate $Z = \dfrac{T + 0.5 - \frac{1}{4}n(n+1)}{\sqrt{\frac{1}{24}n(n+1)(2n+1)}}$, where n is the number of differences.

For a one-tail test at the $100\alpha\%$ significance level the rejection region is $Z \leqslant -z$ where $\Phi(z) = 1 - \alpha$.

For a two-tail test at the $100\alpha\%$ significance level the rejection region is $Z \leqslant -z$ where $\Phi(z) = 1 - \frac{1}{2}\alpha$.

The signed-rank test assumes: in case (a) that the population distribution is symmetrical, in case (b) that the differences have a symmetrical distribution.

Exercise 2A

1   In the past I have found that the median time for my journey to work is 50 minutes. I have decided to try a new route and the times taken (in minutes) for my first 10 journeys are

     43, 41, 39, 108, 52, 42, 38, 45, 39, 51.

   (a)   Plot these values on a number line.

   (b)   Use an appropriate non-parametric test, at the 5% significance level, to test whether the median journey time by the new route is different from 50 minutes. Justify your choice of test.

2   A sign test is used to test the null hypothesis $M = 100$ against the alternative hypothesis $M \neq 100$, where M is the population median. Out of 5 random observations of the variable, only 1 was less than 100 and the rest were greater than 100. Carry out the test, using a 20% significance level.   (OCR)

3   A national survey of 17-year-old school and college students showed that the median number of hours spent in paid employment in a particular week in September 1995 was 3.5. A teacher in a sixth form college did a survey of a random sample of 10 students and this showed that the hours that they had worked in that week were, to the nearest half hour,

     4   7.5   21   0   9   5.5   6   6.5   10   2.5.

Use a sign test, at the 5% significance level, to test whether the median number of hours worked by students in this college was different from the national median.

                                                          (OCR, adapted)

4   A single-sample sign test is used to test the null hypothesis $M = 10$ against the alternative hypothesis $M > 10$, where M is the population median. A random sample of eight observations is taken. It is decided that the null hypothesis will be rejected if six or more of these observations are greater than 10. Given that $M = 10$, find the probability that the null hypothesis is rejected.   (OCR)

5   The numbers of male residents and female residents in eleven randomly selected villages are shown in the table below.

Village	A	B	C	D	E	F	G	H	I	J	K
Male	196	169	335	220	298	215	461	250	370	355	382
Female	220	171	361	248	300	237	434	325	451	345	401

Use a binomial sign test to determine the validity of the hypothesis that there are more female than male residents in villages. Make clear your hypotheses and conduct the test at the 5% significance level.   (OCR, adapted)

6   As part of a paired-sample Wilcoxon signed-rank test, the differences in the paired data were given the signed ranks below. The (+) or (–) beside each rank indicates whether the difference was positive or negative.

     1(–)   2(–)   3(+)   4(–)   5(+)   6(+)   7(+)   8(+)   9(+)   10(+)

Test whether there is a difference in the population medians, using a two-tail test at the 5% significance level.   (OCR)

7 A random sample of times, in hours, for cars driving from Perth to Melbourne is given.

    63.6   55.2   54.1   68.1   52.3   47.1   125.9 60.8   61.4

Assuming that the distribution of times is symmetrical, carry out a single-sample Wilcoxon signed-rank test to test the null hypothesis that the median time for this journey is 55 hours against the alternative hypothesis that the median time for this journey is greater than 55 hours. Use a 5% significance level.

Give a reason why a t-test for the mean journey time may not be appropriate. (OCR)

8 When a Wilcoxon signed-rank test is carried out on a sample of size 30, the value obtained for T is 154. Test whether this result is significant at the 5% level for a one-tail test.

9 A research team has developed a drug which they believe helps older people to retrieve information from their memory. They test this on a group consisting of nine pairs of twins by asking the twins a long series of questions requiring them to remember information from their childhood. One twin from each pair has taken the recommended dose of the drug and the other has not taken the drug. The number of correct answers given by each twin is given below.

Pair of twins	A	B	C	D	E	F	G	H	I
Twin taking drug	94	138	66	142	137	90	123	154	141
Twin not taking drug	83	121	75	157	118	92	105	134	127

Carry out an appropriate Wilcoxon test, at the 5% significance level, to determine whether the drug has improved the ability to recall information. State any assumption that is necessary to justify the use of the test. (OCR)

10 A sociologist is interested in comparing the ages of husbands and wives. He collected the data below, which show the ages for the husband and wife in a randomly chosen sample of nine couples.

Couple	A	B	C	D	E	F	G	H	I
Husband's age (years)	79	39	55	71	37	39	48	63	54
Wife's age (years)	70	36	49	54	38	32	49	52	56

Use these data to test the hypothesis that most men are older than their wives using

(a) a sign test,

(b) a Wilcoxon signed-rank test.

Carry out your tests at the 5% significance level.

(c) What assumptions, if any, are required for each of these tests?

(d) Explain how it is possible for the two tests to give different results.

11 Find the sampling distribution of the Wilcoxon signed-rank statistic, T, for a sample of size 4. What is the significance level for a two-tail test with a rejection region of $T \leqslant 1$?

12 (a) Show that for a sample of size 5 the significance level for a one-tail test with a rejection region of $T \leqslant 2$ is $\dfrac{3}{2^5}$.

(b) What is the significance level for a two-tail test, sample size 6, rejection region $T \leqslant 2$?

(c) What is the significance level for a one-tail test, sample size 8, rejection region $T \leqslant 5$?

2.4 The Wilcoxon rank-sum test

This section introduces a non-parametric alternative to the two-sample t-test for two independent samples. The two-sample t-test tests whether two samples come from populations with the same mean. It requires that the populations are normal with equal variances.

The **Wilcoxon rank-sum test** (or an equivalent test known as the **Mann-Whitney** U **test**) tests whether two samples come from populations with identical distributions and does not require any assumptions about the two populations.

The test works by investigating whether two populations satisfy a condition necessary for them to have identical distributions. Given two populations with identical distributions, if X is a random measurement from the first population and Y is a random measurement from the second population, then $P(X < Y) = \frac{1}{2}$. Therefore, if measurements X and Y from two populations are such that $P(X < Y) \neq \frac{1}{2}$, the populations cannot be distributed identically. The Wilcoxon rank-sum test provides a test of whether measurements from the first population are likely to be higher (or lower) than measurements from the second population.

Consider the following situation.

Each week I visit my local supermarket on either Friday or Saturday at the same time of day but I am not sure which is the better day to shop. I suspect that the time taken is likely to be less on a Friday and I decide to collect data to test this hypothesis. The first line of data below gives the times on four Saturdays and the second row gives the times on three Fridays, to the nearest minute.

Saturday	74	58	61	50
Friday	38	56	60	

Is there any evidence from these data that shopping on Friday is likely to take less time than shopping on Saturday? Appropriate null and alternative hypotheses are respectively

H_0: shopping time has the same distribution on Fridays and Saturdays;
H_1: shopping is likely to take less time on Friday than on Saturday.

The values are listed below in order of increasing size with their ranks underneath them. The letter S or F in the third row indicates whether the value refers to a Saturday or a Friday respectively.

Value	38	50	56	58	60	61	74
Rank	1	2	3	4	5	6	7
Day	F	S	F	S	F	S	S

If shopping on Friday takes less time than shopping on Saturday, then you would expect low ranks in the table above to be associated with the letter F. The sum of the ranks for the F values, $\sum r_F$, is $1 + 3 + 5 = 9$. The highest possible value for $\sum r_F$ is $5 + 6 + 7 = 18$ and the lowest possible value is $1 + 2 + 3 = 6$. The average of these two extremes is 12, so the observed value of $\sum r_F = 9$ is on the low side, suggesting that shopping on Friday may take less time than shopping on Saturday.

If $\sum r_F$ had been on the high side, then there would be no reason to proceed further since the data could not provide evidence that shopping on Friday is quicker than shopping on Saturday.

In order to decide whether the value of $\sum r_F$ is significantly low you need to find the value of $P\left(\sum r_F \leqslant 9\right)$ under the assumption that shopping on the two days takes the same time. Under such an assumption all possible arrangements of Ss and Fs are equally likely. There are $\binom{7}{3} = \binom{7}{4} = 35$ such arrangements. The arrangements in which $\sum r_F \leqslant 9$ are shown below.

1	2	3	4	5	6	7	$\sum r_F$
F	F	F	S	S	S	S	6
F	F	S	F	S	S	S	7
F	S	F	F	S	S	S	8
S	F	F	F	S	S	S	9
F	F	S	S	F	S	S	8
F	S	F	S	F	S	S	9
F	F	S	S	S	F	S	6

There are 7 such arrangements, so $P\left(\sum r_F \leqslant 9\right) = \frac{7}{35} = 0.2$. This result is not significant at, say, the 5% level and so the null hypothesis that the distributions of shopping times are the same on Saturday and Friday would be accepted in this case.

Listing all the possible arrangements would become tedious for larger samples, so you will be pleased to know that you can obtain critical values from the table on page 274. An explanation of how to use the table is given at the top of that page. It is helpful to work through this explanation using the shopping example.

The sizes of the samples are denoted by m and n, where $m \leq n$; so for the shopping example $m = 3$ (Friday) and $n = 4$ (Saturday). The sum of the ranks of the sample of size m is denoted by R_m, so $R_m = 1 + 3 + 5 = 9$. You also need to calculate

$$m(n + m + 1) - R_m = 3(4 + 3 + 1) - 9 = 15.$$

The statistic W is the smaller of the two values 9 and 15, in this case 9.

The quantity $m(n + m + 1) - R_m$ is the rank sum which would have been obtained for the sample of size m if the values had been ranked starting from the largest value rather than the smallest value, as was done above. Taking W to be the smaller of this quantity and R_m ensures that W does not depend on the direction in which you rank the values.

The table on page 274 gives the *largest* value of W which leads to rejection of the null hypothesis. For a one-tail test at the 5% significance level with $m = 3$ and $n = 4$ this is 6, so the rejection region is $W \leq 6$. Since 9 does not lie in the rejection region the null hypothesis is not rejected. This is the same as the result which was obtained by calculating the probability that $\sum r_F \leq 9$.

The following example illustrates a two-tail test.

Example 2.4.1
Two different types of nylon fibre were tested for the amount of stretching under tension. Ten random samples of each fibre, of the same length and diameter, were stretched by applying a standard load. For fibre 1 the increases in length, x mm, were as follows.

> 12.84 14.26 13.23 14.75 15.13 14.15 13.37 12.96 15.02 14.38

For fibre 2 the increases in length, y mm, were as follows.

> 14.27 13.25 14.17 13.11 14.92 12.12 14.21 13.68 15.14 14.81

Test whether the distribution of the increase in length differs for the two types of fibre. Use a 10% significance level.   (OCR, adapted)

A two-tail test is appropriate. The null and alternative hypotheses are

> H_0: the increases in length for the two types of fibre have the same distribution;
> H_1: the increases in length for the two types of fibre have different distributions.

All 20 values are listed below in order of ascending size, together with their ranks. Values for fibre 1 are underlined.

12.12	12.84	12.96	13.11	13.23	13.25	13.37	13.68	14.15	14.17
1	2	3	4	5	6	7	8	9	10
14.21	14.26	14.27	14.38	14.75	14.81	14.92	15.02	15.13	15.14
11	12	13	14	15	16	17	18	19	20

The sums of the ranks for fibre 1 and fibre 2 are 104 and 106 respectively. (It is worth checking that the sum of these values is equal to $1 + 2 + \ldots + 20$.) In this case the sample sizes are equal; that is, $m = n = 10$. The sum of the ranks for the fibre 1 sample is 104, so $R_m = 104$ and $m(n + m + 1) - R_m = 10(10 + 10 + 1) - 104 = 106$. The latter is just the sum of the ranks for the fibre 2 sample, a result which is obtained because the samples have the same size. Thus the test statistic is $W = 104$. For a two-tail test at the 10% significance level with $m = n = 10$ the rejection region is $W \leqslant 82$. Since the observed value of W (= 104) does not lie in the rejection region the null hypothesis that the samples come from identical populations is accepted.

The data in Example 2.4.1 were analysed in S3 Example 4.2.2 using a two-sample t-test for difference between population means. The result of the two-sample t-test was the same; that is, the null hypothesis was accepted. The assumptions which were made in order to carry out the two-sample t-test were that the populations are normally distributed with equal variance. Thus accepting the null hypothesis for this test is equivalent to saying that the samples come from identical populations. If the two-sample t-test is valid, then its probability of a Type II error is lower than that of the Wilcoxon rank-sum test because of the assumptions made about the population distributions in the two-sample t-test. However, the difference is not great and so the Wilcoxon rank-sum test is a useful alternative to the two-sample t-test when you cannot be sure that the conditions for the latter to be valid are met.

For values of m and n greater than 10, the Wilcoxon rank-sum test can be performed using the fact that R_m and $m(n + m + 1) - R_m$ are distributed approximately normally with mean $\frac{1}{2} m(n + m + 1)$ and variance $\frac{1}{12} mn(m + n + 1)$. As for the Wilcoxon signed-rank test, a continuity correction should be applied since a discrete distribution is being approximated by a continuous one.

Suppose, for example, you obtain $W = R_m = 106$ with $m = 12$ and $n = 15$ and wish to carry out a one-tail test at the 1% significance level, where the alternative hypothesis suggests low values of R_m. Under a null hypothesis of identical distributions R_m is distributed normally with

mean $= \frac{1}{2} m(n + m + 1) = \frac{1}{2} \times 12 \times (12 + 15 + 1) = 168$,

variance $= \frac{1}{12} mn(m + n + 1) = \frac{1}{12} \times 12 \times 15(12 + 15 + 1) = 420$.

Using a continuity correction in going from R_m to Z,

$$P(W \leqslant 106) = P(R_m \leqslant 106) \approx P\left(Z \leqslant \frac{106.5 - 168}{\sqrt{420}} \right)$$

$$= P(Z \leqslant -3.000\ldots) = 0.0014.$$

Since $0.0014 < 0.01$ the result is significant and the null hypothesis is rejected.

For a two-tail test you would calculate the probability that W is less than the observed value and then compare this probability with half of the significance level.

In the tests described in Sections 2.3 and 2.4 it is possible for two values to have the same rank. The method then has to be modified, but the modification will not be described here.

The **Wilcoxon rank-sum test** can be used to test the null hypothesis that two samples come from identical populations. The sample sizes are denoted by m and n where $m \leqslant n$.

The steps in carrying out the test are:

Step 1 Rank all the values from both samples in order of increasing size.

Step 2 Find R_m, the sum of the ranks of the items in the sample of size m.

Step 3 Take W as the test statistic, where W is the smaller of R_m and $m(n+m+1) - R_m$.

Step 4 For small samples, find the rejection region from the table on page 274 and reject the null hypothesis if the calculated value of W lies in the rejection region.

For large samples, calculate $Z = \dfrac{W + 0.5 - \frac{1}{2}m(m+n+1)}{\sqrt{\frac{1}{12}mn(m+n+1)}}$.

For a one-tail test at the $100\alpha\%$ significance level the rejection region is $Z \leqslant -z$ where $\Phi(z) = 1 - \alpha$.

For a two-tail test at the $100\alpha\%$ significance level the rejection region is $Z \leqslant -z$ where $\Phi(z) = 1 - \frac{1}{2}\alpha$.

The Wilcoxon rank-sum test for identity of distributions makes no assumptions about the population distributions other than that the data are quantitative.

Exercise 2B

1   The lengths of the femur, in mm, in samples of the mouse *Mus homonunculus* from two sources (Britain and North Africa) are given in the table below.

Britain	12.3	12.7	13.1	10.8	11.3	11.8	12.4	13.2
North Africa	10.6	9.8	11.5	10.0	11.1			

The mean length of the femur is known to be characteristic of each breed of *Mus homonunculus*. Use a non-parametric test at the 5% significance level to test whether the data are consistent with the assumption that *Mus homonunculus* in Britain and North Africa are of the same breed.   (OCR, adapted)

2   Find the sampling distribution of the Wilcoxon rank-sum statistic, W, under the null hypothesis that both samples come from the same distribution for the case $n = 3$, $m = 3$.

3 In a class of 24 Year 6 children, there were 12 girls and 12 boys. The children decided to raise money for the premature baby unit of the local hospital. Each child in the class was sponsored to stay silent. The length of time each succeeded in being silent was recorded. The mathematics coordinator at the school decided to investigate whether boys keep silent longer than girls. After the sponsored silence he examined the data. He decided to use a non-parametric test and ranked the data giving the longest time the rank 1. He found that the sum of the ranks for the times of the boys was 95.

(a) What was the sum of the ranks of the times of the girls?

(b) Carry out a Wilcoxon rank-sum test, or a Mann-Whitney U test, at the 2% level of significance and indicate clearly the inference the teacher may feel justified in making. (OCR)

4 Eleven randomly selected primary school children are weighed. The results, in kg, are shown in the table below.

Girls	43.7	34.4	53.1	38.3	48.5	48.9
Boys	41.4	36.6	34.6	32.5	32.4	

(a) Code B or G as appropriate, and rank the weights, giving weight 32.4 rank 1.

(b) How many different arrangements are there of six Gs and five Bs?

(c) Write down the sum of the ranks of the weights of the boys.

(d) Tables of Wilcoxon's rank-sum statistic indicate that, when $m = 5$, $n = 6$, 'the critical value, at the 5% one-tail level, is 20'. Explain briefly, what you understand by this statement.

(e) Test, at the 1% level, whether the data support the view that, on average, primary school girls have greater weights than primary school boys. (OCR)

5 (a) Calculate the number of distinct possible arrangements of five Ms and eight Fs.

One possible arrangement is shown below.

M	M	F	F	F	M	F	F	M	F	F	F	M
1	2	3	4	5	6	7	8	9	10	11	12	13

In this arrangement, the position of each letter is recorded by noting its rank. The sum, $\sum r_M$, of the ranks of the five Ms is found for each possible arrangement. Assume that each arrangement is equally likely.

(b) Calculate the probability that $\sum r_M \leqslant 17$.

The distance in miles that each of five mothers and eight fathers of primary school children succeeded in running during a sponsored event are shown below.

Mother	4.7	7.6	7.4	4.3	7.0			
Father	6.6	9.8	7.2	8.2	8.0	8.1	7.8	7.7

(c) Use an appropriate test to determine whether there is sufficient evidence at the 5% level of significance to support the hypothesis that, on average, fathers run further than mothers on sponsored events. (OCR, adapted)

6　The table on page 274 gives the rejection region for W for $m = n = 4$ for a one-tail test at the $2\frac{1}{2}\%$ significance level as $W \leqslant 10$. Confirm this by showing that $P(W \leqslant 10) < 0.025$ and $P(W \leqslant 11) > 0.025$ where W is the sum of the ranks for the sample of size m.

7　When a Wilcoxon rank-sum test was carried out the value of the test statistic was $W = 126$ with $m = 13$ and $n = 14$. Is this result significant at the 1% level for a two-tail test?

Miscellaneous exercise 2

1　In a single-sample sign test, the null hypothesis is that the population median is 27.5. A random sample of 10 readings is taken from the population. Assuming that the null hypothesis is true, find the probability that the number of readings greater than 27.5 is 9 or 10. (You may assume that none of the readings is exactly 27.5.)　　(OCR)

2　Describe *briefly* the difference between the procedures for carrying out a single-sample sign test and a single-sample Wilcoxon signed-rank test.

Give one advantage that each test has over the other.

Say why, in a particular situation, you might choose to use one of these non-parametric tests rather than a single-sample t-test.　　(OCR)

3　A bus is timetabled to arrive at 15 35. Its actual arrival time is noted on 10 randomly chosen occasions and the numbers of minutes late or early are recorded, correct to the nearest half-minute. In the table below, positive entries indicate the number of minutes late and negative entries indicate the number of minutes early.

　　0.5　3.0　2.5　–1.0　–3.5　4.0　10.0　5.0　–2.0　7.5

Assuming that the distribution of arrival times is symmetrical, carry out a single-sample Wilcoxon signed-rank test at the 5% significance level to test the claim that the bus is late more often than not.　　(OCR)

4　The publicity accompanying the launch of a new television series claims that children will become more interested in mathematics as a result of watching the programmes. A teacher assessed the level of mathematical interest shown by a group of 13 children before the first programme was broadcast, and again after the children had watched it. The level of interest was measured as the proportion of lesson time for which a child was actively engaged in mathematical activity. The results, expressed as percentages, are shown in the table below.

Child	A	B	C	D	E	F	G	H	I	J	K	L	M
Before	29.1	36.3	33.6	6.0	10.8	23.2	19.6	21.2	8.1	16.8	44.0	44.0	24.4
After	30.4	40.8	38.0	5.2	12.0	25.2	21.2	8.8	4.8	19.6	45.2	48.4	27.6

(a)　Carry out a Wilcoxon signed-rank test at the 5% level of significance to determine whether these data uphold the claim of the publicity.

(b)　What assumption is made in carrying out the test in (a)? Do you think that this assumption is justified in this example?

(c)　An alternative test procedure uses the binomial sign test. Carry out this procedure at the same level of significance.　　(OCR, adapted)

5 A psychologist measured the times taken by a random sample of 12 people to react to a stimulus. The results, in milliseconds, are given below.

  390 395 595 455 580 803 468 588 590 410 683 700

The psychologist believes that the population reaction time used to be 510 milliseconds, and now suspects that it has changed. Tabulate the differences between the reaction times and 510 milliseconds. Assuming that the population of reaction times has a symmetrical distribution, carry out a single-sample Wilcoxon signed-rank test to test the psychologist's suspicion. Use a 5% significance level and give full details of your method.

A *t*-test is to be used with these data to test a null hypothesis concerning the *mean* reaction time of the population against a suitable alternative hypothesis. State a condition required of the population for this *t*-test to be valid. (OCR)

6 Two 400 m runners, Ann and Betty, record the times of their first six races of the season with the following results:

Ann (seconds)	56.2	53.6	56.2	56.8	52.8	57.5
Betty (seconds)	57.2	55.2	59.7	56.5	55.9	58.0

You are asked to investigate whether or not these data indicate that one of these runners is faster than the other over 400 m.

(a) State suitable null and alternative hypotheses.

(b) Calculate W for these data.

(c) Use tables to find the range of values of W for which the null hypothesis should be accepted, using a 5% significance level.

(d) State your conclusion in the context of the problem. (OCR, adapted)

7 A wine producer wishes to test the effect of adding preservative to his wine. A random sample of seven people independently taste the wine with and without preservative and give, in each case, a score on a scale of 1 to 10, 10 being the best. It may be assumed that they do not know whether or not the wine they are tasting contains preservative. The scores given are summarised below.

Person	A	B	C	D	E	F	G
With preservative	4	5	6	3	10	9	5
Without preservative	7	6	8	4	9	10	8

(a) Use a paired-sample sign test to test, at the 10% significance level, the assertion that wine without preservative tastes better than wine with preservative.

(b) State what assumption would have to be made to apply a paired-sample *t*-test to these data. Comment on the reasonableness of this assumption. (OCR)

8 Ten people enrol on a revolutionary slimming course for a week. Their weights (kg), before and after the course, are shown below.

Person	1	2	3	4	5	6	7	8	9	10
Before	75.2	82.6	66.2	70.8	86.9	78.6	94.9	82.0	69.6	88.8
After	74.3	83.7	64.9	68.2	84.6	80.3	92.8	80.5	68.8	89.0

(a) Investigate, at the 5% significance level, whether or not the course is effective using

    (i) a Wilcoxon signed-rank test,   (ii) an appropriate t-test.

(b) State, with a reason, which you regard as the better test for these data.

(OCR, adapted)

9 Following a change in management of a hotel, a random sample of 12 people who stayed in the hotel completed a customer satisfaction questionnaire in which they rated the hotel facilities on a scale of 1 to 10. Of the 12 people, 10 gave a rating greater than 8 and 2 gave a rating less than 8. Before the change in management the median rating for the hotel facilities was 8. Use a sign test to test, at the 10% significance level, the claim that the median rating has increased, giving full details of your method. (OCR)

10 In order to compare the effectiveness of two mail delivery services, A and B, two samples of 12 identical deliveries were arranged. The number of hours taken for each delivery was recorded, to the nearest $\frac{1}{2}$ hour, with the following results.

Delivery	1	2	3	4	5	6	7	8	9	10	11	12
Service A	26.0	21.0	35.0	24.5	26.0	31.0	28.5	18.5	25.0	27.5	15.5	29.5
Service B	26.5	20.0	27.0	27.0	24.5	34.0	33.5	20.5	28.5	32.0	19.5	37.0

(a) It is required to test, at the 5% significance level, whether the data indicate that, on average, service A takes a shorter time for its deliveries than service B.

    (i) Without assuming that the data are samples taken from normal distributions, perform a suitable test, clearly stating your hypotheses.

    (ii) Assuming the data are samples taken from normal distributions, perform a more appropriate test.

(b) Service A claims that its average delivery time is 24 hours. Use a non-parametric test, at the 10% significance level, to test this claim against the alternative hypothesis that the average delivery time exceeds 24 hours. (OCR)

11 (a) (i) Calculate the number of distinct possible arrangements of 4 *F*s and 6 *M*s.

(ii) An arrangement of 4 *F*s and 6 *M*s is listed from left to right and the letters are assigned ranks 1 to 10 by numbering from the left. The total, T_F, of the ranks assigned to the four *F*s is recorded. List all the arrangements for which $T_F \leqslant 11$.

A class of 10 students, 6 male and 4 female, measured their reaction time in seconds. The results are shown below.

Gender	*M*	*M*	*M*	*M*	*M*	*M*	*F*	*F*	*F*	*F*
Time	5.7	3.2	5.3	7.7	4.8	13.5	2.2	4.3	2.1	2.7

(b) (i) Rank the reaction times shown in the table above in ascending order, and find the total of the ranks assigned to female students.

(ii) Use the Wilcoxon rank-sum statistic to test, at the 5% level, whether there is significant evidence that the median reaction time for females is less than the median reaction time for males.

(c) Use a sign test to test the null hypothesis that the median reaction time is 10 seconds against the alternative that it is less than 10 seconds. Conduct your test at the 5% level. (OCR)

12 In order to investigate the difference in wear on front and rear tyres, 6 motorcycles, each initially with new tyres, were ridden for 1000 miles under controlled conditions. After this time, the depth of tread on each tyre was measured and recorded. The results are shown in the table below.

Motorcycle	*A*	*B*	*C*	*D*	*E*	*F*	*G*	*H*
Depth of tread on front tyre (mm)	4.5	3.9	3.9	4.5	4.1	4.2	4.0	3.8
Depth or tread on rear tyre (mm)	4.0	3.1	4.0	3.3	3.9	3.5	4.4	2.8

(a) Test the assertion, at the 10% significance level, that there is no difference in wear for front and rear tyres, using

(i) a paired-sample sign test,   (ii) a paired-sample Wilcoxon signed-rank test.

(b) Give two reasons why the test used in part (ii) is generally preferred to the test used in part (i). (OCR, adapted)

13 A sports retail company decides to test two different makes of golf club (club A and club B) to determine which club strikes a golf ball farther. It is claimed that club A strikes the golf ball greater distances than club B.

Ten golfers used club A to hit a golf ball and 10 different golfers used club B. The distances are recorded in the table below.

| Distance using club A (yards) | 178 | 210 | 165 | 183 | 197 | 182 | 190 | 116 | 151 | 99 |
| Distance using club B (yards) | 158 | 196 | 181 | 173 | 179 | 105 | 147 | 96 | 163 | 207 |

(a) Use a Wilcoxon rank-sum statistic to test whether there is significant evidence, at the 5% level, that club A achieves greater distances than club B. Give the value 96 a rank of 1.

It is discovered subsequently that only 10 golfers were used altogether and that the two entries in each column represent the distances that each golfer achieved using club A and club B. (In each case a fair coin was spun and if it was heads club A was used first, otherwise club B was first.)

(b) Use a binomial sign test to determine whether there is significant evidence that club A strikes the ball farther. State your hypotheses clearly and conduct the test at the 5% level. (OCR)

14 (a) Find the number of distinct arrangements of six Ns and six Ss.

(b) One arrangement is as follows.

N	N	N	N	S	S	N	N	S	S	S	S
1	2	3	4	5	6	7	8	9	10	11	12

In this arrangement the position of each letter is recorded by noting its rank. The sum, $\sum r_N$, of the ranks of the six Ns is calculated for each of the possible arrangements. Calculate the probability that $\sum r_N \leqslant 24$.

(c) Tables of the Wilcoxon rank-sum statistic for $m = 6$ and $n = 6$ indicate that '26 is the critical value at $2\frac{1}{2}$ % level of significance for a one-tail test'. Explain briefly what you understand by the quoted statement.

(d) Twelve people (six smokers and six non-smokers) are randomly selected and have their body temperature measured five minutes after undergoing the same physical exercise. The results are shown below.

| Smokers | 98.4 | 98.7 | 98.8 | 98.9 | 99.2 | 99.3 |
| Non-smokers | 97.9 | 98.1 | 98.2 | 98.5 | 98.6 | 99.0 |

Carry out a Wilcoxon rank-sum test to determine if there is sufficient evidence at the $2\frac{1}{2}$ % level to support the hypothesis that, after exercise, the body temperature of smokers is higher than that of non-smokers. (OCR, adapted)

15 A P.E. teacher wants to determine whether the daytime temperature has any effect on the distances that her students can throw a discus. She selects 10 of her students at random and asks them to throw a discus on two separate days. On the first day, day 1, the temperature was 14 °C and on the second day, day 2, it was 20 °C. The results are given in the table below.

Student no.	1	2	3	4	5	6	7	8	9	10
Day 1	22.1	18.3	20.2	19.3	14.2	38.6	36.7	23.2	35.3	18.3
Day 2	28.3	20.4	21.7	19.7	14.0	40.2	43.1	33.2	40.2	17.5

(a) Explain why the Wilcoxon rank-sum test would not be appropriate in this situation.

(b) Use the Wilcoxon signed-rank test to determine whether the data suggest that the temperature has any effect on the distance thrown. Conduct your test at the 5% level and make your conclusions clear.

(c) Give one suggestion as to how the design of the experiment could be improved.

(OCR, adapted)

3 Probability generating functions

This chapter introduces the concept of a probability generating function. When you have completed it you should be able to

- understand the concept of a probability generating function and construct and use the probability generating function for given distributions (including the discrete uniform, binomial, geometric and Poisson)
- use formulae for the mean and variance of a discrete random variable in terms of its probability generating function, and to use these formulae to calculate the mean and variance of probability distributions
- use the result that the probability generating function of the sum of independent variables is the product of the individual probability generating functions of those variables.

3.1 Defining a probability generating function

In certain cases it is convenient to summarise the values, x_i, taken by a discrete random variable, X, and the probabilities, p_i, associated with these values by a function known as the **probability generating function,** often abbreviated as p.g.f. This function, denoted by $G_X(t)$, involves an arbitrary variable t. $G_X(t)$ is defined as

$$G_X(t) = p_1 t^{x_1} + p_2 t^{x_2} + \ldots = \sum p_i \, t^{x_i} . \qquad (3.1)$$

$G_X(t)$ only exists if this series converges.

You saw in P4 that issues of convergence always arise in dealing with infinite series. In this chapter and the next, certain operations on series, such as rearrangement and term-by-term differentiation, are only justified when the series satisfies, often quite strict, convergence conditions. For the purpose of this Statistics module, although you should realise when your solutions depend on assumptions about convergence, you do not need to worry about the details. You can assume that, unless stated otherwise, all the necessary conditions hold.

Consider the probability generating function for a simple distribution. If X is the throw on a fair dice, then X takes the values 1, 2, 3, 4, 5 and 6, each with probability $\frac{1}{6}$. So in this case

$$G_X(t) = \tfrac{1}{6}t^1 + \tfrac{1}{6}t^2 + \tfrac{1}{6}t^3 + \tfrac{1}{6}t^4 + \tfrac{1}{6}t^5 + \tfrac{1}{6}t^6 .$$

At first sight this does not appear to be a very useful definition, especially since t does not have any obvious meaning. However, you will see in the course of this chapter that it provides a powerful tool for finding the mean and variance of certain probability distributions and also for finding the probability distribution of a sum of independent random variables.

Look again at the definition of $G_X(t)$ in Equation 3.1. You can see that $G_X(t)$ is constructed by multiplying each value of t^X by the associated probability and then summing. Thus $G_X(t)$ is the expected value of t^X; that is,

$$G_X(t) = E(t^X). \qquad (3.2)$$

Substituting $t = 1$ into Equation 3.2 gives

$$G_X(1) = E(1^X) = E(1) = 1.$$

You can see why this must be so by looking back to Equation 3.1. If you substitute $t = 1$ into this equation, you have

$$G_X(1) = p_1 1^{x_1} + p_2 1^{x_2} + \ldots = p_1 + p_2 + \ldots = \sum p_i.$$

Thus $G_X(1)$ is the sum of the probabilities and for a probability distribution this is equal to 1, that is

$$G_X(1) = \sum p_i = 1. \qquad (3.3)$$

Example 3.1.1

(a) The discrete random variable X is the number of throws taken to throw the first six with a fair dice. Find the probability generating function, $G_X(t)$, of X and verify that $G_X(1) = 1$.

(b) Generalise these results to the situation in which the probability of throwing a six is p.

(a) X has a geometric distribution for which

$$P(X = x) = \left(\tfrac{1}{6}\right) \times \left(\tfrac{5}{6}\right)^{x-1} \text{ for } x = 1, 2, 3, \ldots .$$

Thus $G_X(t) = \left(\tfrac{1}{6}\right)t^1 + \left(\tfrac{1}{6}\right) \times \left(\tfrac{5}{6}\right)t^2 + \left(\tfrac{1}{6}\right) \times \left(\tfrac{5}{6}\right)^2 t^3 + \ldots .$

This is an infinite geometric series (see P2 Section 10.3) with first term $\tfrac{1}{6}t$ and common ratio $\tfrac{5}{6}t$. Provided that $\left|\tfrac{5}{6}t\right| < 1$, the series can be summed, giving the probability generating function

$$G_X(t) = \frac{\tfrac{1}{6}t}{1 - \tfrac{5}{6}t} = \frac{t}{6 - 5t}.$$

Substituting $t = 1$ gives $G_X(1) = \dfrac{1}{6 - 5} = 1$.

The value $t = 1$ can be substituted into the expression for $G_X(t)$ since, for this value of t, $\left|\tfrac{5}{6}t\right| = \tfrac{5}{6}$, which is less than 1.

(b) Now $P(X = x) = p \times q^{x-1}$ where $q = 1 - p$.

Thus $G_X(t) = pt^1 + pqt^2 + pq^2 t^3 + \ldots .$

By rewriting this series for $G_X(t)$ in the form

$$G_X(t) = (pt) + (pt)(qt) + (pt)(qt)^2 + \ldots$$

you can see that it is an infinite geometric series with first term pt and common ratio qt. Provided that $|qt| < 1$, the series can be summed, giving

$$G_X(t) = \frac{pt}{1 - qt} = \frac{pt}{1 - (1 - p)t}.$$

Substituting $t = 1$ gives $G_X(1) = \dfrac{p}{1 - (1 - p)} = 1.$

The value $t = 1$ can be substituted since, for this value of t, $|qt| = q < 1$.

Example 3.1.2
X is a discrete random variable taking the values 0, 1, 2, 3, ... The probability generating function of X is given by

$$G_X(t) = \frac{k}{(5 - 2t)^3},$$

where k is a constant.

(a) Show that $k = 27$.
(b) Find $P(X = 2)$.

(a) Since $G_X(1) = 1$, it follows that $\dfrac{k}{(5 - 2)^3} = 1$. Thus $k = 3^3 = 27$.

(b) The required probability is found by first expressing $G_X(t)$ as a series. Recall the binomial expansion

$$(1 + x)^n = 1 + \frac{n}{1}x + \frac{n(n-1)}{1 \times 2}x^2 + \frac{n(n-1)(n-2)}{1 \times 2 \times 3}x^3 + \ldots \text{ (see P3 Section 6.1).}$$

Applying this expansion,

$$G_X(t) = \frac{k}{(5 - 2t)^3} = 27(5 - 2t)^{-3} = \tfrac{27}{125}\left(1 - \tfrac{2}{5}t\right)^{-3}$$

$$= \tfrac{27}{125}\left(1 + (-3) \times \left(-\tfrac{2}{5}t\right) + \frac{(-3) \times (-4)}{1 \times 2}\left(-\tfrac{2}{5}t\right)^2 + \ldots\right).$$

The value of $P(X = 2)$ is given by the coefficient of t^2. So

$$P(X = 2) = \tfrac{27}{125} \times \frac{(-3) \times (-4)}{1 \times 2} \times \left(\tfrac{2}{5}\right)^2 = 0.207\,36.$$

Example 3.1.3

The probability generating function of the discrete random variable X is

$$G_X(t) = k\left(\sqrt{t} + \frac{1}{\sqrt{t}}\right)^4.$$

(a) Find the value of k.

(b) Find the probability distribution of X.

(a) Since $G_X(1) = 1$, it follows that $k\left(\sqrt{1} + \frac{1}{\sqrt{1}}\right)^4 = 16k = 1$. So $k = \frac{1}{16}$.

(b) The probability distribution of X is found by expanding $G_X(t)$ as a power series in t:

$$G_X(t) = \frac{1}{16}\left(\sqrt{t} + \frac{1}{\sqrt{t}}\right)^4$$

$$= \frac{1}{16}\left((\sqrt{t})^4 + 4(\sqrt{t})^3\left(\frac{1}{\sqrt{t}}\right) + 6(\sqrt{t})^2\left(\frac{1}{\sqrt{t}}\right)^2 + 4(\sqrt{t})\left(\frac{1}{\sqrt{t}}\right)^3 + \left(\frac{1}{\sqrt{t}}\right)^4\right)$$

$$= \frac{1}{16}\left(t^2 + 4t + 6 + 4t^{-1} + t^{-2}\right) = \frac{1}{16}t^{-2} + \frac{1}{4}t^{-1} + \frac{3}{8}t^0 + \frac{1}{4}t^1 + \frac{1}{16}t^2.$$

The powers of t in this series give the values taken by X and the coefficients of the terms give the corresponding probabilities. Thus the probability distribution of X is

x	-2	-1	0	1	2
$P(X = x)$	$\frac{1}{16}$	$\frac{1}{4}$	$\frac{3}{8}$	$\frac{1}{4}$	$\frac{1}{16}$

Here is a summary of the results of this section.

> The probability generating function of a
> discrete random variable, X, is defined by
>
> $$G_X(t) = p_1 t^{x_1} + p_2 t^{x_2} + \ldots = E(t^X),$$
>
> provided that this series converges.
>
> $G_X(t)$ has the property that $G_X(1) = 1$.

Exercise 3A

1 A discrete random variable, X, is the throw on a fair six-sided dice; that is, $P(X = x) = \frac{1}{6}$ for $x = 1, 2, 3, 4, 5, 6$. Show that the probability generating function of X can be expressed as $G_X(t) = \dfrac{t(1 - t^6)}{6(1 - t)}$ provided that $t \neq 1$.

2 A discrete random variable, X, has probability generating function $G_X(t) = \dfrac{k}{(2-t)^2}$. Find

(a) the value of k,   (b) $P(X=3)$,   (c) $P(X=x)$.

3 A discrete random variable, X, has probability generating function $G_X(t) = \dfrac{p^2}{\left(1-(1-p)t\right)^2}$
for $x = 0, 1, 2, \ldots$.

(a) Show that $G_X(1) = 1$.

(b) Express $G_X(t)$ as a power series in t and hence show that

   (i) $P(X=3) = 4p^2(1-p)^3$,   (ii) $P(X=x) = (x+1)p^2(1-p)^x$.

4 The discrete random variable X is such that $X \sim \text{Po}(3)$. Show that the probability
generating function of X is $G_X(t) = e^{3(t-1)}$. (Use the Maclaurin expansion for e^x, which is
$e^x = 1 + x + \dfrac{x^2}{2!} + \dfrac{x^3}{3!} + \ldots$ (see P4 Section 7.3).)

5 The discrete random variable X is such that $X \sim \text{B}\left(5, \frac{1}{3}\right)$. Find the probability generating
function of X.

6 Given that the discrete random variable X has probability generating function
$G_X(t) = p_1 t^{x_1} + p_2 t^{x_2} + \ldots$, write down expressions for $G_X(1)$ and $G_X(-1)$ in terms of
$p_1,\ p_2,\ \ldots$. Hence show that the probability that X takes an even value is given by
$\frac{1}{2}\left(1 + G_X(-1)\right)$.

If $X \sim \text{Po}(3)$, use this result to find the probability that X takes an even value. (See
Question 4 for the probability generating function of X.)

3.2 Finding the mean and variance of a discrete random variable

In S1 and S2 you met formulae for the mean and variance of a number of discrete
probability distributions, such as the binomial, geometric and Poisson distributions.
These formulae were stated but not proved. With the aid of the appropriate probability
generating function the proofs of these formulae are relatively straightforward.

The first step is to obtain general results relating the mean and variance of a random
variable, X, to its probability generating function, $G_X(t)$.

Consider the definition of $G_X(t)$,

$$G_X(t) = p_1 t^{x_1} + p_2 t^{x_2} + \ldots .$$

Now differentiate with respect to t. This gives

$$G_X'(t) = p_1 x_1 t^{x_1-1} + p_2 x_2 t^{x_2-1} + \ldots . \qquad (3.4)$$

Such term-by-term differentiation of a series is not always a valid procedure.

Substituting $t=1$ gives

$$G_X'(1) = p_1 x_1 1^{x_1-1} + p_2 x_2 1^{x_2-1} + \ldots .$$

So $\quad G_X'(1) = p_1x_1 + p_2x_2 + \ldots = E(X)$ $\qquad$ (assuming that this series converges).

Thus in order to find the expected value of a random variable it is only necessary to differentiate the probability generating function with respect to t and substitute $t = 1$.

Example 3.2.1

Find the expectation of a random variable, X, such that $X \sim \text{Geo}(p)$.

The probability generating function of a geometric distribution was found in Example 3.1.1. It is

$$G_X(t) = \frac{pt}{1-qt}, \qquad \text{provided that} \qquad |qt| < 1.$$

Differentiating with respect to t gives

$$G_X'(t) = \frac{p(1-qt) - (-q) \times pt}{(1-qt)^2} = \frac{p}{(1-qt)^2}.$$

As $q = 1 - p$ must be less than 1, $|qt|$ will be less than 1 when $t = 1$. Therefore $t = 1$ can be substituted into this expression for $G_X'(t)$.

Thus $E(X) = G_X'(1) = \dfrac{p}{(1-q)^2} = \dfrac{p}{p^2} = \dfrac{1}{p}$.

This is a result which you used without proof in S1.

A similar method can be used to find a variance from a probability generating function. Consider Equation 3.4,

$$G_X'(t) = p_1x_1t^{x_1-1} + p_2x_2t^{x_2-1} + \ldots.$$

Differentiating again with respect to t gives

$$G_X''(t) = p_1x_1(x_1-1)t^{x_1-2} + p_2x_2(x_2-1)t^{x_2-2} + \ldots,$$

and substituting $t = 1$ gives

$$G_X''(1) = p_1x_1(x_1-1) + p_2x_2(x_2-1) + \ldots,$$

or, opening the brackets,

$$\begin{aligned} G_X''(1) &= p_1(x_1^2 - x_1) + p_2(x_2^2 - x_2) + \ldots \\ &= (p_1x_1^2 + p_2x_2^2 + \ldots) - (p_1x_1 + p_2x_2 + \ldots) \\ &= \sum p_i x_i^2 - E(X). \end{aligned}$$

So $\quad G_X''(1) = \sum p_i x_i^2 - E(X).$ $\qquad$ (3.5)

Algebraic manipulations on a series, like those above, are only legitimate if the series meets certain convergence conditions.

Now $\text{Var}(X) = \sum p_i x_i^2 - (\text{E}(X))^2$

$$= (G_X''(1) + \text{E}(X)) - (\text{E}(X))^2 \qquad \text{(using Equation 3.5)}$$

$$= G_X''(1) + G_X'(1) - (G_X'(1))^2.$$

Example 3.2.2
Find the variance of a random variable, X, such that $X \sim \text{Geo}(p)$.

From Example 3.2.1,

$$G_X'(t) = \frac{p}{(1-qt)^2} \qquad \text{and} \qquad G_X'(1) = \frac{1}{p}.$$

Differentiating $G_X'(t)$ with respect to t gives $G_X''(t) = \frac{2qp}{(1-qt)^3}$.

So $\quad G_X''(1) = \frac{2qp}{(1-q)^3} = \frac{2qp}{p^3} = \frac{2q}{p^2}.$

Then

$$\text{Var}(X) = G_X''(1) + G_X'(1) - (G_X'(1))^2$$

$$= \frac{2q}{p^2} + \frac{1}{p} - \left(\frac{1}{p}\right)^2 = \frac{2q + p - 1}{p^2} = \frac{2q - q}{p^2}$$

$$= \frac{q}{p^2} = \frac{1-p}{p^2}.$$

The mean and variance of a discrete random variable, X, with probability generating function $G_X(t)$ are given by

$$\text{E}(X) = G_X'(1), \text{ and}$$

$$\text{Var}(X) = G_X''(1) + G_X'(1) - (G_X'(1))^2.$$

Example 3.2.3
Find the probability generating function of the random variable X where $X \sim \text{Po}(\lambda)$. Hence find the mean and variance of X.

The Poisson probabilities are given by $P(X = x) = e^{-\lambda} \dfrac{\lambda^x}{x!}$ for $x = 0, 1, 2, \ldots$.

$$G_X(t) = p_1 t^{x_1} + p_2 t^{x_2} + \ldots + p_n t^{x_n} + \ldots$$

$$= e^{-\lambda}\lambda^0 t^0 + e^{-\lambda}\frac{\lambda}{1!}t^1 + e^{-\lambda}\frac{\lambda^2}{2!}t^2 + \ldots + e^{-\lambda}\frac{\lambda^n}{n!}t^n + \ldots$$

$$= e^{-\lambda}\left(1 + \frac{\lambda t}{1!} + \frac{\lambda^2 t^2}{2!} + \ldots + \frac{\lambda^n t^n}{n!} + \ldots\right).$$

The terms in the bracket give the Maclaurin expansion for $e^{\lambda t}$ (see P4 Section 7.3), so

$$G_X(t) = e^{-\lambda}e^{\lambda t} = e^{\lambda(t-1)}$$

for a Poisson distribution with parameter λ.

In order to find the mean and variance you need to calculate $G'_X(1)$ and $G''_X(1)$.

$$G'_X(t) = \lambda e^{\lambda(t-1)}, \quad \text{so} \quad G'_X(1) = \lambda.$$

$$G''_X(t) = \lambda^2 e^{\lambda(t-1)}, \quad \text{so} \quad G''_X(1) = \lambda^2.$$

Thus $E(X) = G'_X(1) = \lambda$, and

$$\text{Var}(X) = G''_X(1) + G'_X(1) - (G'_X(1))^2 = \lambda^2 + \lambda - \lambda^2 = \lambda.$$

You met this result for the variance in S2 Section 3.3, but it was not proved there.

Example 3.2.4

Find the probability generating function for the random variable X where $X \sim B(n, p)$, and hence find the mean and variance of X.

The binomial probabilities are given by $P(X = x) = \binom{n}{x}p^x q^{n-x}$,

for $x = 0, 1, 2, \ldots, n$, where $q = 1 - p$.

$$G_X(t) = p_1 t^{x_1} + p_2 t^{x_2} + \ldots + p_r t^{x_r} + \ldots + p_n t^{x_n}$$

$$= \binom{n}{0}p^0 q^n t^0 + \binom{n}{1}p^1 q^{n-1}t^1 + \ldots + \binom{n}{r}p^r q^{n-r}t^r + \ldots + \binom{n}{n}p^n q^0 t^n$$

$$= \binom{n}{0}(pt)^0 q^n + \binom{n}{1}(pt)^1 q^{n-1} + \ldots + \binom{n}{r}(pt)^r q^{n-r} + \ldots + \binom{n}{n}(pt)^n q^0.$$

But this series is just the binomial series for $(pt + q)^n$, so

$$G_X(t) = (pt + q)^n.$$

Now find the mean and variance of X.

Since $G'_X(t) = np(pt + q)^{n-1}$ and $G''_X(t) = n(n-1)p^2(pt + q)^{n-2}$, putting $t = 1$ and recalling that $p + q = 1$ gives

$$G'_X(1) = np(p+q)^{n-1} = np \quad \text{and} \quad G''_X(1) = n(n-1)p^2(p+q)^{n-1} = n(n-1)p^2.$$

So $E(X) = G'_X(1) = np$, and

$$\text{Var}(X) = G''_X(1) + G'_X(1) - (G'_X(1))^2$$

$$= n(n-1)p^2 + np - n^2 p^2 = n^2 p^2 - np^2 + np - n^2 p^2$$

$$= np - np^2 = np(1-p) = npq.$$

Again these are results which you have met before without proof, this time in S1 Section 8.3.

Example 3.2.5

Write down the probability generating function of the discrete random variable X for which $P(X = x) = \frac{1}{5}$ for $x = 1, 2, 3, 4, 5$. Hence find the mean and variance of X.

The probability generating function is

$$G_X(t) = p_1 t^{x_1} + p_2 t^{x_2} + \ldots + p_n t^{x_n}$$
$$= \tfrac{1}{5}t^1 + \tfrac{1}{5}t^2 + \tfrac{1}{5}t^3 + \tfrac{1}{5}t^4 + \tfrac{1}{5}t^5.$$

This is a geometric series which can be summed to give $\dfrac{t}{5}\left(\dfrac{1-t^5}{1-t}\right)$. However, this result is only valid if $t \neq 1$. Since $t = 1$ is just the value which is needed to find the mean and variance from the probability generating function it is not appropriate to use this summation here. Instead the mean and variance must be calculated using the original form of the probability generating function.

The original function is differentiated to give

$$G_X'(t) = \tfrac{1}{5} + \tfrac{2}{5}t + \tfrac{3}{5}t^2 + \tfrac{4}{5}t^3 + t^4,$$

and $\quad G_X''(t) = \tfrac{2}{5} + \tfrac{6}{5}t + \tfrac{12}{5}t^2 + 4t^3$.

Substituting $t = 1$ now gives $G_X'(1) = 3$ and $G_X''(1) = 8$.

So $\quad E(X) = G_X'(1) = 3,\quad$ and

$$\mathrm{Var}(X) = G_X''(1) + G_X'(1) - \left(G_X'(1)\right)^2 = 8 + 3 - 3^2 = 2.$$

The method used in Example 3.2.5 to find $E(X)$ and $\mathrm{Var}(X)$ from the probability generating function is not particularly elegant because the summed form of the probability generating function cannot be used as it was for the geometric, Poisson and binomial distributions.

Exercise 3B

1 A discrete random variable, X, has the probability distribution given below. Write down the probability generating function of X and use this probability generating function to find the mean and variance of X.

x	1	2	3
$P(X = x)$	0.1	0.3	0.6

2 A discrete random variable, X, has probability generating function $G_X(t) = \dfrac{27}{(5 - 2t)^3}$. Find the mean and variance of X.

3 A discrete random variable, X, has probability generating function $G_X(t) = \dfrac{p^2}{\left(1 - (1 - p)t\right)^2}$ for $x = 0, 1, 2, \ldots$. Show that $E(X) = \dfrac{2(1 - p)}{p}$ and $\mathrm{Var}(X) = \dfrac{2(1 - p)}{p^2}$.

4 A discrete random variable, X, has probability generating function $G_X(t) = k\,e^{t+t^2}$. Find

(a) the value of k,   (b) $E(X)$,   (c) $\text{Var}(X)$.

5 A random variable, Y, taking values 0, 1, 2, ... has probability distribution given by

$$P(Y = n) = ka^{-n}, \quad \text{where } a > 1.$$

Show that $k = 1 - \dfrac{1}{a}$, and that the probability generating function of Y may be written in

the form $G(t) = \dfrac{a-1}{a-t}$. Deduce the mean and variance of the distribution.   (OCR)

3.3 The probability generating function of the sum of random variables

The probability generating function has the following useful property.

> The probability generating function of the *sum* of
> independent random variables is equal to the *product*
> of their individual probability generating functions.

You can see why this is so by considering the product of two probability generating functions for two independent random variables X and Y,

$$G_X(t)\,G_Y(t) = \left(p_{x1}t^{x_1} + p_{x2}t^{x_2} + \ldots + p_{xn}t^{x_n} + \ldots\right)\left(p_{y1}t^{y_1} + p_{y2}t^{y_2} + \ldots + p_{yn}t^{y_n} + \ldots\right),$$

where the probability generating functions have been written in series form with $p_{xi} = P(X = x_i)$ and $p_{yi} = P(Y = y_i)$.

Consider the term in t^r in the expansion of this product.

Its coefficient will be the sum of terms like $p_{xi}p_{yj}$ such that $x_i + y_j = r$.

This coefficient is just what you would calculate if you wanted to find $P(X + Y = r)$.

For each pair of values x_i and y_j such that $x_i + y_j = r$ you would multiply the corresponding probabilities to obtain $p_{xi}p_{yj}$ (since X and Y are independent) and then sum these products (since the different pairs are mutually exclusive).

Thus the coefficient of t^r gives $P(X + Y = r)$, so the product of the probability generating functions must be the probability generating function of $X + Y$. This argument can be extended to more than two variables.

The same result can be arrived at more succinctly by using expectation notation. If two variables X and Y are independent, then $E(X)E(Y) = E(XY)$. (This result is proved in Section 6.7.) So $G_X(t)G_Y(t) = E\!\left(t^X\right)E\!\left(t^Y\right) = E\!\left(t^X t^Y\right) = E\!\left(t^{X+Y}\right) = G_{X+Y}(t)$.

This property of probability generating functions gives a powerful method for finding the probability distribution of the sum of independent random variables. In particular it provides a means of proving the results $E(X+Y) = E(X) + E(Y)$ and $\text{Var}(X+Y) = \text{Var}(X) + \text{Var}(Y)$ for independent discrete random variables. These results were used without proof in S3 Chapter 2.

Theorem $E(X+Y) = E(X) + E(Y)$

    Proof   Let $V = X + Y$.

    Then $G_V(t) = G_X(t)G_Y(t)$,   and $G_V'(t) = G_X'(t)G_Y(t) + G_Y'(t)G_X(t)$.

    So $E(V) = G_V'(1) = G_X'(1)G_Y(1) + G_Y'(1)G_X(1)$.

    Recall from Equation 3.3 that $G_X(1) = G_Y(1) = 1$, and substitute these values into the expression for $E(V)$. Then

$$E(V) = G_X'(1) + G_Y'(1) = E(X) + E(Y),$$

    so $E(X+Y) = E(X) + E(Y)$.

Theorem $\text{Var}(X+Y) = \text{Var}(X) + \text{Var}(Y)$

    Proof   By differentiating $G_V'(t) = G_X'(t)G_Y(t) + G_Y'(t)G_X(t)$ again,

$$G_V''(t) = G_X''(t)G_Y(t) + 2G_X'(t)G_Y'(t) + G_Y''(t)G_X(t).$$

    Evaluating $G_V''(t)$ at $t = 1$ gives

$$G_V''(1) = G_X''(1)G_Y(1) + 2G_X'(1)G_Y'(1) + G_Y''(1)G_X(1)$$
$$= G_X''(1) + 2G_X'(1)G_Y'(1) + G_Y''(1).$$

    Then

$$\text{Var}(V) = G_V''(1) + G_V'(1) - \left(G_V'(1)\right)^2$$
$$= \left(G_X''(1) + 2G_X'(1)G_Y'(1) + G_Y''(1)\right) + \left(G_X'(1) + G_Y'(1)\right) - \left(G_X'(1) + G_Y'(1)\right)^2$$
$$= G_X''(1) + 2G_X'(1)G_Y'(1) + G_Y''(1) + G_X'(1) + G_Y'(1)$$
$$- \left(G_X'(1)\right)^2 - 2G_X'(1)G_Y'(1) - \left(G_Y'(1)\right)^2$$
$$= G_X''(1) + G_X'(1) - \left(G_X'(1)\right)^2 + G_Y''(1) + G_Y'(1) - \left(G_Y'(1)\right)^2$$
$$= \text{Var}(X) + \text{Var}(Y),$$

    so $\text{Var}(X+Y) = \text{Var}(X) + \text{Var}(Y)$.

Recall from S3 Section 2.2 that the result $E(X+Y) = E(X) + E(Y)$ is also true for random variables which are not independent, but this result cannot be proved by the method above.

The following example shows how the probability distribution of a sum of random variables can be deduced from the product of the probability generating functions.

Example 3.3.1

Find the probability generating function for the sum, S, of three throws on a fair dice. Hence find $P(S = s)$ for $s = 3, 4, 5$ and 6.

Let X be the result of one throw of the dice. Then X has a uniform distribution with $P(X = x) = \frac{1}{6}$ for $x = 1, 2, 3, 4, 5, 6$.

The probability generating function of X is $G_X(t) = \frac{1}{6}t^1 + \frac{1}{6}t^2 + \ldots + \frac{1}{6}t^6$.

This is a geometric series with first term $\frac{1}{6}t$ and common ratio t. Provided that $t \neq 1$ its sum is given by $\dfrac{t}{6}\dfrac{\left(1 - t^6\right)}{(1 - t)}$.

The summed form of the probability generating function can be used in this example since it will not be necessary to put $t = 1$.

For S, the sum of three throws on the dice, the probability generating function is found by multiplying the probability generating functions for the individual throws, so

$$G_S(t) = \frac{t}{6}\frac{\left(1 - t^6\right)}{(1 - t)} \times \frac{t}{6}\frac{\left(1 - t^6\right)}{(1 - t)} \times \frac{t}{6}\frac{\left(1 - t^6\right)}{(1 - t)} = \frac{1}{216}t^3\frac{\left(1 - t^6\right)^3}{(1 - t)^3}$$

$$= \frac{1}{216}t^3\left(1 - 3t^6 + 3t^{12} - t^{18}\right)\left(1 + 3t + 6t^2 + 10t^3 + \ldots\right)$$

$$= \frac{1}{216}\left(t^3 + 3t^4 + 6t^5 + 10t^6 + \ldots\right).$$

The required probabilities are found from the coefficients of the corresponding powers of t. For example, $P(S = 3)$ is given by the power of t^3. So

$$P(S = 3) = \frac{1}{216}, \ P(S = 4) = \frac{3}{216} = \frac{1}{72}, \ P(S = 5) = \frac{6}{216} = \frac{1}{36}, \ P(S = 6) = \frac{10}{216} = \frac{5}{108}.$$

If two variables have the same distribution, then they also have the same probability generating function. The reverse is also true. If two variables have the same probability generating function, then they also have the same distribution.

Example 3.3.2

Two random variables X and Y are such that $X \sim B\left(5, \frac{1}{3}\right)$ and $Y \sim B\left(10, \frac{1}{3}\right)$.

(a) Write down the probability generating functions of X, Y, and $X + Y$.

(b) Deduce the distribution of $X + Y$.

(a) From Example 3.2.4, the probability generating function of a random variable which is distributed as $B(n, p)$ is $(pt + q)^n$.

Thus the probability generating function of X is $\left(\frac{1}{3}t + \frac{2}{3}\right)^5$ and the probability generating function of Y is $\left(\frac{1}{3}t + \frac{2}{3}\right)^{10}$.

The probability generating function of $X + Y$ is given by the product of these probability generating functions and is thus equal to $\left(\frac{1}{3}t + \frac{2}{3}\right)^5\left(\frac{1}{3}t + \frac{2}{3}\right)^{10} = \left(\frac{1}{3}t + \frac{2}{3}\right)^{15}$.

(b) $X + Y$ has the probability generating function of a variable which has a $B\left(15, \frac{1}{3}\right)$ distribution. Thus $X + Y \sim B\left(15, \frac{1}{3}\right)$.

Example 3.3.3*
Show that the probability generating function of X where $X \sim B(n, p)$ tends to $e^{\lambda(t-1)}$, where λ is constant and equal to np, as n tends to infinity. Deduce the distribution of X as n tends to infinity.

The probability generating function of X is $G_X(t) = (pt + q)^n = (1 + p(t-1))^n$.

Substituting $p = \dfrac{\lambda}{n}$ gives $G_X(t) = \left(1 + \dfrac{\lambda(t-1)}{n}\right)^n$.

Using the result that $\left(1 + \dfrac{x}{n}\right)^n$ tends to e^x as x tends to infinity, you can see that $G_X(t)$ tends to $e^{\lambda(t-1)}$ as n tends to infinity.

But this is the probability generating function of a random variable which has a $\text{Po}(\lambda)$ distribution. Thus the distribution of X tends to the distribution $\text{Po}(\lambda)$, where λ is constant and equal to np, as n tends to infinity.

Exercise 3C

1   A spinning top has five edges numbered $-2, -1, 0, 1, 2$. Show that the probability generating function for the score, X, when the top is spun once can be written $G_X(t) = \frac{1}{5}t^{-2}(1 - t^5)(1 - t)^{-1}$. Hence show that the probability of getting a total score of zero when the top is spun three times is $\frac{19}{125}$.

2   A multiple choice paper consists of 30 questions, each with five possible answers. A candidate is awarded 4 marks for a correct answer but 1 mark is deducted for an incorrect answer. The random variable X is the total number of marks obtained by a candidate who is guessing. Show that the probability generating function of X is $\left(\dfrac{4 + t^5}{5t}\right)^{30}$.

3   In a board game, a player throws a fair six-sided dice repeatedly until a six has been obtained twice. The random variable Y represents the total number of throws up to and including the occurrence of the second six. Find the probability generating function of Y. Hence, or otherwise, find $P(Y = 3)$ and $P(Y = 5)$.   (OCR, adapted)

4   A laboratory reagent kit contains two compounds, A and B, which deteriorate with time at different rates. After one year the probability that A has become useless is 0.2 and the probability that B has become useless is 0.1. A box contains 10 bottles of reagent A and 10 bottles of reagent B. The random variable X represents the total number of useless bottles of reagent in a randomly chosen one-year-old box.

   (a) Find the probability generating function of X, assuming that the bottles of reagent deteriorate independently of each other.

   (b) Use your probability generating function to find $E(X)$.

5 (a) Write down the probability generating function for a Poisson distribution with mean $\lambda_X + \lambda_Y$.

   (b) Two independent random variables, X and Y, are such that $X \sim \text{Po}(\lambda_X)$ and $Y \sim \text{Po}(\lambda_Y)$. Write down the probability generating functions of X and Y and hence find the probability generating function of Z, where $Z = X + Y$.

   (c) Compare your answers to (a) and (b). What can you deduce about the distribution of the sum of two independent Poisson variables? (OCR, adapted)

   (Question 5 gives a result which you met without proof in S3 Section 2.5.)

6 (a) A simple experiment has two outcomes, 'success', which occurs with probability p, and 'failure', which occurs with probability $1 - p$. Given that X_1 is the random variable which gives the number of successes (0 or 1) in this experiment, write down the probability generating function of X_1.

   (b) In a binomial distribution, the random variable X represents the number of successes in n independent trials, and p is the probability of success in each trial. It is given that X can be expressed as the sum $X_1 + X_2 + \ldots + X_n$, where X_r is the number of successes in the rth trial for $r = 1, 2, \ldots, n$. Use part (a) to show that the probability generating function of a binomial distribution with parameters n and p is given by $G_X(t) = ((1 - p) + pt)^n$. (OCR, adapted)

   (Question 6 gives an alternative, and quicker, method to that of Example 3.2.4 for arriving at the probability generating function of $X \sim \text{B}(n, p)$.)

Miscellaneous exercise 3

1 A discrete random variable, X, has the probability distribution given in the following table.

x	1	2	3	4
$P(X = x)$	$\frac{1}{2}$	$\frac{1}{4}$	$\frac{1}{6}$	$\frac{1}{12}$

   (a) Write down the probability generating function of X.

   (b) Use this probability generating function to find the mean and variance of X. (OCR)

2 The probability generating function of the random variable X is $k\left(t + \dfrac{2}{t^2}\right)^3$, where k is a constant.

   (a) Find the value of k.

   (b) Find the probability distribution of X.

   (c) Calculate $E(X)$ and $\text{Var}(X)$.

   Repeated observations of X are taken and Y is the first non-zero value obtained. Find the probability generating function of Y. (OCR)

3 The discrete random variable W has probability generating function given by $G(z) = k(3z^{-2} + 1 + 5z^4)$, where k is a constant. Find

   (a) the value of k,   (b) $P(W = -2)$,

   (c) the modal value of W,   (d) the variance of W. (OCR)

4   The random variable X has a binomial distribution with parameters $n = 6$ and $p = \frac{1}{2}$.
Show that the probability generating function of X is $\frac{1}{64}(1+t)^6$.

Use the generating function to find the mean and variance of X.

The discrete random variable Y, which is independent of X, has the same mean as X and

has probability generating function $\dfrac{t}{a - bt}$. Find the value of each of the constants a and

b, and show that Y has a geometric distribution.

Calculate $P(X + Y = 3)$.   (OCR)

5   In each round of a quiz a contestant can answer up to 3 questions. Each correct answer
scores 1 point and allows the contestant to go on to the next question. A wrong answer
scores nothing and the contestant is allowed no further question in that round once a wrong
answer is given. If all three questions are answered correctly a bonus point of 1 is scored,
making a total score of 4 for the round. For a certain contestant, A, the probability of
giving a correct answer to any question in the round is $\frac{2}{3}$. The random variable X_r is the
number of points scored by A during the rth round. Write down the probability
generating function of X_r and find the mean and variance of X_r.

Write down an expression for the probability generating function of $X_1 + X_2$ and find the
probability that A has a total score of 4 at the end of 2 rounds.   (OCR)

6   The discrete random variable X has probability distribution given by

$$P(X = r) = \frac{k}{r!}, \qquad r = 0, 1, 2, \ldots,$$

where k is a constant.

(a) Find the value of k.

(b) Find the probability generating function of X and hence or otherwise obtain the mean
and variance of X.

(c) $X_1, X_2, \ldots, X_n$ are n independent observations of X, and $Y = \sum_{i=1}^{n} X_i$. Write down the
probability generating function of Y and use it to show that

$$P(Y = r) = \frac{e^{-n}n^r}{r!}, \qquad r = 0, 1, 2, \ldots.$$

Identify the distribution of Y.

In the case $n = 2$, find $P(Y = 3 \mid Y > 0)$, giving your answer correct to 3 decimal places.
                                                                                      (OCR)

7   As part of an advertising campaign, each packet of a new breakfast cereal contains a plastic
model of one of three different dinosaurs. Each packet is equally likely to contain any one
of the three dinosaurs. Jamie opens his first packet of cereal and collects his first dinosaur.
Given that U is the number of extra packets that Jamie opens, up to and including the first

one that contains a different dinosaur, explain why $G_U(t) = \dfrac{\frac{2}{3}t}{1 - \frac{1}{3}t}$.

Once two different dinosaurs have been obtained, V is the number of extra packets
required to get the remaining dinosaur. Find an expression for $G_W(t)$, where $W = U + V$.

Hence find $P(T = 5)$, where T is the total number of cereal packets that Jamie will open in
order to collect all three dinosaurs.   (OCR, adapted)

8 The number of defects is recorded for each digital television which passes through the service department of a store. The number of defects, X, is a random variable which is Poisson distributed with mean λ. However, digital televisions for which $X = 0$ do not pass through the service department and so the observed distribution is a Poisson distribution with $X = 0$ missing; that is, $P(X = x) = \dfrac{k\lambda^x e^{-\lambda}}{x!}$ for $x = 1, 2, 3, \dots$, where λ and k are constants and $\lambda > 0$.

(a) Show that the probability generating function of X is $ke^{-\lambda}\left(e^{\lambda t} - 1\right)$.

(b) Hence show that

(i) $k = \dfrac{e^\lambda}{e^\lambda - 1}$,   (ii) $E(X) = \dfrac{\lambda e^\lambda}{e^\lambda - 1}$,   (iii) $Var(X) = \dfrac{\lambda e^\lambda}{e^\lambda - 1} - \dfrac{\lambda^2 e^\lambda}{\left(e^\lambda - 1\right)^2}$.

9 If $P(X = x) = \alpha\theta^x$ for $x = 0, 1, 2, \dots$, show that $G_X(t) = \dfrac{\alpha}{1 - t\theta}$ and hence show that

(a) $\alpha = 1 - \theta$,   (b) $E(X) = \dfrac{\theta}{1 - \theta}$,   (c) $Var(X) = \dfrac{\theta}{(1 - \theta)^2}$.

10 The discrete random variable X has probability generating function
$G_X(t) = p_1 t^{x_1} + p_2 t^{x_2} + \dots$. Find an expression, in terms of $G_X(-1)$, for the probability that X takes an odd value.

In a game of chance, when a lever is pulled, one of the numbers 1, 2, 3 appears in a window. The lever is pulled 5 times and the total score is recorded. If the probabilities associated with the numbers 1, 2, 3 are $\frac{1}{6}, \frac{1}{3}, \frac{1}{2}$ respectively, write down an expression for the probability generating function for the total score. Hence, or otherwise, find the probability that the total score is odd.   (OCR, adapted)

11* A discrete random variable, X, has probability generating function $G_X(t)$. If the discrete random variable Y is defined by $Y = aX + b$, show that the probability generating function $G_Y(t)$ of Y is related to $G_X(t)$ by $G_Y(t) = t^b G_X\left(t^a\right)$.

Hence prove that $E(Y) = aE(X) + b$ and $Var(Y) = a^2 Var(X)$.

12 In a model of a game of billiards, a player's probability of scoring a point is p and of missing a shot is $q = 1 - p$. The player continues playing until she misses, when the turn passes to her opponent. The number of points she accumulates is the length of her turn, and this can be zero. The random variable X is the number of points scored after r turns.

Show that the probability generating function of X is $\left(\dfrac{q}{1 - pt}\right)^r$.

Hence show that $P(X = x) = \dbinom{x + r - 1}{x} q^r p^x$ and $E(X) = \dfrac{rp}{q}$.

13[†] A random variable, Y, is defined to be the minimum value of k observations, x_1, x_2, ... , x_k of a discrete random variable, X, which takes consecutive integer values. Show that

$$P(Y = y) = \left(P(X > y-1)\right)^k - \left(P(X > y)\right)^k.$$

If X has a distribution defined by $P(X = x) = (1-\theta)\theta^x$ for $x = 0, 1, 2, ...$, show that

$$P(Y = y) = \theta^{yk}\left(1 - \theta^k\right) \text{ for } y = 0, 1, 2, ...$$

Hence show that the probability generating function of Y is $\dfrac{1 - \theta^k}{1 - \theta^k t}$ and find the mean and variance of Y.

14 The random variable X has a geometric distribution given by $P(X = r) = p(1-p)^{r-1}$, $r = 1, 2, ...$. Write down the probability generating function of Y, the sum of k independent observations of X, and show that

$$P(Y = r) = \binom{r-1}{k-1}p^k q^{r-k}, \qquad r = k, k+1, ...$$

Find the mean of Y.

A fair dice is to be thrown until three sixes have been obtained. By the fifth throw only one six has been obtained. Calculate how many throws on average will be needed to obtain the third six.

Given that the third six is obtained on the nth throw, show that the probability that the second six is obtained on the mth throw is $\dfrac{2(m-1)}{(n-1)(n-2)}$, where $2 \leq m < n$.

(OCR, adapted)

4 Moment generating functions

This chapter introduces the concept of a moment generating function. When you have completed it you should be able to

- understand the concept of a moment generating function for both discrete and continuous random variables
- construct the moment generating function for a given distribution
- use the moment generating function of a given distribution to find its mean and variance
- use the result that the moment generating function of the sum of independent random variables is the product of the moment generating functions of the individual variables.

4.1 The moment generating function of a discrete random variable

Like the probability generating function the **moment generating function** (m.g.f.) is a useful tool which can simplify certain calculations dramatically. The moment generating function of a discrete random variable is related to its probability generating function. The definition of the probability generating function is

$$G_X(t) = p_1 t^{x_1} + p_2 t^{x_2} + \ldots = \sum p_i t^{x_i}.$$

The moment generating function, denoted by $M_X(t)$, is defined by replacing t by e^t in this expression to give

$$M_X(t) = p_1 e^{tx_1} + p_2 e^{tx_2} + \ldots = \sum p_i e^{tx_i} \qquad (4.1)$$

provided that this sum converges. Thus $M_X(t) = G_X(e^t) = E(e^{tX})$.

Note that $M_X(0) = \sum p_i = 1$.

As with the probability generating functions which you met in Chapter 3, convergence is an issue when dealing with moment generating functions.

In order to understand the reason for the name 'moment generating function' you first need to know what is meant by a 'moment' in statistics. This is a term borrowed from mechanics.

The first moment of the random variable X is $\sum p_i x_i$, which equals $E(X)$. Each probability is multiplied by the corresponding value of X just as a force is multiplied by the corresponding distance when you calculate its moment.

The first moment given above is 'uncorrected'. You can also define corrected moments which are taken about the mean. For example, the first corrected moment is $\sum p_i(x_i - \mu)$. This equals zero. The second corrected moment is $\sum p_i(x_i - \mu)^2$, which is equal to $\mathrm{Var}(X)$. In this module the term 'moment' will refer to the uncorrected moment.

The second moment of X is $\sum p_i x_i^2$. Since each value of x_i^2 is multiplied by the corresponding probability this can also be written as $E(X^2)$. In general the sth moment of X is given by $\sum p_i x_i^s$.

These moments can be found from the moment generating function $M_X(t)$ by expanding it as a power series in t. You can think of the expansion as 'generating the moments'. From Equation 4.1

$$M_X(t) = \sum p_i e^{tx_i} = p_1 e^{tx_1} + p_2 e^{tx_2} + \dots .$$

Now assume that e^{tx} can be expanded as a series in t, that is $e^{tx} = 1 + tx + \dfrac{(tx)^2}{2!} + \dots .$

Substituting this expansion into the expression for $M_X(t)$ gives

$$M_X(t) = p_1\left(1 + tx_1 + \frac{(tx_1)^2}{2!} + \dots\right) + p_2\left(1 + tx_2 + \frac{(tx_2)^2}{2!} + \dots\right) + \dots$$

$$= (p_1 + p_2 + \dots) + (p_1 x_1 + p_2 x_2 + \dots)t + (p_1 x_1^2 + p_2 x_2^2 + \dots)\frac{t^2}{2!} + \dots .$$

Looking at this series in t you can see that the constant term will always equal 1 since it is the sum of the probabilities. The coefficient of t is the first moment, $E(X)$, and the coefficient of $\dfrac{t^2}{2!}$ is the second moment, $E(X^2)$. The series could be continued to show that the coefficient of $\dfrac{t^s}{s!}$ is the sth moment, $E(X^s)$.

Example 4.1.1
A discrete random variable, X, has the following probability distribution.

x	0	1	2	3
$P(X = x)$	0.1	0.2	0.3	0.4

Write down the moment generating function of X. By expanding the moment generating function as a power series in t, find $E(X)$, $E(X^2)$ and hence $Var(X)$.

The moment generating function is

$$M_X(t) = p_1 e^{x_1 t} + p_2 e^{x_2 t} + \dots = 0.1 e^{0t} + 0.2 e^{1t} + 0.3 e^{2t} + 0.4 e^{3t}$$

$$= 0.1 + 0.2 e^t + 0.3 e^{2t} + 0.4 e^{3t}.$$

Expanding as a power series in t yields

$$M_X(t) = 0.1 + 0.2\left(1 + t + \frac{t^2}{2!} + \dots\right) + 0.3\left(1 + 2t + \frac{(2t)^2}{2!} + \dots\right)$$

$$+ 0.4\left(1 + 3t + \frac{(3t)^2}{2!} + \dots\right).$$

Grouping like terms gives

$$\mathrm{M}_X(t) = (0.1 + 0.2 + 0.3 + 0.4) + (0.2 + 0.6 + 1.2)t + (0.2 + 1.2 + 3.6)\frac{t^2}{2!} + \ldots$$

$$= 1 + 2t + 5 \times \frac{t^2}{2!} + \ldots.$$

Thus $\mathrm{E}(X) = $ coefficient of $t = 2$, and $\mathrm{E}(X^2) = $ coefficient of $\dfrac{t^2}{2!} = 5$.

So $\mathrm{Var}(X) = \sum p_i x_i^2 - \mu^2 = \mathrm{E}(X^2) - (\mathrm{E}(X))^2 = 5 - 2^2 = 1.$

4.2   Finding moments by differentiation

It is often simpler to find moments by differentiating the moment generating function. This is similar to the method which you applied in the last chapter to the probability generating function.

Consider $\mathrm{M}_X(t) = \sum p_i e^{t x_i} = p_1 e^{t x_1} + p_2 e^{t x_2} + \ldots.$

Assuming that term-by-term differentiation is justified

$$\mathrm{M}'_X(t) = p_1 x_1 e^{t x_1} + p_2 x_2 e^{t x_2} + \ldots.$$

Substituting $t = 0$ gives

$$\mathrm{M}'_X(0) = p_1 x_1 + p_2 x_2 + \ldots = \mathrm{E}(X)$$

Differentiating again gives

$$\mathrm{M}''_X(t) = p_1 x_1^2 e^{t x_1} + p_2 x_2^2 e^{t x_2} + \ldots,$$

and again substituting $t = 0$ gives

$$\mathrm{M}''_X(0) = p_1 x_1^2 + p_2 x_2^2 + \ldots = \mathrm{E}(X^2).$$

Thus $\mathrm{Var}(X) = \mathrm{E}(X^2) - (\mathrm{E}(X))^2 = \mathrm{M}''_X(0) - (\mathrm{M}'_X(0))^2.$

Example 4.2.1

Find the mean and variance of the discrete random variable in Example 4.1.1 by differentiating the moment generating function.

From Example 4.1.1

$$\mathrm{M}_X(t) = 0.1 + 0.2e^t + 0.3e^{2t} + 0.4e^{3t}.$$

Differentiating, and then differentiating again, gives

$$\mathrm{M}'_X(t) = 0.2e^t + 0.3 \times 2e^{2t} + 0.4 \times 3e^{3t} = 0.2e^t + 0.6e^{2t} + 1.2e^{3t},$$
$$\mathrm{M}''_X(t) = 0.2e^t + 1.2e^{2t} + 3.6e^{3t}.$$

Putting $t = 0$ gives

$$M'_X(0) = 0.2 + 0.6 + 1.2 = 2,$$
$$M''_X(0) = 0.2 + 1.2 + 3.6 = 5.$$

So   mean $= E(X) = M'_X(0) = 2$, and

$$\text{variance} = \text{Var}(X) = M''_X(0) - \left(M'_X(0)\right)^2 = 5 - 2^2 = 1.$$

As you would expect these results are the same as those obtained in Example 4.1.1.

The moment generating functions of the Poisson, binomial and geometric distributions can be found by substituting e^t for t in their probability generating functions, which were found in Chapter 3. Alternatively they can be found directly from the definition of the moment generating function as shown in the following example.

Example 4.2.2
Find the moment generating function of the discrete random variable X where $X \sim \text{Geo}(p)$. Hence find $E(X)$ and $\text{Var}(X)$.

For a geometric distribution $P(X = x) = q^{x-1}p$ where $q = 1 - p$.

Thus $M_X(t) = \sum p_i e^{tx_i} = p_1 e^{tx_1} + p_2 e^{tx_2} + \ldots = pe^t + qpe^{2t} + q^2 pe^{3t} + \ldots$.

Rewriting the expression for $M_X(t)$ in the form

$$M_X(t) = pe^t + pe^t \times qe^t + pe^t \times \left(qe^t\right)^2 + \ldots$$

shows that this is a geometric series with first term pe^t and common ratio qe^t. Provided that $\left| qe^t \right| < 1$, this series converges to give

$$M_X(t) = \frac{pe^t}{1 - qe^t}.$$

To find $E(X)$ and $\text{Var}(X)$ you need the first and second derivatives of $M_X(t)$:

$$M'_X(t) = \frac{\left(1 - qe^t\right)pe^t - (pe^t)(-qe^t)}{\left(1 - qe^t\right)^2} = \frac{pe^t}{\left(1 - qe^t\right)^2},$$

so $M'_X(0) = \dfrac{p}{(1 - q)^2} = \dfrac{p}{p^2} = \dfrac{1}{p} = E(X).$

Differentiating $M'_X(t)$ again gives

$$M''_X(t) = \frac{\left(1 - qe^t\right)^2 pe^t - (pe^t)(-2qe^t)\left(1 - qe^t\right)}{\left(1 - qe^t\right)^4}$$

$$= \frac{pe^t + pqe^{2t}}{\left(1 - qe^t\right)^3} \qquad \text{(after some manipulation).}$$

Thus $M_X''(0) = \dfrac{p+pq}{(1-q)^3} = \dfrac{p(1+q)}{p^3} = \dfrac{1+q}{p^2} = E\left(X^2\right)$, and

$$\operatorname{Var}(X) = E\left(X^2\right) - (E(X))^2 = \frac{1+q}{p^2} - \frac{1}{p^2} = \frac{q}{p^2} = \frac{1-p}{p^2}.$$

You can see that the calculation of the mean and variance of a geometric distribution is more complicated using the moment generating function than the probability generating function. The particular strength of the moment generating function is in dealing with continuous random variables, as you will see in the next section.

The moment generating function $M_X(t)$ of a discrete random variable, X, is defined by

$$M_X(t) = p_1 e^{tx_1} + p_2 e^{tx_2} + \ldots = E\left(e^{tX}\right)$$

provided that this series converges.

$M_X(t)$ has the following properties.

- If $M_X(t)$ is expanded as a power series in t, then the first moment of X is

    $E(X) = $ coefficient of t,

    and the second moment of X is

    $E\left(X^2\right) = $ coefficient of $\dfrac{t^2}{2!}$.

- Provided that the expression for $M_X(t)$ is valid for $t = 0$,

    $M_X(0) = 1$,

    $E(X) = M_X'(0)$,

    $E\left(X^2\right) = M_X''(0)$,

    $\operatorname{Var}(X) = M_X''(0) - \left(M_X'(0)\right)^2$.

Exercise 4A

1   A fair tetrahedral dice has its four faces numbered 1, 2, 3 and 4. The random variable X represents the score obtained by throwing the dice once. Show that the moment generating function of X is given by $M_X(t) = \frac{1}{4}\left(e^t + e^{2t} + e^{3t} + e^{4t}\right)$.

Hence find the mean and variance of X. (OCR)

2 Show, using Equation 4.1, that the moment generating function of a variable with a Poisson distribution of mean λ is $M_X(t) = e^{\lambda(e^t - 1)}$.

Use this moment generating function to find the mean and variance of X.

3 Show, using Equation 4.1, that the moment generating function of a discrete random variable, X, which is distributed as $B(n, p)$ is $M_X(t) = \left(1 - p + pe^t\right)^n$.

Use this moment generating function to find the mean and variance of X.

4.3 The moment generating function of a continuous random variable

The moment generating function of a continuous random variable, X, with probability density function $f(x)$ is defined by

$$M_X(t) = \int_{-\infty}^{\infty} f(x) e^{tx} \, dx = E\left(e^{tX}\right) \qquad (4.2)$$

where t is an arbitrary variable. This definition assumes that there are values of t for which this integral exists.

There are some probability density functions for which the moment generating function exists for all values of t, some for which the moment generating function exists for some values of t and some probability density functions for which the moment generating function cannot be defined for any value of t. In practice, what is needed is convergence for values of t close to zero.

The moment generating function of a continuous random variable has properties similar to those of the moment generating function of a discrete variable; that is,

$$M_X(0) = 1, \qquad M_X'(0) = E(X), \qquad M_X''(0) = E\left(X^2\right),$$

and if $M_X(t)$ is expanded as a power series in t then the coefficient of $\dfrac{t^s}{s!}$ is the sth moment $E\left(X^s\right)$.

These properties are utilised in the following examples.

Example 4.3.1
The probability density function of X, the length of time taken to serve a customer, is given by

$$f(x) = \begin{cases} \lambda e^{-\lambda x} & x \geqslant 0, \lambda > 0, \\ 0 & \text{otherwise,} \end{cases}$$

where λ is a constant.

Find the moment generating function of X and hence the mean and variance of X.

From Equation 4.2

$$M_X(t) = \int_{-\infty}^{\infty} f(x)\,e^{tx}\,dx = \int_0^{\infty} \lambda e^{-\lambda x}\,e^{tx}\,dx = \int_0^{\infty} \lambda e^{-(\lambda-t)x}\,dx$$

$$= \left[-\frac{\lambda}{\lambda-t}\,e^{-(\lambda-t)x} \right]_0^{\infty}$$

$$= 0 - \left(-\frac{\lambda}{\lambda-t} \right) \qquad \text{(provided that } \lambda - t > 0 \text{, which implies } t < \lambda)$$

$$= \frac{\lambda}{\lambda-t}.$$

The condition $t < \lambda$ will be met when $t = 0$ since $\lambda > 0$. So the mean and variance of X can be found by differentiating and setting $t = 0$ as follows:

$$M_X'(t) = \frac{\lambda}{(\lambda-t)^2}, \text{ giving } M_X'(0) = E(X) = \frac{\lambda}{\lambda^2} = \frac{1}{\lambda}.$$

$$M_X''(t) = \frac{2\lambda}{(\lambda-t)^3}, \text{ giving } M_X''(0) = E(X^2) = \frac{2\lambda}{\lambda^3} = \frac{2}{\lambda^2}.$$

Thus $\text{Var}(X) = E(X^2) - (E(X))^2 = \dfrac{2}{\lambda^2} - \dfrac{1}{\lambda^2} = \dfrac{1}{\lambda^2}.$

Example 4.3.2

A continuous random variable, X, has probability density function

$$f(x) = \begin{cases} \frac{1}{6}x & 0 \leqslant x < 2, \\ \frac{1}{3} & 2 \leqslant x \leqslant 4, \\ 0 & \text{otherwise.} \end{cases}$$

Find the moment generating function of X. Expand this moment generating function as a power series in t and hence find $E(X)$ and $\text{Var}(X)$.

The moment generating function is

$$M_X(t) = \int_{-\infty}^{\infty} f(x)\,e^{tx}\,dx = \int_0^2 \frac{1}{6}x\,e^{tx}\,dx + \int_2^4 \frac{1}{3}e^{tx}\,dx$$

$$= \left[\frac{xe^{tx}}{6t} \right]_0^2 - \int_0^2 \frac{e^{tx}}{6t}\,dx + \left[\frac{e^{tx}}{3t} \right]_2^4 \qquad \text{(provided that } t \neq 0)$$

$$= \left(\frac{e^{2t}}{3t} - 0 \right) - \left[\frac{e^{tx}}{6t^2} \right]_0^2 + \left(\frac{e^{4t}}{3t} - \frac{e^{2t}}{3t} \right)$$

$$= \frac{e^{2t}}{3t} - \left(\frac{e^{2t}}{6t^2} - \frac{1}{6t^2} \right) + \frac{e^{4t}}{3t} - \frac{e^{2t}}{3t} = -\frac{e^{2t}}{6t^2} + \frac{1}{6t^2} + \frac{e^{4t}}{3t}.$$

Expanding $M_X(t)$ as a power series in t gives

$$M_X(t) = \frac{1}{6t^2} \left(\begin{array}{l} 1 - \left(1 + 2t + \frac{(2t)^2}{2!} + \frac{(2t)^3}{3!} + \frac{(2t)^4}{4!} + \cdots \right) \\[2mm] + 2t\left(1 + 4t + \frac{(4t)^2}{2!} + \frac{(4t)^3}{3!} + \cdots \right) \end{array} \right)$$

$$= 1 + \frac{22}{9}t + \frac{62}{9}\frac{t^2}{2!} + \cdots \qquad \text{(after some manipulation)}.$$

The coefficient of $t = E(X) = \frac{22}{9}$.

The coefficient of $\frac{t^2}{2!} = E(X^2) = \frac{62}{9}$.

Thus $\text{Var}(X) = E(X^2) - (E(X))^2 = \frac{62}{9} - \left(\frac{22}{9}\right)^2 = \frac{74}{81}$.

Note that you cannot use differentiation in this example because that method depends on t taking the value of zero, which it cannot here.

Example 4.3.3

The standard normal variable Z has probability density function $\frac{1}{\sqrt{2\pi}} \exp\left(-\frac{1}{2}z^2\right)$ for all values of z. Show that the moment generating function of Z is $M_Z(t) = \exp\left(\frac{1}{2}t^2\right)$. Verify that this moment generating function gives $E(Z) = 0$ and $\text{Var}(Z) = 1$.

Recall that $\exp x \equiv e^x$. The exp notation is used here to avoid tiny letters as indices.

The moment generating function is

$$M_Z(t) = \int_{-\infty}^{\infty} \frac{1}{\sqrt{2\pi}} \exp\left(-\frac{1}{2}z^2\right) \exp(tz)\, dz = \int_{-\infty}^{\infty} \frac{1}{\sqrt{2\pi}} \exp\left(-\frac{1}{2}z^2 + tz\right) dz.$$

It can be shown that this integral exists for all values of t. It can be evaluated by completing the square.

The exponent $-\frac{1}{2}z^2 + zt$ can be written in completed square form as

$$-\frac{1}{2}z^2 + zt = -\frac{1}{2}\left(z^2 - 2zt\right) = -\frac{1}{2}\left(z^2 - 2zt + t^2\right) + \frac{1}{2}t^2 = -\frac{1}{2}(z-t)^2 + \frac{1}{2}t^2.$$

Substituting this expression into the integral gives

$$M_Z(t) = \int_{-\infty}^{\infty} \frac{1}{\sqrt{2\pi}} \exp\left(-\frac{1}{2}(z-t)^2 + \frac{1}{2}t^2\right) dz$$

$$= \exp\left(\frac{1}{2}t^2\right) \int_{-\infty}^{\infty} \frac{1}{\sqrt{2\pi}} \exp\left(-\frac{1}{2}(z-t)^2\right) dz,$$

where the term $\exp\left(\frac{1}{2}t^2\right)$ has been taken outside the integral because it is independent of z.

Making a change of variable $u = z - t$ (for which $\dfrac{du}{dz} = 1$) transforms the integral to

$$\exp\left(\tfrac{1}{2}t^2\right)\int_{-\infty}^{\infty} \frac{1}{\sqrt{2\pi}} \exp\left(-\tfrac{1}{2}(z-t)^2\right) dz = \exp\left(\tfrac{1}{2}t^2\right)\int_{-\infty}^{\infty} \frac{1}{\sqrt{2\pi}} \exp\left(-\tfrac{1}{2}u^2\right) du.$$

The integral $\displaystyle\int_{-\infty}^{\infty} \frac{1}{\sqrt{2\pi}} \exp\left(-\tfrac{1}{2}u^2\right) du$ is the integral of the original probability

density function, with u taking the place of z. As it is the area under a probability

density function, $\displaystyle\int_{-\infty}^{\infty} \frac{1}{\sqrt{2\pi}} \exp\left(-\tfrac{1}{2}u^2\right) du = 1$.

Thus the moment generating function of Z is $M_Z(t) = \exp\left(\tfrac{1}{2}t^2\right)$.

Expanding $M_Z(t)$ as a power series in t gives

$$M_Z(t) = 1 + \tfrac{1}{2}t^2 + \dots.$$

The coefficient of t is 0, so $E(Z) = 0$.

The coefficient of $\dfrac{t^2}{2!}$ is 1, so $E\left(Z^2\right) = 1$.

Thus $\operatorname{Var}(Z) = E\left(Z^2\right) - (E(Z))^2 = 1 - 0 = 1$.

The moment generating function of a continuous random variable, X, with
probability density function $f(x)$ is defined by

$$M_X(t) = \int_{-\infty}^{\infty} f(x)\,e^{tx}\, dx.$$

This definition assumes that there are values of t for which this integral exists.

The properties of the moment generating function of a continuous random
variable are the same as those of a discrete random variable (see page 201).

Exercise 4B

1 The continuous random variable X has probability density function

$$f(x) = \begin{cases} 2x & 0 \leqslant x \leqslant 1, \\ 0 & \text{otherwise.} \end{cases}$$

Find the moment generating function of X and hence find $E(X)$ and $\operatorname{Var}(X)$.

2 The continuous random variable X has probability density function

$$f(x) = \begin{cases} k x e^{-\frac{1}{2}x} & x \geqslant 0, \\ 0 & \text{otherwise,} \end{cases}$$

where k is a constant.

(a) Show that the moment generating function of X is $M_X(t) = \dfrac{4k}{(2t-1)^2}$, giving any restrictions which must be placed on t.

(b) Hence find the value of k and the mean and variance of X.

3 A random variable, Y, has probability density function

$$f(y) = \begin{cases} k & 0 \leqslant y \leqslant 1 \\ 2k & 1 < y \leqslant 2, \\ 0 & \text{otherwise.} \end{cases}$$

(a) Show that the moment generating function of Y is $M_Y(t) = \dfrac{k}{t}\left(2e^{2t} - e^t - 1\right)$ and state any restrictions which must be placed on t.

(b) Find the value of k.

(c) Use the moment generating function to find the mean and variance of Y.

4* A function $H(t)$ is defined by $H(t) = e^{ct} M_X(t)$, where $M_X(t)$ is the moment generating function of a random variable, X, with mean μ and variance σ^2 and c is a constant.

Show that $H'(0) = \mu + c$ and $H''(0) - (H'(0))^2 = \sigma^2$.

Suggest an interpretation for the function $H(t)$.

5† If X is distributed as $N(\mu, \sigma^2)$ then X has probability density function

$$f(x) = \frac{1}{\sigma\sqrt{2\pi}} \exp\left(-\frac{(x-\mu)^2}{2\sigma^2}\right).$$ Show that X has moment generating function

$$M_X(t) = \exp\left(\mu t + \frac{\sigma^2 t^2}{2}\right)$$ by completing the square as in Example 4.3.3.

6 The moment generating function of X where $X \sim N(\mu, \sigma^2)$ is $M_X(t) = \exp\left(\mu t + \dfrac{\sigma^2 t^2}{2}\right)$.

Use this moment generating function to show that $E(X) = \mu$ and $\text{Var}(X) = \sigma^2$.

4.4 The moment generating function of the sum of random variables

The moment generating function has a useful property analogous to that shown by the probability generating function.

> For both discrete and continuous random variables the moment generating function of the sum of independent random variables is equal to the product of their individual moment generating functions.

This result can be demonstrated using expectation notation. If two random variables, X and Y, have moment generating functions $M_X(t)$ and $M_Y(t)$, then

$$M_X(t)M_Y(t) = E\left(e^{tX}\right)E\left(e^{tY}\right).$$

If X and Y are independent, then

$$E\left(e^{tX}\right)E\left(e^{tY}\right) = E\left(e^{tX}e^{tY}\right) = E\left(e^{t(X+Y)}\right),$$

which is the moment generating function of $X + Y$.

The following examples illustrate the application of this property.

Example 4.4.1

(a) A Bernoulli trial is one in which there are only two possible mutually exclusive outcomes, which can be labelled 'success' and 'failure'. X is a random variable which takes the value 0 for a failure and 1 for a success. Write down the moment generating function of X given that the probability of a success is p.

(b) In a binomial distribution Y represents the number of successes in n trials where p is the probability of success at each trial. By considering Y as a sequence of independent Bernoulli trials show that the moment generating function of Y is
$M_Y(t) = \left(1 - p + pe^t\right)^n$.

(a) $M_X(t) = \sum_i p_i e^{tx_i} = (1-p)e^{0t} + pe^{1t} = (1-p) + pe^t$.

(b) The number of successes in n trials is given by

$$Y = X_1 + X_2 + \ldots + X_n,$$

where X_i represents the result of the ith Bernoulli trial.

Provided that the Bernoulli trials are independent, the moment generating function of Y is equal to the product of the moment generating functions of the Bernoulli trials, so

$$M_Y(t) = \left(1 - p + pe^t\right)^n$$

This is the same as the result which would be obtained by replacing t with e^t in the probability generating function found in Example 3.2.4.

Example 4.4.2

(a) Example 4.3.1 gave the probability density function for X, the time taken to serve a customer. Find the moment generating function for Y, the time taken to serve two consecutive customers, assuming that the serving times are independent.

(b) Find the moment generating function for the random variable V which has probability density function

$$f(v) = \begin{cases} \lambda^2 v e^{-\lambda v} & v \geq 0, \ \lambda > 0, \\ 0 & \text{otherwise,} \end{cases}$$

where λ is a constant.

(a) The time taken to serve two consecutive customers is given by $Y = X_1 + X_2$ where X_1 and X_2 each have the moment generating function found in Example 4.3.1. Thus the moment generating function of Y is given by the product of these moment generating functions; that is,

$$M_Y(t) = \left(\frac{\lambda}{\lambda - t}\right)^2.$$

(b) The moment generating function of V is given by

$$M_V(t) = \int_0^\infty \lambda^2 v e^{-\lambda v} e^{tv} \, dv$$

$$= \left[-\frac{\lambda^2}{\lambda - t} v e^{-v(\lambda - t)}\right]_0^\infty - \int_0^\infty -\frac{\lambda^2}{\lambda - t} e^{-v(\lambda - t)} \, dv$$

$$= (0 - 0) - \left[\frac{\lambda^2}{(\lambda - t)^2} e^{-v(\lambda - t)}\right]_0^\infty \qquad \text{(provided that } \lambda - t > 0)$$

$$= \frac{\lambda^2}{(\lambda - t)^2}.$$

You will notice that the answers to parts (a) and (b) of Example 4.4.2 are the same. An important theorem in statistics says that if X and Y have the same moment generating function, then they also have the same distribution. Thus you can deduce that the time taken to serve two consecutive customers has the distribution given in part (b) of Example 4.4.2.

Exercise 4C

1 A random variable, R, is distributed exponentially with mean equal to 2. Its probability density function is

$$f_R(x) = \begin{cases} 2e^{-2x} & x \geqslant 0, \\ 0 & \text{otherwise.} \end{cases}$$

The random variable S, which is independent of R, is distributed exponentially with mean equal to 3.

(a) Determine the moment generating function of $M_R(t)$ for R, stating any restriction that must be placed on t.

(b) Determine the moment generating function for the random variable represented by $R + S$.

(c) Hence find the mean and variance of $R + S$.   (OCR, adapted)

2 (a) Given that the moment generating function of X where $X \sim N(\mu, \sigma^2)$ is

$$M_X(t) = \exp\left(\mu t + \frac{\sigma^2 t^2}{2}\right) \text{ (see Exercise 4B Question 5), find the moment generating}$$

function of Y where Y is the sum of n independent observations of X, that is $Y = X_1 + X_2 + \ldots + X_n$.

  (b) Write down the moment generating function of S where $S \sim N(n\mu, n\sigma^2)$.

  (c) Compare your answers for (a) and (b). What conclusion can you draw about the distribution of the sum of n independent observations of a normally distributed random variable?

3 (a) Consider the situation described in Example 4.4.2. Let W denote the time taken to serve three customers. Write down the moment generating function for W.

  (b) What form do you think the probability density function of W will take? Check whether you are correct by finding the moment generating function of your suggested probability density function and comparing it with your answer to part (a).

  (c) Generalise your result to the situation where there are n customers.

Miscellaneous exercise 4

1 A continuous random variable, X, has moment generating function given by

$$M_X(t) = \frac{1}{(1-t)^2}.$$

Expand $M_X(t)$ as a series of ascending powers of t, up to and including the term in t^2, and hence find the mean and variance of X.   (OCR)

2 The continuous random variable X has moment generating function given by

$$M_X(t) = e^{\alpha t + \beta t^2},$$

where α and β are constants. Find $E(X)$ and $Var(X)$.   (OCR)

3 The continuous random variable X has probability density function given by

$$f(x) = \begin{cases} 2e^{-x} & 0 \le x \le b, \\ 0 & \text{otherwise,} \end{cases}$$

where b is a constant.

  (a) Show that the moment generating function of X is given by $M_X(t) = \dfrac{2}{1-t}\left(1 - e^{-b}e^{bt}\right)$.

  (b) Show that $b = \ln 2$.

  (c) Expand $M_X(t)$ as a power series in t, up to and including the terms in t^2. (Standard expressions may be used for e^{bt} and $(1-t)^{-1}$.)

  (d) Hence show that $E(X) = 1 - \ln 2$ and find $Var(X)$.   (OCR, adapted)

4 A mathematician often does calculations without a calculator. To simplify the calculations she rounds each number down to the nearest integer below; so, for example, 4.81 would become 4.

(a) The random variable X, which represents the magnitude of the error resulting from this rounding process, has probability density function given by

$$f(x) = \begin{cases} 1 & 0 \leqslant x \leqslant 1, \\ 0 & \text{otherwise.} \end{cases}$$

Show that the moment generating function of X is given by $M_X(t) = \dfrac{e^t - 1}{t}$.

(b) A random variable Y has probability density function given by

$$g(y) = \begin{cases} y & 0 \leqslant y < 1, \\ 2 - y & 1 \leqslant y < 2, \\ 0 & \text{otherwise.} \end{cases}$$

Find the moment generating function of Y.

(c) The mathematician adds two numbers together. The magnitude of the error in the answer from having rounded down each of the numbers before adding is denoted by W. Use moment generating functions to show that W has the same distribution as Y.

(OCR)

5 A discrete random variable is such that $P(X = x_i) = p_i$. The probability generating function is defined by $P_X(t) = \sum p_i t^{x_i}$.

Show that the moment generating function of X is given by $M_X(t) = P_X(e^t)$.

A discrete random variable has a distribution defined by $P(X = x) = \dfrac{1}{n}$ for $x = 0, 1, 2, \ldots, n-1$.

Show that the moment generating function $M_X(t)$ of X is given by $M_X(t) = \dfrac{e^{nt} - 1}{n(e^t - 1)}$, stating any restrictions that must be placed on t.

6 A continuous random variable, X, has probability density function

$$f(x) = \begin{cases} e^{-ax}\left(1 - e^{-bx}\right) & x \geqslant 0, \\ 0 & \text{otherwise,} \end{cases}$$

where a and b are constants and $a > 0$, $b > 0$.

(a) Find the moment generating function $M_X(t)$ of X, stating any restrictions on the value of t, and hence find b in terms of a.

(b) Find the mean and variance of X from the moment generating function.

7[†] A continuous random variable, X, has probability density function defined by

$$f(x) = \begin{cases} \frac{1}{4}|x| & -2 \leqslant x \leqslant 2, \\ 0 & \text{otherwise,} \end{cases}$$

and the random variable Y is defined by $Y = X^2$. Show that the moment generating function of Y is $\dfrac{e^{4t} - 1}{4t}$.

Find the mean and variance of Y.

(OCR)

8 The random variable X has moment generating function $M(t)$. State how $M(t)$ may be used to find $E(X)$, where r is a positive integer.

It is given that $M(t) = \dfrac{e^{\frac{1}{2}\pi t} + e^{-\frac{1}{2}\pi t}}{2(1+t^2)}$.

(a) Show that the mean of X is 0.   (b) Find the variance of X.   (OCR)

9 The random variable X has a uniform distribution on the interval $\alpha \leqslant x \leqslant \beta$. Find the values of α and β given that the moment generating function of X is $\dfrac{2}{t}\left(e^{\frac{1}{2}t} - 1\right)$.

The random variables X_1 and X_2 are independent observations of X. Write down the moment generating function of $Y = X_1 + X_2$ and use it to find the mean and variance of Y.

                                                             (OCR, adapted)

5 Estimators

This chapter builds on the ideas about estimators which you first met in S2. When you have completed it you should be able to

- understand that an estimator of a parameter is a random variable and understand the meaning of the terms 'biased' and 'unbiased' as applied to estimators
- determine in simple cases whether an estimator is biased or unbiased, and find the variance of an estimator
- determine which of two unbiased estimators is more efficient by comparing their variances and understand why the more efficient estimator is generally to be preferred.

5.1 Unbiased and biased estimators

You met the concept of an estimator in S2 and again in S3. There the work concentrated mainly on the sample mean, $\overline{X}$, as an estimator of the population mean, μ. The sample mean is a random variable since its value varies from one sample to the next. As a result $\overline{X}$ has a probability distribution of its own. This is known as the sampling distribution of the mean. You have used the result that $E(\overline{X})$, the mean of the sampling distribution of the mean, is equal to μ, or in other words that $\overline{X}$ is an **unbiased estimator** of the population mean μ.

You have met other examples of unbiased estimators. In S3 Section 3.5 you used the sample proportion, P_s, as an unbiased estimator of the population proportion, p. This estimator is unbiased because, although its value varies from sample to sample, $E(P_s) = p$. In S2 Section 4.7 you used $\dfrac{\sum (X_i - \overline{X})^2}{n-1}$ as an unbiased estimator of the population variance, σ^2. Again the value taken by $\dfrac{\sum (X_i - \overline{X})^2}{n-1}$ varies from one sample to the next, but its expected value is equal to σ^2. (A proof of this result is given in Section 5.4.) In general an unbiased estimator is defined as follows.

> For an unknown population parameter α, the estimator M is unbiased if $E(M) = \alpha$, where the expected value is taken over all possible samples of a given size.

Any estimator which is not unbiased is said to be **biased**.

5.2 Testing for bias

You may remember from S2 that intuitive choices of estimators often prove to be biased. One way of deciding whether or not an estimator is biased is to find its sampling distribution and hence its expected value. This is illustrated in the following example.

Example 5.2.1

A population consists of a large number of cards. The number 1 is written on 40% of the cards and the number 2 on the remaining 60%. A sample of size 3 is taken and its median noted. List all possible samples and hence find the sampling distribution of M, the sample median. Is M an unbiased estimator of the population median?

Table 5.1 shows the possible sample values and their associated probabilities. Since there are a large number of cards it is reasonable to say that the probability of selecting a 1 or 2 remains constant for each selection.

Sample	Probability	m, Value of M
1,1,1	$0.4^3 = 0.064$	1
1,1,2 (in any order)	$3 \times 0.4^2 \times 0.6 = 0.288$	1
1,2,2 (in any order)	$3 \times 0.4 \times 0.6^2 = 0.432$	2
2,2,2	$0.6^3 = 0.216$	2

Table 5.1. Possible sample values for a sample of size 3.

The sampling distribution of M is shown in Table 5.2.

m	1	2
$P(M = m)$	0.352	0.648

Table 5.2. Sampling distribution of M.

Thus $E(M) = 1 \times 0.352 + 2 \times 0.648 = 1.648$.

Although the number of cards in the population is not given you should see that, because more cards are labelled 2 than 1, the middle value will be 2 when the cards are arranged in numerical order, however many cards there are. Thus the median of the population is 2. The sample median is therefore a biased estimator of the population median since $E(M) \neq 2$.

If the population distribution is symmetrical, then the sample median is an unbiased estimator of the population median. For instance, if in Example 5.2.1 there were equal numbers of cards with 1 and 2 on them, the median would be an unbiased estimator of the population median (see Exercise 5A Question 2).

Obviously a method which tests an estimator for bias by evaluating it on all samples is only possible if the variable is discrete and then only practicable for small sample sizes. Another approach is to use computer simulation. Using the estimator which is to be tested, an estimate is calculated for each of a large number of random samples drawn from a population for which the parameter is known. An estimate of the population parameter is calculated from each sample. If the mean of these estimates is close to the known value of the parameter, then this test would suggest that the estimator being used is unbiased.

Computer activity   Imagine that you arrive at the railway station in a large city. You have been told that the taxis in this city each bear a registration plate. These plates are numbered consecutively, starting at 1. You want to estimate how many taxis there are in the city so you note down the registration numbers of the first three taxis which you see (ignoring any taxi which you see twice). Devise at least four estimators for the highest registration number, N.

Now choose a value for N, the highest registration number. For a particular sample size, generate a large number of samples from the population of N taxis. For each sample calculate the value of one of your estimators. Test whether this estimator of N appears to be unbiased by calculating the mean of your estimates. Make a note also of the variance of the sampling distribution of this estimator, that is the variance of the estimates. Repeat for your other estimators.

5.3   Testing for bias algebraically

Suppose that the continuous random variable X has probability density function

$$f(x) = \begin{cases} \dfrac{1}{k} & 1 \leqslant x \leqslant k+1, \\ 0 & \text{otherwise,} \end{cases}$$

and you wish to find an unbiased estimator for k. You might decide to tackle this problem by first finding $E(X)$:

$$E(X) = \int_1^{k+1} x \times \frac{1}{k}\,dx = \left[\frac{x^2}{2k}\right]_1^{k+1} = \frac{(k+1)^2}{2k} - \frac{1^2}{2k} = \tfrac{1}{2}k + 1.$$

Rearranging gives $k = 2(E(X)-1)$, which suggests that $2(X-1)$ might be an unbiased estimator of k. You can check this by finding $E(2(X-1))$:

$$E(2(X-1)) = \int_1^{k+1} 2(x-1) \times \frac{1}{k}\,dx = \left[\frac{(x-1)^2}{k}\right]_1^{k+1} = \frac{(k)^2}{k} - \frac{0^2}{k} = k.$$

So $2(X-1)$ *is* an unbiased estimator of k.

This approach to finding an unbiased estimator will always be successful if $E(X) = b\alpha + c$ where α is the parameter which you are trying to estimate. In this situation you take $\dfrac{X-c}{b}$ as your estimator. It will be unbiased because

$$E\left(\frac{X-c}{b}\right) = \frac{1}{b}E(X) - \frac{c}{b} = \frac{b\alpha+c}{b} - \frac{c}{b} = \alpha.$$

This approach will not be successful, however, if $E(X)$ is not a linear function of the parameter to be estimated. Consider the geometric distribution. For this distribution $E(X) = \dfrac{1}{p}$, and you might hope that as a result $\dfrac{1}{X}$ is an unbiased estimator of p. The following example shows that this is not the case.

Example 5.2.2

If $X \sim \text{Geo}(p)$, show that $\dfrac{1}{X}$ is a biased estimator of p.

The formula for the expectation of a function of a discrete random variable is analogous to that for a continuous variable; that is,

$$E(g(x)) = \sum_x g(x)P(X = x).$$

For a geometric distribution $P(X = x) = q^{x-1}p$ where $p = 1 - q$, so

$$E\left(\frac{1}{X}\right) = \sum_x \frac{1}{x}P(X = x) = \sum_x \frac{1}{x}q^{x-1}p = p + \tfrac{1}{2}qp + \tfrac{1}{3}q^2p + \tfrac{1}{4}q^3p + \ldots$$

$$= \frac{p}{q}\left(q + \tfrac{1}{2}q^2 + \tfrac{1}{3}q^3 + \tfrac{1}{4}q^4 + \ldots\right)$$

$$= -\frac{p}{q}\ln(1-q)$$

$$= -\frac{p}{q}\ln p = \frac{p}{q}\ln\frac{1}{p}.$$

Since $E\left(\dfrac{1}{X}\right) \neq \dfrac{1}{p}$, $\dfrac{1}{X}$ is a biased estimator of p.

The bias in this estimator is quite large. For example, if $p = 0.5$, $E\left(\dfrac{1}{X}\right) = 0.69$.

The preceding analysis should convince you that spotting a suitable estimator is not a straightforward process. There are mathematical techniques for doing this which you will encounter if you continue your study of statistics.

Exercise 5A

1 A box contains 10 beads which are identical apart from their colour. Seven of the beads are red and the remainder are black. Four beads are selected at random without replacement.

   (a) Find the sampling distribution of P_s, the proportion of the beads in the sample which are red.

   (b) Show that P_s is an unbiased estimator of the proportion of beads in the box which are red.

2 Show that if Example 5.2.1 is altered so that there are equal numbers of cards with 1 and 2 on them, the sample median is an unbiased estimator of the population median.

3 What do you understand by the phrase 'an unbiased estimate of population variance'?

(a) An infinite population consists of the numbers 1, 2, 3 in equal proportions. Write down the population mean, and calculate the population variance.

(b) Random samples of size two are obtained from the population. Write down all the possible samples of size two. Hence, write down the probability distribution of the means of samples of size two. Obtain the expected value of the sample mean and determine if the 'sample mean' is an unbiased estimator of the population mean in this case.

(c) Obtain the sampling distribution of $S^2 = \dfrac{\sum\left(X_i - \overline{X}\right)^2}{n-1}$ and show that S^2 is an unbiased estimator of population variance in this case.

(d) Obtain the sampling distribution of $S = \sqrt{S^2}$ and show that S is a biased estimator of population standard deviation.

(e) Is the sample maximum an unbiased estimate of the population maximum? Justify your response.   (OCR, adapted)

4 Two independent random samples of observations containing n_1 and n_2 values respectively are made of a random variable, X, which has mean μ and variance σ^2.

Unbiased estimates of σ^2 are calculated from each sample. These are denoted by S_1^2 and S_2^2 respectively.

Show that $\dfrac{\left(n_1 - 1\right)S_1^2 + \left(n_2 - 1\right)S_2^2}{n_1 + n_2 - 2}$ is also an unbiased estimator of σ^2.

(You used this estimator in the two-sample t-test, described in S3 Section 4.2.)

5 A continuous random variable, X, has probability density function

$$f(x) = \begin{cases} \dfrac{2x}{\theta^2} & 0 \leqslant x \leqslant \theta, \\ 0 & \text{otherwise,} \end{cases}$$

where θ is an unknown constant.

Show that $\frac{3}{2}X$ is an unbiased estimator of θ.

6 Show that the sample mean $\overline{X} = \dfrac{1}{n}\left(X_1 + X_2 + \ldots + X_n\right)$ is an unbiased estimator of the population mean μ.

7 The continuous random variable X has probability density function

$$f(x) = \begin{cases} \dfrac{2\alpha^2}{x^3} & x \geqslant \alpha, \\ 0 & \text{otherwise,} \end{cases}$$

where α is an unknown parameter. Show that

(a) $E(X) = 2\alpha$,

(b) $\frac{1}{2}X$ is an unbiased estimator of α.

8 A continuous random variable, X, has probability density function

$$f(x) = \begin{cases} \dfrac{x}{\theta^2} e^{-x/\theta} & x \geqslant 0, \\ 0 & \text{otherwise,} \end{cases}$$

where θ is an unknown parameter. If $X_1, X_2, \ldots, X_n$ is a random sample from this distribution, show that $\dfrac{1}{2n}\sum X_i$ is an unbiased estimator of θ.

9 In surveys it is hard to obtain truthful answers to embarrassing questions like 'Have you ever stolen anything?' A method of overcoming this problem is the technique of 'randomised response'. In one version of this the person being interviewed is presented with two questions, the second of which is not embarrassing, for example

    A: Have you ever stolen anything?

    B: Is your birthday an even-numbered date in the month?

The person is asked to toss a coin but not to tell the interviewer the result. The person is instructed that if the coin comes down heads to answer question A, if it comes down tails to answer question B. The idea is that people are more likely to answer truthfully when the interviewer does not know which question they are answering.

Assuming that birthdays occur at random the proportion of people who should answer 'yes' to question B is $\frac{1}{2}$ (ignoring the slight differences in lengths of months). Suppose that the proportion of people in the population who should answer 'yes' to question A is p where p is unknown. Let R be the proportion in a random sample who answer 'yes'.

(a) Express $E(R)$ in terms of p.

(b) Hence find an unbiased estimator for p and verify that it is unbiased.

10 A biased coin has a probability p that it gives a head when it is spun. The random variable Y is the number of throws of the coin up to and including the second head.

(a) Show that $P(Y = y) = (y-1)(1-p)^{y-2}p^2$ for $y \geqslant 2$.

(b) Hence show that $\dfrac{1}{Y-1}$ is an unbiased estimator of p.

5.4 Comparing different estimators

If you carried out the computer activity in Section 5.2, then you may have found a number of different estimators for the number of taxis, N. Some unbiased estimators of N are $2\overline{X}-1$, $2M-1$ where M is the median, $\frac{4}{3}X_{\max}-1$ where $X_{\max}$ is the highest value and $X_{\max} + X_{\min} - 1$ where $X_{\min}$ is the minimum value. It is not possible here to give the exact sampling distributions for these estimators when the number of taxis is realistically large, but the following example compares the sampling distributions in the situation when $N = 6$.

Example 5.4.1

A population consists of the numbers 1, 2, 3, 4, 5, 6. The following estimators are
suggested for the maximum value in the population:

(a) $2\bar{X} - 1$,

(b) $2M - 1$ where M is the median,

(c) $\frac{4}{3}X_{\max} - 1$ where $X_{\max}$ is the highest value,

(d) $X_{\max} + X_{\min} - 1$ where $X_{\min}$ is the minimum value,

for samples of size 3 taken without replacement.

Find the sampling distribution of each estimator and hence show that the expected value
of each estimator is 6.

Table 5.3 lists the possible samples together with the value taken by each of the
estimators.

Sample	Value of			
	$2\bar{X} - 1$	$2M - 1$	$\frac{4}{3}X_{\max} - 1$	$X_{\max} + X_{\min} - 1$
1, 2, 3	3	3	3	3
1, 2, 4	$3\frac{2}{3}$	3	$4\frac{1}{3}$	4
1, 2, 5	$4\frac{1}{3}$	3	$5\frac{2}{3}$	5
1, 2, 6	5	3	7	6
1, 3, 4	$4\frac{1}{3}$	5	$4\frac{1}{3}$	4
1, 3, 5	5	5	$5\frac{2}{3}$	5
1, 3, 6	$5\frac{2}{3}$	5	7	6
1, 4, 5	$5\frac{2}{3}$	7	$5\frac{2}{3}$	5
1, 4, 6	$6\frac{1}{3}$	7	7	6
1, 5, 6	7	9	7	6
2, 3, 4	5	5	$4\frac{1}{3}$	5
2, 3, 5	$5\frac{2}{3}$	5	$5\frac{2}{3}$	6
2, 3, 6	$6\frac{1}{3}$	5	7	7
2, 4, 5	$6\frac{1}{3}$	7	$5\frac{2}{3}$	6
2, 4, 6	$7\frac{2}{3}$	7	7	7
2, 5, 6	7	9	7	7
3, 4, 5	$7\frac{2}{3}$	7	$5\frac{2}{3}$	7
3, 4, 6	7	7	7	8
3, 5, 6	$8\frac{1}{3}$	9	7	8
4, 5, 6	9	9	7	9

Table 5.3. Possible samples for Example 5.4.1.

It is left as an exercise for you to check that the expected value of each estimator is 6,
indicating that all the estimators give unbiased estimates of the maximum value.

In Example 5.4.1 you have a choice of four different unbiased estimators for the largest value in the population. In this situation which is the best choice of estimator? The answer is that you should choose the estimator whose sampling distribution is clustered most closely about the value which you are trying to estimate. This will be the estimator with the smallest variance. You can verify for yourself that the variances of the four estimators are

$$\text{Var}\left(2\overline{X}-1\right)=2\tfrac{1}{3}, \qquad\qquad \text{Var}\left(2M-1\right)=4\tfrac{1}{5},$$

$$\text{Var}\left(\tfrac{4}{3}X_{\max}-1\right)=1\tfrac{2}{5}, \qquad \text{Var}\left(X_{\max}+X_{\min}-1\right)=2\tfrac{1}{10}.$$

So among these the best estimator of the largest value is $\tfrac{4}{3}X_{\max}-1$. It is said to be the **most efficient** estimator.

> Where there is a choice of unbiased estimators the estimator with the smallest variance is said to be the **most efficient** estimator.

If you carried out the computer activity in Section 5.2, compare variances to pick out the most efficient of any unbiased estimators which you found.

Sometimes an estimator can give an estimate which is unrealistic. For example, the second sample, 1, 2, 4, in Table 5.2 gives $3\tfrac{2}{3}$ as an estimate of the maximum value if you use the estimator $2\overline{X}-1$. This estimate is unrealistic since the value of 4 in the sample indicates that the maximum value must be at least 4. The problem does not arise if samples of size 2 are taken. Check this for yourself and show also that $\text{Var}\left(2\overline{X}-1\right)=4\tfrac{2}{3}$ for samples of size 2. In this case, even though $2\overline{X}-1$ is a less efficient estimator for the smaller sample size, it would be the better choice if you had only these two estimators to choose between. In practice, of course, there is no problem because you already know that $\tfrac{4}{3}X_{\max}-1$ is a more efficient estimator and Table 5.3 shows that the estimates which it provides are not unrealistic.

In Example 5.4.1 the sampling was done without replacement. If the sampling had been made *with* replacement, then the conclusions might have been different. You might like to explore this for yourself. In practice populations usually have many more than 6 members and as a result the sample size is usually much less than the population size. In these circumstances it is not necessary to make any distinction between the results 'with replacement' and 'without replacement'.

The following examples give other situations in which different unbiased estimators are possible.

Example 5.4.2
(a) Three independent measurements, X_1, X_2 and X_3, are made of a random variable X with $\text{E}(X)=\mu$ and $\text{Var}(X)=\sigma^2$. Show that
    (i) $\tfrac{1}{3}\left(X_1+X_2+X_3\right)$,   (ii) $\tfrac{1}{6}\left(X_1+2X_2+3X_3\right)$,   (iii) $\tfrac{1}{4}\left(X_1+2X_2+X_3\right)$,
are all unbiased estimators of μ.
(b) Find the variance of each estimator and hence state which is the most efficient.

(a)   (i) $E\left(\frac{1}{3}(X_1 + X_2 + X_3)\right) = \frac{1}{3}E(X_1) + \frac{1}{3}E(X_2) + \frac{1}{3}E(X_3)$

$$= \frac{1}{3}\mu + \frac{1}{3}\mu + \frac{1}{3}\mu = \mu.$$

(ii) $E\left(\frac{1}{6}(X_1 + 2X_2 + 3X_3)\right) = \frac{1}{6}E(X_1) + \frac{2}{6}E(X_2) + \frac{3}{6}E(X_3)$

$$= \frac{1}{6}\mu + \frac{2}{6}\mu + \frac{3}{6}\mu = \mu.$$

(iii) $E\left(\frac{1}{4}(X_1 + 2X_2 + X_3)\right) = \frac{1}{4}E(X_1) + \frac{2}{4}E(X_2) + \frac{1}{4}E(X_3)$

$$= \frac{1}{4}\mu + \frac{2}{4}\mu + \frac{1}{4}\mu = \mu.$$

Since all the expected values are equal to μ, all three estimators are unbiased.

(b)   (i)   As the measurements are independent

$$\text{Var}\left(\frac{1}{3}(X_1 + X_2 + X_3)\right) = \frac{1}{3^2}\text{Var}(X_1) + \frac{1}{3^2}\text{Var}(X_2) + \frac{1}{3^2}\text{Var}(X_3)$$

$$= \frac{1}{9}\sigma^2 + \frac{1}{9}\sigma^2 + \frac{1}{9}\sigma^2 = \frac{1}{3}\sigma^2.$$

(ii) $\text{Var}\left(\frac{1}{6}(X_1 + 2X_2 + 3X_3)\right) = \frac{1}{6^2}\text{Var}(X_1) + \left(\frac{2}{6}\right)^2\text{Var}(X_2) + \left(\frac{3}{6}\right)^2\text{Var}(X_3)$

$$= \frac{1}{36}\sigma^2 + \frac{4}{36}\sigma^2 + \frac{9}{36}\sigma^2 = \frac{7}{18}\sigma^2.$$

(iii) $\text{Var}\left(\frac{1}{4}(X_1 + 2X_2 + X_3)\right) = \frac{1}{4^2}\text{Var}(X_1) + \left(\frac{2}{4}\right)^2\text{Var}(X_2) + \frac{1}{4^2}\text{Var}(X_3)$

$$= \frac{1}{16}\sigma^2 + \frac{4}{16}\sigma^2 + \frac{1}{16}\sigma^2 = \frac{3}{8}\sigma^2.$$

Since the first estimator has the smallest variance it is the most efficient.

You may have spotted that for this example the most efficient estimator of the population mean is the sample mean.

Example 5.4.3
In order to estimate the mean of a population, two observations, X_1 and X_2, are made of the random variable X, which has mean μ and variance σ^2.
(a) Show that $kX_1 + (1-k)X_2$ is an unbiased estimator of μ.
(b) Find the value of k for which this estimator is most efficient.

(a) $E(kX_1 + (1-k)X_2) = kE(X_1) + (1-k)E(X_2)$

$$= k\mu + (1-k)\mu = \mu.$$

Hence $kX_1 + (1-k)X_2$ is an unbiased estimator of μ.

(b) $\text{Var}(kX_1 + (1-k)X_2) = k^2\text{Var}(X_1) + (1-k)^2\text{Var}(X_2)$

$$= k^2\sigma^2 + (1-k)^2\sigma^2.$$

The minimum value of this expression can be found by thinking of the variance as a function of k, that is $V(k)$. Then

$$\frac{dV}{dk} = 2k\sigma^2 - 2(1-k)\sigma^2 = (4k-2)\sigma^2,$$

giving $\frac{dV}{dk} = 0$ when $k = \frac{1}{2}$. It is left as an exercise for you to check that this value of k gives a minimum.

Example 5.4.4

Two independent observations, X_1 and X_2, are made of a random variable with probability density function

$$f(x) = \begin{cases} \dfrac{1}{\theta} & 0 \leqslant x \leqslant \theta, \\ 0 & \text{otherwise,} \end{cases}$$

where θ is an unknown constant.

Two estimators are proposed for θ. The first is S where $S = X_1 + X_2$, and the second is $\frac{3}{2}L$ where L is the larger of X_1 and X_2.

(a) Show that both S and L are unbiased estimators of θ.
(b) Determine which estimator is the more efficient.

(a) Consider S first:

$$E(S) = E(X_1 + X_2) = E(X_1) + E(X_2) = 2E(X), \text{ and}$$

$$E(X) = \int_0^\theta x\frac{1}{\theta}\,dx = \left[\frac{x^2}{2\theta}\right]_0^\theta = \tfrac{1}{2}\theta.$$

Therefore $E(S) = 2E(X) = 2 \times \tfrac{1}{2}\theta = \theta$ and S is an unbiased estimator of θ.

Now consider L. First you have to find the probability density function of L. This can be obtained by considering the cumulative distribution function of L. For $0 \leqslant l \leqslant \theta$

$$F_L(l) = P(L \leqslant l) = P(\text{both } X_1 \text{ and } X_2 \leqslant l)$$
$$= P(X_1 \leqslant l) \times P(X_2 \leqslant l) \quad \text{(since the observations are independent).}$$

Fig. 5.4 shows the probability density function of X with $P(X \leqslant l)$ shaded. It is clear that the shaded area is equal to $\dfrac{l}{\theta}$, so

$$F_L(l) = P(X_1 \leqslant l) \times P(X_2 \leqslant l)$$
$$= \frac{l}{\theta} \times \frac{l}{\theta} = \frac{l^2}{\theta^2}.$$

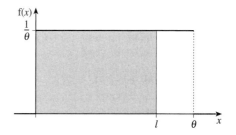

Fig. 5.4. Diagram illustrating Example 5.4.4.

Outside the interval of interest, define $F_L(l) = 0$ for $l < 0$ and $F_L(l) = 1$ for $l > \theta$.

The probability density function of L is found by differentiating its cumulative distribution function to obtain

$$f_L(l) = F_L'(l) = \begin{cases} \dfrac{2l}{\theta^2} & 0 \leqslant l \leqslant \theta, \\ 0 & \text{otherwise.} \end{cases}$$

Now $E(L) = \displaystyle\int_0^\theta l \times \frac{2l}{\theta^2} \, dl = \left[\frac{2l^3}{3\theta^2}\right]_0^\theta = \frac{2}{3}\theta$, so

$$E\left(\tfrac{3}{2}L\right) = \tfrac{3}{2} \times \tfrac{2}{3}\theta = \theta.$$

Thus $\tfrac{3}{2}L$ is also an unbiased estimator of θ.

(b) To compare the efficiencies of the estimators you need to find their variances.

$$\begin{aligned} \mathrm{Var}(S) &= \mathrm{Var}(X_1 + X_2) = \mathrm{Var}(X_1) + \mathrm{Var}(X_2) \\ &= 2\mathrm{Var}(X) \quad \text{(since the observations are independent).} \end{aligned}$$

$$\mathrm{Var}(X) = \int_0^\theta x^2 \frac{1}{\theta} \, dx - \left(\tfrac{1}{2}\theta\right)^2 = \left[\frac{x^3}{3\theta}\right]_0^\theta - \tfrac{1}{4}\theta^2 = \tfrac{1}{12}\theta^2, \text{ so}$$

$$\mathrm{Var}(S) = 2\mathrm{Var}(X) = 2 \times \tfrac{1}{12}\theta^2 = \tfrac{1}{6}\theta^2.$$

The variance of L is given by

$$\mathrm{Var}(L) = \int_0^\theta l^2 \times \frac{2l}{\theta^2} \, dl - \left(\tfrac{2}{3}\theta\right)^2 = \left[\frac{2l^4}{4\theta^2}\right]_0^\theta - \tfrac{4}{9}\theta^2 = \tfrac{1}{2}\theta^2 - \tfrac{4}{9}\theta^2 = \tfrac{1}{18}\theta^2.$$

Thus $\mathrm{Var}\left(\tfrac{3}{2}L\right) = \left(\tfrac{3}{2}\right)^2 \mathrm{Var}\left(\tfrac{3}{2}L\right) = \tfrac{9}{4} \times \tfrac{1}{18}\theta^2 = \tfrac{1}{8}\theta^2.$

Since the second estimator has the smaller variance it is the more efficient estimator.

Exercise 5B

1 (a) Three independent measurements, X_1, X_2 and X_3, are made of a random variable X with $E(X) = \mu$ and $\mathrm{Var}(X) = \sigma^2$. Show that the following are unbiased estimators of μ.

(i) $\tfrac{1}{3}(2X_1 + 2X_2 - X_3)$ (ii) $\tfrac{1}{2}(X_1 - 2X_2 + 3X_3)$ (iii) $X_1 - 2X_2 + 2X_3$

(b) Find the variance of each estimator and hence state which is the most efficient estimator.

2 Two independent random samples of observations containing n_1 and n_2 values respectively are made of a random variable, X, which has mean μ and variance σ^2. The means of the samples are denoted by $\overline{X}_1$ and $\overline{X}_2$.

(a) Show that $c\overline{X}_1 + (1-c)\overline{X}_2$ is an unbiased estimator of μ.

(b) Find the value of c for which this estimator is most efficient and show that for this

value of c the estimator is $\dfrac{n_1\overline{X}_1 + n_2\overline{X}_2}{n_1 + n_2}$.

3 The proportion, p, of fish in a lake which are below a certain size can be estimated by catching a random sample of the fish. The random variable X_1 is the number of fish in a

sample of size n_1 which are below the specified size. Show that P_1, where $P_1 = \dfrac{X_1}{n_1}$, is an unbiased estimator of p and find the variance of P_1.

A further sample of size n_2 is taken and the random variable X_2 is defined to be the

number of undersized fish in this sample. If $P_2 = \dfrac{X_2}{n_2}$ and $P = \frac{1}{2}(P_1 + P_2)$, show that P is also an unbiased estimator of p.

For what values of $\dfrac{n_1}{n_2}$ is P a more efficient estimator than either of P_1 or P_2?

4 The continuous random variable X has a uniform distribution on the interval $0 \leqslant x \leqslant a$, where the value of the parameter a is unknown. Three observations, X_1, X_2 and X_3, of X are taken.

(a) An estimator θ is defined by $\theta = \frac{2}{3}(X_1 + X_2 + X_3)$. Show that θ is an unbiased estimator of a and find $\mathrm{Var}(\theta)$ in terms of a.

(b) Another estimator ϕ is based on the greatest of the three values X_1, X_2 and X_3. Denoting the greatest of the three values by the variable G, use the fact that, for any value x between 0 and a,

$$G \leqslant x \Leftrightarrow \left(X_1 \leqslant x \text{ and } X_2 \leqslant x \text{ and } X_3 \leqslant x\right)$$

to write down the cumulative distribution function of G, and hence to obtain the probability density function of G.

Hence show that, if $\phi = \frac{4}{3}G$, then ϕ is an unbiased estimator of a, and determine which of θ and ϕ is the more efficient estimator.   (OCR, adapted)

5 A discrete random variable, X, takes values 0, 1, 2 with probabilities $1 - 2\alpha$, α, α respectively, where α is an unknown constant such that $0 \leqslant \alpha \leqslant \frac{1}{2}$. A random sample of n observations is made of X. Two estimators are proposed for α. The first is $\frac{1}{3}\overline{X}$, and the second is $\frac{1}{2}Y$ where Y is the proportion of observations in the sample which are not equal to 0.

(a) Show that $\frac{1}{3}\overline{X}$ and $\frac{1}{2}Y$ are both unbiased estimators of α.

(b) Show that $\frac{1}{2}Y$ is the more efficient estimator.

(c) Which, if either, estimator could lead to an unrealistic estimate of α?

5.5* Proof that $S^2 = \dfrac{\sum (X_i - \overline{X})^2}{n-1}$ is an unbiased estimator of σ^2

You may omit this section if you wish.

Let n independent observations be made of a random variable, X, with mean μ and variance σ^2.

$$S^2 = \frac{\sum (X_i - \overline{X})^2}{n-1} = \frac{n}{n-1} \left(\frac{\sum X_i^2}{n} - \overline{X}^2 \right) = \frac{1}{n-1} \left(\sum X_i^2 - n\overline{X}^2 \right).$$

Consider

$$E\left(\sum X_i^2 - n\overline{X}^2 \right) = E(X_1^2) + E(X_2^2) + \ldots + E(X_n^2) - nE(\overline{X}^2)$$
$$= nE(X^2) - nE(\overline{X}^2). \qquad (5.1)$$

Now $\mathrm{Var}(X) = \sigma^2 = E(X^2) - (E(X))^2 = E(X^2) - \mu^2$, so

$$E(X^2) = \sigma^2 + \mu^2. \qquad (5.2)$$

As $\overline{X}$ has mean μ and variance $\dfrac{\sigma^2}{n}$,

$$\mathrm{Var}(\overline{X}) = E(\overline{X}^2) - (E(\overline{X}))^2 \quad \Leftrightarrow \quad \frac{\sigma^2}{n} = E(\overline{X}^2) - \mu^2,$$

giving giving $E(\overline{X}^2) = \dfrac{\sigma^2}{n} + \mu^2. \qquad (5.3)$

Substituting from Equations 5.2 and 5.3 into Equation 5.1 gives

$$E\left(\sum X_i^2 - n\overline{X}^2 \right) = n(\sigma^2 + \mu^2) - n\left(\frac{\sigma^2}{n} + \mu^2 \right) = (n-1)\sigma^2.$$

So $E(S^2) = E\left(\dfrac{1}{n-1} \left(\sum X_i^2 - n\overline{X}^2 \right) \right) = \sigma^2$ and $S^2 = \dfrac{\sum (X_i - \overline{X})^2}{n-1}$ is an unbiased estimator of σ^2.

███████████ Miscellaneous exercise 5 ███████████

1 A continuous random variable, X, has probability density function

$$f(x) = \begin{cases} \dfrac{k}{(x+\theta)^4} & x \geqslant 0, \\ 0 & x < 0, \end{cases}$$

where k and θ are positive constants.

(a) (i) Show that $k = 3\theta^3$. (ii) Obtain expressions for $E(X)$ and $\mathrm{Var}(X)$ in terms of θ.

(b) To estimate θ a random sample $X_1, X_2, \ldots, X_n$ is taken from the distribution of X. Show that $\dfrac{2}{n} \sum_{i=1}^{n} X_i$ is an unbiased estimator of θ, and find the variance of this estimator. (OCR, adapted)

2 A continuous random variable, X, has probability density function

$$f(x) = \begin{cases} \frac{1}{2}\alpha^3 x^2 e^{-\alpha x} & x \geqslant 0, \\ 0 & \text{otherwise,} \end{cases}$$

where α is a positive constant.

Show that $\dfrac{2}{X}$ is an unbiased estimator of α.

3 Two separate independent samples are taken from a large population in order to estimate the proportion, p, of people in the population with blood group O. If the sample sizes are denoted by n_1 and n_2 and the corresponding sample proportions for blood group O by P_1 and P_2, show that P', where $P' = (1-c)P_1 + cP_2$ and c is a constant, is an unbiased estimator of p. Find the value of c for which this estimator is most efficient. Show that for this value of c, $P' = \dfrac{n_1 P_1 + n_2 P_2}{n_1 + n_2}$.

(You used this estimator in testing for a difference between two population proportions in S3 Section 4.4.)

4 The breaking strength, k, of elastic bands is estimated by observing a related random variable, Z, which has probability density function

$$f(z) = \begin{cases} \dfrac{3z^2}{k^3} & 0 \leqslant z \leqslant k \\ 0 & \text{otherwise.} \end{cases}$$

(a) Show that $\frac{4}{3}Z$ is an unbiased estimator of k and that it has variance $\frac{1}{15}k^2$.

The breaking strength can also be estimated by making observations of a random variable, X, which has mean $\frac{1}{2}k$ and variance $\frac{1}{12}k^2$. Let $Y = X_1 + X_2 + X_3$ where X_1, X_2 and X_3 are three independent observations of X.

(b) What is the value of the constant c such that cY is an unbiased estimator of k?

(c) Of the unbiased estimators $\frac{4}{3}Z$ and cY which do you prefer and why?

(OCR, adapted)

5 The continuous random variable Y has probability density function

$$f(z) = \begin{cases} \frac{2}{9}(\beta + 3 - y) & \beta \leqslant y \leqslant \beta + 3, \\ 0 & \text{otherwise,} \end{cases}$$

where β is an unknown constant.

(a) Find an unbiased estimator for β.

In a single observation Y is found to be 5.

(b) Find an unbiased estimate of β.

(OCR, adapted)

6 A random variable, U, has probability density function

$$f(u) = \begin{cases} \dfrac{1}{k} & 0 \leqslant u \leqslant k, \\ 0 & \text{otherwise,} \end{cases}$$

where k is a constant. $U_1, U_2, \ldots, U_n$, are n independent observations of U.

(a) Calculate the probability that $U_1, U_2, \ldots, U_n$ are all at most l where $0 < l < k$.

(b) Determine the probability density function for L, the largest observation of n independent observations of U.

(c) Calculate the expected value of L in a random sample of n observations.

(d) Suggest a possible unbiased estimator for k based on your answer to (c) and check whether your estimator is unbiased.

(e) Find $E(\overline{U})$ where $\overline{U}$ is the mean of n independent observations of U.

(f) Suggest another possible unbiased estimator for k based on your answer to (e) and check whether your estimator is unbiased.

(g) Calculate the variance of each of your estimators. Hence show that L is the more efficient estimator whatever the sample size.

7 The continuous random variable X is uniformly distributed over the interval $a \leqslant x \leqslant a + b$ where a and b are unknown constants.

If X_1, X_2 and X_3 are three independent observations of X, where $X_1 < X_2 < X_3$, show that the probability density function of X_1 is

$$f(x_1) = \begin{cases} \dfrac{3}{b^3}(a+b-x_1)^2 & a \leqslant x_1 \leqslant a+b, \\ 0 & \text{otherwise.} \end{cases}$$

Find the value of $E(X_1)$.

By considering the values of $E(X_1)$ and $E(X_3)$, obtain estimates of a and b when $x_1 = 7$ and $x_3 = 11$.   (OCR, adapted)

8[†] Two populations have the same mean μ but different variances σ_1^2, σ_2^2. A random observation, X_1, is taken from the first population and another, X_2, from the second population.

(a) Show that if, in the linear function $T = c_1 X_1 + c_2 X_2$, c_1 and c_2 are chosen so that T is an unbiased estimator of μ and T has minimum variance, then

$$c_1 = \frac{\sigma_2^2}{\sigma_1^2 + \sigma_2^2} \quad \text{and} \quad c_2 = \frac{\sigma_1^2}{\sigma_1^2 + \sigma_2^2}.$$

Two instruments are used in a laboratory to measure a particular property of metals. From long experience it has been found that both instruments give unbiased readings and that determinations by instrument A have a variance that is twice that by instrument B. Random samples were taken from an ingot of metal and divided between the two instruments. The mean of 12 determinations by instrument A was 6.0, in appropriate units, while the mean of 9 determinations by instrument B was 6.5.

(b) Estimate the common mean from these data by using the linear function of the two means that is unbiased and has minimum variance.   (OCR)

9 The emissions of particles from a radioactive source occur at random. The mean number of emissions per second is an unknown constant λ. The number of particles emitted from the source is observed for two separate time intervals, the first of length t_1 seconds and the second of t_2 seconds. Let the random variables X_1 and X_2 be the numbers of particles observed in the first and second time intervals respectively.

(a) Show that $\dfrac{X_1 + X_2}{t_1 + t_2}$ and $\dfrac{1}{2}\left(\dfrac{X_1}{t_1} + \dfrac{X_2}{t_2}\right)$ are both unbiased estimators of λ.

(b)[†] Show that the first estimator is always more efficient than the second one.

10[†] The random variable X is distributed as $B(n, p)$. If $P_s = \dfrac{X}{n}$, show that $\text{Var}(P_s) = \dfrac{p(1-p)}{n}$.

Show also that $\dfrac{P_s(1 - P_s)}{n - 1}$ is an unbiased estimator of $\text{Var}(P_s)$.

(The estimator P_s was mentioned in S3 Section 3.5, in connection with the confidence interval for a proportion.)

11[†] Explain what is meant by an unbiased estimator.

A random sample is drawn from a large population in which a proportion p have a certain rare disease. Sampling continues until a predetermined number b of the sample are found to have the disease. The random variable R is the sample size at this stage. Find an expression for $P(R = r)$ and hence show that $\dfrac{b-1}{R-1}$ is an unbiased estimator of p.

(OCR, adapted)

6 Discrete bivariate distributions

This chapter extends the work on probability distributions of discrete random variables to the situation in which there are two such variables. When you have completed it you should be able to

- understand the joint probability distribution of a pair of discrete random variables and find and use marginal distributions
- determine and use the distribution of one variable conditional on a particular value of the other variable
- determine whether or not two variables are independent
- calculate the covariance for a pair of discrete random variables and understand the relation between zero covariance and independence
- use the formula $\text{Var}(aX \pm bY) = a^2 \text{Var}(X) + b^2 \text{Var}(Y) \pm 2ab\,\text{Cov}(X,Y)$.

6.1 Bivariate distributions

The probability distributions for discrete random variables which you have met so far dealt with only one random variable at a time. However, in many situations you might be interested in specifying the values of two random variables for each member of a population, often because you think there is a relation between them. A probability distribution which depends on two random variables is called **bivariate**.

A similar situation arose when you studied correlation in S1 Chapter 9. There the variables concerned were continuous, for example height and mass of a person, and you investigated the relation between values of the two variables for a sample. This chapter looks only at discrete variables and looks at probability distributions rather than samples.

The probability distribution of two random variables is given in the form of a **joint probability distribution**.

Table 6.1 gives an example which refers to a population of households. The table specifies the joint probability distribution of two discrete random variables X and Y, where X denotes the number of members of a household and Y denotes the number of bedrooms in a household's dwelling place.

For a household chosen at random the probability that X takes the value x_i and Y takes the value y_j is denoted by $P(X = x_i, Y = y_j)$. For example, the probability that a household chosen at random has 2 members and 3 bedrooms is denoted by $P(X = 2, Y = 3)$; from Table 6.1 this probability is 0.10.

The total of all the probabilities in a joint probability distribution must equal one.

		X, Number of members			
		1	2	3	4	5
	1	0.03	0.02	0.02	0.02	0.01
Y, Number of	2	0.04	0.06	0.06	0.03	0.01
bedrooms	3	0.02	0.10	0.15	0.12	0.11
	4	0.01	0.02	0.02	0.08	0.07

Table 6.1. Joint probability distribution for X, number of household members, and Y, number of bedrooms.

Check that you agree with following probabilities, obtained from Table 6.1.

$P(X = 1, Y = 4) = 0.01$, $P(X = 4, Y = 1) = 0.02$,
$P(X = 5, Y = 4) = 0.07$, $P(X = 2, Y = 2) = 0.06$.

In earlier modules you found the distribution of a random variable by thinking about possible outcomes and then using the laws of probability. This approach can be extended to the situation in which two variables are recorded for each experiment.

Example 6.1.1
A fair coin is spun until either a head is obtained or the coin has been spun four times. Two random variables are defined as X, the number of spins, and Y, the number of tails. Find the joint probability distribution of X and Y.

The possible sequences of spins are listed below, together with the probability of each sequence and the values taken by X and Y. The letter T denotes a tail and the letter H a head.

Sequence	Probability	Value of X	Value of Y
H	$\frac{1}{2}$	1	0
TH	$\frac{1}{2} \times \frac{1}{2} = \frac{1}{4}$	2	1
TTH	$\frac{1}{2} \times \frac{1}{2} \times \frac{1}{2} = \frac{1}{8}$	3	2
TTTH	$\frac{1}{2} \times \frac{1}{2} \times \frac{1}{2} \times \frac{1}{2} = \frac{1}{16}$	4	3
TTTT	$\frac{1}{2} \times \frac{1}{2} \times \frac{1}{2} \times \frac{1}{2} = \frac{1}{16}$	4	4

The joint probability distribution of X and Y is

		1	2	3	4
			X, Number of spins		
	0	$\frac{1}{2}$	0	0	0
	1	0	$\frac{1}{4}$	0	0
Y, Number	2	0	0	$\frac{1}{8}$	0
of tails	3	0	0	0	$\frac{1}{16}$
	4	0	0	0	$\frac{1}{16}$

6.2 Marginal distributions

Table 6.2 reproduces Table 6.1 but with row and column totals given.

		X, Number of members					
		1	2	3	4	5	
	1	0.03	0.02	0.02	0.02	0.01	0.10
Y, Number of	2	0.04	0.06	0.06	0.03	0.01	0.20
bedrooms	3	0.02	0.10	0.15	0.12	0.11	0.50
	4	0.01	0.02	0.02	0.08	0.07	0.20
		0.10	0.20	0.25	0.25	0.20	1.00

Table 6.2. Marginal probability distributions for Table 6.1, where X is number of household members and Y is number of bedrooms.

The row totals form what is known as the **marginal distribution of Y**. This gives the probability that Y takes a given value, irrespective of the value of X. The probability that Y takes the value y_i irrespective of the value of X is denoted by $P_Y(Y = y_i)$. For example, $P_Y(Y = 3)$ denotes the probability that a household chosen at random has 3 bedrooms, however many household members there are, and from Table 6.2 this probability is 0.50.

Similarly the column totals give the **marginal distribution of X**, from which, for example, $P_X(X = 2)$ is 0.20. This is the probability that a household chosen at random has 2 members, irrespective of the number of bedrooms it has.

The marginal distributions allow you to calculate the mean and variance for each variable taken separately. Table 6.3 shows the marginal distribution for $P_X(X = x)$, the number of household members, together with the relevant calculations needed to find $E(X)$ and $Var(X)$.

x	1	2	3	4	5	Total
$P_X(X = x)$	0.10	0.20	0.25	0.25	0.20	1.00
$x\,P_X(X = x)$	0.10	0.40	0.75	1.00	1.00	3.25
$x^2\,P_X(X = x)$	0.10	0.80	2.25	4.00	5.00	12.15

Table 6.3. Calculation of the mean and variance of the marginal distribution of X in Table 6.2.

$$E(X) = \sum x\,P_X(X = x) = 3.25.$$

$$\mathrm{Var}(X) = \sum x^2 P_X(X = x) - (E(X))^2 = 12.15 - 3.25^2 = 1.5875.$$

So the average number of members in a household is 3.25 and the variance of the number of members is 1.5875.

It is left as an exercise for you to use the marginal distribution of Y to show that $E(Y) = 2.8$ and $\mathrm{Var}(Y) = 0.76$.

6.3   Conditional distributions

The joint probability distribution also allows you to deduce the probability that X takes a particular value given that Y takes a particular value. For example, for the distribution in Table 6.2 you can find the probability that a household chosen at random has 1 bedroom given that the household has 4 members. Using the notation for conditional probability this can be written as $P(Y = 1 \mid X = 4)$. Its value can be found using Chapter 1 Equation 1.4.

Since $P(A \mid B) = \dfrac{P(A \cap B)}{P(B)}$,

$$P(Y = 1 \mid X = 4) = \frac{P(Y = 1, X = 4)}{P_X(X = 4)} = \frac{0.02}{0.25} = 0.08.$$

In a similar way you can find the probability that Y takes the values 2, 3 and 4, given that $X = 4$ in each case, by dividing the probabilities in the column for $X = 4$ by the total of that column. You should check that the values of these probabilities are

$$P(Y = 2 \mid X = 4) = 0.12, \quad P(Y = 3 \mid X = 4) = 0.48, \quad P(Y = 4 \mid X = 4) = 0.32.$$

These probabilities allow you to write down the **probability distribution of Y conditional on the value $X = x$**, where in this case $x = 4$, shown in Table 6.4.

y	1	2	3	4	Total
$P(Y = y \mid X = 4)$	0.08	0.12	0.48	0.32	1.00

Table 6.4. Probability distribution of Y conditional on the value $X = 4$.

From this distribution you can calculate the mean and variance for the number of bedrooms for households with $X = 4$ members. The relevant calculations are shown in Table 6.5.

y	1	2	3	4	Total
$P(Y = y \mid X = 4)$	0.08	0.12	0.48	0.32	1.00
$y\,P(Y = y \mid X = 4)$	0.08	0.24	1.44	1.28	3.04
$y^2\,P(Y = y \mid X = 4)$	0.08	0.48	4.32	5.12	10.00

Table 6.5. Calculation of the mean and variance of the distribution of Y conditional on $X = 4$.

So $E(Y \mid X = 4) = 3.04$ and $\mathrm{Var}\,(Y \mid X = 4) = 10 - 3.04^2 = 0.7584$.

Note that these values are not the same as those for the marginal distribution of Y, which were 2.8 and 0.76 respectively. You can see that $E(Y \mid X = 4)$ is greater than $E(Y)$. Stated in words this means that households with 4 members have, on average, more bedrooms than households in general, a result which seems sensible.

In a similar way you can find the **probability distribution of X conditional on the value $Y = y$**. For example, the probability distribution of X conditional on the value $Y = 3$ is found by dividing the probabilities in the row for $Y = 3$ by the total of that row. Thus $P(X = 1 \mid Y = 3) = \dfrac{0.02}{0.50} = 0.04$ and so on. The complete probability distribution of X conditional on the value $Y = 3$ is shown in Table 6.6.

x	1	2	3	4	5	Total
$P(X = x \mid Y = 3)$	0.04	0.2	0.3	0.24	0.22	1.00

Table 6.6. Probability distribution of X conditional on the value $Y = 3$.

Check that you agree with these values and verify that the mean and variance of this conditional distribution are 3.4 and 1.32 respectively.

Exercise 6A

You will need the answers to this exercise in Exercise 6B.

1 The table below shows the joint probability distribution of two random variables B and C.

			B	
		1	2	3
	1	0.02	0.05	k
C	2	0.06	0.15	0.09
	3	0.12	0.30	0.18

(a) Find the value of k.

(b) Give the values of the probabilities

   (i) $P(B = 1 \mid C = 2)$,   (ii) $P(B = 2 \mid C = 1)$,

   (iii) $P(B = 3 \mid C = 3)$,   (iv) $P(B = 3 \mid C = 2)$.

2 The table shows the joint probability distribution of discrete random variables R and S.

		\multicolumn{4}{c}{R}			
		1	2	3	4
S	0	0.20	0.05	0.02	0.03
	1	0.15	0.11	0.03	0.02
	2	0.13	0.07	0.06	0.01
	3	0.07	0.03	0.02	0

(a) Write down the marginal distribution of R and calculate $E(R)$ and $Var(R)$.

(b) Write down the marginal distribution of S and calculate $E(S)$ and $Var(S)$.

(c) Write the values of the following probabilities.

   (i) $P(R=1 | S=2)$ (ii) $P(R=2 | S=1)$

   (iii) $P(S=3 | R=3)$ (iv) $P(S=3 | R=4)$

(d) Write down the distribution of S conditional on $R=3$ and hence find the expected value and variance of S given that $R=3$.

(e) Write down the distribution of R conditional on $S=3$ and hence find the expected value and variance of R given that $S=3$.

3 Two fair spinners, one red and one blue, are spun together. Both spinners are numbered 1, 2, 3. The two random variables X and Y are defined as the score on the red spinner and the sum of the scores on the two spinners respectively.

(a) Write down the joint probability distribution of X and Y.

(b) Write down the marginal distributions of X and Y and hence find $E(X)$ and $E(Y)$.

(c) Write down the conditional distribution of X given that $Y=3$ and hence find the expected value of X given that $Y=3$.

4 A couple decide that they will continue to have children until they have one child of each sex or until they have four children, whichever occurs sooner. If B denotes the number of boys in the final family and G the number of girls, write down the joint probability distribution of G and B. You may assume that boys and girls are equally likely.

(a) Write down the marginal distribution of B and find $E(B)$.

(b) Write down the distribution of B conditional on $G=1$ and hence find the expected number of boys in a family given that the number of girls is 1.

5 Three fair coins are tossed. The coins which land 'heads' are removed and the remaining coins are tossed again.

The random variables H and T are defined as the number of heads on the first toss and the total number of heads for both tosses respectively.

(a) Write down the joint probability distribution of H and T.

(b) Write down the marginal distribution of T and calculate $E(T)$ and $Var(T)$.

(c) Find the expected number of heads on the first toss if the total number of heads is 3.

6.4* Proof that $E(X+Y) = E(X) + E(Y)$

You may omit this section if you wish.

The introduction of a notation to describe joint probability distributions provides a convenient opportunity to prove a result for discrete random variables which has been stated and used before but not proved. This is that

$$E(X+Y) = E(X) + E(Y)$$

for all pairs of variables, whether or not they are independent.

In order to simplify the explanation the proof will be given in the first instance for two discrete variables X and Y where X takes three values and Y takes four values. The joint probability distribution is shown in Table 6.7.

		X		
		x_1	x_2	x_3
Y	y_1	$P(X = x_1, Y = y_1)$	$P(X = x_2, Y = y_1)$	$P(X = x_3, Y = y_1)$
	y_2	$P(X = x_1, Y = y_2)$	$P(X = x_2, Y = y_2)$	$P(X = x_3, Y = y_2)$
	y_3	$P(X = x_1, Y = y_3)$	$P(X = x_2, Y = y_3)$	$P(X = x_3, Y = y_3)$
	y_4	$P(X = x_1, Y = y_4)$	$P(X = x_2, Y = y_4)$	$P(X = x_3, Y = y_4)$

Table 6.7. Joint probability distribution for two random variables.

In order to find the value of $E(X+Y)$ it is necessary to calculate the value of $x + y$ for each cell in Table 6.7, then multiply by the corresponding probability and finally sum the resulting products. The step of multiplying the value of $x + y$ for each cell in the table by the corresponding probability is shown in Table 6.8.

		X		
		x_1	x_2	x_3
Y	y_1	$(x_1 + y_1)P(X = x_1, Y = y_1)$	$(x_2 + y_1)P(X = x_2, Y = y_1)$	$(x_3 + y_1)P(X = x_3, Y = y_1)$
	y_2	$(x_1 + y_2)P(X = x_1, Y = y_2)$	$(x_2 + y_2)P(X = x_2, Y = y_2)$	$(x_3 + y_2)P(X = x_3, Y = y_2)$
	y_3	$(x_1 + y_3)P(X = x_1, Y = y_3)$	$(x_2 + y_3)P(X = x_2, Y = y_3)$	$(x_3 + y_3)P(X = x_3, Y = y_3)$
	y_4	$(x_1 + y_4)P(X = x_1, Y = y_4)$	$(x_2 + y_4)P(X = x_2, Y = y_4)$	$(x_3 + y_4)P(X = x_3, Y = y_4)$

Table 6.8. Joint probability distribution for two random variables showing the products required to calculate E(X + Y).

The quantity in each cell can be split into two terms, for example

$$(x_1 + y_2)P(X = x_1, Y = y_2) = x_1\,P(X = x_1, Y = y_2) + y_2\,P(X = x_1, Y = y_2).$$

Table 6.9 shows the first of these terms for each cell, the one containing the x-value. There are corresponding terms for the y-value, which are shown in Table 6.10.

	X		
	x_1	x_2	x_3
y_1	$x_1\,\mathrm{P}(X=x_1,Y=y_1)$	$x_2\,\mathrm{P}(X=x_2,Y=y_1)$	$x_3\,\mathrm{P}(X=x_3,Y=y_1)$
Y y_2	$x_1\,\mathrm{P}(X=x_1,Y=y_2)$	$x_2\,\mathrm{P}(X=x_2,Y=y_2)$	$x_3\,\mathrm{P}(X=x_3,Y=y_2)$
y_3	$x_1\,\mathrm{P}(X=x_1,Y=y_3)$	$x_2\,\mathrm{P}(X=x_2,Y=y_3)$	$x_3\,\mathrm{P}(X=x_3,Y=y_3)$
y_4	$x_1\,\mathrm{P}(X=x_1,Y=y_4)$	$x_2\,\mathrm{P}(X=x_2,Y=y_4)$	$x_3\,\mathrm{P}(X=x_3,Y=y_4)$

Table 6.9. Joint probability distribution for two random variables showing the x-terms of the products required to calculate E($X+Y$).

Now consider what happens when you sum each column in Table 6.9. Look at the first column, for example. The terms contain the common factor x_1 so the sum can be written as

$$x_1\left(\mathrm{P}(X=x_1,Y=y_1)+\mathrm{P}(X=x_1,Y=y_2)+\mathrm{P}(X=x_1,Y=y_3)+\mathrm{P}(X=x_1,Y=y_4)\right).$$

Since the expression in the outer brackets is the sum of the probabilities in the first column of the probability distribution in Table 6.7 it is equal to $\mathrm{P}_X(X=x_1)$. Thus the sum of the terms in the first column of Table 6.9 is equal to $x_1\,\mathrm{P}_X(X=x_1)$. Similarly the sums of the terms in the second and third columns of Table 6.9 are $x_2\,\mathrm{P}_X(X=x_2)$ and $x_3\,\mathrm{P}_X(X=x_3)$. This means that the sum of all the terms in Table 6.9 is given by

$$x_1\,\mathrm{P}_X(X=x_1)+x_2\,\mathrm{P}_X(X=x_2)+x_3\,\mathrm{P}_X(X=x_3).$$

This sum is equal to E(X).

Table 6.10 shows the second term in each cell from Table 6.8, that is the one which contains the y-value.

	X		
	x_1	x_2	x_3
y_1	$y_1\,\mathrm{P}(X=x_1,Y=y_1)$	$y_1\,\mathrm{P}(X=x_2,Y=y_1)$	$y_1\,\mathrm{P}(X=x_3,Y=y_1)$
Y y_2	$y_2\,\mathrm{P}(X=x_1,Y=y_2)$	$y_2\,\mathrm{P}(X=x_2,Y=y_2)$	$y_2\,\mathrm{P}(X=x_3,Y=y_2)$
y_3	$y_3\,\mathrm{P}(X=x_1,Y=y_3)$	$y_3\,\mathrm{P}(X=x_2,Y=y_3)$	$y_3\,\mathrm{P}(X=x_3,Y=y_3)$
y_4	$y_4\,\mathrm{P}(X=x_1,Y=y_4)$	$y_4\,\mathrm{P}(X=x_2,Y=y_4)$	$y_4\,\mathrm{P}(X=x_3,Y=y_4)$

Table 6.10. Joint probability distribution for two random variables showing the y-terms of the products required to calculate E($X+Y$).

By summing across the rows and using an argument similar to that given above you can deduce that the sum of all the terms in Table 6.10 is equal to E(Y). Thus the sum of all the products in Table 6.8 is E(X)+E(Y), giving

$$\mathrm{E}(X+Y)=\mathrm{E}(X)+\mathrm{E}(Y).$$

This proof can be generalised to any number of rows and columns by letting X take m values $x_1,\ x_2,\ \dots,\ x_m$ and Y take n values $y_1,\ y_2,\ \dots,\ y_n$ and following the argument through in the same way.

6.5 Determining whether two random variables are independent

Table 6.11 reproduces Table 6.2 showing the joint probability distribution of the number of members, X, in a household and the number of bedrooms, Y.

		\multicolumn{5}{c}{X, Number of members}
		1	2	3	4	5
Y, Number of bedrooms	1	0.03	0.02	0.02	0.02	0.01	0.10
	2	0.04	0.06	0.06	0.03	0.01	0.20
	3	0.02	0.10	0.15	0.12	0.11	0.50
	4	0.01	0.02	0.02	0.08	0.07	0.20
		0.10	0.20	0.25	0.25	0.20	1.00

Table 6.11. Joint probability distribution for X, number of household members, and Y, number of bedrooms.

If the two variables X and Y are independent, then, from Chapter 1 Equation 1.6,

$$P\left(X = x_i, Y = y_j\right) = P_X\left(X = x_i\right) \times P_Y\left(Y = y_j\right) = P_X\left(X = x_i\right) P_Y\left(Y = y_j\right) \text{ for all } i \text{ and } j.$$

Consider, in Table 6.11, however, the situation when $X = 3$ and $Y = 2$:

$$P(X = 3, Y = 2) = 0.06 \quad \text{and} \quad P_X(X = 3) \times P_Y(Y = 2) = 0.25 \times 0.20 = 0.05.$$

Since $P(X = 3, Y = 2) \neq P_X(X = 3) P_Y(Y = 2)$, X and Y cannot be independent. So to show that X and Y are not independent you only have to find one instance in which $P\left(X = x_i, Y = y_j\right) \neq P_X\left(X = x_i\right) P_Y\left(Y = y_j\right)$.

However, to show that X and Y *are* independent you have to show that $P\left(X = x_i, Y = y_j\right) = P_X\left(X = x_i\right) P_Y\left(Y = y_j\right)$ for *all* i and j.

An alternative way of determining whether X and Y are independent is by comparing the conditional distribution of Y for each value of X with the marginal distribution of Y. If each conditional distribution is the same as the marginal distribution, then the conditional distributions of Y do not depend on the value of X, and so X and Y are independent. The method would be equally valid if you found the conditional distributions for X and compared them with the marginal distribution of X.

Consider the joint probability distribution given in Table 6.12, where the marginal distributions of X and Y are also given.

		\multicolumn{4}{c}{X}
		1	2	3	4
Y	1	0.03	0.06	0.09	0.12	0.3
	2	0.02	0.04	0.06	0.08	0.2
	3	0.05	0.10	0.15	0.20	0.5
		0.1	0.2	0.3	0.4	1.0

Table 6.12. Table to demonstrate that X and Y *are* independent.

The distribution of X conditional on $Y = 1$ is shown in Table 6.13.

x	1	2	3	4
$P(X = x \mid Y = 1)$	$\dfrac{0.03}{0.30} = 0.1$	$\dfrac{0.06}{0.30} = 0.2$	$\dfrac{0.09}{0.30} = 0.3$	$\dfrac{0.12}{0.30} = 0.4$

Table 6.13. Probability distribution of X conditional on the value $Y = 1$.

This distribution is the same as the marginal distribution of X. You can check that the distributions of X conditional on $Y = 2$, 3 and 4 are also the same as the marginal distribution. It follows that X and Y are independent.

Exercise 6B

For each of the joint probability distributions in Exercise 6A decide whether the two variables are independent and justify your answers.

6.6 Covariance

In the previous section it was shown that the two discrete random variables X, number of household members, and Y, number of bedrooms, are not independent. This is not surprising given the nature of the variables. Table 6.14 reproduces Table 6.1.

		X, Number of members				
		1	2	3	4	5
	1	0.03	0.02	0.02	0.02	0.01
Y, Number of	2	0.04	0.06	0.06	0.03	0.01
bedrooms	3	0.02	0.10	0.15	0.12	0.11
	4	0.01	0.02	0.02	0.08	0.07

Table 6.14. Joint probability distribution for X, number of household members, and Y, number of bedrooms.

You can see from this table that low values of X are more likely to be associated with low values of Y and high values of X with high values of Y. This is what you would expect: the more members in a household, the more bedrooms the household requires. This joint variability is measured by the **covariance**. It is the average of the product of the deviation of X from its mean and the deviation of Y from its mean. Thus the covariance, $\mathrm{Cov}(X, Y)$, of two random variables X and Y is defined as

$$\mathrm{Cov}(X, Y) = \mathrm{E}\big((X - \mu_X)(Y - \mu_Y)\big) \qquad (6.1)$$

where $\mu_X = \mathrm{E}(X)$ is the mean of X and $\mu_Y = \mathrm{E}(Y)$ is the mean of Y.

You may remember meeting the concept of covariance briefly in S1 Chapter 9, in the discussion on correlation. In that case the covariance of a sample was calculated.

If Y tends to be higher than its mean when X is higher than its mean, then the covariance will be positive. If, on the other hand, Y tends to be lower than its mean when X is higher than its mean, then the covariance will be negative.

Another version of Equation 6.1 is easier to use in calculations. It can be derived as follows.

$$\text{Cov}(X, Y) = \text{E}\big((X - \mu_X)(Y - \mu_Y)\big) = \text{E}\big(XY - \mu_X Y - \mu_Y X + \mu_X \mu_Y\big)$$
$$= \text{E}(XY) - \mu_X \text{E}(Y) - \mu_Y \text{E}(X) + \mu_X \mu_Y$$
$$= \text{E}(XY) - \mu_X \mu_Y - \mu_Y \mu_X + \mu_X \mu_Y$$
$$= \text{E}(XY) - \mu_X \mu_Y.$$

So $\quad \text{Cov}(X, Y) = \text{E}(XY) - \mu_X \mu_Y.$ $\qquad$ (6.2)

Example 6.6.1

Calculate the covariance of X and Y for the probability distribution in Table 6.14.

The expected value of XY is found by multiplying each value of XY by the corresponding probability and then summing. Reading across the rows in Table 6.14 this gives

$$
\begin{aligned}
\text{E}(XY) = (1 \times 1) \times 0.03 + (1 \times 2) \times 0.02 + (1 \times 3) \times 0.02 + (1 \times 4) \times 0.02 \\
+ (1 \times 5) \times 0.01 \\
+ (2 \times 1) \times 0.04 + (2 \times 2) \times 0.06 + (2 \times 3) \times 0.06 + (2 \times 4) \times 0.03 \\
+ (2 \times 5) \times 0.01 \\
+ (3 \times 1) \times 0.02 + (3 \times 2) \times 0.10 + (3 \times 3) \times 0.15 + (3 \times 4) \times 0.12 \\
+ (3 \times 5) \times 0.11 \\
+ (4 \times 1) \times 0.01 + (4 \times 2) \times 0.02 + (4 \times 3) \times 0.02 + (4 \times 4) \times 0.08 \\
+ (4 \times 5) \times 0.07 \\
= 9.5.
\end{aligned}
$$

The expected values of X and Y were calculated in Section 6.2. They are $\text{E}(X) = 3.25$ and $\text{E}(Y) = 2.8$. Therefore from Equation 6.2 the covariance of X and Y is

$$\text{Cov}(X, Y) = \text{E}(XY) - \mu_X \mu_Y = 9.5 - (3.25 \times 2.8) = 9.5 - 9.1 = 0.4.$$

Thus the covariance is positive as expected.

If two variables, X and Y, are independent, then $\text{E}(XY) = \mu_X \mu_Y$. (A proof is given in Section 6.7.) As a result, when X and Y are independent their covariance is zero. This is what you would expect because covariance measures the association between two variables.

The converse is not true, however. A zero value for the covariance does *not* imply that the two variables are independent. This is illustrated in the following example.

Example 6.6.2
The joint probability distribution of two discrete random variables is given in the table.

		X		
		0	1	2
	0	$\frac{1}{8}$	0	$\frac{1}{8}$
Y	1	0	$\frac{1}{2}$	0
	2	$\frac{1}{8}$	0	$\frac{1}{8}$

(a) Demonstrate that X and Y are not independent.
(b) Find the covariance of X and Y.

(a) The marginal distributions of X and Y are shown in the table below.

		X			
		0	1	2	
	0	$\frac{1}{8}$	0	$\frac{1}{8}$	$\frac{1}{4}$
Y	1	0	$\frac{1}{2}$	0	$\frac{1}{2}$
	2	$\frac{1}{8}$	0	$\frac{1}{8}$	$\frac{1}{4}$
		$\frac{1}{4}$	$\frac{1}{2}$	$\frac{1}{4}$	1

From this table $P(X = 1, Y = 1) = \frac{1}{2}$ and $P(X = 1)P(Y = 1) = \frac{1}{2} \times \frac{1}{2} = \frac{1}{4}$. Since $P(X = 1, Y = 1) \neq P(X = 1)P(Y = 1)$, X and Y are not independent.

(b) Both of the marginal distributions are symmetrical about the value 1, so

$$E(X) = E(Y) = 1.$$

Omitting terms for which either the probability is 0 or the value of XY is 0 (since these make no contribution to the sum),

$$E(XY) = (1 \times 1) \times \frac{1}{2} + (2 \times 2) \times \frac{1}{8} = 1.$$

Therefore $Cov(XY) = E(X)E(Y) - \mu_X \mu_Y = 1 - (1 \times 1) = 0$.

So the covariance of X and Y is zero even though the variables are not independent. This corresponds to the situation which you met in S1 where the correlation coefficient was 0 because there was no linear correlation although the scatter diagram showed a relation of another type, for example a quadratic relation.

6.7* Proof that $E(XY) = E(X)E(Y) = \mu_X \mu_Y$ for independent random variables

You may omit this section if you wish.

As in Section 6.4, the proof will be given in the first instance for two discrete variables X and Y where X takes three values and Y takes four values. X and Y have the joint probability distribution shown in Table 6.7.

In order to find the value of $E(XY)$ it is necessary to calculate the value of xy for each cell in Table 6.7, then multiply by the corresponding probability and finally sum the resulting products. The step of calculating xy and multiplying by the corresponding probability is shown in Table 6.15.

| | | X | |
	x_1	x_2	x_3
y_1	$x_1 y_1\, P(X = x_1, Y = y_1)$	$x_2 y_1\, P(X = x_2, Y = y_1)$	$x_3 y_1\, P(X = x_3, Y = y_1)$
Y y_2	$x_1 y_2\, P(X = x_1, Y = y_2)$	$x_2 y_2\, P(X = x_2, Y = y_2)$	$x_3 y_2\, P(X = x_3, Y = y_2)$
y_3	$x_1 y_3\, P(X = x_1, Y = y_3)$	$x_2 y_3\, P(X = x_2, Y = y_3)$	$x_3 y_3\, P(X = x_3, Y = y_3)$
y_4	$x_1 y_4\, P(X = x_1, Y = y_4)$	$x_2 y_4\, P(X = x_2, Y = y_4)$	$x_3 y_4\, P(X = x_3, Y = y_4)$

Table 6.15. Joint probability distribution for two random variables showing the products required to calculate E(XY).

If X and Y are independent,

$$P(X = x_i, Y = y_j) = P(X = x_i)P(Y = y_j) \text{ for all } i, j.$$

Table 6.16 reproduces Table 6.15 with the probabilities written as products of two independent probabilities.

| | | X | |
	x_1	x_2	x_3
y_1	$x_1 y_1\, P_X(X = x_1)P_Y(Y = y_1)$	$x_2 y_1\, P_X(X = x_2)P_Y(Y = y_1)$	$x_3 y_1\, P_X(X = x_3)P_Y(Y = y_1)$
Y y_2	$x_1 y_2\, P_X(X = x_1)P_Y(Y = y_2)$	$x_2 y_2\, P_X(X = x_2)P_Y(Y = y_2)$	$x_3 y_2\, P_X(X = x_3)P_Y(Y = y_2)$
y_3	$x_1 y_3\, P_X(X = x_1)P_Y(Y = y_3)$	$x_2 y_3\, P_X(X = x_2)P_Y(Y = y_3)$	$x_3 y_3\, P_X(X = x_3)P_Y(Y = y_3)$
y_4	$x_1 y_4\, P_X(X = x_1)P_Y(Y = y_4)$	$x_2 y_4\, P_X(X = x_2)P_Y(Y = y_4)$	$x_3 y_4\, P_X(X = x_3)P_Y(Y = y_4)$

Table 6.16. Joint probability distribution for two random variables showing the products required to calculate E(XY) assuming that X and Y are independent.

Consider the first column in Table 6.16. The terms have the common factor $x_1 P_X(X = x_1)$ and so the sum of the terms in this column can be written

$$x_1 P_X(X = x_1)\big(y_1 P_Y(Y = y_1) + y_2 P_Y(Y = y_2) + y_3 P_Y(Y = y_3) + y_4 P_Y(Y = y_4)\big).$$

The sum of the terms in the outer brackets is $E(Y)$, so the sum of the terms in the first column is $x_1 P_X(X = x_1) E(Y)$. Similarly the sums of the terms in the second and third columns are $x_2 P_X(X = x_2) E(Y)$ and $x_3 P_X(X = x_3) E(Y)$ respectively. Thus the sum of all the terms in Table 6.16 is

$$x_1 P_X(X = x_1) E(Y) + x_2 P_X(X = x_2) E(Y) + x_3 P_X(X = x_3) E(Y),$$

which can be factorised to give

$$= (x_1 P_X(X = x_1) + x_2 P_X(X = x_2) + x_3 P_X(X = x_3)) E(Y)$$
$$= E(X) E(Y).$$

This proves that $E(XY) = E(X)E(Y)$, and since $E(X) = \mu_X$ and $E(Y) = \mu_Y$ it follows that $E(XY) = \mu_X \mu_Y$.

As in Section 6.4 this proof can be generalised to any number of rows and columns by letting X take m values $x_1, x_2, \ldots, x_m$ and Y take n values $y_1, y_2, \ldots, y_n$ and following the argument through in the same way.

6.8 The relation between variance and covariance

The covariance of two random variables is a way of characterising the extent to which the variables fail to be independent. It can be used to adjust the relation $\operatorname{Var}(aX \pm bY) = a^2 \operatorname{Var}(X) + b^2 \operatorname{Var}(Y)$, which you met for two *independent* random variables in S3 Section 2.2. The more general relation is

$$\operatorname{Var}(aX \pm bY) = a^2 \operatorname{Var}(X) + b^2 \operatorname{Var}(Y) \pm 2ab \operatorname{Cov}(X, Y), \qquad (6.3)$$

which is true for all pairs of variables. This relation reverts to the previous one when X and Y are independent since in this case $\operatorname{Cov}(X, Y) = 0$.

Equation 6.3 is straightforward to prove.

$$\operatorname{Var}(aX \pm bY) = E\left((aX \pm bY)^2\right) - (E(aX \pm bY))^2$$
$$= E\left(a^2 X^2 \pm 2abXY + b^2 Y^2\right) - (a\mu_X \pm b\mu_Y)^2$$
$$= a^2 E\left(X^2\right) \pm 2ab E(XY) + b^2 E\left(Y^2\right) - \left(a^2 \mu_X^2 \pm 2ab\mu_X \mu_Y + b^2 \mu_Y^2\right)$$
$$= a^2 \left(E\left(X^2\right) - \mu_X^2\right) + b^2 \left(E\left(Y^2\right) - b^2 \mu_Y^2\right) \pm 2ab\left(E(XY) - \mu_X \mu_Y\right)$$
$$= a^2 \operatorname{Var}(X) + b^2 \operatorname{Var}(Y) \pm 2ab \operatorname{Cov}(X, Y).$$

Example 6.8.1
A fair six-sided dice has two faces painted blue and the remainder red. The dice is thrown six times. Two random variables are defined as R, the number of times a red face is uppermost, and B, the number of times a blue face is uppermost in the same sequence of six throws.
(a) Write down the values of $\operatorname{Var}(R)$, $\operatorname{Var}(B)$ and $\operatorname{Var}(R + B)$ and hence find $\operatorname{Cov}(R, B)$.
(b) If each throw of red scores 3 and each throw of blue scores 4, find the variance of the total score, S, for a sequence of six throws.

(a) The random variable R has a binomial distribution with $n = 6$ and $p = \frac{2}{3}$, so $\operatorname{Var}(R) = npq = 6 \times \frac{1}{3} \times \frac{2}{3} = \frac{4}{3}$. By similar reasoning $\operatorname{Var}(B) = \frac{4}{3}$. Since the sum of R and B is always 6 in any sequence of six throws it follows that $\operatorname{Var}(R + B) = 0$.

From Equation 6.3

$$\mathrm{Var}\,(R+B) = \mathrm{Var}\,(R) + \mathrm{Var}\,(B) + 2\,\mathrm{Cov}\,(R,B).$$

Substituting the values above gives

$$0 = \tfrac{4}{3} + \tfrac{4}{3} + 2\,\mathrm{Cov}\,(R,B), \quad \text{giving} \quad \mathrm{Cov}\,(R,B) = -\tfrac{4}{3}.$$

(b) The total score S is given by $S = 3R + 4S$. From Equation 6.3

$$\mathrm{Var}\,(3R+4S) = 3^2\,\mathrm{Var}\,(R) + 4^2\,\mathrm{Var}\,(B) + 2\times 3\times 4\times \mathrm{Cov}\,(R,B).$$

Substituting the values above for $\mathrm{Var}\,(R)$, $\mathrm{Var}\,(B)$ and $\mathrm{Cov}\,(R,B)$ gives

$$\mathrm{Var}\,(3R+4S) = 3^2\times\tfrac{4}{3} + 4^2\times\tfrac{4}{3} + 2\times 3\times 4\times\left(-\tfrac{4}{3}\right) = \tfrac{4}{3}.$$

- The covariance $\mathrm{Cov}\,(X,Y)$ of two random variables X and Y is defined by

  $$\mathrm{Cov}\,(X,Y) = \mathrm{E}\big((X-\mu_X)(Y-\mu_Y)\big),$$

  where $\mu_X = \mathrm{E}(X)$ is the mean of X and $\mu_Y = \mathrm{E}(Y)$ is the mean of Y.

- The covariance of X and Y can also be calculated using the equation

  $$\mathrm{Cov}\,(X,Y) = \mathrm{E}(XY) - \mu_X\mu_Y.$$

- If two variables are independent, then their covariance is zero.

- The converse is not true: zero covariance does not imply independence.

- The relation between variance and covariance is

  $$\mathrm{Var}\,(aX\pm bY) = a^2\mathrm{Var}\,(X) + b^2\mathrm{Var}\,(Y) \pm 2ab\,\mathrm{Cov}\,(X,Y)$$

  for all pairs of variables.

- If X and Y are independent, this relation becomes

  $$\mathrm{Var}\,(aX\pm bY) = a^2\mathrm{Var}\,(X) + b^2\mathrm{Var}\,(Y).$$

Exercise 6C

1 Two random variables X and Y have the joint probability distribution below.

		X	
		1	2
Y	1	0.1	0.3
	2	0.4	0.2

(a) Show that X and Y are not independent.

(b) Calculate $\mathrm{Cov}\,(X,Y)$.

2 Two random variables U and V have the joint probability distribution given below.

			U		
		0	1	2	3
	0	0.06	0.06	0.06	0.02
V	1	0.12	0.12	0.12	0.04
	2	0.09	0.09	0.09	0.03
	3	0.03	0.03	0.03	0.01

(a) Show that U and V are independent by comparing the marginal and conditional distributions of U.

(b) Calculate $E(U)$, $E(V)$ and $E(UV)$. Hence calculate $\text{Cov}(U,V)$ and confirm that it is equal to 0.

3 Two random variables X and Y have the joint probability distribution below.

			X	
		1	2	3
Y	1	0.1	0.25	0.35
	2	0.15	0.1	0.05

Find the covariance of X and Y. Are X and Y independent?

4 Two fair spinners, one red and one blue, are spun together. Both spinners are numbered 1, 2, 3. The two random variables X and Y are the score on the red spinner and the sum of the scores on the two spinners respectively. The joint probability distribution of X and Y is given below (see Exercise 6A Question 3).

			X	
		1	2	3
	2	$\frac{1}{9}$	0	0
	3	$\frac{1}{9}$	$\frac{1}{9}$	0
Y	4	$\frac{1}{9}$	$\frac{1}{9}$	$\frac{1}{9}$
	5	0	$\frac{1}{9}$	$\frac{1}{9}$
	6	0	0	$\frac{1}{9}$

Calculate $\text{Cov}(X,Y)$. What does your answer tell you about the independence of X and Y?

5 A couple decide that they will continue to have children until they have one child of each sex or until they have four children, whichever occurs sooner. The joint probability distribution of G and B, where B is the number of boys in the final family and G is the number of girls, is given below (see Exercise 6A Question 4).

		G				
		0	1	2	3	4
	0	0	0	0	0	$\frac{1}{16}$
	1	0	$\frac{1}{2}$	$\frac{1}{8}$	$\frac{1}{16}$	0
B	2	0	$\frac{1}{8}$	0	0	0
	3	0	$\frac{1}{16}$	0	0	0
	4	$\frac{1}{16}$	0	0	0	0

Calculate $\mathrm{Cov}(G, B)$.

6 The variances of two random variables S and T are 3 and 2 respectively and $\mathrm{Cov}(S, T) = 4$. Find

(a) $\mathrm{Var}(S + T)$,

(b) $\mathrm{Var}(S - T)$,

(c) $\mathrm{Var}(2S + 3T)$,

(d) $\mathrm{Var}(3S - T + 1)$.

7 A bin contains a large number of seeds of which 20% will produce a plant with a red flower and 30% will produce a plant with a yellow flower. The rest will not germinate. Two seeds are chosen at random. R and Y are the random variables denoting, respectively, the number of red and yellow flowers that will be produced from the seeds. The following table gives the joint probability distribution of R and Y.

		R		
		0	1	2
	0	0.25	0.20	0.04
Y	1	a	b	0
	2	0.09	0	0

(a) Find the values of a and b.

(b) Find the marginal distributions of R and Y.

(c) Show that $\mathrm{E}(R) = 0.4$ and find $\mathrm{E}(Y)$.

(d) Find the mean and variance of $R + Y$.

(e) Find $\mathrm{Cov}(R, Y)$ and deduce that $\mathrm{Var}(R + Y) \neq \mathrm{Var}(R) + \mathrm{Var}(Y)$.   (OCR, adapted)

8 Two random variables U and V have the joint probability distribution below

		U		
		0	1	2
	0	a	b	a
V	1	b	0	b
	2	a	b	a

where a and b are constants between 0 and 1.

(a) Show that $a + b = \frac{1}{4}$.

(b) Find $\text{Cov}(U, V)$.

(c) Are U and V independent? Justify your answer.

(d) Find $\text{Var}(U + V)$ in terms of b.

9 Show that $\text{Cov}(X, X) = \text{Var}(X)$.

10† X and Y are two independent random variables, with variances σ_x^2 and σ_y^2 respectively. Two other variables W and Z are defined by $W = X + Y$ and $Z = X - Y$.

Show that

(a) $\text{Cov}(X, Z) = \sigma_x^2$,

(b) $\text{Cov}(W, Z) = \sigma_x^2 - \sigma_y^2$.

11† Two discrete random variables X and Y are related by $Y = aX + b$. Show that

$$\frac{\text{Cov}(X, Y)}{\sqrt{\text{Var}(X)\text{Var}(Y)}} = 1.$$

Miscellaneous exercise 6

1 Two discrete random variables have the joint probability distribution given in the table.

		X		
		1	2	3
	0	0.12	0.20	0.10
Y	1	0.10	0.12	0.14
	2	0.12	0	0.10

Show that $\text{Cov}(X, Y) = 0$, but that X and Y are not independent. (OCR)

2 Two discrete random variables X and Y have a joint probability distribution defined by

$$P(X = x, Y = y) = \begin{cases} k(x + y) & \text{for } x = 0, 1, 2 \text{ and } y = 0, 1, 2, \\ 0 & \text{otherwise.} \end{cases}$$

(a) Find the value of k.

(b) Tabulate the joint probability distribution of X and Y.

(c) Calculate $\text{Cov}(X, Y)$.

3 Two fair tetrahedral dice have their faces numbered 1, 2, 3, 4. When a dice is thrown the score is the number on the bottom face. Let X and Y denote the two scores when the dice are thrown simultaneously. Two discrete random variables, M and D, are defined by:

M = the lower of X and Y, or their common value if they are equal;

$D = |X - Y|$.

(a) Find the joint probability distribution of M and D.

(b) Calculate $\text{Cov}(M, D)$.

(c) Calculate $\text{Var}(M + D)$.

(d) Find the expected value and variance of D given $M = 1$.

(e) Find the expected value and variance of M given $D = 2$.

4 In a board game a player throws a fair tetrahedral dice with its faces numbered 1, 2, 3, 4. The number on the face which lands downwards determines the number of 'steps' which the player will make on that turn. Each step can be either forwards or backwards. A coin is thrown to determine the direction of each step. If the coin gives a head, the step is taken forwards, and if the coin gives a tail, the step is taken backwards. For example, if a player throws a 3 with the dice and then head, tail, tail with the coin, that player moves one step forwards and two backwards.

Let S denote the throw on the dice and hence the number of steps moved and D denote the distance in steps, without regard to sign, from the player's starting point at the beginning of the turn. In the example above, $S = 3$ and $D = 1$.

(a) Copy and complete the table below showing the joint probability distribution of S and D.

			S		
		1	2	3	4
	0	0			
	1	$\frac{1}{4}$		$\frac{3}{16}$	
D	2			0	
	3				
	4				

(b) Calculate the mean and variance of D.   (c) Calculate $\text{Cov}(D, S)$.

5 A large batch of tulip bulbs contains 50% which have white flowers, 30% which have yellow flowers and 20% which have mauve flowers. Three bulbs are selected at random. The random variables M and Y are defined as the numbers of bulbs out of the sample of three which give mauve flowers and yellow flowers respectively.

(a) How are M, Y and $M + Y$ distributed?

(b) Calculate $\text{Var}(M)$, $\text{Var}(Y)$ and $\text{Var}(M + Y)$ and hence deduce $\text{Cov}(M, Y)$.

(c) Find the joint probability distribution of M and Y.

(d) Calculate the value of $\text{Cov}(M, Y)$ from the joint probability distribution and verify that your answer is the same as you obtained in (b).

6 The tops of bottles of milk are equally likely to be red or blue. The random variable X denotes the total number of bottles of milk delivered to a certain house on a randomly chosen day. The random variable Y denotes the number of red-topped bottles of milk delivered to that house on that day. The marginal distribution of X is given by

$$P(X = r) = \begin{cases} k(4 - r) & r = 0, 1, 2, 3, \\ 0 & \text{otherwise.} \end{cases}$$

(a) Determine the value of k.

(b) Tabulate the joint probability distribution of X and Y.

(c) Tabulate the marginal distribution of Y.

(d) Show that $P(X = 2 \mid Y = 2) = \frac{4}{7}$.

(e) Find $\text{Cov}(X, Y)$.

(f) It is known that there was exactly one red-topped bottle of milk delivered to the house on that day. Determine the expected total number of bottles of milk delivered to that house on that day. (OCR)

7 The discrete random variable X can take values 0, 1, 2 and 3 with equal probabilities. The random variables X_1 and X_2 are independent observations of X, and the random variables Y and Z are defined as follows:

Y = the larger of X_1 and X_2, or their common value if they are equal;

$Z = |X_1 - X_2|$.

Draw up a table giving the joint distribution of Y and Z.

(a) Show that $P(Y > Z) = \frac{9}{16}$.

(b) Write down the marginal distributions of Y and Z.

(c) Show that $E(Y^2) = \frac{43}{8}$ and find $E(Z^2)$.

(d) Calculate $\text{Cov}(Y^2, Z^2)$. (OCR)

8 A computer is programmed to display three independent digits, A, B and C, each of which can be 0 with probability p or 1 with probability $q = 1 - p$. The random variables X and Y are defined by $X = A + B$ and $Y = B + C$.

(a) Construct a table giving the joint probability distribution of X and Y, in terms of p and q, simplifying the entries in the table.

(b) Using the probabilities in the table, find the marginal distributions of X and Y, and show that X and Y have the same binomial distribution.

(c) State, with a reason, whether X and Y are independent.

Out of 1000 such displays generated, the number of times the combination $X = 0$ and $Y = 0$ occurred was 231.

(d) Test the hypothesis that $p = 0.6$, at the 5% significance level, against the alternative hypothesis that $p \neq 0.6$. (OCR, adapted)

9[†] A barrel contains a large number of grapes. Each of two green-grocers, X and Y, takes a grape at random from the barrel. The masses x and y of the chosen grapes are recorded, the grapes are then eaten and two new grapes are chosen. For each pair of values x and y the difference $d = x - y$ is calculated. The first four values of d that are obtained are all different in magnitude. These values are then replaced by their signed ranks. The statistic S is equal to the lesser of A and B, where A is the number of positive ranks and B is the number of negative ranks. The statistic T is equal to the lesser of G and $|H|$, where G is the sum of the positive ranks and H is the sum of the negative ranks.

(a) Copy and complete the table below showing the joint distribution of S and T.

		T					
		0	1	2	3	4	5
S	0	$\frac{1}{8}$	0	0	0	0	0
	1	0	$\frac{1}{8}$	$\frac{1}{8}$			
	2						

(b) Show that $\operatorname{Var}(S) = \frac{7}{16}$ and that $\operatorname{Var}(T) = \frac{39}{16}$.

(c) Calculate $\operatorname{Cov}(S, T)$.

(d) Find the largest integer $t*$ such that $P(T \leqslant t*) < 0.4$ and the largest integer $s*$ such that $P(S \leqslant s*) < 0.4$.

Find $P(S \leqslant s* \mid T \leqslant t*)$.

(OCR, adapted)

10[†] All trains from A stop at B. There are three types of train: express, semi-express and commuter trains (denoted by E, S and C in the table). The times taken by the trains for the journey from A to B are respectively 50 minutes, 60 minutes and 75 minutes, and all trains run to time. There is a train from A to B every 10 minutes. A traveller arrives at A immediately after a train has left for B. The joint probability distribution for the types of the next two trains is given in the table.

		Second train		
		E	S	C
First	E	0	0.01	0.08
train	S	0.01	0	0.16
	C	0.08	0.16	0.50

(a) Determine the probability that the traveller arrives at B within 81 minutes of his or her arrival at A,

   (i) given that the traveller catches the first train,

   (ii) given that if the first train is a commuter train then the traveller catches the second train.

Let Y denote the length of time that elapses from the traveller arriving at A to the traveller arriving at B.

(b) In each of the cases (i) and (ii) above, find $E(Y)$.

Denote by X the time taken for the first train to travel between A and B.

(c) Find, for (ii) above, the joint probability distribution of X and Y.   (OCR, adapted)

Revision exercise 2

1 (a) Show that, if the events D and E are independent then so are the events D' and E'.

(b) A delicatessen shop sells both green olives and black olives. The probability that, at any time, the shop is out of stock of green olives is 0.05 and of black olives is 0.03. The probability that it is out of stock of at least one of these items is 0.06. The events 'the shop is out of stock of green olives' and 'the shop is out of stock of black olives' are denoted by G and B respectively. Calculate $P(B \cap G)$ and $P(G' \mid B')$.

Determine whether G and B are independent.

2 When Aruna leaves the house she may wear a coat, a hat or gloves. The events C, H and G are defined for when Aruna leaves the house on a randomly chosen day.

C: Aruna wears a coat

H: Aruna wears a hat

G: Aruna wears gloves

It is given that $P(C) = 0.75$, $P(H) = 0.3$, $P(G) = 0.25$, $P(H \cup C) = 0.85$,

$P(H \cap G) = 0.10$, $P(G \cap C) = 0.15$ and $P\big((H \cup C \cup G)'\big) = 0.1$.

(a) Find $P(H \cap C)$ and $P(C \mid H')$.

(b) Express, in terms of the above events, the probability that Aruna wears neither a hat nor a coat, and calculate this probability.

(c) Find the probability that Aruna wears all three items.

(d) If Aruna leaves the house without a hat, find the least value of the probability that she is wearing either a coat or gloves or both coat and gloves.

3 The average breaking strength of a wire is supposed to be at least 500 N. A random sample of 12 lengths of the wire, selected from a large batch, were tested and the forces, in newtons, at which they broke were as follows.

474   513   458   488   518   479   490   484   503   491   486   469

The sign test is used to test the hypothesis that the average breaking strength of the wire is at least 500 N.

(a) State which average (mean, median, mode) is referred to in the hypothesis.

(b) Carry out the test at the 5% significance level.

(c) Use the Wilcoxon signed-rank test, to test the same hypothesis at the same significance level.

(d) State, giving a reason, which of the two tests should give a more reliable conclusion.

4 In order to compare the quality of the water bottled at two springs, A and B, situated in nearby regions of Trentino, random samples of 5 bottles from A and 6 bottles from B were selected. Each was tasted by two experts who did not know which springs produced the water. They then agreed a rank order for the quality of the water according to criteria laid down. The following table gives the rank and the spring for each of the bottles.

Rank	1	2	3	4	5	6	7	8	9	10	11
Spring	A	A	B	A	A	B	B	B	A	B	B

Test, at the 10% significance level, whether there is a difference in the quality of the water from the two springs.

A extra bottle is selected from spring A and tasted to see which rank it should have in relation to the other 11. Determine possible ranks of the extra bottle if its inclusion leads to acceptance, at the 10% significance level, that there is a difference in the quality of the water from the two springs.

5 State circumstances under which a non-parametric test of significance should be used in preference to a parametric test.

It is generally believed by husbands that they are more knowledgeable politically than their wives. In order to test this belief a random sample of 16 married couples was selected and each person was given the same 20 political questions to answer. The results were as follows, where H denotes that the husband answered more questions correctly and W denotes that the wife answered more questions correctly.

$$W \quad W \quad H \quad W \quad H \quad H \quad H \quad W \quad H \quad W \quad W \quad W \quad W \quad W \quad W \quad W$$

(a) Explain why, whatever the level of significance, it cannot be concluded from the data that, on average, husbands are more politically knowledgeable that their wives.

(b) Test, at the 5% significance level, whether (on average) husbands are less politically knowledgeable than their wives.

The actual values for the husband's score minus the wife's score are as follows.

$$-18 \ -13 \ +7 \ -2 \ +4 \ +5 \ +10 \ -8 \ +6 \ -9 \ -1 \ -15 \ -12 \ -17 \ -11 \ -19$$

Carry out another non-parametric test, at the 5% significance level, of whether (on average) husbands are less politically knowledgeable than their wives. (OCR, adapted)

6 Alice and Randip are each learning to shoot at a target with a bow and arrow. The probability that Alice scores an inner with any shot is $\frac{1}{3}$ and the probability that Randip scores an inner with any shot is $\frac{1}{4}$. They shoot consecutively, Alice first, until an inner is scored. The number of shots required (including the one for the inner) is denoted by X. Assuming that the shots are independent, show that the probability generating function of X is $\dfrac{2t+t^2}{6\left(1-\frac{1}{2}t^2\right)}$. Use the probability generating function to find

(a) $E(X)$, (b) $Var(X)$, (c) $P(X=12)$.

7 The random variable X has probability density function given by

$$f(x) = \tfrac{1}{2} a e^{-a|x|} \qquad -\infty < x < \infty,$$

where a is a positive constant.

(a) Sketch the graph of $f(x)$ and state the value of $E(X)$.

(b) Show that the moment generating function of X is $\dfrac{a^2}{a^2 - t^2}$.

(c) Use the moment generating function to find $E(X^2)$.

The *kurtosis* of a distribution measures the extent to which it is peaked or flat. A statistic sometimes used is denoted by α_4, where

$$\alpha_4 = \frac{E\big((X-\mu)^4\big)}{(\mathrm{Var}(X))^2}.$$

For a normal distribution, $\alpha_4 = 3$. When $\alpha_4 < 3$ the distribution is flatter (platykurtic) and when $\alpha_4 > 3$ the distribution is more peaked (leptokurtic).

Find α_4 for the above distribution and comment on its value.

8 Show that the probability generating function of X where $X \sim B(n, p)$ is $(1 - p + pt)^n$.

If $Y \sim B(m, p)$, write down the probability generating function of the sum of an observation of X and an independent observation of Y. Identify the distribution of $X + Y$.

(a) Show that $\tfrac{1}{2}\left(\dfrac{X}{n} + \dfrac{Y}{m}\right)$ is an unbiased estimator of p.

(b) Find the variance of the estimator.

9 The random variable X has unknown mean μ and unknown variance σ^2. The random variable Y has unknown mean 2μ and unknown variance $2\sigma^2$. The mean of 10 random observations of X is denoted by $\overline{X}$, and an unbiased estimate of the variance of X is denoted by S_x^2. The mean of 5 random observations of Y is denoted by $\overline{Y}$, and an unbiased estimate of the variance of Y is denoted by S_y^2. The statistic T_1 is given by $T_1 = \lambda \overline{X} + \tfrac{1}{2}(1 - \lambda)\overline{Y}$, where λ is a constant.

(a) Show that T_1 is an unbiased estimator of μ.

(b) Find the value of λ for which the variance of T_1 is a minimum, and find this variance.

Show that the statistics T_2 and T_3 given by $T_2 = \tfrac{1}{3}\big(S_x^2 + S_y^2\big)$ and $T_3 = S_y^2 - S_x^2$ are both unbiased estimators of σ^2 and determine which is more efficient.

10 The random variables X and Y have the joint probability distribution function given in the table below, from which two entries have been omitted.

		X		
		0	1	2
	1	0.2	0.3	0.15
Y	2	0.1	0.1	
	3	0.05		0.1

Find

(a) the missing values,

(b) the marginal distributions of X and Y,

(c) $\text{Cov}(X,Y)$.

State, giving a reason, whether X and Y are independent.

Find the value of $\dfrac{\text{Cov}(X,Y)}{\sqrt{\text{Var}(X)\,\text{Var}(Y)}}$ for this distribution.

11 A bag contains three red counters, two blue counters and one green counter. A random sample of three counters is drawn from the bag without replacement. The numbers of red and blue counters drawn are denoted by R and B respectively. Below is a table showing the joint probability distribution of R and B.

		R			
		0	1	2	3
	0	0	0	0.15	0.05
B	1	0	0.3	0.3	0
	2	0.05	0.15	0	0

(a) Show how the value of $P(R=1 \text{ and } B=1)$ which is given in the table can be obtained.

(b) Find the marginal distributions of R and B.

(c) Find $\text{Cov}(R,B)$.

(d) Find the expectation and variance of X, where $X = R + B$.

(e) Find the probability that the sample contains one green counter given that it contains at least one red counter.

Mock examination 1 for S4

Time 1 hour 20 minutes

Answer all the questions.
You are permitted to use a graphic calculator in this paper.

1 An unbiased coin is tossed until a head is obtained. The number of tosses required is denoted by X. Show that the probability generating function of X is $\dfrac{t}{2-t}$. [2]

Five people each toss an unbiased coin until they each obtain a head. Write down the probability generating function of Y, the total number of tosses required by the five people. [1]

Calculate $P(Y = 6)$. [2]

2 A new drug for treating leukaemia is tested using 11 rats, each at an advanced stage of the disease. Six of the rats are treated with the drug and the remaining five rats (the control group) are not treated. The times, in months, that the rats survived after the commencement of the test are as follows.

Untreated rats	2.4	1.8	2.8	1.7	2.0	
Treated rats	1.1	2.5	4.8	5.4	3.2	5.6

  (i)   State suitable hypotheses for a non-parametric test of whether the drug can be claimed to be effective. [1]

  (ii) Carry out the test at the 5% significance level. [5]

3 Explain why unbiased estimators of a population parameter, θ, are usually preferred to others. [1]

Two unbiased estimators are proposed. How do you decide which is more efficient? [1]

The random variable X has known mean μ but unknown variance σ^2. A sample of n independent observations, X_1, X_2, ... , X_n, is obtained. The statistic T is defined by

$$T = k\sum_{i=1}^{n}(X_i - \mu)^2, \text{ where } k \text{ is a constant.}$$

Show that $\dfrac{1}{n}$ is the only value of k for which T is an unbiased estimator of σ^2. [3]

Suppose that five independent observations of $X \sim N(0,\sigma^2)$ are
$$-2.1 \quad -0.8 \quad -0.9 \quad 1.4 \quad 2.3$$

  (i)   Find an unbiased estimate of σ^2. [1]

  (ii) Estimate the probability that the sum of five random observations of X exceeds 1.5. [2]

4 The moment generating function of the random variable X, which has a χ^2 distribution with ν degrees of freedom, is given by

$$M_X(t) = (1-2t)^{-\frac{1}{2}\nu}.$$

(i) Show that $E(X) = \nu$. [2]

(ii) Find $\text{Var}(X)$. [2]

(iii) Obtain the moment generating function of the sum Y of two independent χ^2 random variables, one with 4 degrees of freedom and the other with 10 degrees of freedom. [1]

(iv) Identify the distribution of Y. [2]

(v) Estimate $P(Y \geqslant 21)$. [2]

5 A diagnostic test has been developed to detect the presence of a disease which occurs in 9% of the population. When given to a randomly chosen person the test gives a positive result (which indicates that the person has the disease) with probability p when the person actually has the disease, and with probability 0.08 when the person does not have the disease. D and A denote the events 'the person has the disease' and 'the test result is positive', respectively.

(i) Find, in terms of p,

(a) $P(A)$, [2]

(b) $P(D \mid A)$. [2]

(ii) Show that, for varying p, $P(D \mid A)$ has a greatest value and give this value. [3]

(iii) For the case $p = 0.95$, find the probability that the test gives an incorrect result. [3]

6 The times between successive arrivals of customers at a particular city cash-point were measured one Wednesday afternoon. The first 30 intervals (in minutes) were as follows.

```
0.6   2.1   3.4   0.4   0.7   1.7   4.8   1.8   2.9   3.2
5.3   8.1   6.4   0.2   2.4   2.8   1.9   5.2   0.8   2.6
1.3   3.6   1.5   4.3   7.3   2.5   1.3   6.2   0.2   1.9
```

(i) Draw a stem-and-leaf diagram for the data. [2]

(ii) The average time interval between successive arrivals at a similar cash-point in another part of the city is 1.75 minutes for Wednesday afternoons. It is required to test whether the average interval for the above cash-point is greater than 1.75 minutes.

(a) Explain why it is advisable to use a non-parametric test. [1]

(b) State, giving a reason, whether Wilcoxon's signed-rank test would be suitable for the test. [2]

(ii) Carry out a suitable test, at the 10% significance level. [5]

7 The discrete random variables X and Y take integer values with joint probability distribution given by

$$f(x,y) = \begin{cases} a(y-x+1) & 0 \leqslant x \leqslant y \leqslant 2, \\ 0 & \text{otherwise}, \end{cases}$$

where a is a constant.

(i)   Tabulate the distribution and show that $a = 0.1$.   [2]

(ii) Find the marginal distributions of X and Y.   [2]

(iii) Calculate $\text{Cov}(X,Y)$.   [3]

(iv) State, giving a reason, whether X and Y are independent.   [2]

(v)   Calculate $E(Y \mid X = 1)$.   [3]

Mock examination 2 for S4

Time 1 hour 20 minutes

Answer all the questions.
You are permitted to use a graphic calculator in this paper.

1 The students at a medical seminar on smoking comprised 6 smokers and 12 non-smokers. Their pulse rates, in beats per minute, were measured with the following results, which are ordered for convenience.

Non-smokers: 60   62   63   65   68   70   72   78   80   82   91   94

Smokers: 64   74   76   88   92   102

Assuming that the students were random samples of smokers and non-smokers, test, at the 5% significance level, whether there is a difference in the median pulse rates of smokers and non-smokers. [6]

2 For the events A and B, $P(A) = 0.6$, $P(B') = 0.2$ and $P(A \mid B) = 0.5$.

  (i)   Calculate $P(B \mid A)$. [2]

 (ii)   Show that A' and B' are mutually exclusive. [2]

A third event C is independent of A, B and $A \cap B$. Show that $P(A \cup B \cup C) = 1$. [3]

3 Find the moment generating function of the random variable X which has a uniform distribution over the interval $[-1, 1]$.

The sum of two independent observations of X is denoted by Y.

  (i)   Write down $M_Y(t)$, the moment generating function of Y. [1]

 (ii)   Expand $M_Y(t)$ in ascending powers of t as far as the term in t^4. Hence calculate $\mathrm{Var}(Y^2)$. [5]

4 A factory produces compact discs and there are two machines which press the same number of CDs each day. In a quality control exercise the numbers of faulty CDs produced by the machines were monitored over a period of 28 days. On 9 days machine B produced more faulty discs than machine A, and on 19 days machine A produced more faulty discs than machine B.

  (i)   Test, at the 5% significance level, whether machine A produces, on average, more faulty CDs than machine B. [7]

 (ii)   State, giving a reason, the type of error that could *not* have arisen in the test conclusion. [1]

5 The probability generating function of the random variable X is $\frac{1}{27}\left(t + \frac{2}{t}\right)^3$.

  (i)   Find $E(X)$ and $\mathrm{Var}(X)$. [5]

 (ii)   By finding the probability distribution of X, or otherwise, show that $\frac{1}{2}(X + 3)$ has a $B(n, p)$ distribution and give the values of n and p. [5]

6 An unbiased coin is tossed three times. The number of sequences of heads is denoted by X and the number of sequences of tails is denoted by Y. A sequence of heads begins and ends with a head so that for the outcome HHT $X = 1$ and $Y = 1$, and for THT $X = 1$ and $Y = 2$.

   (i)   Show that $P(X = 1, Y = 1) = \frac{1}{2}$ and obtain all other related probabilities.   [2]

   (ii) Show that the marginal distributions of X and Y are identical.   [2]

   (iii) By considering $P(X = 1 \mid Y = 1)$ show that X and Y are not independent.   [2]

   (iv) Show that $\text{Cov}(X, Y) = 0$ and comment on this in view of the result of part (iii).   [3]

7 The lifetime of a certain brand of TV tube can be modelled by a random variable X with probability density function given by

$$f(x) = \begin{cases} \dfrac{3a^3}{x^4} & x \geqslant a, \\ 0 & \text{otherwise,} \end{cases}$$

where a is an unknown constant.

The lifetimes of two randomly chosen tubes are X_1 and X_2 and an estimator T is defined by $T = \frac{1}{3}(X_1 + X_2)$.

   (i)   Show that T is an unbiased estimator of a.   [3]

   (ii) Given that $X_1 = 4.5$ and $X_2 = 9.9$, show that the value of T for this sample is an unrealistic estimate of a.   [1]

   (iii) Find the variance of T.   [3]

   (iv) The smaller of x_1 and x_2 is denoted by S. Explain why the cumulative distribution function of S is given by

$$G(s) = 1 - (1 - F(s))^2 \qquad \text{over } s \geqslant a,$$

   where $F(x)$ is the cumulative distribution function of X.   [1]

   (v)   Show that the probability density function of S is given by

$$g(s) = \begin{cases} \dfrac{6a^6}{s^7} & s \geqslant a, \\ 0 & \text{otherwise.} \end{cases}$$ [2]

   (vi) Show that $U = \frac{5}{6}S$ is also an unbiased estimator of a and determine which of T and U is more efficient.   [4]

Cumulative Binomial Probabilities

n = 5

p	0.05	0.10	0.15	1/6	0.20	0.25	0.30	1/3	0.35	0.40	0.45	0.50	0.55	0.60	0.65	2/3	0.70	0.75	0.80	5/6	0.85	0.90	0.95
x = 0	0.7738	0.5905	0.4437	0.4019	0.3277	0.2373	0.1681	0.1317	0.1160	0.0778	0.0503	0.0313	0.0185	0.0102	0.0053	0.0041	0.0024	0.0010	0.0003	0.0001	0.0001	0.0000	0.0000
1	0.9774	0.9185	0.8352	0.8038	0.7373	0.6328	0.5282	0.4609	0.4284	0.3370	0.2562	0.1875	0.1312	0.0870	0.0540	0.0453	0.0308	0.0156	0.0067	0.0033	0.0022	0.0005	0.0000
2	0.9988	0.9914	0.9734	0.9645	0.9421	0.8965	0.8369	0.7901	0.7648	0.6826	0.5931	0.5000	0.4069	0.3174	0.2352	0.2099	0.1631	0.1035	0.0579	0.0355	0.0266	0.0086	0.0012
3	1.0000	0.9995	0.9978	0.9967	0.9933	0.9844	0.9692	0.9547	0.9460	0.9130	0.8688	0.8125	0.7438	0.6630	0.5716	0.5391	0.4718	0.3672	0.2627	0.1962	0.1648	0.0815	0.0226
4	1.0000	1.0000	0.9999	0.9999	0.9997	0.9990	0.9976	0.9959	0.9947	0.9898	0.9815	0.9688	0.9497	0.9222	0.8840	0.8683	0.8319	0.7627	0.6723	0.5981	0.5563	0.4095	0.2262
5	1.0000	1.0000	1.0000	1.0000	1.0000	1.0000	1.0000	1.0000	1.0000	1.0000	1.0000	1.0000	1.0000	1.0000	1.0000	1.0000	1.0000	1.0000	1.0000	1.0000	1.0000	1.0000	1.0000

n = 6

p	0.05	0.10	0.15	1/6	0.20	0.25	0.30	1/3	0.35	0.40	0.45	0.50	0.55	0.60	0.65	2/3	0.70	0.75	0.80	5/6	0.85	0.90	0.95
x = 0	0.7351	0.5314	0.3771	0.3349	0.2621	0.1780	0.1176	0.0878	0.0754	0.0467	0.0277	0.0156	0.0083	0.0041	0.0018	0.0014	0.0007	0.0002	0.0001	0.0000	0.0000	0.0000	0.0000
1	0.9672	0.8857	0.7765	0.7368	0.6554	0.5339	0.4202	0.3512	0.3191	0.2333	0.1636	0.1094	0.0692	0.0410	0.0223	0.0178	0.0109	0.0046	0.0016	0.0007	0.0004	0.0001	0.0000
2	0.9978	0.9842	0.9527	0.9377	0.9011	0.8306	0.7443	0.6804	0.6471	0.5443	0.4415	0.3438	0.2553	0.1792	0.1174	0.1001	0.0705	0.0376	0.0170	0.0087	0.0059	0.0013	0.0001
3	0.9999	0.9987	0.9941	0.9913	0.9830	0.9624	0.9295	0.8999	0.8826	0.8208	0.7447	0.6563	0.5585	0.4557	0.3529	0.3196	0.2557	0.1694	0.0989	0.0623	0.0473	0.0159	0.0022
4	1.0000	0.9999	0.9996	0.9993	0.9984	0.9954	0.9891	0.9822	0.9777	0.9590	0.9308	0.8906	0.8364	0.7667	0.6809	0.6488	0.5798	0.4661	0.3446	0.2632	0.2235	0.1143	0.0328
5	1.0000	1.0000	1.0000	1.0000	0.9999	0.9998	0.9993	0.9986	0.9982	0.9959	0.9917	0.9844	0.9723	0.9533	0.9246	0.9122	0.8824	0.8220	0.7379	0.6651	0.6229	0.4686	0.2649
6	1.0000	1.0000	1.0000	1.0000	1.0000	1.0000	1.0000	1.0000	1.0000	1.0000	1.0000	1.0000	1.0000	1.0000	1.0000	1.0000	1.0000	1.0000	1.0000	1.0000	1.0000	1.0000	1.0000

n = 7

p	0.05	0.10	0.15	1/6	0.20	0.25	0.30	1/3	0.35	0.40	0.45	0.50	0.55	0.60	0.65	2/3	0.70	0.75	0.80	5/6	0.85	0.90	0.95
x = 0	0.6983	0.4783	0.3206	0.2791	0.2097	0.1335	0.0824	0.0585	0.0490	0.0280	0.0152	0.0078	0.0037	0.0016	0.0006	0.0005	0.0002	0.0001	0.0000	0.0000	0.0000	0.0000	0.0000
1	0.9556	0.8503	0.7166	0.6698	0.5767	0.4449	0.3294	0.2634	0.2338	0.1586	0.1024	0.0625	0.0357	0.0188	0.0090	0.0069	0.0038	0.0013	0.0004	0.0001	0.0001	0.0000	0.0000
2	0.9962	0.9743	0.9262	0.9042	0.8520	0.7564	0.6471	0.5706	0.5323	0.4199	0.3164	0.2266	0.1529	0.0963	0.0556	0.0453	0.0288	0.0129	0.0047	0.0020	0.0012	0.0002	0.0000
3	0.9998	0.9973	0.9879	0.9824	0.9667	0.9294	0.8740	0.8267	0.8002	0.7102	0.6083	0.5000	0.3917	0.2898	0.1998	0.1733	0.1260	0.0706	0.0333	0.0176	0.0121	0.0027	0.0002
4	1.0000	0.9998	0.9988	0.9980	0.9953	0.9871	0.9712	0.9547	0.9444	0.9037	0.8471	0.7734	0.6836	0.5801	0.4677	0.4294	0.3529	0.2436	0.1480	0.0958	0.0738	0.0257	0.0038
5	1.0000	1.0000	0.9999	0.9999	0.9996	0.9987	0.9962	0.9931	0.9910	0.9812	0.9643	0.9375	0.8976	0.8414	0.7662	0.7366	0.6706	0.5551	0.4233	0.3302	0.2834	0.1497	0.0444
6	1.0000	1.0000	1.0000	1.0000	1.0000	0.9999	0.9998	0.9995	0.9994	0.9984	0.9963	0.9922	0.9848	0.9720	0.9510	0.9415	0.9176	0.8665	0.7903	0.7209	0.6794	0.5217	0.3017
7	1.0000	1.0000	1.0000	1.0000	1.0000	1.0000	1.0000	1.0000	1.0000	1.0000	1.0000	1.0000	1.0000	1.0000	1.0000	1.0000	1.0000	1.0000	1.0000	1.0000	1.0000	1.0000	1.0000

n = 8

p	0.05	0.10	0.15	1/6	0.20	0.25	0.30	1/3	0.35	0.40	0.45	0.50	0.55	0.60	0.65	2/3	0.70	0.75	0.80	5/6	0.85	0.90	0.95
x = 0	0.6634	0.4305	0.2725	0.2326	0.1678	0.1001	0.0576	0.0390	0.0319	0.0168	0.0084	0.0039	0.0017	0.0007	0.0002	0.0002	0.0001	0.0000	0.0000	0.0000	0.0000	0.0000	0.0000
1	0.9428	0.8131	0.6572	0.6047	0.5033	0.3671	0.2553	0.1951	0.1691	0.1064	0.0632	0.0352	0.0181	0.0085	0.0036	0.0026	0.0013	0.0004	0.0001	0.0000	0.0000	0.0000	0.0000
2	0.9942	0.9619	0.8948	0.8652	0.7969	0.6785	0.5518	0.4682	0.4278	0.3154	0.2201	0.1445	0.0885	0.0498	0.0253	0.0197	0.0113	0.0042	0.0012	0.0004	0.0002	0.0000	0.0000
3	0.9996	0.9950	0.9786	0.9693	0.9437	0.8862	0.8059	0.7414	0.7064	0.5941	0.4770	0.3633	0.2604	0.1737	0.1061	0.0879	0.0580	0.0273	0.0104	0.0046	0.0029	0.0004	0.0000
4	1.0000	0.9996	0.9971	0.9954	0.9896	0.9727	0.9420	0.9121	0.8939	0.8263	0.7396	0.6367	0.5230	0.4059	0.2936	0.2586	0.1941	0.1138	0.0563	0.0307	0.0214	0.0050	0.0004
5	1.0000	1.0000	0.9998	0.9996	0.9988	0.9958	0.9887	0.9803	0.9747	0.9502	0.9115	0.8555	0.7799	0.6846	0.5722	0.5318	0.4482	0.3215	0.2031	0.1348	0.1052	0.0381	0.0058
6	1.0000	1.0000	1.0000	1.0000	0.9999	0.9996	0.9987	0.9974	0.9964	0.9915	0.9819	0.9648	0.9368	0.8936	0.8309	0.8049	0.7447	0.6329	0.4967	0.3953	0.3428	0.1869	0.0572
7	1.0000	1.0000	1.0000	1.0000	1.0000	1.0000	0.9999	0.9998	0.9998	0.9993	0.9983	0.9961	0.9916	0.9832	0.9681	0.9610	0.9424	0.8999	0.8322	0.7674	0.7275	0.5695	0.3366
8	1.0000	1.0000	1.0000	1.0000	1.0000	1.0000	1.0000	1.0000	1.0000	1.0000	1.0000	1.0000	1.0000	1.0000	1.0000	1.0000	1.0000	1.0000	1.0000	1.0000	1.0000	1.0000	1.0000

Cumulative Binomial Probabilities

n = 9

p	0.05	0.10	0.15	1/6	0.20	0.25	0.30	1/3	0.35	0.40	0.45	0.50	0.55	0.60	0.65	2/3	0.70	0.75	0.80	5/6	0.85	0.90	0.95
x = 0	0.6302	0.3874	0.2316	0.1938	0.1342	0.0751	0.0404	0.0207	0.0260	0.0101	0.0046	0.0020	0.0008	0.0003	0.0001	0.0001	0.0000	0.0000	0.0000	0.0000	0.0000	0.0000	0.0000
1	0.9288	0.7748	0.5995	0.5427	0.4362	0.3003	0.1960	0.1211	0.1431	0.0705	0.0385	0.0195	0.0091	0.0038	0.0014	0.0010	0.0004	0.0001	0.0000	0.0000	0.0000	0.0000	0.0000
2	0.9916	0.9470	0.8591	0.8217	0.7382	0.6007	0.4628	0.3373	0.3772	0.2318	0.1495	0.0898	0.0498	0.0250	0.0112	0.0083	0.0043	0.0013	0.0003	0.0001	0.0000	0.0000	0.0000
3	0.9994	0.9917	0.9661	0.9520	0.9144	0.8343	0.7297	0.6089	0.6503	0.4826	0.3614	0.2539	0.1658	0.0994	0.0536	0.0424	0.0253	0.0100	0.0031	0.0011	0.0006	0.0001	0.0000
4	1.0000	0.9991	0.9944	0.9910	0.9804	0.9511	0.9012	0.8283	0.8552	0.7334	0.6214	0.5000	0.3786	0.2666	0.1717	0.1448	0.0988	0.0489	0.0196	0.0090	0.0056	0.0009	0.0000
5	1.0000	0.9999	0.9994	0.9989	0.9969	0.9900	0.9747	0.9464	0.9576	0.9006	0.8342	0.7461	0.6386	0.5174	0.3911	0.3497	0.2703	0.1657	0.0856	0.0480	0.0339	0.0083	0.0006
6	1.0000	1.0000	1.0000	0.9999	0.9997	0.9987	0.9957	0.9888	0.9917	0.9750	0.9502	0.9102	0.8505	0.7682	0.6627	0.6228	0.5372	0.3993	0.2618	0.1783	0.1409	0.0530	0.0084
7	1.0000	1.0000	1.0000	1.0000	1.0000	0.9999	0.9996	0.9986	0.9990	0.9962	0.9909	0.9805	0.9615	0.9295	0.8789	0.8569	0.8040	0.6997	0.5638	0.4573	0.4005	0.2252	0.0712
8	1.0000	1.0000	1.0000	1.0000	1.0000	1.0000	1.0000	0.9999	0.9999	0.9997	0.9992	0.9980	0.9954	0.9899	0.9793	0.9740	0.9596	0.9249	0.8658	0.8062	0.7684	0.6126	0.3698
9	1.0000	1.0000	1.0000	1.0000	1.0000	1.0000	1.0000	1.0000	1.0000	1.0000	1.0000	1.0000	1.0000	1.0000	1.0000	1.0000	1.0000	1.0000	1.0000	1.0000	1.0000	1.0000	1.0000

n = 10

p	0.05	0.10	0.15	1/6	0.20	0.25	0.30	1/3	0.35	0.40	0.45	0.50	0.55	0.60	0.65	2/3	0.70	0.75	0.80	5/6	0.85	0.90	0.95
x = 0	0.5987	0.3487	0.1969	0.1615	0.1074	0.0563	0.0282	0.0135	0.0173	0.0060	0.0025	0.0010	0.0003	0.0001	0.0000	0.0000	0.0000	0.0000	0.0000	0.0000	0.0000	0.0000	0.0000
1	0.9139	0.7361	0.5443	0.4845	0.3758	0.2440	0.1493	0.0860	0.1040	0.0464	0.0233	0.0107	0.0045	0.0017	0.0005	0.0004	0.0001	0.0000	0.0000	0.0000	0.0000	0.0000	0.0000
2	0.9885	0.9298	0.8202	0.7752	0.6778	0.5256	0.3828	0.2616	0.2991	0.1673	0.0996	0.0547	0.0274	0.0123	0.0048	0.0034	0.0016	0.0004	0.0001	0.0000	0.0000	0.0000	0.0000
3	0.9990	0.9872	0.9500	0.9303	0.8791	0.7759	0.6496	0.5138	0.5593	0.3823	0.2660	0.1719	0.1020	0.0548	0.0260	0.0197	0.0106	0.0035	0.0009	0.0003	0.0001	0.0000	0.0000
4	0.9999	0.9984	0.9901	0.9845	0.9672	0.9219	0.8497	0.7515	0.7869	0.6331	0.5044	0.3770	0.2616	0.1662	0.0949	0.0766	0.0473	0.0197	0.0064	0.0024	0.0014	0.0001	0.0000
5	1.0000	0.9999	0.9986	0.9976	0.9936	0.9803	0.9527	0.9051	0.9234	0.8338	0.7384	0.6230	0.4956	0.3669	0.2485	0.2131	0.1503	0.0781	0.0328	0.0155	0.0099	0.0016	0.0001
6	1.0000	1.0000	0.9999	0.9997	0.9991	0.9965	0.9894	0.9740	0.9803	0.9452	0.8980	0.8281	0.7340	0.6177	0.4862	0.4407	0.3504	0.2241	0.1209	0.0697	0.0500	0.0128	0.0010
7	1.0000	1.0000	1.0000	1.0000	0.9999	0.9996	0.9984	0.9952	0.9966	0.9877	0.9726	0.9453	0.9004	0.8327	0.7384	0.7009	0.6172	0.4744	0.3222	0.2248	0.1798	0.0702	0.0115
8	1.0000	1.0000	1.0000	1.0000	1.0000	1.0000	0.9999	0.9995	0.9996	0.9983	0.9955	0.9893	0.9767	0.9536	0.9140	0.8960	0.8507	0.7560	0.6242	0.5155	0.4557	0.2639	0.0861
9	1.0000	1.0000	1.0000	1.0000	1.0000	1.0000	1.0000	1.0000	1.0000	0.9999	0.9997	0.9990	0.9975	0.9940	0.9865	0.9827	0.9718	0.9437	0.8926	0.8385	0.8031	0.6513	0.4013
10	1.0000	1.0000	1.0000	1.0000	1.0000	1.0000	1.0000	1.0000	1.0000	1.0000	1.0000	1.0000	1.0000	1.0000	1.0000	1.0000	1.0000	1.0000	1.0000	1.0000	1.0000	1.0000	1.0000

n = 12

p	0.05	0.10	0.15	1/6	0.20	0.25	0.30	1/3	0.35	0.40	0.45	0.50	0.55	0.60	0.65	2/3	0.70	0.75	0.80	5/6	0.85	0.90	0.95
x = 0	0.5404	0.2824	0.1422	0.1122	0.0687	0.0317	0.0138	0.0057	0.0077	0.0022	0.0008	0.0002	0.0001	0.0000	0.0000	0.0000	0.0000	0.0000	0.0000	0.0000	0.0000	0.0000	0.0000
1	0.8816	0.6590	0.4435	0.3813	0.2749	0.1584	0.0850	0.0424	0.0540	0.0196	0.0083	0.0032	0.0011	0.0003	0.0001	0.0000	0.0000	0.0000	0.0000	0.0000	0.0000	0.0000	0.0000
2	0.9804	0.8891	0.7358	0.6774	0.5583	0.3907	0.2528	0.1513	0.1811	0.0834	0.0421	0.0193	0.0079	0.0028	0.0008	0.0005	0.0002	0.0000	0.0000	0.0000	0.0000	0.0000	0.0000
3	0.9978	0.9744	0.9078	0.8748	0.7946	0.6488	0.4925	0.3467	0.3931	0.2253	0.1345	0.0730	0.0356	0.0153	0.0056	0.0039	0.0017	0.0004	0.0001	0.0000	0.0000	0.0000	0.0000
4	0.9998	0.9957	0.9761	0.9636	0.9274	0.8424	0.7237	0.5833	0.6315	0.4382	0.3044	0.1938	0.1117	0.0573	0.0255	0.0188	0.0095	0.0028	0.0006	0.0002	0.0001	0.0000	0.0000
5	1.0000	0.9995	0.9954	0.9921	0.9806	0.9456	0.8822	0.7873	0.8223	0.6652	0.5269	0.3872	0.2607	0.1582	0.0846	0.0664	0.0386	0.0143	0.0039	0.0013	0.0007	0.0001	0.0000
6	1.0000	0.9999	0.9993	0.9987	0.9961	0.9857	0.9614	0.9154	0.9336	0.8418	0.7393	0.6128	0.4731	0.3348	0.2127	0.1777	0.1178	0.0544	0.0194	0.0079	0.0046	0.0005	0.0000
7	1.0000	1.0000	0.9999	0.9998	0.9994	0.9972	0.9905	0.9745	0.9812	0.9427	0.8883	0.8062	0.6956	0.5618	0.4167	0.3685	0.2763	0.1576	0.0726	0.0364	0.0239	0.0043	0.0002
8	1.0000	1.0000	1.0000	1.0000	0.9999	0.9996	0.9983	0.9944	0.9961	0.9847	0.9644	0.9270	0.8655	0.7747	0.6533	0.6069	0.5075	0.3512	0.2054	0.1252	0.0922	0.0256	0.0022
9	1.0000	1.0000	1.0000	1.0000	1.0000	1.0000	0.9998	0.9992	0.9995	0.9972	0.9921	0.9807	0.9579	0.9166	0.8487	0.8189	0.7472	0.6093	0.4417	0.3226	0.2642	0.1109	0.0196
10	1.0000	1.0000	1.0000	1.0000	1.0000	1.0000	1.0000	0.9999	1.0000	0.9997	0.9989	0.9968	0.9917	0.9804	0.9576	0.9460	0.9150	0.8416	0.7251	0.6187	0.5565	0.3410	0.1184
11	1.0000	1.0000	1.0000	1.0000	1.0000	1.0000	1.0000	1.0000	1.0000	1.0000	0.9999	0.9998	0.9992	0.9978	0.9943	0.9923	0.9862	0.9683	0.9313	0.8878	0.8578	0.7176	0.4596

Cumulative Binomial Probabilities

$n = 14$

p	0.05	0.10	0.15	1/6	0.20	0.25	0.30	1/3	0.35	0.40	0.45	0.50	0.55	0.60	0.65	2/3	0.70	0.75	0.80	5/6	0.85	0.90	0.95
$x=0$	0.4877	0.2288	0.1028	0.0779	0.0440	0.0178	0.0068	0.0034	0.0024	0.0008	0.0002	0.0001	0.0000	0.0000	0.0000	0.0000	0.0000	0.0000	0.0000	0.0000	0.0000	0.0000	0.0000
1	0.8470	0.5846	0.3567	0.2960	0.1979	0.1010	0.0475	0.0274	0.0205	0.0081	0.0029	0.0009	0.0003	0.0001	0.0000	0.0000	0.0000	0.0000	0.0000	0.0000	0.0000	0.0000	0.0000
2	0.9699	0.8416	0.6479	0.5795	0.4481	0.2811	0.1608	0.1053	0.0839	0.0398	0.0170	0.0065	0.0022	0.0006	0.0001	0.0001	0.0000	0.0000	0.0000	0.0000	0.0000	0.0000	0.0000
3	0.9958	0.9559	0.8535	0.8063	0.6982	0.5213	0.3552	0.2612	0.2205	0.1243	0.0632	0.0287	0.0114	0.0039	0.0011	0.0007	0.0002	0.0000	0.0000	0.0000	0.0000	0.0000	0.0000
4	0.9996	0.9908	0.9533	0.9310	0.8702	0.7415	0.5842	0.4755	0.4227	0.2793	0.1672	0.0898	0.0426	0.0175	0.0060	0.0040	0.0017	0.0003	0.0000	0.0000	0.0000	0.0000	0.0000
5	1.0000	0.9985	0.9885	0.9809	0.9561	0.8883	0.7805	0.6898	0.6405	0.4859	0.3373	0.2120	0.1189	0.0583	0.0243	0.0174	0.0083	0.0022	0.0004	0.0001	0.0000	0.0000	0.0000
6	1.0000	0.9998	0.9978	0.9959	0.9884	0.9617	0.9067	0.8505	0.8164	0.6925	0.5461	0.3953	0.2586	0.1501	0.0753	0.0576	0.0315	0.0103	0.0024	0.0007	0.0003	0.0000	0.0000
7	1.0000	1.0000	0.9997	0.9993	0.9976	0.9897	0.9685	0.9424	0.9247	0.8499	0.7414	0.6047	0.4539	0.3075	0.1836	0.1495	0.0933	0.0383	0.0116	0.0041	0.0022	0.0002	0.0000
8	1.0000	1.0000	1.0000	0.9999	0.9996	0.9978	0.9917	0.9826	0.9757	0.9417	0.8811	0.7880	0.6627	0.5141	0.3595	0.3102	0.2195	0.1117	0.0439	0.0191	0.0115	0.0015	0.0000
9	1.0000	1.0000	1.0000	1.0000	1.0000	0.9997	0.9983	0.9960	0.9940	0.9825	0.9574	0.9102	0.8328	0.7207	0.5773	0.5245	0.4158	0.2585	0.1298	0.0690	0.0467	0.0092	0.0004
10	1.0000	1.0000	1.0000	1.0000	1.0000	1.0000	0.9998	0.9993	0.9989	0.9961	0.9886	0.9713	0.9368	0.8757	0.7795	0.7388	0.6448	0.4787	0.3018	0.1937	0.1465	0.0441	0.0042
11	1.0000	1.0000	1.0000	1.0000	1.0000	1.0000	1.0000	0.9999	0.9999	0.9994	0.9978	0.9935	0.9830	0.9602	0.9161	0.8947	0.8392	0.7189	0.5519	0.4205	0.3521	0.1584	0.0301
12	1.0000	1.0000	1.0000	1.0000	1.0000	1.0000	1.0000	1.0000	1.0000	0.9999	0.9997	0.9991	0.9971	0.9919	0.9795	0.9726	0.9525	0.8990	0.8021	0.7040	0.6433	0.4154	0.1530
13	1.0000	1.0000	1.0000	1.0000	1.0000	1.0000	1.0000	1.0000	1.0000	1.0000	1.0000	0.9999	0.9998	0.9992	0.9976	0.9966	0.9932	0.9822	0.9560	0.9221	0.8972	0.7712	0.5123
14	1.0000	1.0000	1.0000	1.0000	1.0000	1.0000	1.0000	1.0000	1.0000	1.0000	1.0000	1.0000	1.0000	1.0000	1.0000	1.0000	1.0000	1.0000	1.0000	1.0000	1.0000	1.0000	1.0000

$n = 16$

p	0.05	0.10	0.15	1/6	0.20	0.25	0.30	1/3	0.35	0.40	0.45	0.50	0.55	0.60	0.65	2/3	0.70	0.75	0.80	5/6	0.85	0.90	0.95
$x=0$	0.4401	0.1853	0.0743	0.0541	0.0281	0.0100	0.0033	0.0015	0.0010	0.0003	0.0001	0.0000	0.0000	0.0000	0.0000	0.0000	0.0000	0.0000	0.0000	0.0000	0.0000	0.0000	0.0000
1	0.8108	0.5147	0.2839	0.2272	0.1407	0.0635	0.0261	0.0137	0.0098	0.0033	0.0010	0.0003	0.0001	0.0000	0.0000	0.0000	0.0000	0.0000	0.0000	0.0000	0.0000	0.0000	0.0000
2	0.9571	0.7892	0.5614	0.4868	0.3518	0.1971	0.0994	0.0594	0.0451	0.0183	0.0066	0.0021	0.0006	0.0001	0.0000	0.0000	0.0000	0.0000	0.0000	0.0000	0.0000	0.0000	0.0000
3	0.9930	0.9316	0.7899	0.7291	0.5981	0.4050	0.2459	0.1659	0.1339	0.0651	0.0281	0.0106	0.0035	0.0009	0.0002	0.0001	0.0000	0.0000	0.0000	0.0000	0.0000	0.0000	0.0000
4	0.9991	0.9830	0.9209	0.8866	0.7982	0.6302	0.4499	0.3391	0.2892	0.1666	0.0853	0.0384	0.0149	0.0049	0.0013	0.0008	0.0003	0.0000	0.0000	0.0000	0.0000	0.0000	0.0000
5	0.9999	0.9967	0.9765	0.9622	0.9183	0.8103	0.6598	0.5469	0.4900	0.3288	0.1976	0.1051	0.0486	0.0191	0.0062	0.0040	0.0016	0.0003	0.0000	0.0000	0.0000	0.0000	0.0000
6	1.0000	0.9995	0.9944	0.9899	0.9733	0.9204	0.8247	0.7374	0.6881	0.5272	0.3660	0.2272	0.1241	0.0583	0.0229	0.0159	0.0071	0.0016	0.0002	0.0000	0.0000	0.0000	0.0000
7	1.0000	0.9999	0.9989	0.9979	0.9930	0.9729	0.9256	0.8735	0.8406	0.7161	0.5629	0.4018	0.2559	0.1423	0.0671	0.0500	0.0257	0.0075	0.0015	0.0004	0.0002	0.0000	0.0000
8	1.0000	1.0000	0.9998	0.9996	0.9985	0.9925	0.9743	0.9500	0.9329	0.8577	0.7441	0.5982	0.4371	0.2839	0.1594	0.1265	0.0744	0.0271	0.0070	0.0021	0.0011	0.0001	0.0000
9	1.0000	1.0000	1.0000	1.0000	0.9998	0.9984	0.9929	0.9841	0.9771	0.9417	0.8759	0.7728	0.6340	0.4728	0.3119	0.2626	0.1753	0.0796	0.0267	0.0101	0.0056	0.0005	0.0000
10	1.0000	1.0000	1.0000	1.0000	1.0000	0.9997	0.9984	0.9960	0.9938	0.9809	0.9514	0.8949	0.8024	0.6712	0.5100	0.4531	0.3402	0.1897	0.0817	0.0378	0.0235	0.0033	0.0001
11	1.0000	1.0000	1.0000	1.0000	1.0000	1.0000	0.9997	0.9992	0.9987	0.9951	0.9851	0.9616	0.9147	0.8334	0.7108	0.6609	0.5501	0.3698	0.2018	0.1134	0.0791	0.0170	0.0009
12	1.0000	1.0000	1.0000	1.0000	1.0000	1.0000	1.0000	0.9999	0.9998	0.9991	0.9965	0.9894	0.9719	0.9349	0.8661	0.8341	0.7541	0.5950	0.4019	0.2709	0.2101	0.0684	0.0070
13	1.0000	1.0000	1.0000	1.0000	1.0000	1.0000	1.0000	1.0000	1.0000	0.9999	0.9994	0.9979	0.9934	0.9817	0.9549	0.9406	0.9006	0.8029	0.6482	0.5132	0.4386	0.2108	0.0429
14	1.0000	1.0000	1.0000	1.0000	1.0000	1.0000	1.0000	1.0000	1.0000	1.0000	0.9999	0.9997	0.9990	0.9967	0.9902	0.9863	0.9739	0.9365	0.8593	0.7728	0.7161	0.4853	0.1892
15	1.0000	1.0000	1.0000	1.0000	1.0000	1.0000	1.0000	1.0000	1.0000	1.0000	1.0000	1.0000	0.9999	0.9997	0.9990	0.9985	0.9967	0.9900	0.9719	0.9459	0.9257	0.8147	0.5599
16	1.0000	1.0000	1.0000	1.0000	1.0000	1.0000	1.0000	1.0000	1.0000	1.0000	1.0000	1.0000	1.0000	1.0000	1.0000	1.0000	1.0000	1.0000	1.0000	1.0000	1.0000	1.0000	1.0000

Cumulative Binomial Probabilities

$n = 18$

p	0.05	0.10	0.15	1/6	0.20	0.25	0.30	1/3	0.35	0.40	0.45	0.50	0.55	0.60	0.65	2/3	0.70	0.75	0.80	5/6	0.85	0.90	0.95
$x = 0$	0.3972	0.1501	0.0536	0.0376	0.0180	0.0056	0.0016	0.0007	0.0004	0.0001	0.0000	0.0000	0.0000	0.0000	0.0000	0.0000	0.0000	0.0000	0.0000	0.0000	0.0000	0.0000	0.0000
1	0.7735	0.4503	0.2241	0.1728	0.0991	0.0395	0.0142	0.0068	0.0046	0.0013	0.0003	0.0001	0.0000	0.0000	0.0000	0.0000	0.0000	0.0000	0.0000	0.0000	0.0000	0.0000	0.0000
2	0.9419	0.7338	0.4797	0.4027	0.2713	0.1353	0.0600	0.0326	0.0236	0.0082	0.0025	0.0007	0.0001	0.0000	0.0000	0.0000	0.0000	0.0000	0.0000	0.0000	0.0000	0.0000	0.0000
3	0.9891	0.9018	0.7202	0.6479	0.5010	0.3057	0.1646	0.1017	0.0783	0.0328	0.0120	0.0038	0.0010	0.0002	0.0000	0.0000	0.0000	0.0000	0.0000	0.0000	0.0000	0.0000	0.0000
4	0.9985	0.9718	0.8794	0.8318	0.7164	0.5187	0.3327	0.2311	0.1886	0.0942	0.0411	0.0154	0.0049	0.0013	0.0003	0.0001	0.0000	0.0000	0.0000	0.0000	0.0000	0.0000	0.0000
5	0.9998	0.9936	0.9581	0.9347	0.8671	0.7175	0.5344	0.4122	0.3550	0.2088	0.1077	0.0481	0.0183	0.0058	0.0014	0.0009	0.0003	0.0000	0.0000	0.0000	0.0000	0.0000	0.0000
6	1.0000	0.9988	0.9882	0.9794	0.9487	0.8610	0.7217	0.6085	0.5491	0.3743	0.2258	0.1189	0.0537	0.0203	0.0062	0.0039	0.0014	0.0002	0.0000	0.0000	0.0000	0.0000	0.0000
7	1.0000	0.9998	0.9973	0.9947	0.9837	0.9431	0.8593	0.7767	0.7283	0.5634	0.3915	0.2403	0.1280	0.0576	0.0212	0.0144	0.0061	0.0012	0.0002	0.0000	0.0000	0.0000	0.0000
8	1.0000	1.0000	0.9995	0.9989	0.9957	0.9807	0.9404	0.8924	0.8609	0.7368	0.5778	0.4073	0.2527	0.1347	0.0597	0.0433	0.0210	0.0054	0.0009	0.0002	0.0001	0.0000	0.0000
9	1.0000	1.0000	0.9999	0.9998	0.9991	0.9946	0.9790	0.9567	0.9403	0.8653	0.7473	0.5927	0.4222	0.2632	0.1391	0.1076	0.0596	0.0193	0.0043	0.0011	0.0005	0.0000	0.0000
10	1.0000	1.0000	1.0000	1.0000	0.9998	0.9988	0.9939	0.9856	0.9788	0.9424	0.8720	0.7597	0.6085	0.4366	0.2717	0.2233	0.1407	0.0569	0.0163	0.0053	0.0027	0.0002	0.0000
11	1.0000	1.0000	1.0000	1.0000	1.0000	0.9998	0.9986	0.9961	0.9938	0.9797	0.9463	0.8811	0.7742	0.6257	0.4509	0.3915	0.2783	0.1390	0.0513	0.0206	0.0118	0.0012	0.0000
12	1.0000	1.0000	1.0000	1.0000	1.0000	1.0000	0.9997	0.9991	0.9986	0.9942	0.9817	0.9519	0.8923	0.7912	0.6450	0.5878	0.4656	0.2825	0.1329	0.0653	0.0419	0.0064	0.0002
13	1.0000	1.0000	1.0000	1.0000	1.0000	1.0000	1.0000	0.9999	0.9997	0.9987	0.9951	0.9846	0.9589	0.9058	0.8114	0.7689	0.6673	0.4813	0.2836	0.1682	0.1206	0.0282	0.0015
14	1.0000	1.0000	1.0000	1.0000	1.0000	1.0000	1.0000	1.0000	1.0000	0.9998	0.9990	0.9962	0.9880	0.9672	0.9217	0.8983	0.8354	0.6943	0.4990	0.3521	0.2798	0.0982	0.0109
15	1.0000	1.0000	1.0000	1.0000	1.0000	1.0000	1.0000	1.0000	1.0000	1.0000	0.9999	0.9993	0.9975	0.9918	0.9764	0.9674	0.9400	0.8647	0.7287	0.5973	0.5203	0.2662	0.0581
16	1.0000	1.0000	1.0000	1.0000	1.0000	1.0000	1.0000	1.0000	1.0000	1.0000	1.0000	0.9999	0.9997	0.9987	0.9954	0.9932	0.9858	0.9605	0.9009	0.8272	0.7759	0.5497	0.2265
17	1.0000	1.0000	1.0000	1.0000	1.0000	1.0000	1.0000	1.0000	1.0000	1.0000	1.0000	1.0000	1.0000	0.9999	0.9996	0.9993	0.9984	0.9944	0.9820	0.9624	0.9464	0.8499	0.6028
18	1.0000	1.0000	1.0000	1.0000	1.0000	1.0000	1.0000	1.0000	1.0000	1.0000	1.0000	1.0000	1.0000	1.0000	1.0000	1.0000	1.0000	1.0000	1.0000	1.0000	1.0000	1.0000	1.0000

Cumulative Binomial Probabilities

$n = 20$

p	0.05	0.10	0.15	1/6	0.20	0.25	0.30	1/3	0.35	0.40	0.45	0.50	0.55	0.60	0.65	2/3	0.70	0.75	0.80	5/6	0.85	0.90	0.95
$x=0$	0.3585	0.1216	0.0388	0.0261	0.0115	0.0032	0.0008	0.0003	0.0002	0.0000	0.0000	0.0000	0.0000	0.0000	0.0000	0.0000	0.0000	0.0000	0.0000	0.0000	0.0000	0.0000	0.0000
1	0.7358	0.3917	0.1756	0.1304	0.0692	0.0243	0.0076	0.0033	0.0021	0.0005	0.0001	0.0000	0.0000	0.0000	0.0000	0.0000	0.0000	0.0000	0.0000	0.0000	0.0000	0.0000	0.0000
2	0.9245	0.6769	0.4049	0.3287	0.2061	0.0913	0.0355	0.0176	0.0121	0.0036	0.0009	0.0002	0.0000	0.0000	0.0000	0.0000	0.0000	0.0000	0.0000	0.0000	0.0000	0.0000	0.0000
3	0.9841	0.8670	0.6477	0.5665	0.4114	0.2252	0.1071	0.0604	0.0444	0.0160	0.0049	0.0013	0.0003	0.0000	0.0000	0.0000	0.0000	0.0000	0.0000	0.0000	0.0000	0.0000	0.0000
4	0.9974	0.9568	0.8298	0.7687	0.6296	0.4148	0.2375	0.1515	0.1182	0.0510	0.0189	0.0059	0.0015	0.0003	0.0000	0.0000	0.0000	0.0000	0.0000	0.0000	0.0000	0.0000	0.0000
5	0.9997	0.9887	0.9327	0.8982	0.8042	0.6172	0.4164	0.2972	0.2454	0.1256	0.0553	0.0207	0.0064	0.0016	0.0003	0.0002	0.0000	0.0000	0.0000	0.0000	0.0000	0.0000	0.0000
6	1.0000	0.9976	0.9781	0.9629	0.9133	0.7858	0.6080	0.4793	0.4166	0.2500	0.1299	0.0577	0.0214	0.0065	0.0015	0.0009	0.0003	0.0000	0.0000	0.0000	0.0000	0.0000	0.0000
7	1.0000	0.9996	0.9941	0.9887	0.9679	0.8982	0.7723	0.6615	0.6010	0.4159	0.2520	0.1316	0.0580	0.0210	0.0060	0.0037	0.0013	0.0002	0.0000	0.0000	0.0000	0.0000	0.0000
8	1.0000	0.9999	0.9987	0.9972	0.9900	0.9591	0.8867	0.8095	0.7624	0.5956	0.4143	0.2517	0.1308	0.0565	0.0196	0.0130	0.0051	0.0009	0.0001	0.0000	0.0000	0.0000	0.0000
9	1.0000	1.0000	0.9998	0.9994	0.9974	0.9861	0.9520	0.9081	0.8782	0.7553	0.5914	0.4119	0.2493	0.1275	0.0532	0.0376	0.0171	0.0039	0.0006	0.0001	0.0000	0.0000	0.0000
10	1.0000	1.0000	1.0000	0.9999	0.9994	0.9961	0.9829	0.9624	0.9468	0.8725	0.7507	0.5881	0.4086	0.2447	0.1218	0.0919	0.0480	0.0139	0.0026	0.0006	0.0002	0.0000	0.0000
11	1.0000	1.0000	1.0000	1.0000	0.9999	0.9991	0.9949	0.9870	0.9804	0.9435	0.8692	0.7483	0.5857	0.4044	0.2376	0.1905	0.1133	0.0409	0.0100	0.0028	0.0013	0.0001	0.0000
12	1.0000	1.0000	1.0000	1.0000	1.0000	0.9998	0.9987	0.9963	0.9940	0.9790	0.9420	0.8684	0.7480	0.5841	0.3990	0.3385	0.2277	0.1018	0.0321	0.0113	0.0059	0.0004	0.0000
13	1.0000	1.0000	1.0000	1.0000	1.0000	1.0000	0.9997	0.9991	0.9985	0.9935	0.9786	0.9423	0.8701	0.7500	0.5834	0.5207	0.3920	0.2142	0.0867	0.0371	0.0219	0.0024	0.0000
14	1.0000	1.0000	1.0000	1.0000	1.0000	1.0000	1.0000	0.9998	0.9997	0.9984	0.9936	0.9793	0.9447	0.8744	0.7546	0.7028	0.5836	0.3828	0.1958	0.1018	0.0673	0.0113	0.0003
15	1.0000	1.0000	1.0000	1.0000	1.0000	1.0000	1.0000	1.0000	1.0000	0.9997	0.9985	0.9941	0.9811	0.9490	0.8818	0.8485	0.7625	0.5852	0.3704	0.2313	0.1702	0.0432	0.0026
16	1.0000	1.0000	1.0000	1.0000	1.0000	1.0000	1.0000	1.0000	1.0000	1.0000	0.9997	0.9987	0.9951	0.9840	0.9556	0.9396	0.8929	0.7748	0.5886	0.4335	0.3523	0.1330	0.0159
17	1.0000	1.0000	1.0000	1.0000	1.0000	1.0000	1.0000	1.0000	1.0000	1.0000	1.0000	0.9998	0.9991	0.9964	0.9879	0.9824	0.9645	0.9087	0.7939	0.6713	0.5951	0.3231	0.0755
18	1.0000	1.0000	1.0000	1.0000	1.0000	1.0000	1.0000	1.0000	1.0000	1.0000	1.0000	1.0000	0.9999	0.9995	0.9979	0.9967	0.9924	0.9757	0.9308	0.8696	0.8244	0.6083	0.2642
19	1.0000	1.0000	1.0000	1.0000	1.0000	1.0000	1.0000	1.0000	1.0000	1.0000	1.0000	1.0000	1.0000	1.0000	0.9998	0.9997	0.9992	0.9968	0.9885	0.9739	0.9612	0.8784	0.6415
20	1.0000	1.0000	1.0000	1.0000	1.0000	1.0000	1.0000	1.0000	1.0000	1.0000	1.0000	1.0000	1.0000	1.0000	1.0000	1.0000	1.0000	1.0000	1.0000	1.0000	1.0000	1.0000	1.0000

Cumulative Binomial Probabilities

$n = 25$

p	0.05	0.10	0.15	1/6	0.20	0.25	0.30	1/3	0.35	0.40	0.45	0.50	0.55	0.60	0.65	2/3	0.70	0.75	0.80	5/6	0.85	0.90	0.95
x = 0	0.2774	0.0718	0.0172	0.0105	0.0038	0.0008	0.0001	0.0000	0.0000	0.0000	0.0000	0.0000	0.0000	0.0000	0.0000	0.0000	0.0000	0.0000	0.0000	0.0000	0.0000	0.0000	0.0000
1	0.6424	0.2712	0.0931	0.0629	0.0274	0.0070	0.0016	0.0005	0.0003	0.0001	0.0000	0.0000	0.0000	0.0000	0.0000	0.0000	0.0000	0.0000	0.0000	0.0000	0.0000	0.0000	0.0000
2	0.8729	0.5371	0.2537	0.1887	0.0982	0.0321	0.0090	0.0035	0.0021	0.0004	0.0001	0.0000	0.0000	0.0000	0.0000	0.0000	0.0000	0.0000	0.0000	0.0000	0.0000	0.0000	0.0000
3	0.9659	0.7636	0.4711	0.3816	0.2340	0.0962	0.0332	0.0149	0.0097	0.0024	0.0005	0.0001	0.0000	0.0000	0.0000	0.0000	0.0000	0.0000	0.0000	0.0000	0.0000	0.0000	0.0000
4	0.9928	0.9020	0.6821	0.5937	0.4207	0.2137	0.0905	0.0462	0.0320	0.0095	0.0023	0.0005	0.0001	0.0000	0.0000	0.0000	0.0000	0.0000	0.0000	0.0000	0.0000	0.0000	0.0000
5	0.9988	0.9666	0.8385	0.7720	0.6167	0.3783	0.1935	0.1120	0.0826	0.0294	0.0086	0.0020	0.0004	0.0001	0.0000	0.0000	0.0000	0.0000	0.0000	0.0000	0.0000	0.0000	0.0000
6	0.9998	0.9905	0.9305	0.8908	0.7800	0.5611	0.3407	0.2215	0.1734	0.0736	0.0258	0.0073	0.0016	0.0003	0.0000	0.0000	0.0000	0.0000	0.0000	0.0000	0.0000	0.0000	0.0000
7	1.0000	0.9977	0.9745	0.9553	0.8909	0.7265	0.5118	0.3703	0.3061	0.1536	0.0639	0.0216	0.0058	0.0012	0.0002	0.0001	0.0000	0.0000	0.0000	0.0000	0.0000	0.0000	0.0000
8	1.0000	0.9995	0.9920	0.9843	0.9532	0.8506	0.6769	0.5376	0.4668	0.2735	0.1340	0.0539	0.0174	0.0043	0.0008	0.0004	0.0001	0.0000	0.0000	0.0000	0.0000	0.0000	0.0000
9	1.0000	0.9999	0.9979	0.9953	0.9827	0.9287	0.8106	0.6956	0.6303	0.4246	0.2424	0.1148	0.0440	0.0132	0.0029	0.0016	0.0005	0.0000	0.0000	0.0000	0.0000	0.0000	0.0000
10	1.0000	1.0000	0.9995	0.9988	0.9944	0.9703	0.9022	0.8220	0.7712	0.5858	0.3843	0.2122	0.0960	0.0344	0.0093	0.0056	0.0018	0.0002	0.0000	0.0000	0.0000	0.0000	0.0000
11	1.0000	1.0000	0.9999	0.9997	0.9985	0.9893	0.9558	0.9082	0.8746	0.7323	0.5426	0.3450	0.1827	0.0778	0.0255	0.0164	0.0060	0.0009	0.0001	0.0000	0.0000	0.0000	0.0000
12	1.0000	1.0000	1.0000	0.9999	0.9996	0.9966	0.9825	0.9585	0.9396	0.8462	0.6937	0.5000	0.3063	0.1538	0.0604	0.0415	0.0175	0.0034	0.0004	0.0001	0.0000	0.0000	0.0000
13	1.0000	1.0000	1.0000	1.0000	0.9999	0.9991	0.9940	0.9836	0.9745	0.9222	0.8173	0.6550	0.4574	0.2677	0.1254	0.0918	0.0442	0.0107	0.0015	0.0003	0.0001	0.0000	0.0000
14	1.0000	1.0000	1.0000	1.0000	1.0000	0.9998	0.9982	0.9944	0.9907	0.9656	0.9040	0.7878	0.6157	0.4142	0.2288	0.1780	0.0978	0.0297	0.0056	0.0012	0.0005	0.0000	0.0000
15	1.0000	1.0000	1.0000	1.0000	1.0000	1.0000	0.9995	0.9984	0.9971	0.9868	0.9560	0.8852	0.7576	0.5754	0.3697	0.3044	0.1894	0.0713	0.0173	0.0047	0.0021	0.0001	0.0000
16	1.0000	1.0000	1.0000	1.0000	1.0000	1.0000	0.9999	0.9996	0.9992	0.9957	0.9826	0.9461	0.8660	0.7265	0.5332	0.4624	0.3231	0.1494	0.0468	0.0157	0.0080	0.0005	0.0000
17	1.0000	1.0000	1.0000	1.0000	1.0000	1.0000	1.0000	0.9999	0.9998	0.9988	0.9942	0.9784	0.9361	0.8464	0.6939	0.6297	0.4882	0.2735	0.1091	0.0447	0.0255	0.0023	0.0000
18	1.0000	1.0000	1.0000	1.0000	1.0000	1.0000	1.0000	1.0000	1.0000	0.9997	0.9984	0.9927	0.9742	0.9264	0.8266	0.7785	0.6593	0.4389	0.2200	0.1092	0.0695	0.0095	0.0002
19	1.0000	1.0000	1.0000	1.0000	1.0000	1.0000	1.0000	1.0000	1.0000	0.9999	0.9996	0.9980	0.9914	0.9706	0.9174	0.8880	0.8065	0.6217	0.3833	0.2280	0.1615	0.0334	0.0012
20	1.0000	1.0000	1.0000	1.0000	1.0000	1.0000	1.0000	1.0000	1.0000	1.0000	0.9999	0.9995	0.9977	0.9905	0.9680	0.9538	0.9095	0.7863	0.5793	0.4063	0.3179	0.0980	0.0072
21	1.0000	1.0000	1.0000	1.0000	1.0000	1.0000	1.0000	1.0000	1.0000	1.0000	1.0000	0.9999	0.9995	0.9976	0.9903	0.9851	0.9668	0.9038	0.7660	0.6184	0.5289	0.2364	0.0341
22	1.0000	1.0000	1.0000	1.0000	1.0000	1.0000	1.0000	1.0000	1.0000	1.0000	1.0000	1.0000	0.9999	0.9996	0.9979	0.9965	0.9910	0.9679	0.9018	0.8113	0.7463	0.4629	0.1271
23	1.0000	1.0000	1.0000	1.0000	1.0000	1.0000	1.0000	1.0000	1.0000	1.0000	1.0000	1.0000	1.0000	0.9999	0.9997	0.9995	0.9984	0.9930	0.9726	0.9371	0.9069	0.7288	0.3576
24	1.0000	1.0000	1.0000	1.0000	1.0000	1.0000	1.0000	1.0000	1.0000	1.0000	1.0000	1.0000	1.0000	1.0000	1.0000	1.0000	0.9999	0.9992	0.9962	0.9895	0.9828	0.9282	0.7226
25	1.0000	1.0000	1.0000	1.0000	1.0000	1.0000	1.0000	1.0000	1.0000	1.0000	1.0000	1.0000	1.0000	1.0000	1.0000	1.0000	1.0000	1.0000	1.0000	1.0000	1.0000	1.0000	1.0000

Cumulative Binomial Probabilities

$n = 30$

p / x	0.05	0.10	0.15	1/6	0.20	0.25	0.30	1/3	0.35	0.40	0.45	0.50	0.55	0.60	0.65	2/3	0.70	0.75	0.80	5/6	0.85	0.90	0.95
0	0.2146	0.0424	0.0076	0.0042	0.0012	0.0002	0.0000	0.0000	0.0000	0.0000	0.0000	0.0000	0.0000	0.0000	0.0000	0.0000	0.0000	0.0000	0.0000	0.0000	0.0000	0.0000	0.0000
1	0.5535	0.1837	0.0480	0.0295	0.0105	0.0020	0.0003	0.0001	0.0000	0.0000	0.0000	0.0000	0.0000	0.0000	0.0000	0.0000	0.0000	0.0000	0.0000	0.0000	0.0000	0.0000	0.0000
2	0.8122	0.4114	0.1514	0.1028	0.0442	0.0106	0.0021	0.0007	0.0003	0.0000	0.0000	0.0000	0.0000	0.0000	0.0000	0.0000	0.0000	0.0000	0.0000	0.0000	0.0000	0.0000	0.0000
3	0.9392	0.6474	0.3217	0.2396	0.1227	0.0374	0.0093	0.0033	0.0019	0.0003	0.0000	0.0000	0.0000	0.0000	0.0000	0.0000	0.0000	0.0000	0.0000	0.0000	0.0000	0.0000	0.0000
4	0.9844	0.8245	0.5245	0.4243	0.2552	0.0979	0.0302	0.0122	0.0075	0.0015	0.0002	0.0000	0.0000	0.0000	0.0000	0.0000	0.0000	0.0000	0.0000	0.0000	0.0000	0.0000	0.0000
5	0.9967	0.9268	0.7106	0.6164	0.4275	0.2026	0.0766	0.0355	0.0233	0.0057	0.0011	0.0002	0.0000	0.0000	0.0000	0.0000	0.0000	0.0000	0.0000	0.0000	0.0000	0.0000	0.0000
6	0.9994	0.9742	0.8474	0.7765	0.6070	0.3481	0.1595	0.0838	0.0586	0.0172	0.0040	0.0007	0.0001	0.0000	0.0000	0.0000	0.0000	0.0000	0.0000	0.0000	0.0000	0.0000	0.0000
7	0.9999	0.9922	0.9302	0.8863	0.7608	0.5143	0.2814	0.1668	0.1238	0.0435	0.0121	0.0026	0.0004	0.0000	0.0000	0.0000	0.0000	0.0000	0.0000	0.0000	0.0000	0.0000	0.0000
8	1.0000	0.9980	0.9722	0.9494	0.8713	0.6736	0.4315	0.2860	0.2247	0.0940	0.0312	0.0081	0.0016	0.0002	0.0000	0.0000	0.0000	0.0000	0.0000	0.0000	0.0000	0.0000	0.0000
9	1.0000	0.9995	0.9903	0.9803	0.9389	0.8034	0.5888	0.4317	0.3575	0.1763	0.0694	0.0214	0.0050	0.0009	0.0001	0.0000	0.0000	0.0000	0.0000	0.0000	0.0000	0.0000	0.0000
10	1.0000	0.9999	0.9971	0.9933	0.9744	0.8943	0.7304	0.5848	0.5078	0.2915	0.1350	0.0494	0.0138	0.0029	0.0004	0.0002	0.0000	0.0000	0.0000	0.0000	0.0000	0.0000	0.0000
11	1.0000	1.0000	0.9992	0.9980	0.9905	0.9493	0.8407	0.7239	0.6548	0.4311	0.2327	0.1002	0.0334	0.0083	0.0014	0.0007	0.0002	0.0000	0.0000	0.0000	0.0000	0.0000	0.0000
12	1.0000	1.0000	0.9998	0.9995	0.9969	0.9784	0.9155	0.8340	0.7802	0.5785	0.3592	0.1808	0.0714	0.0212	0.0045	0.0025	0.0006	0.0001	0.0000	0.0000	0.0000	0.0000	0.0000
13	1.0000	1.0000	1.0000	0.9999	0.9991	0.9918	0.9599	0.9102	0.8737	0.7145	0.5025	0.2923	0.1356	0.0481	0.0124	0.0072	0.0021	0.0002	0.0000	0.0000	0.0000	0.0000	0.0000
14	1.0000	1.0000	1.0000	1.0000	0.9998	0.9973	0.9831	0.9565	0.9348	0.8246	0.6448	0.4278	0.2309	0.0971	0.0301	0.0188	0.0064	0.0008	0.0001	0.0000	0.0000	0.0000	0.0000
15	1.0000	1.0000	1.0000	1.0000	0.9999	0.9992	0.9936	0.9812	0.9699	0.9029	0.7691	0.5722	0.3552	0.1754	0.0652	0.0435	0.0169	0.0027	0.0002	0.0000	0.0000	0.0000	0.0000
16	1.0000	1.0000	1.0000	1.0000	1.0000	0.9998	0.9979	0.9928	0.9876	0.9519	0.8644	0.7077	0.4975	0.2855	0.1263	0.0898	0.0401	0.0082	0.0009	0.0001	0.0000	0.0000	0.0000
17	1.0000	1.0000	1.0000	1.0000	1.0000	0.9999	0.9994	0.9975	0.9955	0.9788	0.9286	0.8192	0.6408	0.4215	0.2198	0.1660	0.0845	0.0216	0.0031	0.0005	0.0002	0.0000	0.0000
18	1.0000	1.0000	1.0000	1.0000	1.0000	1.0000	0.9998	0.9993	0.9986	0.9917	0.9666	0.8998	0.7673	0.5689	0.3452	0.2761	0.1593	0.0507	0.0095	0.0020	0.0008	0.0000	0.0000
19	1.0000	1.0000	1.0000	1.0000	1.0000	1.0000	1.0000	0.9998	0.9996	0.9971	0.9862	0.9506	0.8650	0.7085	0.4922	0.4152	0.2696	0.1057	0.0256	0.0067	0.0029	0.0001	0.0000
20	1.0000	1.0000	1.0000	1.0000	1.0000	1.0000	1.0000	1.0000	0.9999	0.9991	0.9950	0.9786	0.9306	0.8237	0.6425	0.5683	0.4112	0.1966	0.0611	0.0197	0.0097	0.0005	0.0000
21	1.0000	1.0000	1.0000	1.0000	1.0000	1.0000	1.0000	1.0000	1.0000	0.9998	0.9984	0.9919	0.9688	0.9060	0.7753	0.7140	0.5685	0.3264	0.1287	0.0506	0.0278	0.0020	0.0000
22	1.0000	1.0000	1.0000	1.0000	1.0000	1.0000	1.0000	1.0000	1.0000	1.0000	0.9996	0.9974	0.9879	0.9565	0.8762	0.8332	0.7186	0.4857	0.2392	0.1137	0.0698	0.0078	0.0001
23	1.0000	1.0000	1.0000	1.0000	1.0000	1.0000	1.0000	1.0000	1.0000	1.0000	0.9999	0.9993	0.9960	0.9828	0.9414	0.9162	0.8405	0.6519	0.3930	0.2235	0.1526	0.0258	0.0006
24	1.0000	1.0000	1.0000	1.0000	1.0000	1.0000	1.0000	1.0000	1.0000	1.0000	1.0000	0.9998	0.9989	0.9943	0.9767	0.9645	0.9234	0.7974	0.5725	0.3836	0.2894	0.0732	0.0033
25	1.0000	1.0000	1.0000	1.0000	1.0000	1.0000	1.0000	1.0000	1.0000	1.0000	1.0000	1.0000	0.9998	0.9985	0.9925	0.9878	0.9698	0.9021	0.7448	0.5757	0.4755	0.1755	0.0156
26	1.0000	1.0000	1.0000	1.0000	1.0000	1.0000	1.0000	1.0000	1.0000	1.0000	1.0000	1.0000	1.0000	0.9997	0.9981	0.9967	0.9907	0.9626	0.8773	0.7604	0.6783	0.3526	0.0608
27	1.0000	1.0000	1.0000	1.0000	1.0000	1.0000	1.0000	1.0000	1.0000	1.0000	1.0000	1.0000	1.0000	1.0000	0.9997	0.9993	0.9979	0.9894	0.9558	0.8972	0.8486	0.5886	0.1878
28	1.0000	1.0000	1.0000	1.0000	1.0000	1.0000	1.0000	1.0000	1.0000	1.0000	1.0000	1.0000	1.0000	1.0000	1.0000	0.9999	0.9997	0.9980	0.9895	0.9705	0.9520	0.8163	0.4465
29	1.0000	1.0000	1.0000	1.0000	1.0000	1.0000	1.0000	1.0000	1.0000	1.0000	1.0000	1.0000	1.0000	1.0000	1.0000	1.0000	1.0000	0.9998	0.9988	0.9958	0.9924	0.9576	0.7854
30	1.0000	1.0000	1.0000	1.0000	1.0000	1.0000	1.0000	1.0000	1.0000	1.0000	1.0000	1.0000	1.0000	1.0000	1.0000	1.0000	1.0000	1.0000	1.0000	1.0000	1.0000	1.0000	1.0000

Cumulative Poisson Probabilities

λ	0.01	0.02	0.03	0.04	0.05	0.06	0.07	0.08	0.09
$x = 0$	0.9900	0.9802	0.9704	0.9608	0.9512	0.9418	0.9324	0.9231	0.9139
1	1.0000	0.9998	0.9996	0.9992	0.9988	0.9983	0.9977	0.9970	0.9962
2	1.0000	1.0000	1.0000	1.0000	1.0000	1.0000	0.9999	0.9999	0.9999
3	1.0000	1.0000	1.0000	1.0000	1.0000	1.0000	1.0000	1.0000	1.0000

λ	0.10	0.20	0.30	0.40	0.50	0.60	0.70	0.80	0.90
$x = 0$	0.9048	0.8187	0.7408	0.6703	0.6065	0.5488	0.4966	0.4493	0.4066
1	0.9953	0.9825	0.9631	0.9384	0.9098	0.8781	0.8442	0.8088	0.7725
2	0.9998	0.9989	0.9964	0.9921	0.9856	0.9769	0.9659	0.9526	0.9371
3	1.0000	0.9999	0.9997	0.9992	0.9982	0.9966	0.9942	0.9909	0.9865
4	1.0000	1.0000	1.0000	0.9999	0.9998	0.9996	0.9992	0.9986	0.9977
5	1.0000	1.0000	1.0000	1.0000	1.0000	1.0000	0.9999	0.9998	0.9997
6	1.0000	1.0000	1.0000	1.0000	1.0000	1.0000	1.0000	1.0000	1.0000

λ	1.00	1.10	1.20	1.30	1.40	1.50	1.60	1.70	1.80	1.90
$x = 0$	0.3679	0.3329	0.3012	0.2725	0.2466	0.2231	0.2019	0.1827	0.1653	0.1496
1	0.7358	0.6990	0.6626	0.6268	0.5918	0.5578	0.5249	0.4932	0.4628	0.4337
2	0.9197	0.9004	0.8795	0.8571	0.8335	0.8088	0.7834	0.7572	0.7306	0.7037
3	0.9810	0.9743	0.9662	0.9569	0.9463	0.9344	0.9212	0.9068	0.8913	0.8747
4	0.9963	0.9946	0.9923	0.9893	0.9857	0.9814	0.9763	0.9704	0.9636	0.9559
5	0.9994	0.9990	0.9985	0.9978	0.9968	0.9955	0.9940	0.9920	0.9896	0.9868
6	0.9999	0.9999	0.9997	0.9996	0.9994	0.9991	0.9987	0.9981	0.9974	0.9966
7	1.0000	1.0000	1.0000	0.9999	0.9999	0.9998	0.9997	0.9996	0.9994	0.9992
8	1.0000	1.0000	1.0000	1.0000	1.0000	1.0000	1.0000	0.9999	0.9999	0.9998
9	1.0000	1.0000	1.0000	1.0000	1.0000	1.0000	1.0000	1.0000	1.0000	1.0000

λ	2.00	2.10	2.20	2.30	2.40	2.50	2.60	2.70	2.80	2.90
$x = 0$	0.1353	0.1225	0.1108	0.1003	0.0907	0.0821	0.0743	0.0672	0.0608	0.0550
1	0.4060	0.3796	0.3546	0.3309	0.3084	0.2873	0.2674	0.2487	0.2311	0.2146
2	0.6767	0.6496	0.6227	0.5960	0.5697	0.5438	0.5184	0.4936	0.4695	0.4460
3	0.8571	0.8386	0.8194	0.7993	0.7787	0.7576	0.7360	0.7141	0.6919	0.6696
4	0.9473	0.9379	0.9275	0.9162	0.9041	0.8912	0.8774	0.8629	0.8477	0.8318
5	0.9834	0.9796	0.9751	0.9700	0.9643	0.9580	0.9510	0.9433	0.9349	0.9258
6	0.9955	0.9941	0.9925	0.9906	0.9884	0.9858	0.9828	0.9794	0.9756	0.9713
7	0.9989	0.9985	0.9980	0.9974	0.9967	0.9958	0.9947	0.9934	0.9919	0.9901
8	0.9998	0.9997	0.9995	0.9994	0.9991	0.9989	0.9985	0.9981	0.9976	0.9969
9	1.0000	0.9999	0.9999	0.9999	0.9998	0.9997	0.9996	0.9995	0.9993	0.9991
10	1.0000	1.0000	1.0000	1.0000	1.0000	0.9999	0.9999	0.9999	0.9998	0.9998
11	1.0000	1.0000	1.0000	1.0000	1.0000	1.0000	1.0000	1.0000	1.0000	0.9999
12	1.0000	1.0000	1.0000	1.0000	1.0000	1.0000	1.0000	1.0000	1.0000	1.0000

Cumulative Poisson Probabilities

λ	3.00	3.10	3.20	3.30	3.40	3.50	3.60	3.70	3.80	3.90
$x = 0$	0.0498	0.0450	0.0408	0.0369	0.0334	0.0302	0.0273	0.0247	0.0224	0.0202
1	0.1991	0.1847	0.1712	0.1586	0.1468	0.1359	0.1257	0.1162	0.1074	0.0992
2	0.4232	0.4012	0.3799	0.3594	0.3397	0.3208	0.3027	0.2854	0.2689	0.2531
3	0.6472	0.6248	0.6025	0.5803	0.5584	0.5366	0.5152	0.4942	0.4735	0.4532
4	0.8153	0.7982	0.7806	0.7626	0.7442	0.7254	0.7064	0.6872	0.6678	0.6484
5	0.9161	0.9057	0.8946	0.8829	0.8705	0.8576	0.8441	0.8301	0.8156	0.8006
6	0.9665	0.9612	0.9554	0.9490	0.9421	0.9347	0.9267	0.9182	0.9091	0.8995
7	0.9881	0.9858	0.9832	0.9802	0.9769	0.9733	0.9692	0.9648	0.9599	0.9546
8	0.9962	0.9953	0.9943	0.9931	0.9917	0.9901	0.9883	0.9863	0.9840	0.9815
9	0.9989	0.9986	0.9982	0.9978	0.9973	0.9967	0.9960	0.9952	0.9942	0.9931
10	0.9997	0.9996	0.9995	0.9994	0.9992	0.9990	0.9987	0.9984	0.9981	0.9977
11	0.9999	0.9999	0.9999	0.9998	0.9998	0.9997	0.9996	0.9995	0.9994	0.9993
12	1.0000	1.0000	1.0000	1.0000	0.9999	0.9999	0.9999	0.9999	0.9998	0.9998
13	1.0000	1.0000	1.0000	1.0000	1.0000	1.0000	1.0000	1.0000	1.0000	0.9999
14	1.0000	1.0000	1.0000	1.0000	1.0000	1.0000	1.0000	1.0000	1.0000	1.0000

λ	4.00	4.10	4.20	4.30	4.40	4.50	4.60	4.70	4.80	4.90
$x = 0$	0.0183	0.0166	0.0150	0.0136	0.0123	0.0111	0.0101	0.0091	0.0082	0.0074
1	0.0916	0.0845	0.0780	0.0719	0.0663	0.0611	0.0563	0.0518	0.0477	0.0439
2	0.2381	0.2238	0.2102	0.1974	0.1851	0.1736	0.1626	0.1523	0.1425	0.1333
3	0.4335	0.4142	0.3954	0.3772	0.3594	0.3423	0.3257	0.3097	0.2942	0.2793
4	0.6288	0.6093	0.5898	0.5704	0.5512	0.5321	0.5132	0.4946	0.4763	0.4582
5	0.7851	0.7693	0.7531	0.7367	0.7199	0.7029	0.6858	0.6684	0.6510	0.6335
6	0.8893	0.8786	0.8675	0.8558	0.8436	0.8311	0.8180	0.8046	0.7908	0.7767
7	0.9489	0.9427	0.9361	0.9290	0.9214	0.9134	0.9049	0.8960	0.8867	0.8769
8	0.9786	0.9755	0.9721	0.9683	0.9642	0.9597	0.9549	0.9497	0.9442	0.9382
9	0.9919	0.9905	0.9889	0.9871	0.9851	0.9829	0.9805	0.9778	0.9749	0.9717
10	0.9972	0.9966	0.9959	0.9952	0.9943	0.9933	0.9922	0.9910	0.9896	0.9880
11	0.9991	0.9989	0.9986	0.9983	0.9980	0.9976	0.9971	0.9966	0.9960	0.9953
12	0.9997	0.9997	0.9996	0.9995	0.9993	0.9992	0.9990	0.9988	0.9986	0.9983
13	0.9999	0.9999	0.9999	0.9998	0.9998	0.9997	0.9997	0.9996	0.9995	0.9994
14	1.0000	1.0000	1.0000	1.0000	0.9999	0.9999	0.9999	0.9999	0.9999	0.9998
15	1.0000	1.0000	1.0000	1.0000	1.0000	1.0000	1.0000	1.0000	1.0000	0.9999
16	1.0000	1.0000	1.0000	1.0000	1.0000	1.0000	1.0000	1.0000	1.0000	1.0000

Cumulative Poisson Probabilities

λ	5.00	5.50	6.00	6.50	7.00	7.50	8.00	8.50	9.00	9.50
$x = 0$	0.0067	0.0041	0.0025	0.0015	0.0009	0.0006	0.0003	0.0002	0.0001	0.0001
1	0.0404	0.0266	0.0174	0.0113	0.0073	0.0047	0.0030	0.0019	0.0012	0.0008
2	0.1247	0.0884	0.0620	0.0430	0.0296	0.0203	0.0138	0.0093	0.0062	0.0042
3	0.2650	0.2017	0.1512	0.1118	0.0818	0.0591	0.0424	0.0301	0.0212	0.0149
4	0.4405	0.3575	0.2851	0.2237	0.1730	0.1321	0.0996	0.0744	0.0550	0.0403
5	0.6160	0.5289	0.4457	0.3690	0.3007	0.2414	0.1912	0.1496	0.1157	0.0885
6	0.7622	0.6860	0.6063	0.5265	0.4497	0.3782	0.3134	0.2562	0.2068	0.1649
7	0.8666	0.8095	0.7440	0.6728	0.5987	0.5246	0.4530	0.3856	0.3239	0.2687
8	0.9319	0.8944	0.8472	0.7916	0.7291	0.6620	0.5925	0.5231	0.4557	0.3918
9	0.9682	0.9462	0.9161	0.8774	0.8305	0.7764	0.7166	0.6530	0.5874	0.5218
10	0.9863	0.9747	0.9574	0.9332	0.9015	0.8622	0.8159	0.7634	0.7060	0.6453
11	0.9945	0.9890	0.9799	0.9661	0.9467	0.9208	0.8881	0.8487	0.8030	0.7520
12	0.9980	0.9955	0.9912	0.9840	0.9730	0.9573	0.9362	0.9091	0.8758	0.8364
13	0.9993	0.9983	0.9964	0.9929	0.9872	0.9784	0.9658	0.9486	0.9261	0.8981
14	0.9998	0.9994	0.9986	0.9970	0.9943	0.9897	0.9827	0.9726	0.9585	0.9400
15	0.9999	0.9998	0.9995	0.9988	0.9976	0.9954	0.9918	0.9862	0.9780	0.9665
16	1.0000	0.9999	0.9998	0.9996	0.9990	0.9980	0.9963	0.9934	0.9889	0.9823
17	1.0000	1.0000	0.9999	0.9998	0.9996	0.9992	0.9984	0.9970	0.9947	0.9911
18	1.0000	1.0000	1.0000	0.9999	0.9999	0.9997	0.9993	0.9987	0.9976	0.9957
19	1.0000	1.0000	1.0000	1.0000	1.0000	0.9999	0.9997	0.9995	0.9989	0.9980
20	1.0000	1.0000	1.0000	1.0000	1.0000	1.0000	0.9999	0.9998	0.9996	0.9991
21	1.0000	1.0000	1.0000	1.0000	1.0000	1.0000	1.0000	0.9999	0.9998	0.9996
22	1.0000	1.0000	1.0000	1.0000	1.0000	1.0000	1.0000	1.0000	0.9999	0.9999
23	1.0000	1.0000	1.0000	1.0000	1.0000	1.0000	1.0000	1.0000	1.0000	0.9999
24	1.0000	1.0000	1.0000	1.0000	1.0000	1.0000	1.0000	1.0000	1.0000	1.0000

Cumulative Poisson Probabilities

λ	10.00	11.00	12.00	13.00	14.00	15.00	16.00	17.00	18.00	19.00
$x = 0$	0.0000	0.0000	0.0000	0.0000	0.0000	0.0000	0.0000	0.0000	0.0000	0.0000
1	0.0005	0.0002	0.0001	0.0000	0.0000	0.0000	0.0000	0.0000	0.0000	0.0000
2	0.0028	0.0012	0.0005	0.0002	0.0001	0.0000	0.0000	0.0000	0.0000	0.0000
3	0.0103	0.0049	0.0023	0.0011	0.0005	0.0002	0.0001	0.0000	0.0000	0.0000
4	0.0293	0.0151	0.0076	0.0037	0.0018	0.0009	0.0004	0.0002	0.0001	0.0000
5	0.0671	0.0375	0.0203	0.0107	0.0055	0.0028	0.0014	0.0007	0.0003	0.0002
6	0.1301	0.0786	0.0458	0.0259	0.0142	0.0076	0.0040	0.0021	0.0010	0.0005
7	0.2202	0.1432	0.0895	0.0540	0.0316	0.0180	0.0100	0.0054	0.0029	0.0015
8	0.3328	0.2320	0.1550	0.0998	0.0621	0.0374	0.0220	0.0126	0.0071	0.0039
9	0.4579	0.3405	0.2424	0.1658	0.1094	0.0699	0.0433	0.0261	0.0154	0.0089
10	0.5830	0.4599	0.3472	0.2517	0.1757	0.1185	0.0774	0.0491	0.0304	0.0183
11	0.6968	0.5793	0.4616	0.3532	0.2600	0.1848	0.1270	0.0847	0.0549	0.0347
12	0.7916	0.6887	0.5760	0.4631	0.3585	0.2676	0.1931	0.1350	0.0917	0.0606
13	0.8645	0.7813	0.6815	0.5730	0.4644	0.3632	0.2745	0.2009	0.1426	0.0984
14	0.9165	0.8540	0.7720	0.6751	0.5704	0.4657	0.3675	0.2808	0.2081	0.1497
15	0.9513	0.9074	0.8444	0.7636	0.6694	0.5681	0.4667	0.3715	0.2867	0.2148
16	0.9730	0.9441	0.8987	0.8355	0.7559	0.6641	0.5660	0.4677	0.3751	0.292
17	0.9857	0.9678	0.9370	0.8905	0.8272	0.7489	0.6593	0.5640	0.4686	0.3784
18	0.9928	0.9823	0.9626	0.9302	0.8826	0.8195	0.7423	0.6550	0.5622	0.4695
19	0.9965	0.9907	0.9787	0.9573	0.9235	0.8752	0.8122	0.7363	0.6509	0.5606
20	0.9984	0.9953	0.9884	0.9750	0.9521	0.9170	0.8682	0.8055	0.7307	0.6472
21	0.9993	0.9977	0.9939	0.9859	0.9712	0.9469	0.9108	0.8615	0.7991	0.7255
22	0.9997	0.9990	0.9970	0.9924	0.9833	0.9673	0.9418	0.9047	0.8551	0.7931
23	0.9999	0.9995	0.9985	0.9960	0.9907	0.9805	0.9633	0.9367	0.8989	0.8490
24	1.0000	0.9998	0.9993	0.9980	0.9950	0.9888	0.9777	0.9594	0.9317	0.8933
25	1.0000	0.9999	0.9997	0.9990	0.9974	0.9938	0.9869	0.9748	0.9554	0.9269
26	1.0000	1.0000	0.9999	0.9995	0.9987	0.9967	0.9925	0.9848	0.9718	0.9514
27	1.0000	1.0000	0.9999	0.9998	0.9994	0.9983	0.9959	0.9912	0.9827	0.9687
28	1.0000	1.0000	1.0000	0.9999	0.9997	0.9991	0.9978	0.9950	0.9897	0.9805
29	1.0000	1.0000	1.0000	1.0000	0.9999	0.9996	0.9989	0.9973	0.9941	0.9882
30	1.0000	1.0000	1.0000	1.0000	0.9999	0.9998	0.9994	0.9986	0.9967	0.9930
31	1.0000	1.0000	1.0000	1.0000	1.0000	0.9999	0.9997	0.9993	0.9982	0.9960
32	1.0000	1.0000	1.0000	1.0000	1.0000	1.0000	0.9999	0.9996	0.9990	0.9978
33	1.0000	1.0000	1.0000	1.0000	1.0000	1.0000	0.9999	0.9998	0.9995	0.9988
34	1.0000	1.0000	1.0000	1.0000	1.0000	1.0000	1.0000	0.9999	0.9998	0.9994
35	1.0000	1.0000	1.0000	1.0000	1.0000	1.0000	1.0000	1.0000	0.9999	0.9997
36	1.0000	1.0000	1.0000	1.0000	1.0000	1.0000	1.0000	1.0000	0.9999	0.9998
37	1.0000	1.0000	1.0000	1.0000	1.0000	1.0000	1.0000	1.0000	1.0000	0.9999
38	1.0000	1.0000	1.0000	1.0000	1.0000	1.0000	1.0000	1.0000	1.0000	1.0000

The Normal Distribution Function

If Z has a normal distribution with mean 0 and
variance 1 then, for each value of z, the table
gives the value of $\Phi(z)$, where

$$\Phi(z) = P(Z \leqslant z).$$

For negative values of z use $\Phi(-z) = 1 - \Phi(z)$.

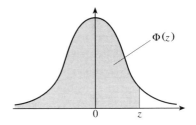

z	0	1	2	3	4	5	6	7	8	9	1	2	3	4	5	6	7	8	9
															ADD				
0.0	0.5000	0.5040	0.5080	0.5120	0.5160	0.5199	0.5239	0.5279	0.5319	0.5359	4	8	12	16	20	24	28	32	36
0.1	0.5398	0.5438	0.5478	0.5517	0.5557	0.5596	0.5636	0.5675	0.5714	0.5753	4	8	12	16	20	24	28	32	36
0.2	0.5793	0.5832	0.5871	0.5910	0.5948	0.5987	0.6026	0.6064	0.6103	0.6141	4	8	12	15	19	23	27	31	35
0.3	0.6179	0.6217	0.6255	0.6293	0.6331	0.6368	0.6406	0.6443	0.6480	0.6517	4	7	11	14	18	22	25	29	32
0.4	0.6554	0.6591	0.6628	0.6664	0.6700	0.6736	0.6772	0.6808	0.6844	0.6879	4	7	11	14	18	22	25	29	32
0.5	0.6915	0.6950	0.6985	0.7019	0.7054	0.7088	0.7123	0.7157	0.7190	0.7224	3	7	10	14	17	20	24	27	31
0.6	0.7257	0.7291	0.7324	0.7357	0.7389	0.7422	0.7454	0.7486	0.7517	0.7549	3	7	10	13	16	19	23	26	29
0.7	0.7580	0.7611	0.7642	0.7673	0.7704	0.7734	0.7764	0.7794	0.7823	0.7852	3	6	9	12	15	18	21	24	27
0.8	0.7881	0.7910	0.7939	0.7967	0.7995	0.8023	0.8051	0.8078	0.8106	0.8133	3	5	8	11	14	16	19	22	25
0.9	0.8159	0.8186	0.8212	0.8238	0.8264	0.8289	0.8315	0.8340	0.8365	0.8389	3	5	8	10	13	15	18	20	23
1.0	0.8413	0.8438	0.8461	0.8485	0.8508	0.8531	0.8554	0.8577	0.8599	0.8621	2	5	7	9	12	14	16	19	21
1.1	0.8643	0.8665	0.8686	0.8708	0.8729	0.8749	0.8770	0.8790	0.8810	0.8830	2	4	6	8	10	12	14	16	18
1.2	0.8849	0.8869	0.8888	0.8907	0.8925	0.8944	0.8962	0.8980	0.8997	0.9015	2	4	6	7	9	11	13	15	17
1.3	0.9032	0.9049	0.9066	0.9082	0.9099	0.9115	0.9131	0.9147	0.9162	0.9177	2	3	5	6	8	10	11	13	14
1.4	0.9192	0.9207	0.9222	0.9236	0.9251	0.9265	0.9279	0.9292	0.9306	0.9319	1	3	4	6	7	8	10	11	13
1.5	0.9332	0.9345	0.9357	0.9370	0.9382	0.9394	0.9406	0.9418	0.9429	0.9441	1	2	4	5	6	7	8	10	11
1.6	0.9452	0.9463	0.9474	0.9484	0.9495	0.9505	0.9515	0.9525	0.9535	0.9545	1	2	3	4	5	6	7	8	9
1.7	0.9554	0.9564	0.9573	0.9582	0.9591	0.9599	0.9608	0.9616	0.9625	0.9633	1	2	3	4	4	5	6	7	8
1.8	0.9641	0.9649	0.9656	0.9664	0.9671	0.9678	0.9686	0.9693	0.9699	0.9706	1	1	2	3	4	4	5	6	6
1.9	0.9713	0.9719	0.9726	0.9732	0.9738	0.9744	0.9750	0.9756	0.9761	0.9767	1	1	2	2	3	4	4	5	5
2.0	0.9772	0.9778	0.9783	0.9788	0.9793	0.9798	0.9803	0.9808	0.9812	0.9817	0	1	1	2	2	3	3	4	4
2.1	0.9821	0.9826	0.9830	0.9834	0.9838	0.9842	0.9846	0.9850	0.9854	0.9857	0	1	1	2	2	2	3	3	4
2.2	0.9861	0.9864	0.9868	0.9871	0.9875	0.9878	0.9881	0.9884	0.9887	0.9890	0	1	1	1	2	2	2	3	3
2.3	0.9893	0.9896	0.9898	0.9901	0.9904	0.9906	0.9909	0.9911	0.9913	0.9916	0	1	1	1	1	2	2	2	2
2.4	0.9918	0.9920	0.9922	0.9925	0.9927	0.9929	0.9931	0.9932	0.9934	0.9936	0	0	1	1	1	1	1	2	2
2.5	0.9938	0.9940	0.9941	0.9943	0.9945	0.9946	0.9948	0.9949	0.9951	0.9952	0	0	0	1	1	1	1	1	1
2.6	0.9953	0.9955	0.9956	0.9957	0.9959	0.9960	0.9961	0.9962	0.9963	0.9964	0	0	0	0	1	1	1	1	1
2.7	0.9965	0.9966	0.9967	0.9968	0.9969	0.9970	0.9971	0.9972	0.9973	0.9974	0	0	0	0	0	1	1	1	1
2.8	0.9974	0.9975	0.9976	0.9977	0.9977	0.9978	0.9979	0.9979	0.9980	0.9981	0	0	0	0	0	0	0	1	1
2.9	0.9981	0.9982	0.9982	0.9983	0.9984	0.9984	0.9985	0.9985	0.9986	0.9986	0	0	0	0	0	0	0	0	0

Critical values for the normal distribution

If Z has a normal distribution with mean 0 and variance 1 then, for each value of p, the
table gives the value of z such that $P(Z \leqslant z) = p$.

p	0.75	0.90	0.95	0.975	0.99	0.995	0.9975	0.999	0.9995
z	0.674	1.282	1.645	1.960	2.326	2.576	2.807	3.090	3.291

Critical Values for the *t* Distribution

If T has a t distribution with v degrees of freedom then, for each pair of values of p and v, the table gives the value of t such that

$$P(T \leqslant t) = p.$$

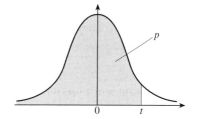

p	0.75	0.90	0.95	0.975	0.99	0.995	0.9975	0.999	0.9995
$v = 1$	1.000	3.078	6.314	12.71	31.82	63.66	127.3	318.3	636.6
2	0.816	1.886	2.920	4.303	6.965	9.925	14.09	22.33	31.60
3	0.765	1.638	2.353	3.182	4.541	5.841	7.453	10.21	12.92
4	0.741	1.533	2.132	2.776	3.747	4.604	5.598	7.173	8.610
5	0.727	1.476	2.015	2.571	3.365	4.032	4.773	5.894	6.869
6	0.718	1.440	1.943	2.447	3.143	3.707	4.317	5.208	5.959
7	0.711	1.415	1.895	2.365	2.998	3.499	4.029	4.785	5.408
8	0.706	1.397	1.860	2.306	2.896	3.355	3.833	4.501	5.041
9	0.703	1.383	1.833	2.262	2.821	3.250	3.690	4.297	4.781
10	0.700	1.372	1.812	2.228	2.764	3.169	3.581	4.144	4.587
11	0.697	1.363	1.796	2.201	2.718	3.106	3.497	4.025	4.437
12	0.695	1.356	1.782	2.179	2.681	3.055	3.428	3.930	4.318
13	0.694	1.350	1.771	2.160	2.650	3.012	3.372	3.852	4.221
14	0.692	1.345	1.761	2.145	2.624	2.977	3.326	3.787	4.140
15	0.691	1.341	1.753	2.131	2.602	2.947	3.286	3.733	4.073
16	0.690	1.337	1.746	2.120	2.583	2.921	3.252	3.686	4.015
17	0.689	1.333	1.740	2.110	2.567	2.898	3.222	3.646	3.965
18	0.688	1.330	1.734	2.101	2.552	2.878	3.197	3.610	3.922
19	0.688	1.328	1.729	2.093	2.539	2.861	3.174	3.579	3.883
20	0.687	1.325	1.725	2.086	2.528	2.845	3.153	3.552	3.850
21	0.686	1.323	1.721	2.080	2.518	2.831	3.135	3.527	3.819
22	0.686	1.321	1.717	2.074	2.508	2.819	3.119	3.505	3.792
23	0.685	1.319	1.714	2.069	2.500	2.807	3.104	3.485	3.768
24	0.685	1.318	1.711	2.064	2.492	2.797	3.091	3.467	3.745
25	0.684	1.316	1.708	2.060	2.485	2.787	3.078	3.450	3.725
26	0.684	1.315	1.706	2.056	2.479	2.779	3.067	3.435	3.707
27	0.684	1.314	1.703	2.052	2.473	2.771	3.057	3.421	3.689
28	0.683	1.313	1.701	2.048	2.467	2.763	3.047	3.408	3.674
29	0.683	1.311	1.699	2.045	2.462	2.756	3.038	3.396	3.660
30	0.683	1.310	1.697	2.042	2.457	2.750	3.030	3.385	3.646
40	0.681	1.303	1.684	2.021	2.423	2.704	2.971	3.307	3.551
60	0.679	1.296	1.671	2.000	2.390	2.660	2.915	3.232	3.460
120	0.677	1.289	1.658	1.980	2.358	2.617	2.860	3.160	3.373
∞	0.674	1.282	1.645	1.960	2.326	2.576	2.807	3.090	3.291

Critical Values for the χ^2 Distribution

If X has a χ^2 distribution with v degrees of freedom then, for each pair of values of p and v, the table gives the value of x such that

$$P(X \leqslant x) = p.$$

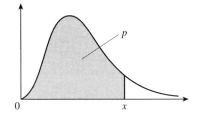

p	0.01	0.025	0.05	0.9	0.95	0.975	0.99	0.995	0.999
$v = 1$	0.0^31571	0.0^39821	0.0^23932	2.706	3.841	5.024	6.635	7.8794	10.83
2	0.02010	0.05064	0.1026	4.605	5.991	7.378	9.210	10.60	13.82
3	0.1148	0.2158	0.3518	6.251	7.815	9.348	11.34	12.84	16.27
4	0.2971	0.4844	0.7107	7.779	9.488	11.14	13.28	14.86	18.47
5	0.5543	0.8312	1.145	9.236	11.07	12.83	15.09	16.75	20.51
6	0.8721	1.237	1.635	10.64	12.59	14.45	16.81	18.55	22.46
7	1.239	1.690	2.167	12.02	14.07	16.01	18.48	20.28	24.32
8	1.647	2.180	2.733	13.36	15.51	17.53	20.09	21.95	26.12
9	2.088	2.700	3.325	14.68	16.92	19.02	21.67	23.59	27.88
10	2.558	3.247	3.940	15.99	18.31	20.48	23.21	25.19	29.59
11	3.053	3.816	4.575	17.28	19.68	21.92	24.73	26.76	31.26
12	3.571	4.404	5.226	18.55	21.03	23.34	26.22	28.30	32.91
13	4.107	5.009	5.892	19.81	22.36	24.74	27.69	29.82	34.53
14	4.660	5.629	6.571	21.06	23.68	26.12	29.14	31.32	36.12
15	5.229	6.262	7.261	22.31	25.00	27.49	30.58	32.80	37.70
16	5.812	6.908	7.962	23.54	26.30	28.85	32.00	34.27	39.25
17	6.408	7.564	8.672	24.77	27.59	30.19	33.41	35.72	40.79
18	7.015	8.231	9.390	25.99	28.87	31.53	34.81	37.16	42.31
19	7.633	8.907	10.12	27.20	30.14	32.85	36.19	38.58	43.82
20	8.260	9.591	10.85	28.41	31.41	34.17	37.57	40.00	45.31
21	8.897	10.28	11.59	29.62	32.67	35.48	38.93	41.40	46.80
22	9.542	10.98	12.34	30.81	33.92	36.78	40.29	42.80	48.27
23	10.20	11.69	13.09	32.01	35.17	38.08	41.64	44.18	49.73
24	10.86	12.40	13.85	33.20	36.42	39.36	42.98	45.56	51.18
25	11.52	13.12	14.61	34.38	37.65	40.65	44.31	46.93	52.62
30	14.95	16.79	18.49	40.26	43.77	46.98	50.89	53.67	59.70
40	22.16	24.43	26.51	51.81	55.76	59.34	63.69	66.77	73.40
50	29.71	32.36	34.76	63.17	67.50	71.42	76.15	79.49	86.66
60	37.48	40.48	43.19	74.40	79.08	83.30	88.38	91.95	99.61
70	45.44	48.76	51.74	85.53	90.53	95.02	100.4	104.2	112.3
80	53.54	57.15	60.39	96.58	101.9	106.6	112.3	116.3	124.8
90	61.75	65.65	69.13	107.6	113.1	118.1	124.1	128.3	137.2
100	70.06	74.22	77.93	118.5	124.3	129.6	135.8	140.2	149.4

Wilcoxon Signed-Rank Test

P is the sum of the ranks corresponding to the positive differences,

Q is the sum of the ranks corresponding to the negative differences,

T is the smaller of P and Q.

For each value of n the table gives the **largest** value of T which will lead to rejection of the null hypothesis at the level of significance indicated.

Critical values of T

	Level of significance			
One tail	0.05	0.025	0.01	0.005
Two tail	0.1	0.05	0.02	0.01
$n = 6$	2	0		
7	3	2	0	
8	5	3	1	0
9	8	5	3	1
10	10	8	5	3
11	13	10	7	5
12	17	13	9	7
13	21	17	12	9
14	25	21	15	12
15	30	25	19	15
16	35	29	23	19
17	41	34	27	23
18	47	40	32	27
19	53	46	37	32
20	60	52	43	37

For larger values of n, each of P and Q can be approximated by the normal distribution with mean $\frac{1}{4}n(n+1)$ and variance $\frac{1}{24}n(n+1)(2n+1)$.

Wilcoxon Rank-Sum Test

The two samples have sizes m and n, where $m \leqslant n$.

R_m is the sum of the ranks of the items in the sample of size m.

W is the smaller of R_m and $m(n + m + 1) - R_m$.

For each pair of values of m and n, the table gives the **largest** value of W which will lead to rejection of the null hypothesis at the level of significance indicated.

Critical values of W

	Level of significance											
One tail	0.05	0.025	0.01	0.05	0.025	0.01	0.05	0.025	0.01	0.05	0.025	0.01
Two tail	0.1	0.05	0.02	0.1	0.05	0.02	0.1	0.05	0.02	0.1	0.05	0.02
n	$m = 3$			$m = 4$			$m = 5$			$m = 6$		
3	6	–	–									
4	6	–	–	11	10	–						
5	7	6	–	12	11	10	19	17	16			
6	8	7	–	13	12	11	20	18	17	28	26	24
7	8	7	6	14	13	11	21	20	18	29	27	25
8	9	8	6	15	14	12	23	21	19	31	29	27
9	10	8	7	16	14	13	24	22	20	33	31	28
10	10	9	7	17	15	13	26	23	21	35	32	29

	Level of significance											
One tail	0.05	0.025	0.01	0.05	0.025	0.01	0.05	0.025	0.01	0.05	0.025	0.01
Two tail	0.1	0.05	0.02	0.1	0.05	0.02	0.1	0.05	0.02	0.1	0.05	0.02
n	$m = 7$			$m = 8$			$m = 9$			$m = 10$		
7	39	36	34									
8	41	38	35	51	49	45						
9	43	40	37	54	51	47	66	62	59			
10	45	42	39	56	53	49	69	65	61	82	78	74

For larger values of m and n, the normal distribution with mean $\frac{1}{2}m(n + m + 1)$ and variance $\frac{1}{12}mn(m + n + 1)$ should be used as an approximation to the distribution of R_m.

Answers to S3

Most non-exact numerical answers are given correct to 3 significant figures.

1 Continuous random variables

Exercise 1A (page 6)

1 (b) $\frac{2}{3}$ (c) $\frac{7}{12}$ (d) $\frac{7}{9}$ (e) $\frac{37}{162}$

2 (b) $\frac{1}{9}$ (c) $\frac{2}{9}$ (d) $\frac{43}{72}$ (e) 3 (f) $\frac{3}{2}$

3 (b) $\frac{3}{14}$ (c) $\frac{65}{112}$ (d) $\frac{15}{7}$ (e) $\frac{177}{245}$

4 (b) $\frac{1}{3}$ (c) $\frac{5}{8}$ (d) 2 (e) $\frac{5}{6}$

5 (b) $\frac{8}{15}$ (c) $\frac{7}{12}$ (d) $\frac{26}{45}$ (e) $\frac{3553}{4050}$

6 (a) (ii) $\frac{11}{20}$ (iii) 2000 hours
  (b) (i) 2000 hours
    (ii) For example, the first model sets an upper bound to the lifetimes.

7 (b) $\dfrac{1}{a^2}$ (d) a

Exercise 1B (page 13)

1 (a)
$$F(x)=\begin{cases}0 & x<0, \\ \frac{1}{16}x^2 & 0\leqslant x\leqslant 4, \\ 1 & x>4.\end{cases}$$

  (b) 2.83

2 (a)
$$F(x)=\begin{cases}0 & x<0, \\ \frac{2}{3}x & 0\leqslant x<1, \\ \frac{1}{3}\left(4x-x^2-1\right) & 1\leqslant x\leqslant 2, \\ 1 & x>2.\end{cases}$$

  (b) $\frac{3}{8}$ (c) $\frac{4}{3}$

3 (a)
$$F(x)=\begin{cases}0 & x<0, \\ \frac{3}{28}x^2 & 0\leqslant x<2, \\ \frac{1}{28}\left(6x^2-x^3-4\right) & 2\leqslant x\leqslant 4, \\ 1 & x>4.\end{cases}$$

  (b) 2.17 (c) $\frac{41}{224}$

4 (a)
$$F(x)=\begin{cases}0 & x<0, \\ \frac{1}{16}\left(24x^2-16x^3+3x^4\right) & 0\leqslant x\leqslant 2, \\ 1 & x>2.\end{cases}$$

  (b) 7700

5
$$f(x)=\begin{cases}\frac{1}{6}x-\frac{1}{36}x^3 & 0\leqslant x\leqslant 6, \\ 0 & \text{otherwise.}\end{cases}$$

6
$$f(x)=\begin{cases}\frac{1}{9}x & 0\leqslant x<3, \\ \frac{2}{3}-\frac{1}{9}x & 3\leqslant x\leqslant 6, \\ 0 & \text{otherwise.}\end{cases}$$

Exercise 1C (page 18)

2 (a)
$$f(y)=\begin{cases}\frac{1}{10}y^{-\frac{1}{2}} & 1\leqslant y\leqslant 36, \\ 0 & \text{otherwise.}\end{cases}$$

  (b) $\frac{43}{3}$ (c) $\frac{43}{3}$ (d) Because $Y=X^2$

3 $f(y)=\dfrac{1}{6\sqrt{\pi}y}$ for $\pi\leqslant y\leqslant 16\pi$

4 $0,\ \frac{1}{5},0,\ \frac{3}{35}$

5 0

6 12, 3, 16

7 40.5, $\frac{2}{3}\ln 2$

Miscellaneous exercise 1 (page 19)

1 (b) $\frac{11}{9},\ \frac{31}{18}$ (c) $\frac{17}{48}$

2 $F(t)=\frac{1}{2}k(t-2)^2$ for $2\leqslant t\leqslant 4$; $\frac{1}{2}$

3 $\frac{1}{32}$; $f(x)=\frac{3}{32}\left(4x-x^2\right)$ for $0\leqslant x\leqslant 4$; 2

4
$$f(x)=\begin{cases}\frac{1}{9}(3-x)^2 & 0\leqslant x\leqslant 3, \\ 0 & \text{otherwise;}\end{cases}$$
$\frac{3}{4}$

5 -15, $f(x)=\begin{cases}8-2x & 3\leqslant x\leqslant 4, \\ 0 & \text{otherwise.}\end{cases}$

6 (b) $F(x)=\ln x$ for $1\leqslant x\leqslant e$ (c) $1-\dfrac{1}{e}$

7 (b) 1, $\frac{5}{6}$ (c) $\frac{1}{4}$

8 (a) $\frac{1}{4}$ (b) 0.134
  (c) $f(x)=\begin{cases}2(1-x) & 0\leqslant x\leqslant 1, \\ 0 & \text{otherwise.}\end{cases}$

9 $f(y)=\begin{cases}e^y & y<0, \\ 0 & \text{otherwise;}\end{cases}$
  -1

10 $\frac{3}{2}f\leqslant v\leqslant 2f$; $f(1+\ln 2)$, $\frac{5}{3}f$

2 Linear combinations of random variables

Exercise 2A (page 26)

1 0.5, 0.25; 0.48, 0.16; 0.3, 0.37, 0.2, 0.04; 1, $\frac{1}{2}$, 0.8, 0.48, 1.8, 0.98

2 3.1, 3.69; 0.2, 0.16, 0.1, 0.14, 0.2

3 24, 12, 6, 24

4 8 mm, 0.14 mm^2

5 $3.5, \frac{35}{12}, 3, 9, 6.5, \frac{143}{12}$

6 $\frac{51}{8}, \frac{213}{64}$

7 $82.5, 311$

Exercise 2B (page 31)

1 0.0592

2 0.0638

3 0.0228

4 0.127

5 0.362

6 0.0317

7 $\mu = 16, \sigma^2 = 9$

8 (a) 5, 5   (b) 1, 5   (c) 11, 27
(a) is Poisson

9 0.165

10 0.242

Miscellaneous exercise 2 (page 32)

1 10, 50

2 (a) $1, \frac{4}{5}$ (b) $\frac{3}{5}, \frac{6}{25}$ (c) 11.2, 7.28

3 Values: $-3, 0, 3, 6$; probabilities: p^3, $3p^2(1-p)$, $3p(1-p)^2$, $(1-p)^3$
450 pence, 30 pence

4 2, 1; 4, 3

5 $\frac{1}{15}, \frac{2}{3}, \frac{34}{45}; \frac{4}{3}, \frac{68}{45}$

6 12 kg, 57 g, 3.97%, 765 g

7 0.121

8 (a) 0.189   (b) 0.308   (c) 0.184

9 (a) 0.132   (b) 0.228

10 (a) 0.655   (b) 0.314

11 (a) 0.681   (b) 0.113   (c) 0.159

12 (a) 0.309
(b) 0.235; 0 because
$P(N > 3.5n) = P\left(z > \frac{1}{4}\sqrt{n}\right) = 1 - \Phi\left(\frac{1}{4}\sqrt{n}\right).$

3 Confidence intervals and the *t* distribution

Exercise 3A (page 41)

1 $[496.5, 504.5]$, 190

2 $[0.981, 1.028]$; 0.0233 litres

3 (a) 5.155   (b) 8.48   (c) 10.10

4 $[169.4, 181.0]$; no, 178 is within the interval.

5 (a) $[5.013, 5.057]$
(b) 5.00 cm is outside the interval and indicates that the mean has increased.

6 (a) $[15.67, 16.17]$ (b) Six more

Exercise 3B (page 44)

1 (a) $[4.73, 5.62]$
(b) Assume sample mean has a normal distribution, which is justified by the central limit theorem (sample size large); also that the sample variance is a good estimate of the population variance, which is justified by the large sample size.

2 (a) 498.1 g, 4.839 g^2 (b) $[497.7, 498.5]$
The confidence interval will not contain the mean 5% of the time.

3 (a) 2.43, 2.288   (b) $[2.18, 2.68]$

4 (a) 5.968 m^2 (b) $[6.44, 8.22]$
$[5.10, 6.88]$

5 (a) $[84.1, 89.1]$ (b) Interval is only valid for mean of 8-year-olds attending the clinic.

6 (a) $[61.0, 62.5]$
(b) No, both limits greater than 60.

Exercise 3C (page 48)

1 (a) Yes   (b) No   (c) Yes

2 $[0.024, 0.176]$, $[0.238, 0.762]$

3 $[28.5, 39.5]$

4 (a) $[0.144, 0.224]$ (b) Sample is random.
(c) For example, all cars passing under the bridge over a specified period
(d) 49

5 $[0.322, 0.424]$; $n = 971$; variance is estimate and normal approximation is used.

6 (a) $[0.045, 0.155]$, $[0.159, 0.316]$
(b) Indicates $p_1 < p_2$ since intervals do not intersect, with that for p_1 lower than that for p_2.

Exercise 3D (page 51)

1 (a) 1.796   (b) 2.262   (c) 2.492
(d) 2.9 approximately, by interpolation (n is large enough to use a normal distribution)

2 [14.66, 15.20]; assumes alcohol content has a normal distribution.

3 $[2725.8, 2967.4]$; 10% chance that interval will not contain population mean.

4 (a) $[3.65, 4.75]$; assumes a normal population and a random sample
(b) Class appears better than average, suggesting that they are not a random sample.

5 (a) 9.806 (b) $[9.756, 9.856]$
  (c) Interval is exact; neither the distribution nor parameters are approximated.

6 (a) $[18.3, 19.9]$
  (b) $\Phi(-3.14) \approx 0.001$; most unlikely to be fully-grown

Exercise 3E (page 56)

1 $H_0: \mu = 6.32$, $H_1: \mu \neq 6.32$;
  $t = 0.665 \in [-2.145, 2.145]$; accept mean is 6.32.

2 $H_0: \mu = 4.8$, $H_1: \mu < 4.8$; $t = -3.643 < -2.365$;
  accept H_1, mean has reduced.

3 (a) $H_0: \mu = 5$, $H_1: \mu > 5$; $t = 2.414 > 1.711$;
    accept H_1, glass acceptable.
  (b) $0.01 < p < 0.025$

4 $H_0: \mu = 5.7$, $H_1: \mu < 5.7$; $t = -2.994 < -3.365$;
  accept H_0, mean not less than 5.7.

5 $H_0: \mu = 14.2$, $H_1: \mu \neq 14.2$;
  $t = 1.410 \in [-2.262, 2.262]$, accept mean is 14.2.

6 $\left| \dfrac{3.207 - \mu_0}{0.461/\sqrt{20}} \right| < 1.729$; $3.029 < \mu_0 < 3.385$; a symmetric 90% confidence interval for μ

Miscellaneous exercise 3 (page 57)

1 (a) For example, number all members and use a table of random numbers or a random number generator.
  (b) 5.64, 3.158
  (c) $[4.37, 6.91]$; population distributed normally.
  (d) 95

2 (a) $3.357\sigma/\sqrt{n}$ (b) $3.306\sigma/\sqrt{n}$
  (c) $3.29\sigma/\sqrt{n}$

These confirm that a symmetric confidence interval has shortest width.

3 (a) $[124.22, 125.71]$ (b) $[124.13, 125.80]$

4 (a) 1.791, 0.6615
  (b) $[1.696, 1.886]$, $[0.149, 0.241]$

No, the confidence interval indicates a mean greater than 10%.

5 $[5.111, 5.169]$, 0.043 mg

6 (a) 1.04 litres, 0.0192 litres^2 (b) $[1.02, 1.06]$
Note that the limits are the same correct to 3 significant digits using either a z- or a t-value.
  (c) 520

7 (a) Assumes burning times are normally distributed; $[37.58, 40.02]$
  (b) $H_0: \mu = 40$, $H_1: \mu < 40$;
    $t = -2.103 < -1.761$; reject H_0, accept $\mu < 40$.
The confidence interval includes 40.0, but it corresponds to a two-tail test at the 5% level. If a two-tail test had been carried out, H_0 would not have been rejected at the 5% level.

8 $[22.8, 24.6]$; normal distribution of sample mean is approximate (central limit theorem) and variance estimate is used.

9 $[0.640, 0.860]$, $n = 180$

10 (a) 3.439 (b) 284

11 (a) $[0.0362, 0.0738]$
  (b) Between 2710 and 5520 based on confidence interval; 3640 based on p_s

12 Assumes weights normally distributed;
  $H_0: \mu = 3$, $H_1: \mu < 3$; $t = -2.639 < -1.796$;
  accept that $\mu < 3$ and reject batch.

13 (a) $t = -2.515 \notin [-1.753, 1.753]$; reject null hypothesis, mean is not 4 kg.
  (b) $\mu < 1.97$, $\mu > 3.83$

14 (a) Confidence interval for p is [0.426, 0.560]; average.
  (b) 95% confidence interval $[0.413, 0.573]$; yes

15 (a) $H_0: \mu = 750$, $H_1: \mu < 750$;
    $t = -2.483 > -2.998$; accept that the mean is at least 750 g.
  (b) Melons will be selected to have weights around 750 g and are likely to have a normal distribution truncated at the extremes.

16 $[1.38, 2.12]$; $P(T < 0) = 0.132$, not small enough; sample large enough for the central limit theorem to apply, so the interval is valid for most reasonable distributions.

4 Testing for differences between populations

Exercise 4A (page 66)

1 $H_0: \mu_x = \mu_y$, $H_1: \mu_x > \mu_y$; $z = 0.448 < 1.645$, so accept H_0, μ_x is not greater than μ_y.

2 $H_0: \mu_A = \mu_B$, $H_1: \mu_A \neq \mu_B$; $z = 2.269$; rejection region is $|Z| \geq 1.96$, so reject H_0 and accept that the population means are different. Not necessary for populations to be normal since sample sizes are large enough for the central limit theorem to hold.

3 (a) $H_0: \mu_1 = \mu_2$, $H_1: \mu_1 \neq \mu_2$; $z = 0.641$,
$p = 2 \times 0.261 = 0.522$
(b) Accept that means are equal.

4 (a) $H_0: \mu_S = \mu_N$, $H_1: \mu_S > \mu_N$;
$z = 1.510 < 1.645$, so accept H_0, the means
are equal.
(b) The numbers of book-shops in each region

5 (a) $H_0: \mu_x = \mu_y$, $H_1: \mu_x \neq \mu_y$; $z = -1.588$;
rejection region is $|Z| \geq 1.645$, so accept
H_0, the mean has not changed.
(b) $z = 1.790$, so reject H_0 and accept that the
mean has changed.
The second test is more reliable since the
variance may well have altered.

6 (a) $H_0: \mu_E = \mu_C$, $H_1: \mu_E > \mu_C$;
$z = 3.134 > 2.326$, so reject H_0 and accept
that $\mu_E > \mu_C$.
(b) $H_0: \mu_E - \mu_C = 2$, $H_1: \mu_E - \mu_C > 2$;
$z = 1.527 > 1.282$, so reject H_0 and accept
that $\mu_E - \mu_C > 2$.

Exercise 4B (page 72)

1 (a) 5.57
(b) $t = 1.089$; rejection region is $|T| \geq 2.086$,
so accept that $\mu_x = \mu_y$.

2 $H_0: \mu_A = \mu_B$, $H_1: \mu_A < \mu_B$; $t = -2.089$; p-value
approximately 0.025.

3 $H_0: \mu_N = \mu_S$, $H_1: \mu_N > \mu_S$; $t = 2.444$; rejection
region is $T \geq 1.895$, so reject H_0 and accept
that mean moisture in southern half is less than in
northern half; assume two populations are normal
with common variance.

4 (a) Assume the weights have normal
distributions with a common variance;
$H_0: \mu_K = \mu_J$, $H_1: \mu_K > \mu_J$; $t = 3.562$,
which is significant at the 0.25% level,
which implies strong evidence for H_1.
(b) $H_0: \mu_K - \mu_J = 10$, $H_1: \mu_K - \mu_J > 10$;
$t = 0.822 < 1.761$, so accept H_0,
$\mu_K - \mu_J = 10$ (or less), so Kapil's carrots
are not more than 10 g heavier than Jack's
on average.

5 (a) For example, all children taught by the two
teachers for that examination over a period
of years
(b) $s_G^2 = 89.33$, $s_J^2 = 78.99$
(c) 83.51
(d) $H_0: \mu_G = \mu_J$, $H_1: \mu_G \neq \mu_J$; $t = 1.361$;
rejection region is $|T| \geq 2.04$
(approximately), so accept H_0, there is no
difference in the means.

6 (a) $\text{Est}(\mu_1) = 11.65$, $s_1^2 = 10.027$,
$\text{Est}(\mu_2) = 9.3$, $s_2^2 = 6.529$
(b) $H_0: \mu_1 = \mu_2$, $H_1: \mu_1 > \mu_2$; $t = 1.539$;
p-value is between 0.05 and 0.10

Exercise 4C (page 77)

1 $H_0: \mu_1 = \mu_2$, $H_1: \mu_1 > \mu_2$; $\bar{d} = 2.625$;
$s^2 = 33.70$; $t = 1.279 < 1.895$, so accept H_0, the
belief is not supported.

2 $t = 2.547 > 2.105$, so accept that $\mu_D > 40$.

3 $s^2 = 159.63$, $z = 1.704$; p-value = 0.044

4 $H_0: \mu_D = 10$, $H_1: \mu_D > 10$; $t = 3.162 > 2.821$, so
reject H_0 and accept that $\mu_D > 10$.

5 $H_0: \mu_O - \mu_C = 0$, $H_1: \mu_O - \mu_C \neq 0$; $t = -0.661$;
rejection region is $|T| \geq 2.228$, so accept H_0,
there is no difference in the effects of organic and
chemical fertilisers.

6 $H_0: \mu_D = 0$, $H_1: \mu_D > 0$; sample size large
enough to use normal test; $z = 1.554 < 1.645$, so
accept H_0, there is no difference in means of the
two populations.
t-test would be valid; $t = 1.554$; rejection region
is $T \geq a$ where $a > 1.645$, so H_0 still accepted.

Exercise 4D (page 81)

1 $H_0: p_N - p_R = 0$, $H_1: p_N - p_R < 0$;
$z = -1.680 < -1.645$, so reject H_0 and accept
that manufacturer's claim is supported.

2 $H_0: p_2 - p_1 = 0$, $H_1: p_2 - p_1 > 0$;
$z = 2.412 > 1.282$, so there is evidence of an
increase in the candidate's share of votes; the
campaign was successful.
$H_0: p_2 - p_1 = 0.05$, $H_1: p_2 - p_1 > 0.05$;
$z = 1.337 > 1.282$, so accept H_1, the increase is
greater than 5%.

3 $H_0: p_L - p_B = 0$, $H_1: p_L - p_B \neq 0$; $z = -1.457$;
rejection region is $|Z| \geq 1.96$, so accept H_0,
there is no difference in the proportions.

4 $H_0: p_A - p_B = 0$, $H_1: p_A - p_B \neq 0$; $z = -0.721$;
rejection region is $|Z| \geq 1.645$, so accept H_0,
there is no difference between the claim rates.

5 $H_0: p_1 - p_2 = 0$, $H_1: p_1 - p_2 \neq 0$; $z = -0.755$;
p-value = $2 \times 0.2251 = 0.450$; drop-out rates are
not significantly different. Variance estimate is
used and normal distribution is approximate.

6 $H_0: p_N - p_C = 0.1$, $H_1: p_N - p_C > 0.1$;
$z = 2.407 > 2.054$; significant at less than 2%
level, so company should market the new pill.

Exercise 4E (page 85)

1 (a) $[-0.354, 0.054]$
(b) No, since zero is inside the interval.

2 $[-0.095, 0.315]$

3 (a) 0.461

(b) $[-0.342, 0.7957]$ for $\mu_{US} - \mu_{UK}$

4 $[-4.72, 17.06]$

5 $[0.04, 8.22]$; the interval does not contain zero and so a two-tail test at the 10% significance level would accept a difference in means. Zero is to the left of the interval, so at 5% level it would be accepted that $\mu_1 > \mu_2$.

6 $[0.38, 1.65]$; it indicates that eldest sons tend to be taller that their fathers.

In 1885, Francis Galton reported the results of a study which he carried out on parents and their children. He found that, on average, tall parents have shorter children but short parents have taller children.

Exercise 4F (page 88)

1 $[0.045, 0.275]$

2 $[0.055, 0.345]$

3 $[-0.107, 0.125]$. No, since the confidence interval includes zero.

Miscellaneous exercise 4 (page 89)

1 (a) Independent samples and $\sigma_x = \sigma_y$.

(b) X_i and Y_i are paired and $X_i - Y_i$ has a normal distribution.

Use test (a) assuming normal distributions with equal variances; $H_0: \mu_y = \mu_x$, $H_1: \mu_y > \mu_x$; $t = 1.193 < 1.860$, so accept H_0.

Use each mixture on all 10 cars and use test (b). It is better since it only assumes differences are distributed normally, and removes variation between individual cars.

2 Assumes data comprise random samples and difference in weight loss has a normal distribution; $[0.10, 0.42]$.

3 $P_s \sim N\left(p, \dfrac{p(1-p)}{n}\right)$ approximately

$z = 2.349$; p-value $= 2 \times 0.0094 = 0.0188$, so conclude that there is no difference. $[0.0038, 0.0579]$

4 $H_0: \mu_S = \mu_P$, $H_1: \mu_S > \mu_P$; $z = -2.458 < -1.645$, so reject H_0 and accept that principal's office receives fewer letters.

5 Assumes daily takings in each year were distributed normally with a common variance; $H_0: \mu_x = \mu_y$, $H_1: \mu_x < \mu_y$; $t = -0.671 > -1.753$, so accept H_0 and accept average daily takings have not changed.

6 Assumes normally distributed populations with a common variance; $H_0: \mu_V = \mu_P$, $H_1: \mu_V > \mu_P$; $t = 1.412 < 1.701$, so accept H_0.

Choose pairs of children with matched IQs and use a paired-sample t-test.

7 (a) $z = 2.475 > 2.326$, so reject H_0 and accept that mean increased.

(b) No change; sample sizes are large enough for the central limit theorem to hold, so sample means have approximate normal distributions.

8 (a) (i) Assume variance unchanged and random samples

(ii) $H_0: \mu_1 = \mu_2$, $H_1: \mu_1 > \mu_2$; $z = 3.315 > 1.282$, so reject H_0 and accept mean had decreased.

(b) $[0.028, 0.112]$

9 $H_0: \mu_A = \mu_B$, $H_1: \mu_A > \mu_B$; $t = 2.315$; p-value $= 0.02$ approximately. Reject H_0 and accept that the course improves memory.

10 $H_0: p_A = p_B$, $H_1: p_A \neq p_B$; $z = 2.123 > 1.96$, so reject H_0 and accept that one ointment is superior.

If the two doctors had similar patients and assessed the results by the same criteria, then interpretation would be unaffected.

11 (a) $H_0: p_1 = p_2$, $H_1: p_1 > p_2$; $z = 2.128 > 1.96$, so accept that $p_1 > p_2$.

(b) $[0.006, 0.146]$

12 $[-6.98, 16.73]$; no evidence of a difference at the 5% significance level since confidence interval contains zero.

13 $[-0.0174, 0.0224]$; sample large so sample means have approximate normal distributions. $H_0: p_A = p_B$, $H_1: p_A < p_B$; $z = -1.023$; p-value $= 0.154$ approximately.

14 (a) Assumes students form a random sample and $T_1 - T_2$ has a normal distribution; $H_0: \mu_1 - \mu_2 = 0$, $H_1: \mu_1 - \mu_2 > 0$; $t = 2.504 > 1.833$, so reject H_0 and accept that there is a reduction in the mean time.

(b) $[0.66, 12.92]$, to 2 decimal places

15 (a) Assumes amounts spent per month have normal distributions with a common variance

$H_0: \mu_g = \mu_b$, $H_1: \mu_g > \mu_b$; $t = 2.558 > 1.721$, so reject H_0 and accept that girls spend more than boys each month.

(b) Use $\dfrac{7.5 - a}{2.932} > 1.323$; $a = 3$

(c) College may have a catchment area biased towards a particular socio-economic group.

5 Chi-squared tests

In all these exercises, the answers are presented in the format: distribution under H_0; expected frequencies (after combination of classes if necessary); X^2; critical values; accept or reject H_0. Your estimated frequencies and values of X^2 may differ from those given, depending on how much estimated parameters are rounded. This should not affect your conclusions.

Exercise 5A (page 105)

1 All $\frac{1}{6}$; all 10; 3.4; 11.07; accept H_0.

2 $p_1 = \frac{9}{16}$, $p_2 = p_3 = \frac{3}{16}$, $p_4 = \frac{1}{16}$; 90, 30, 30, 10; 1.84; 11.34; accept H_0.

3 (a) $B\left(4, \frac{1}{4}\right)$; 63.28, 84.38, 42.19, 10.16; 241.86; 7.82; reject H_0.
   (b) $B(4, 0.465)$; 16.38, 56.96, 74.27, 43.03, 9.35; 3.68; 7.82; accept H_0.

4 $B\left(6, \frac{5}{18}\right)$; 8.52, 19.65, 18.89, 12.94; 2.35; 9.21; accept H_0.

5 $\text{Geo}\left(\frac{1}{2}\right)$; 25, 12.5, 6.25, 6.25; 2.24; 6.25; accept H_0.

6 All $\frac{1}{10}$; all 9; 16; 14.68; reject H_0.

7 $\text{Po}\left(\frac{13}{15}\right)$; 37.83, 32.79, 14.21, 5.17; 4.91; 5.99; accept H_0.

8 All $\frac{1}{7}$; all 85.71; 3.10; 12.59; accept H_0.

9 $p_1 = \frac{9}{49}$, remainder $\frac{10}{49}$; 110.2, remainder 122.45; 3.04; 7.78; accept H_0.

10 $B(5, 0.424)$; 14.84, 17.18, 12.64, 5.34; 2.47; 5.99; accept H_0.

11 (a) $\text{Po}(1)$; 30.90, 30.90, 15.45, 6.75; 26.84; 7.82; reject H_0.
   (b) $\text{Po}\left(\frac{67}{42}\right)$; 17.04, 27.18, 21.69, 11.53, 6.55; 1.80; 7.82; accept H_0.

12 $\text{Po}\left(\frac{45}{52}\right)$; 21.87, 18.94, 11.16, 4.05; 5.02; accept H_0.

Exercise 5B (page 110)

1 $N\left(50, 10^2\right)$; 15.87, 34.13, 34.13, 15.87; 0.89; 9.35; accept H_0.

2 $N\left(698.3, 18.83^2\right)$; 7.95, 8.05, 10.26, 9.93, 7.29, 6.51; 3.35; 7.82; accept H_0.

3 (a) $N\left(100, 15^2\right)$; 6.84, 40.77, 120.39, 120.39, 40.77, 6.84; 17.60; 11.07; reject H_0.
   (b) $N\left(96.6, 15^2\right)$; 10.59, 54.47, 110.00, 90.11, 32.99; 2.90; 7.82; accept H_0.

4 $N\left(172.2, 7.31^2\right)$; 8.98, 11.41, 13.31, 9.89, 6.41; 0.17; 5.99; accept H_0.

5 $N\left(2.915, 1.77^2\right)$; 13.96, 16.30, 21.68, 21.09, 15.05, 11.94; 18.39; 16.27; reject H_0.

6 $f(w) = 0.0002w^3(10 - w)$; 8.70, 24.99, 40.03, 26.27; 7.33; 6.25; reject H_0.

Exercise 5C (page 118)

1 No association; 101.31, 82.28, 123.41, 149.16, 121.14, 181.7, 79.53, 64.59, 96.88; 44.29; 13.28; reject H_0.

2 No association; 32.64, 20.4, 14.96, 15.36, 9.6, 7.04; 2.6; 7.38; accept H_0.

3 No association; 71.5, 53.6, 69.9, 85.1, 63.8, 83.1, 48.8, 36.6, 47.6, 14.7, 11, 14.3; 29.0; 22.46; reject H_0.

4 No association; 32.5, 68.25, 29.25, 17.5, 36.75, 15.75; 2.44; 5.99; accept H_0.

5 No association; 9, 24, 27, 36, 96, 108, 30, 80, 90; 18.99; 9.49; reject H_0.

6 No association; 23.83, 45.16, 163.06, 164.95, 14.17, 26.84, 96.94, 98.05; 124.1; 16.27; reject H_0.

7 No association; 30.8, 9.2, 26.2, 7.8; 0.15; 3.84; accept H_0.

8 No association; 397, 163, 312, 128; 6.03; 3.84; reject H_0.

Miscellaneous exercise 5 (page 120)

1 All $\frac{1}{10}$; all 8; 12.65; 14.68; accept H_0.

2 $p_1 = p_4 = 0.16$, $p_2 = 0.48$, $p_3 = 0.2$; 128, 384, 160, 128; 4.95; 7.82; accept H_0. 256, 768, 320, 256; 9.90; 7.82; reject H_0.

3 (a) $B\left(5, \frac{1}{6}\right)$; 80.4, 80.4, 32.2, 7.1; 7.9; 7.82; reject H_0.
   (b) $B(5, 0.2)$; 65.5, 81.9, 41.0, 11.6; 0.04; 5.99; accept H_0.

4 $B(4, 0.4)$; 12.96, 34.56, 34.56, 17.92; 11.1; 9.21; reject H_0.

5 $\text{Po}(2)$; 16.24, 32.48, 32.48, 21.65, 10.83, 6.32; 12.24; 9.49; reject H_0.

6 $\text{Geo}\left(\frac{2}{3}\right)$; 133.3, 44.4, 14.8, 7.4; 2.71; 4.61; accept H_0.

7 $N\left(69.95, 1.26^2\right)$; 6.7, 25.7, 61.3, 80.2, 57.7, 22.8, 5.6; 1.93; 9.49; accept H_0.

8 $N\left(1.03, 1^2\right)$; 6.30, 8.85, 14.66, 19.00, 19.28, 15.32, 9.52, 7.08; 4.91; 16.81; accept H_0.

9 $f(x) = \lambda e^{-\lambda x}$, $\lambda = \frac{5}{52}$; 7.98, 6.50, 5.15, 5.37; 1.34; 5.99; accept H_0.

10 No association; 202.2, 260.7, 318.1, 184.8, 238.3, 290.9; 2.01; 5.99; accept H_0.

11 Tabulate sample against answer. No association; 66.7, 33.3, 53.3, 26.7; 6.75; 3.84; reject H_0.

Revision exercise 1
(page 123)

1 (b) Less, since $P(X \leqslant 6) = 0.6 > 0.5$
 (c) 5.4 tonnes
 5.28 tonnes
 (e) £7.11
 (f) It would take about 112 months to recoup the investment, so it is not a good idea.

2 (a) 2 (b) $G(a) = \dfrac{2a}{\pi} - \dfrac{a^2}{\pi^2}$, for $0 \leqslant a \leqslant \pi$

 (c) $g(a) = \dfrac{2}{\pi} - \dfrac{2a}{\pi^2}$, for $0 \leqslant a \leqslant \pi$

 (d) $\frac{1}{3}\pi$, $\frac{1}{18}\pi^2$; 1

3 0.010, 0.098(5)

4 (a) As both diagrams appear to be reasonably symmetric, there is no reason to doubt normality.
 (b) Without assuming equal variances $z = 5.191 > 3.291$, so H_0 rejected at a significance level smaller than 0.05%.
 (c) $[9.67, 28.73]$
 (d) Not necessary since sample sizes are large enough for the sample means to be distributed normally.

5 (b) H_0: binomial distribution fits data, H_1: binomial distribution does not fit data; $X^2 = 1.719 < 4.605$, so accept H_0.
 (c) The binomial distribution requires independence, so no reason to doubt this.

6 $[0.326, 0.410]$
 H_0: $p_{UK} - p_F = 0$, H_1: $p_{UK} - p_F \neq 0$; $z = 1.588$; rejection region is $|Z| \geqslant 1.645$, so accept H_0, there is no difference between the proportions.

7 Assume differences are random samples from a normal distribution. H_0: $\mu_D = 0$, H_1: $\mu_D < 0$, where $D = $ End BMI $-$ Beginning BMI.
 $t = -3.464 < -1.895$, so reject H_0 and accept that BMI has decreased.
 Type I error might have occurred, (a) when H_1 is true, (b) when H_1 is false.

8 0.504; $[0.410, 0.534]$; since 0.504 is inside this interval there is no reason to doubt the randomness.
 H_0: pairs equally likely, H_1: pairs not equally likely; $X^2 = 7.102 < 16.92$, so accept H_0 that digit pairs are equally likely.

9 H_0: $\mu = 3.80$, H_1: $\mu < 3.80$;
 $t = -1.549 < -1.318$, so reject H_0 and accept that the requirement is not met.
 H_0: $\mu_1 = \mu_2$, H_1: $\mu_1 \neq \mu_2$; $t = -1.857 > -2.021$, so accept H_0, there is no change in the mean length.

10 (a) H_0: responses independent of drug used, H_1: responses depend on drug
 (b) 54.52, 81.78, 4.70, 61.48, 92.22, 5.30
 (c) One of the expected values is less than 5.
 (d) Combining Improved and Much Improved; $X^2 = 4.550 < 5.024$, so accept H_0, responses are independent of drug used.
 (e) Without Yates' correction $X^2 = 5.071$, so H_0 is rejected.

Mock examinations

Mock examination 1 for S3 (page 127)

1 (i) Poisson (ii) 33.9 (iii) $e^{-33.9} \dfrac{33.9^{40}}{40!}$

2
$$G(Y) = \begin{cases} 0 & y < 0, \\ \frac{1}{3}(e^y - 1) & 0 \leqslant y \leqslant \ln 4, \\ 1 & y > \ln 4; \end{cases}$$
 $g(y) = \frac{1}{3}e^y$ for $0 \leqslant y \leqslant \ln 4$.

3 (i) $[42.6, 59.4]$
 (ii) Normality required for the test statistic to have a t distribution. It is used in finding the value 3.25.

4 0.986; assumption is that the probability that the extra passenger is male is $\frac{185}{391}$, and probability of female is $\frac{206}{391}$. The assumption is reasonable.

5 8.49, 3.56
 H_0: data fit model, H_1: data do not fit model; $X^2 = 8.23 > 6.251$, so reject H_0.

6 (i) H_0: $p_N - p_D = 0$; H_1: $p_N - p_D > 0$; $z = 1.062 < 1.645$, so accept H_0, the proportion of defectives is not greater on night shifts.
 (ii) $[0.0375, 0.0885]$

7 (i) $E(X) = 3$ (ii) $\frac{1}{8}$ (iii) $a = 32$

Mock examination 2 for S3 (page 129)

1 0.305

2 (i) $\dfrac{2y+2}{y+9}$ for $-1 \leqslant y \leqslant 7$ (ii) 1

3 (i) B(50,0.2) (iii) $a = 1$

4 (i) 0.192   (ii) 0.176
The assumption of independence is made in the calculation of variances.

5 Discrete; P_s takes values $\dfrac{1}{250} r$ for
  $r = 1, 2, \ldots, 250$
  (i) [28.1, 39.9]
  (ii) Variance is estimate; discrete variable is approximated by continuous variable; distribution is approximately normal.
  Approximate sample size is 2380;
  99% probability that error is less than $2\frac{1}{2}\%$.

6 (i) H_0: hair colour of husbands and wives independent, H_1: hair colour of husbands and wives not independent
  (ii) $62 \times \dfrac{122}{200}$
  (iii) Value 2.9 is less than 5.
  (iv) $X^2 = 1.388$ (with Yates' correction) < 3.841, so accept H_0, the sociologist's belief is not supported.

7 $2n - 2$
  (i) Variance unknown and sample sizes too small for the central limit theorem.
  (ii) [72.5, 79.4]
  (iii) 78.6

Answers to S4

Most non-exact numerical answers are given correct to 3 significant figures.

1 Probability

Exercise 1A (page 138)

1 (a) $\{4,5,6\}$ (b) $\{1,2,6\}$
    (c) $\{3\}$ (d) $\{4,5\}$
    (e) $\{6\}$ (f) $\{1,2,4,5,6\}$
    (g) $\{1,2,4,5,6\}$ (h) $\{6\}$

2 (a) 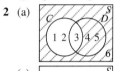   (b)

   (c)   (d)

   (e) 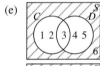   (f)

   (g) 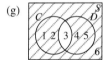   (h)

4 (a) $A=\{1,3,5,7,9\}$, $B=\{0,2,4,6,8\}$
       $C=\{2,3,5,7\}$, $D=\{0,3,6,9\}$; A and B
   (b) $A'=\{0,2,4,6,8\}$, $B'=\{1,3,5,7,9\}$,
       $C'=\{0,1,4,6,8,9\}$, $D'=\{1,2,4,5,7,8\}$
   (c) (i) $\{1,2,3,5,7,9\}$ (ii) $\{0,1,2,4,5,6,7,8\}$
       (iii) $\{0,1,2,3,4,5,6,7,8,9\}$ (iv) $\{0,2,4,8\}$
   (d) (i) $\{3,5,7\}$ (ii) $\{2,4,8\}$
       (iii) $\{0,2,4,6,8\}$ (iv) $\{0,2,3,5,6,7,9\}$
   (e) (i) $\{3\}$ (ii) $\{0,1,2,3,5,6,7,8,9\}$ (iii) $\{\,\}$

5 (a) $\{0,1,2,3,4,5,6,7\}$
   (b) $E=\{0,2,4,6\}$, $F=\{0,3,6\}$, $G=\{0,4\}$
   (c) (i) $\{0\}$ (ii) $\{0,2,3,4,6\}$ (iii) $\{0,4,6\}$
       (iv) $\{0,4,6\}$ (v) $\{0,2,4,6\}$
       (vi) $\{0,4\}$ (vii) $\{1,5,7\}$

Exercise 1B (page 145)

1 (a) 0.9   (b) 0.2

2 Yes, since $P(C\cup D)=P(C)+P(D)$.
   (a) 0.9   (b) 0.7

3 (a) 0.9   (b) 0.2   (c) 0.1   (d) 0.5

4 $P(B)=0.3$, $P(C)=0.4$, $P(B\cup C)=0.6$
   (a) 0.1   (b) 0.2   (c) 0.4   (d) 0.5

5 (a) 0.75   (b) 1   (c) 0.58   (d) 0.35

6 0.16

Exercise 1C (page 150)

1 (a) 0.44   (b) 0.38

2 (a) 0.075   (b) 0.375

3 $\frac{14}{45}$

4 (a) (i) $\frac{5}{24}$ (ii) $\frac{1}{24}$ (iii) $\frac{5}{6}$ (iv) $\frac{1}{12}$
   (b) (i) Not independent since
       $P(A)P(B)\neq P(A\cap B)$.
      (ii) Not mutually exclusive since
       $P(A\cap B)\neq 0$.

5 (a) $\frac{1}{5}$ (b) $\frac{5}{13}$ (c) $\frac{17}{25}$
   (d) $\frac{8}{25}$ (e) $\frac{8}{25}$

6 (a) 0.58   (b) 0.6

7 (a) $\frac{1}{64}$ (b) $\frac{21}{64}$

8 (a) $\frac{5}{24}$ (b) $\frac{1}{8}$

Exercise 1D (page 153)

1 (a) 0.33   (b) $\frac{4}{11}$

2 0.16

3 0.593

4 $\frac{2}{3}$

5 0.000 099. Even with this extra piece of evidence it is most unlikely that the prisoner is guilty.

6 $\dfrac{23p}{22p+1}$

Miscellaneous exercise 1 (page 155)

1 $\frac{1}{25}$

2 $\frac{21}{40}$

3 maximum $\frac{2}{3},\frac{3}{4}$; minimum $\frac{5}{12},1$

4 (a) 0.5   (b) $5p$, $4p$ (c) $\frac{1}{40}$

5 $\frac{2}{3}$

6 (a) The student did not obtain two heads.
   (b) (i) $\frac{1}{4}$ (ii) p (iii) $\frac{1}{4}p$ (iv) $\frac{3}{4}(1-p)$
   (d) An estimate of p is 0.78; 78% enjoyed the lecture.

7 0.000 28; 0.893

8 (a) $\frac{4}{7}$ (b) $\frac{1}{2}$

9 (a) (i) 0.04   (ii) 0.12   (iii) 0.16
   (b) 0.75

10 (a) (i) $P(A \cap B) = \frac{1}{12} \neq 0$ so A and B are not
mutually exclusive.
(ii) $P(A)P(B) = \frac{1}{6} \neq P(A \cap B)$, so not
independent.
(b) (i) $\frac{1}{4}$ (ii) $\frac{5}{8}$

11 (a) 0.125 (b) $\frac{5}{32}$ (c) 0.769

12 (a) $\frac{2}{3}$ (b) $\frac{1}{6}$ (c) $\frac{5}{18}$ (d) $\frac{1}{4}$ (e) $\frac{3}{5}$

13 (a) 0.69 (b) 0.84
$\frac{7}{20}, \frac{1}{10}$

14 (a) (ii) $\frac{1}{3}, \frac{1}{8}$
(iii) No, since $P(A_1 \cap A_2) \neq P(A_1)P(A_2)$
(b) (i) $\frac{9}{20}$ (ii) $\frac{2}{3}$

2 Non-parametric tests

Exercise 2A (page 166)

1 (b) H_0: median = 50, H_1: median $\neq$ 50. Use a
sign test since the distribution is not
symmetrical. $P(X \leqslant 3) = 0.1719 > 0.025$,
so accept H_0, there is no evidence that
median journey time by new route differs
from 50 minutes.

2 $P(X \leqslant 1) = 0.1875 > 0.10$. Result is not
significant at 10 % level, two-tail test. Accept
null hypothesis that the median is 100.

3 $H_0: M = 3.5$, $H_1: M \neq 3.5$;
$P(X \leqslant 2) = 0.0547 > 0.025$. Result is not
significant at 5% level. Accept null hypothesis
that the median is 3.5.

4 $P(X \geqslant 6) = 0.1445$

5 $P(X \leqslant 2) = 0.0327 < 0.05$. Result is significant
at 5% level, one-tail test. Reject H_0; most
villages have more females than males.

6 H_0: population medians are equal,
H_1: population medians are not equal.
$T = 7 \leqslant 8$. Reject H_0; the population medians
are not equal.

7 $T = 11 \geqslant 8$. Accept H_0; median is 55 hours. The
times are not normally distributed. Note the
outlier 125.9.

8 $z = -1.604 > -1.645$. Result is not significant at
5% level.

9 H_0: drug has no effect, H_1: drug improves
memory. $T = 8 \leqslant 8$. Reject H_0. There is
evidence that drug improves memory.

10 H_0: no difference in age, H_1: wives are younger
on average.
(a) $P(X \leqslant 3) = 0.2539 > 0.05$. Accept H_0; no
age difference.
(b) $T = 7 \leqslant 8$. Reject H_0; wives are younger
than their husbands.
(c) Test in (a) requires no assumptions, test in
(b) requires distribution of differences to be
symmetrical.
(d) The test in (b) is more discriminating than
that in (a) because it uses more information
from the sample. It has a lower probability
of giving a Type II error because it detects
that the minus deviations are all much
smaller than the positive deviations.

11

t	0	1	2	3	4	5
$P(T = t)$	$\frac{1}{8}$	$\frac{1}{8}$	$\frac{1}{8}$	$\frac{1}{4}$	$\frac{1}{4}$	$\frac{1}{8}$

25%

12 (a) $\frac{3}{32}$ (b) $\frac{3}{32}$ (c) $\frac{5}{128}$

Exercise 2B (page 172)

1 H_0: *Mus homonunculus* are of same breed in two
regions, H_1: *Mus homonunculus* are not of same
breed in two regions. $W = 18 \leqslant 21$. Reject H_0.
Mice in two regions are of different breeds.

2

w	3	4	5	6	7
$P(W = w)$	0.1	0.1	0.2	0.3	0.3

3 (a) 205
(b) H_0: on average, boys and girls stay silent
equal times, H_1: on average, boys stay silent
longer than girls. $W = 95$, $z = 3.147 > 2.053$.
Reject H_0. There is evidence that boys stay
silent longer than girls.

4 (a)

1	2	3	4	5	6	7	8	9	10	11
B	*B*	*G*	*B*	*B*	*G*	*B*	*G*	*G*	*G*	*G*

(b) 462 (c) 19
(d) If $W \leqslant 20$, conclude at the 5% level that
one distribution is, on average, lower than
the other.
(e) $19 > 17$. Accept H_0. The data do not
support the view that, on average, primary
school girls have greater weights than
primary school boys.

5 (a) 1287 (b) $\frac{4}{1287}$
(c) H_0: on average, fathers and mothers run
equal distances, H_1: on average, fathers run
further than mothers. $W = 20 \leqslant 23$. Reject H_0.
There is evidence that, on average, fathers run
further than mothers.

6 $P(W \le 10) = \frac{1}{70}$, $P(W \le 11) = \frac{2}{70}$

7 Yes, $z = -2.693 < -2.326$

Miscellaneous exercise 2 (page 174)

1 0.0107

2 Single-sample sign test makes no assumptions about population distribution whereas single-sample Wilcoxon signed-rank test requires that population distribution is symmetrical. Single-sample Wilcoxon signed-rank test is a more powerful test because it uses more information from the sample.
It is preferable to use a non-parametric test for small samples when the population does not have a normal distribution.

3 $H_0: M = 0$, $H_1: M > 0$. $T = 11 > 10$. Accept H_0
Insufficient evidence to say that the bus is late more often than not.

4 (a) H_0: programme does not affect mathematical activity, H_1: programme increases mathematical activity.
$T = 23 > 21$. Accept H_0.
(b) The test assumes that the population of differences has a symmetrical distribution. A dot plot of the sample suggests that this may not be true.
(c) $P(X \le 3) = 0.0461 < 0.05$. Reject H_0.

5 $H_0: \mu = 510$, $H_1: \mu \ne 510$. $T = 27 > 13$. Accept H_0. There is insufficient evidence to say that reaction time has changed. t-test assumes that the population is distributed normally.

6 (a) H_0: on average, Ann and Betty run at the same speed, H_1: on average, Ann and Betty run at different speeds.
(b) $W = 32$
(c) $W > 26$
(d) Accept H_0. There is insufficient evidence to say that Ann and Betty run at different speeds.

7 (a) H_0: preservative has no effect on taste, H_1: wine without preservative tastes better than wine with preservative.
$P(X \le 1) = 0.0625 < 0.1$. Reject H_0. There is evidence that wine without preservative tastes better than wine with preservative.
(b) To apply the paired-sample t-test to these data, the differences between paired values would have to be distributed normally. This is not reasonable since the values are discrete.

8 (a) H_0: course is not effective, H_1: course is effective. (i) $T = 12 > 10$. Accept H_0.
(ii) $T = 1.862 > 1.833$. Reject H_0 (just).
(b) A t-test is better since it is more powerful and it does not seem unreasonable to assume that differences come from a distribution that is approximately normal; *or* the Wilcoxon signed-rank test is better because it does not assume that the data come from a population which is distributed normally.

9 $H_0: M = 8$, $H_1: M \ne 8$. $P(X \le 2) = 0.0193 < 0.1$
Reject H_0. There is evidence that the median rating has increased.

10 (a) (i) Use Wilcoxon matched-pairs signed-rank test. H_0: there is no difference in average delivery times for A and B, H_1: A takes a shorter time than B. $T = 17 \le 17$. Reject H_0 There is evidence that A takes a shorter time than B.
(ii) $H_0: \mu_d = 0$, $H_1: \mu_d < 0$.
$t = 1.59 < 1.796$. Accept H_0. There is no difference in average delivery times for A and B.
(b) Use sign test (since there are tied ranks). H_0: median $= 24$, H_1: median > 24.
$P(X \le 3) = 0.0730 < 0.1$. Reject H_0. The median delivery time for A is greater than 24 hours.

11 (a) (i) 210
(ii) *FFFFMMMMMM, FFFMFMMMMM*
(b) (i) 11
(ii) H_0: on average, reaction times for males and females are equal, H_1: on average, reaction times are lower for females than for males.
$P(X \le 11) = \frac{2}{210} = 0.0095 < 0.050$.
Reject H_0. There is sufficient evidence to say that the median reaction time for females is less than that for males.
(c) $P(X \le 1) = 0.0107 < 0.05$. Accept H_1 that the median reaction time is less than 10 seconds.

12 (a) H_0: there is no difference in wear for front and rear tyres, H_1: there is a difference in wear for front and rear tyres.
(i) $P(X \le 2) = 0.1445 > 0.05$. Accept H_0.
(ii) $T = 4 \le 5$. Reject H_0.
(b) Test (i) uses information about the shape of the distribution; test (ii) takes into account the sizes of the deviations.

13 (a) H_0: clubs A and B achieve equal distances, H_1: club A achieves greater distances than club B. $W = 95 > 82$. Accept H_0. There is insufficient evidence to say that club A achieves greater distances than club B.

(b) $P(X \leqslant 1) = 0.0107 < 0.05$. Reject H_0. There is significant evidence that club A strikes the ball further.

14 (a) 924   (b) $\frac{7}{924}$

(d) H_0: on average, the body temperature of smokers and non-smokers is the same after exercise, H_1: on average, the body temperature of smokers is higher than that of non-smokers after exercise. $W = 27 > 26$. Accept H_0. There is insufficient evidence to say that, on average, the body temperature of smokers is higher than that of non-smokers after exercise.

15 (a) The Wilcoxon rank sum test is not appropriate because the samples are paired, not independent.

(b) H_0: temperature has no effect on the distance thrown, H_1: temperature does have an effect on the distance thrown. $T = 4 \leqslant 8$. Reject H_0. Temperature does have an effect on the distance thrown.

(c) With the present design the greater distance thrown on the second day may be due to improvement with practice rather than temperature difference. It would be better if data were also collected in the situation where the temperature on the second day was lower than that on the first.

3 Probability generating functions

Exercise 3A (page 183)

2 (a) 1   (b) $\frac{1}{2}$ (c) $\dfrac{x+1}{2^x}$

5 $G_X(t) = \left(\frac{2}{3} + \frac{1}{3}t\right)^5$

6 0.501

Exercise 3B (page 188)

1 $G_X(t) = 0.1t + 0.3t^2 + 0.6t^3$, 2.5, 0.45

2 2, $3\frac{1}{3}$

4 (a) $\dfrac{1}{e^2}$ (b) 3   (c) 5

5 $\dfrac{1}{\alpha-1}$, $\dfrac{\alpha}{(\alpha-1)^2}$

Exercise 3C (page 192)

3 $\left(\dfrac{t}{6-5t}\right)^2$, $\dfrac{10}{6^3}$, $\dfrac{4 \times 5^3}{6^5}$

4 (a) $\left(0.72 + 0.26t + 0.02t^2\right)^{10}$

(b) 3

5 (a) $\exp\!\left((\lambda_x + \lambda_y)(t-1)\right)$

(b) $\exp(\lambda_x(t-1))$, $\exp(\lambda_y(t-1))$, $\exp\!\left((\lambda_x + \lambda_y)(t-1)\right)$

(c) The sum of two variables which have a Poisson distribution also has a Poisson distribution with a mean equal to the sum of the means of the individual distributions.

6 (a) $1 - p + pt$

Miscellaneous exercise 3 (page 193)

1 (a) $G_X(t) = \frac{1}{2}t + \frac{1}{4}t^2 + \frac{1}{6}t^3 + \frac{1}{12}t^4$

(b) $\frac{11}{6}$, $\frac{35}{36}$

2 (a) $\frac{1}{27}$

(b)

x	-6	-3	0	3
$P(X = x)$	$\frac{8}{27}$	$\frac{12}{27}$	$\frac{6}{27}$	$\frac{1}{27}$

(c) $-3, 6$

$G_Y(t) = \frac{8}{21}t^{-6} + \frac{12}{21}t^{-3} + \frac{1}{21}t^3$

3 (a) $\frac{1}{9}$ (b) $\frac{1}{3}$ (c) 4   (d) $\frac{632}{81}$

4 3, $\frac{3}{2}$; $a = 3$, $b = 2$; $\frac{175}{1728}$

5 $\frac{1}{3} + \frac{2}{9}t + \frac{4}{27}t^2 + \frac{8}{27}t^4$, $\frac{46}{27}$, $\frac{1934}{729}$

$\left(\frac{1}{3} + \frac{2}{9}t + \frac{4}{27}t^2 + \frac{8}{27}t^4\right)^2$, $\frac{160}{729}$

6 (a) $\dfrac{1}{e}$ (b) $G_X(t) = e^{t-1}$, 1, 1

(c) $G_Y(t) = e^{n(t-1)}$; $Y \sim \text{Po}(n)$; 0.209

7 $U \sim \text{Geo}\!\left(\frac{2}{3}\right)$; $\dfrac{2t^2}{(3-2t)(3-t)}$; $\dfrac{14}{81}$

10 $\frac{1}{2}(1 - G_X(-1))$; $\left(\frac{1}{6}t + \frac{1}{3}t^2 + \frac{1}{2}t^3\right)^5$; $\frac{122}{243}$

13 $\dfrac{\theta^k}{1-\theta^k}$, $\dfrac{\theta^k}{\left(1-\theta^k\right)^2}$

14 $G_X(t) = \left(\dfrac{pt}{1-qt}\right)^k$; $\dfrac{k}{p}$;

12, in addition to first 5 throws.

4 Moment generating functions

Exercise 4A (page 201)

1 2.5, 1.25

2 λ, λ

3 np, $np(1-p)$

Exercise 4B (page 205)

1 $M_X(t) = \dfrac{2}{t}e^t - \dfrac{2}{t^2}e^t + \dfrac{2}{t^2}, t \neq 0$; $\frac{2}{3}$, $\frac{1}{18}$

2 (a) $t < \frac{1}{2}$ (b) $\frac{1}{4}$; 4, 8

3 (a) $t \neq 0$ (b) $\frac{1}{3}$ (c) $\frac{7}{6}$, $\frac{11}{36}$

4 $H(t)$ is the moment generating function of $X + c$.

Exercise 4C (page 208)

1 (a) $\dfrac{2}{2-t}, t < 2$ (b) $\dfrac{6}{(t-2)(t-3)}$

(c) $\frac{5}{6}$, $\frac{13}{36}$

2 (a) $\exp\left(n\mu t + \frac{1}{2}n\sigma^2 t^2\right)$

(b) $\exp\left(n\mu t + \frac{1}{2}n\sigma^2 t^2\right)$

(c) The sum of n independent observations of $X \sim N\left(\mu, \sigma^2\right)$ is distributed as $X \sim N\left(n\mu, n\sigma^2\right)$.

3 (a) $\left(\dfrac{\lambda}{\lambda - t}\right)^3$ (b) $f(w) = \frac{1}{2}\lambda^3 w^2 e^{-\lambda w}$

(c) $f(y) = \dfrac{1}{(n-1)!}\lambda^n y^{n-1}e^{-\lambda y}$, where Y is the time taken to serve n customers.

Miscellaneous exercise 4 (page 209)

1 $1 + 2t + 3t^2 + \ldots$; 2, 2

2 α, 2β

3 (c) $1 + (1-b)t + \frac{1}{2}t^2\left(2 - 2b - b^2\right) + \ldots$
(d) $1 - 2(\ln 2)^2$

4 (b) $\dfrac{e^{2t} - 2e^t + 1}{t^2}$

(c) $M_W(t) = \left(M_X(t)\right)^2 = M_Y(t)$

5 $t \neq 0$

6 (a) $\dfrac{1}{a-t} - \dfrac{1}{a+b-t}, t < a$; $\dfrac{a^2}{1-a}$

(b) $\dfrac{2-a}{a}, \dfrac{2-2a+a^2}{a^2}$

7 2, $\frac{4}{3}$

8 (b) $\frac{1}{4}\pi^2 - 2$

9 0, $\frac{1}{2}$; $\dfrac{4\left(e^{\frac{1}{2}t} - 1\right)^2}{t^2}$, $\frac{1}{2}$, $\frac{1}{24}$

5 Estimators

Exercise 5A (page 215)

1 (a)

p_s	0	0.25	0.5	0.75
$P(P_s = p)$	$\frac{5}{30}$	$\frac{15}{30}$	$\frac{9}{30}$	$\frac{1}{30}$

3 An estimate obtained from an unbiased estimator, that is an estimator with expectation equal to the population variance

(a) 2, $\frac{2}{3}$

(b)

x	1	1.5	2	2.5	3
$P(\overline{X} = x)$	$\frac{1}{9}$	$\frac{2}{9}$	$\frac{3}{9}$	$\frac{2}{9}$	$\frac{1}{9}$

2; yes, unbiased

(c)

s^2	0	0.5	2
$P(S^2 = s^2)$	$\frac{3}{9}$	$\frac{4}{9}$	$\frac{2}{9}$

(d)

s	0	$\frac{1}{2}\sqrt{2}$	$\sqrt{2}$
$P(S = s)$	$\frac{3}{9}$	$\frac{4}{9}$	$\frac{2}{9}$

$E(S) = \frac{4}{9}\sqrt{2} \neq \sqrt{\frac{2}{3}}$.

(e) The population maximum is 3. However, the distribution of the sample maximum will include values lower than this. For example, for the sample (1,2) the sample maximum is 2. Hence the expected value of the sample maximum will be less than 3.

9 (a) $\frac{1}{2}\left(p + \frac{1}{2}\right)$ (b) $2R - \frac{1}{2}$

Exercise 5B (page 222)

1 (b) $\sigma^2, \frac{7}{2}\sigma^2, 9\sigma^2$; (i)

2 (b) $\frac{1}{2}$

3 $\dfrac{p(1-p)}{n_1}$; $\frac{1}{3} < \dfrac{n_1}{n_2} < 3$

4 (a) $\frac{1}{9}a^2$

(b)
$$f(g) = \begin{cases} \dfrac{3g^2}{a^3} & 0 \leqslant g \leqslant a, \\ 0 & \text{otherwise.} \end{cases}$$

$\text{Var}(\phi) = \frac{1}{15}a^2 < \frac{1}{9}a^2$, so ϕ is the more efficient estimator.

5 (c) For $n = 1$ the sample 2 gives $\frac{1}{3}\overline{x} = \frac{2}{3}$, but $\alpha \leqslant \frac{1}{2}$.

Miscellaneous exercise 5 (page 224)

1 (a) (ii) $\frac{1}{2}\theta, \frac{3}{4}\theta^2$ (b) $\dfrac{30\theta^2}{n}$

4 (b) $\frac{2}{3}$

(c) $\frac{4}{3}Z$ is the more efficient estimator because $\text{Var}\,Y > \text{Var}\left(\frac{4}{3}Z\right)$.

5 (a) $Y-1$ or $\bar{Y}-1$ (b) 4

6 (a) $\left(\dfrac{u}{k}\right)^n$ (b) $\mathrm{f}(l) = \begin{cases} \dfrac{nl^{n-1}}{k^n} & 0 \leq l \leq k, \\ 0 & \text{otherwise.} \end{cases}$

(c) $\dfrac{nk}{n+1}$ (d) $\dfrac{(n+1)L}{n}$ (e) $\frac{1}{2}k$ (f) $2\bar{U}$

(g) $\text{Var}\left(\dfrac{(n+1)}{n}L\right) = \dfrac{k^2}{n(n+2)}$; $\text{Var}(2\bar{U}) = \dfrac{k^2}{3n}$

$\text{Var}\left(\dfrac{(n+1)}{n}L\right) \leq \text{Var}(2\bar{U})$ for all positive

integral values of n.

7 $a + \frac{1}{4}b$; $a = 5, b = 8$

8 6.3

11 $P(R = r) = \dbinom{r-1}{b-1}p^b(1-p)^{r-b}$

6 Discrete bivariate distributions

Exercise 6A (page 232)

1 (a) 0.03

(b) (i) 0.06 (ii) 0.05 (iii) 0.18 (iv) 0.09

2 (a)

r	1	2	3	4
$P_R(R=r)$	0.55	0.26	0.13	0.06

1.7, 0.83

(b)

s	0	1	2	3
$P_S(S=s)$	0.30	0.31	0.27	0.12

1.21, 1.0059

(c) (i) $\frac{13}{27}$ (ii) $\frac{11}{31}$ (iii) $\frac{2}{13}$ (iv) 0

(d)

s	0	1	2	3
$P(S=s\mid R=3)$	$\frac{2}{13}$	$\frac{3}{13}$	$\frac{6}{13}$	$\frac{2}{13}$

$\frac{21}{13}, \frac{144}{169}$

(e)

r	1	2	3
$P(R=r\mid S=3)$	$\frac{7}{12}$	$\frac{1}{4}$	$\frac{1}{6}$

$\frac{19}{12}, \frac{83}{144}$

3 (a)

		X		
		1	2	3
Y	2	$\frac{1}{9}$	0	0
	3	$\frac{1}{9}$	$\frac{1}{9}$	0
	4	$\frac{1}{9}$	$\frac{1}{9}$	$\frac{1}{9}$
	5	0	$\frac{1}{9}$	$\frac{1}{9}$
	6	0	0	$\frac{1}{9}$

(b)

x	1	2	3
$P_X(X=x)$	$\frac{1}{3}$	$\frac{1}{3}$	$\frac{1}{3}$

$E(X) = 2$

y	2	3	4	5	6
$P_Y(Y=y)$	$\frac{1}{9}$	$\frac{2}{9}$	$\frac{1}{3}$	$\frac{2}{9}$	$\frac{1}{9}$

$E(Y) = 4$

(c)

x	1	2
$P_Y(X=x\mid Y=3)$	$\frac{1}{2}$	$\frac{1}{2}$

1.5

4

		G				
		0	1	2	3	4
B	0	0	0	0	0	$\frac{1}{16}$
	1	0	$\frac{1}{2}$	$\frac{1}{8}$	$\frac{1}{16}$	0
	2	0	$\frac{1}{8}$	0	0	0
	3	0	$\frac{1}{16}$	0	0	0
	4	$\frac{1}{16}$	0	0	0	0

(a)

b	0	1	2	3	4
$P_B(B=b)$	$\frac{1}{16}$	$\frac{11}{16}$	$\frac{1}{8}$	$\frac{1}{16}$	$\frac{1}{16}$

1.375

(b)

b	1	2	3
$P(B=b\mid G=1)$	$\frac{8}{11}$	$\frac{2}{11}$	$\frac{1}{11}$

$1\frac{4}{11}$

5 (a)

		H			
		0	1	2	3
T	0	$\frac{1}{64}$	0	0	0
	1	$\frac{3}{64}$	$\frac{3}{32}$	0	0
	2	$\frac{3}{64}$	$\frac{3}{16}$	$\frac{3}{16}$	0
	3	$\frac{1}{64}$	$\frac{3}{32}$	$\frac{3}{16}$	$\frac{1}{8}$

(b)

t	0	1	2	3
$P_T(T=t)$	$\frac{1}{64}$	$\frac{9}{64}$	$\frac{27}{64}$	$\frac{27}{64}$

$\frac{9}{4}, \frac{9}{16}$

(c) 2

Exercise 6B (page 237)

The pair of variables in Exercise 6A Question 1 are independent; the remaining pairs are not independent.

Exercise 6C (page 242)

1 (b) -0.1

2 (b) $1.2, 1.3, 1.56$

3 -0.145, no

4 $\frac{2}{3}$; $\text{Cov}(X,Y) \neq 0$, so X and Y not independent.

5 $-\frac{33}{64}$

6 (a) 13 (b) -3 (c) 78 (d) 5

7 (a) $0.3, 0.12$

(b)

r	0	1	2
$P_R(R=r)$	0.64	0.32	0.04

y	0	1	2
$P_Y(Y=y)$	0.49	0.42	0.09

(c) 0.6   (d) $1, 0.5$ (e) -0.12

8 (b) 0

(c) No, for example
$P(U=0) \neq P(U=0 \mid V=0)$

(d) $2-4b$

Miscellaneous exercise 6 (page 245)

2 (a) $k = \frac{1}{18}$

(b)

		X		
		0	1	2
	0	0	$\frac{1}{18}$	$\frac{1}{9}$
Y	1	$\frac{1}{18}$	$\frac{1}{9}$	$\frac{1}{6}$
	2	$\frac{1}{9}$	$\frac{1}{6}$	$\frac{2}{9}$

(c) $-\frac{1}{9}$

3 (a)

		M			
		1	2	3	4
	0	$\frac{1}{16}$	$\frac{1}{16}$	$\frac{1}{16}$	$\frac{1}{16}$
D	1	$\frac{1}{8}$	$\frac{1}{8}$	$\frac{1}{8}$	0
	2	$\frac{1}{8}$	$\frac{1}{8}$	0	0
	3	$\frac{1}{8}$	0	0	0

(b) $-\frac{15}{32}$ (c) $\frac{55}{64}$ (d) $\frac{12}{7}, \frac{52}{49}$ (e) $\frac{3}{2}, \frac{1}{4}$

4 (a)

		S			
		1	2	3	4
	0	0	$\frac{1}{8}$	0	$\frac{3}{32}$
	1	$\frac{1}{4}$	0	$\frac{3}{16}$	0
D	2	0	$\frac{1}{8}$	0	$\frac{1}{8}$
	3	0	0	$\frac{1}{16}$	0
	4	0	0	0	$\frac{1}{32}$

(b) $\frac{5}{4}, \frac{15}{16}$ (c) $\frac{1}{4}$

5 (a) $M \sim B(3, 0.2)$, $Y \sim B(3, 0.3)$,
$M + Y \sim B(3, 0.5)$

(b) $0.48, 0.63, 0.75, -0.18$.

(c)

		M			
		0	1	2	3
	0	0.125	0.150	0.060	0.008
Y	1	0.225	0.180	0.036	0
	2	0.135	0.054	0	0
	3	0.027	0	0	0

6 (a) 0.1

(b)

		X			
		0	1	2	3
	0	0.4	0.15	0.05	0.0125
Y	1	0	0.15	0.10	0.0375
	2	0	0	0.05	0.0375
	3	0	0	0	0.0125

(c)

y	0	1	2	3
$P_Y(Y=y)$	0.6125	0.2875	0.0875	0.0125

(e) $\frac{1}{2}$ (f) $\frac{37}{23}$

7

		Y			
		0	1	2	3
	0	$\frac{1}{16}$	$\frac{1}{16}$	$\frac{1}{16}$	$\frac{1}{16}$
	1	0	$\frac{1}{8}$	$\frac{1}{8}$	$\frac{1}{8}$
Z	2	0	0	$\frac{1}{8}$	$\frac{1}{8}$
	3	0	0	0	$\frac{1}{8}$

(b)

y	0	1	2	3
$P_Y(Y=y)$	$\frac{1}{16}$	$\frac{3}{16}$	$\frac{5}{16}$	$\frac{7}{16}$

z	0	1	2	3
$P_Z(Z=z)$	$\frac{1}{4}$	$\frac{3}{8}$	$\frac{1}{4}$	$\frac{1}{8}$

(c) $\frac{5}{2}$ (d) $\frac{79}{16}$

8 (a)

		X		
		0	1	2
	0	p^3	$p^2 q$	0
Y	1	$p^2 q$	pq	pq^2
	2	0	pq^2	q^3

(b)

x	0	1	2
$P_X(X=x)$	p^2	$2pq$	q^2

Marginal distribution of Y is the same. Both X and Y are $B(2, q)$.

(c) No, since e.g. $P(X=2, Y=0) = 0$, which is not equal to $P_X(X=2) \times P_Y(Y=0) = p^2 q^2$.

(d) Under H_0, no. of times $\sim B(1000, 0.6)$; approximate by $N(216, 169.344)$, then $z = 1.114$; since critical region is $|Z| \geqslant 1.96$, accept H_0.

9 (a)

				T			
		0	1	2	3	4	5
	0	$\frac{1}{8}$	0	0	0	0	0
S	1	0	$\frac{1}{8}$	$\frac{1}{8}$	$\frac{1}{8}$	$\frac{1}{8}$	0
	2	0	0	0	$\frac{1}{8}$	$\frac{1}{8}$	$\frac{1}{8}$

  (c) $\frac{13}{16}$ (d) $2, 0; \frac{1}{3}$

10 (a) (i) 0.26 (ii) 0.50
  (b) 80.2 minutes, 83.2 minutes
  (c)

		X	
	50	60	75
60	0.09	0	0
70	0	0.17	0.08
80	0	0	0.16
95	0	0	0.50

(with Y labelling the rows 60, 70, 80, 95)

Revision exercise 2
(page 250)

1 (b) $\frac{1}{50}, \frac{94}{97}$; not independent

2 (a) $0.2, \frac{11}{14}$ (b) 0.15
  (c) 0.05   (d) $\frac{6}{7}$

3 (a) Median
  (b) H_0: median = 500, H_1: median < 500;

$$P\left(X \leqslant 3 \mid X \sim B\left(12, \tfrac{1}{2}\right)\right) = 0.073 > 0.05,\text{ so}$$

    accept H_0, the median is at least 500 N.
  (c) $T = 14 < 17$, so reject H_0, and accept that the median is less than 500 N.
  (d) The Wilcoxon test uses more information, and so should be more reliable.

4 H_0: average quality same at A and B,
  H_1: average quality not the same; $W = 21 > 20$, so accept H_0.
  The new rejection region is $W \leqslant 28$. Any rank less than 7.

5 When sampled population distribution unknown or not normal.
  (a) Fewer husbands than wives answered more questions correctly.
  (b) H_0: $p_H = \frac{1}{2}$, H_1: $p_H < \frac{1}{2}$,

$$P\left(X \leqslant 5 \mid X \sim B\left(16, \tfrac{1}{2}\right)\right) = 0.1051 > 0.05,\text{ so}$$

    accept H_0.
  H_0: median$(H - W) = 0$,
  H_1: median$(H - W) < 0$; $T = 27 < 35$, so accept H_1.

6 (a) $3\frac{1}{3}$ (b) $8\frac{2}{9}$ (c) $\frac{1}{192}$

7 (a) $E(X) = 0$ (c) $\dfrac{2}{a^2}$
  $\alpha_4 = 6$; distribution is leptokurtic for all $a > 0$.

8 $(1 - p + pt)^{m+n}$, $B(m+n, p)$
  (b) $\dfrac{(n+m)p(1-p)}{4mn}$

9 (b) $\lambda = \frac{1}{2}, \frac{1}{20}\sigma^2$
  T_2 is more efficient.

10 (a) Both 0
  (b)

x	0	1	2
$P(X = x)$	0.35	0.4	0.25

y	1	2	3
$P(Y = y)$	0.65	0.2	0.15

  (c) 0.05
  Not independent since $\mathrm{Cov}(X,Y) \neq 0$.
  0.0878

11 (a) $P(R = 1 \text{ and } B = 1) = \frac{3}{6} \times \frac{2}{5} \times \frac{1}{4} \times 3!$
  (b)

r	0	1	2	3
$P(R = r)$	0.05	0.45	0.45	0.05

b	0	1	2
$P(B = b)$	0.2	0.6	0.2

  (c) -0.3 (d) $2.5, 0.25$ (e) $\frac{9}{19}$

Mock examinations

Mock examination 1 for S4 (page 254)

1 $G_Y(t) = \dfrac{t^5}{(2-t)^5}$; $\dfrac{5}{64}$

2 (i) H_0: distributions of survival times for untreated and treated are identical, H_1: treated have greater average survival time.
  (ii) Wilcoxon rank-sum test; $W = 21$; the 5% rejection region is $\leqslant 20$, so accept H_0, the drug is not effective.

3 Unbiased estimators have expectation equal to the parameter. Biased estimators tend to underestimate or overestimate the parameter. The more efficient estimator has a smaller variance.
  (i) 2.62
  (ii) 0.34

4 (ii) $2v$
  (iii) $\dfrac{1}{(1-2t)^7}$
  (iv) χ^2 with $v = 14$
  (v) 0.1

5 (i) (a) $0.09p + 0.0728$

(b) $\dfrac{0.09p}{0.09p + 0.0728}$

(ii) 0.553

(iii) 0.0773

6 (i)

```
0 | 6  4  7  2  8  2            (6)
1 | 7  8  9  3  5  3  9         (7)
2 | 1  9  4  8  6  5            (6)
3 | 4  2  6                     (3)
4 | 8  3                        (2)
5 | 3  2                        (2)
6 | 4  2                        (2)
7 | 3                           (1)
8 | 1                           (1)
```

Key: $5\,|\,2$ means 5.2 minutes

(ii) (a) Distribution does not appear to be normal.

(b) No, distribution appears to be highly skewed.

(iii) Using sign test H_0: median $= 1.75$, H_1: median > 1.75; the number less than 1.75 is 10.
$P(X \leqslant 10 \mid X \sim B(30, \tfrac{1}{2})) = 0.0494 < 0.1$, so reject H_0 and accept that median is greater than 1.75 minutes.

7 (i)

		X		
		0	1	2
	0	a	0	0
Y	1	$2a$	a	0
	2	$3a$	$2a$	a

(ii)

x	0	1	2
$P(X=x)$	0.6	0.3	0.1

y	0	1	2
$P(Y=y)$	0.1	0.3	0.6

(iii) $\mathrm{Cov}(X,Y) = 0.15$

(iv) Not independent since $\mathrm{Cov}(X,Y) \neq 0$.

(v) $\tfrac{5}{3}$

3 $\dfrac{1}{2t}\left(e^t - e^{-t}\right)$

(i) $\dfrac{1}{4t^2}\left(e^t - e^{-t}\right)^2$

(ii) $1 + \tfrac{1}{3}t^2 + \tfrac{2}{45}t^4$; $\tfrac{28}{45}$

4 (i) H_0: A and B produce the same number of faulty CDs, H_1: A produces more faulty CDs than B; $X \sim B(28, \tfrac{1}{2}) \approx N(14, 7)$ $P(X \geqslant 19)$ gives $z = 1.701 > 1.645$, so accept H_1, machine A produces more faulty CDs.

(ii) Type II error, because the null hypothesis was rejected.

5 (i) -1, $\tfrac{8}{3}$ (ii) $B(3, \tfrac{1}{3})$

6 (i)

		X		
		0	1	2
	0	0	$\tfrac{1}{8}$	0
Y	1	$\tfrac{1}{8}$	$\tfrac{1}{2}$	$\tfrac{1}{8}$
	2	0	$\tfrac{1}{8}$	0

(ii)

x	0	1	2
$P(X=x)$	$\tfrac{1}{8}$	$\tfrac{3}{4}$	$\tfrac{1}{8}$

y	0	1	2
$P(Y=y)$	$\tfrac{1}{8}$	$\tfrac{3}{4}$	$\tfrac{1}{8}$

(iii) $P(X=1 \mid Y=1) = \tfrac{2}{3} \neq P(X=1) = \tfrac{3}{4}$

(iv) It shows that $\mathrm{Cov}(X,Y) = 0$ does not imply that X and Y are independent.

7 (ii) $t = 4.8$; this estimate of a implies that $P(X \leqslant 4.8) = 0$, but $x_1 = 4.5$.

(iii) $\tfrac{1}{6}a^2$

(iv) $P(S \leqslant s) = P(\text{at least one of } X_1 \text{ and } X_2 \leqslant s)$ $= P(\text{not both } X_1 \text{ and } X_2 > s)$

(vi) U is more efficient.

Mock examination 2 for S4 (page 257)

1 H_0: medians equal, H_1: medians not equal; for Wilcoxon rank-sum test, $W \approx N(57, 114)$; $P(W \leqslant 43) \approx P(Z \leqslant -1.264)$; rejection region is $|Z| \geqslant 1.96$, so accept H_0, medians are equal.

2 (i) $\tfrac{2}{3}$

Index

The page numbers refer to the first mention of each term, or the shaded box if there is one.